Lockheed
C-130
Hercules

Lockheed C-130

Hercules

THE WORLD'S FAVOURITE MILITARY TRANSPORT

Peter C. Smith

Airlife
England

First published in the UK in 2001
by Airlife Publishing Ltd

British Library Cataloguing-in-Publication Data
A catalogue record for this book
is available from the British Library

ISBN 1 84037 197 8

Typeset by Servis Filmsetting Ltd, Manchester
Printed in Hong Kong

Airlife Publishing Ltd
101 Longden Road, Shrewsbury, SY3 9EB, England
E-mail: airlife@airlifebooks.com
Website: www.airlifebooks.com

By the same Author

Destroyer Leader – The Story of HMS Faulknor *1934–46*
Task Force 57 – The British Pacific Fleet 1944–45
Pedestal – The Malta Convoy of August 1942
Stuka at War
Hard Lying – The Birth of the Destroyer 1893–1914
British Battle Cruisers
War in the Aegean
The Story of the Torpedo Bomber
Heritage of the Sea
Royal Navy Ships' Badges
RAF Squadron Badges
Battles of the Malta Striking Forces
Per Mare, Per Terram
Fighting Flotilla
Arctic Victory
Battle of Midway
The Great Ships Pass
Hit First, Hit Hard. HMS Renown *1916–48*
Destroyer Action
Impact! – The Dive Bomber Pilots Speak
Action Imminent
Cruisers in Action
Dive Bomber!
Hold the Narrow Sea – Naval Warfare in the English Channel 1939–45
HMS Wild Swan
Into the Assault: Famous Dive-Bomber Aces of the Second World War
Vengeance! – The Vultee Vengeance Dive Bomber
Jungle Dive Bombers at War
Victoria's Victories – Seven Classic Battles of the British Army
  1849–1884
The Royal Marines – A Pictorial History
Massacre at Tobruk
Dive Bombers in Action
Battleship Royal Sovereign
Stuka Squadron: StG77 – The Luftwaffe's Fire Brigade
T-6: The Harvard, Texan & Wirraway
Eagle's War: The War Diary of an Aircraft Carrier
Douglas SBD Dauntless
Stuka Spearhead
Stukas over the Steppe
Ship Strike! – The History of Air-to-Sea Weapons Systems
Curtiss SB2C Helldiver
Junkers Ju 87 Stuka
Aichi D3A1/A2 Val
Douglas AD Skyraider
Stukas over the Mediterranean
Fairchild-Republic A-10 Thunderbolt II
Straight Down! The North American A-36 Dive Bomber
The Sea Eagles – The Luftwaffe's Maritime Operations 1939–45

For more information on these titles contact www.dive-bombers.co.uk

Acknowledgements

To list in full the kind and helpful people who have contributed their knowledge and expertise to the compilation of this book would require about as much space as the cargo hold of a 'stretched' Hercules! Few aircraft generate such a warmth of affection and eagerness of response than the Herk, and this has been reflected in the enormous help I have been freely given. The majority of these contributors, mainly serving personnel, aircrew and ground crew, engineers and constructors alike, have requested anonymity, but I know who they are and to them all I extend my gratitude and indebtedness. Especially to all those who were so helpful during my visits to various locations in Washington DC; in Maryland and Virginia; in Atlanta, Georgia; in Seattle and Redmond, Washington State; in San Diego, Long Beach and San Francisco, California; in Pensacola and Fort Myers, Florida; in Portland, Oregon and at Hill AFB, Utah; around Nagoya, Japan, especially Norio Aoki at the Kakamigahara Air & Space Museum; the Directorate of Public Information at the Department of Defence, Canberra ACT, Australia; National Oceanic and Atmospheric Administration, at Rockville, Maryland; Smithsonian Museum, Washington DC; the United States Marine Corps Museum, USMCB Quantico, Virginia; and the United Nations Office, New York. I hasten to add that any mistakes I accept entirely as my own.

I would also like to thank by name a few of the people who went out of their way to assist me, and these include Mollie Angel, RAAF Historical Records, Canberra ACT; Norio Aoki and 401st Hikotai, JASDF, Komaki Air Base, Japan; Captain Dave Becker, South African Air Force Museum, Pretoria, RSA; Major Donald L. Black, Director, Media Division, United States Air Force, Headquarters Tactical Air Command, Langley Air Force Base, Virginia; Martin W. Bowman, Norwich; Colonel A. C. J. Collocott, South African Defence Force, Pretoria, RSA; J. C. David, United States Department of Commerce, National Oceanic and Atmospheric Administration, Rockville, Maryland; Eric F. Deylius, 731st Tactical Airlift Squadron (AFRES), Peterson Air Force Base, Colorado; D. L. Dick, Headquarters Third Air Force (USAFE), RAF Mildenhall, Suffolk, UK; Russell D. Egnor, News Photo Branch, Office of Information, Department of the Navy, Washington DC; Mark Farrar, *Flightpath*; Giancarlo Garello, Venice, Italy; Jeffrey S. Halik, Chief Media Relations, Office of Public Affairs, Headquarters 5135th Tactical Airlift Wing (USAFE), RAF Mildenhall, Suffolk, UK; Mario Isack, Hellenhahn, Germany; Lieutenant Alena Kotas, Air Force Headquarters, Pretoria, RSA; Stephanie Mitchell, Pima Air & Space Museum, Tucson, Arizona; Seán O'Brien, Shannon Airport, Eire; K. O'Donoghue, Safair Freighters, Kempton Park, RSA; Lars Olausson, Satenas, Sweden; Audrey Pearcy, Sharnbrook, for the free use of the late Arthur Pearcy's photographs, letters and documents; Sharon Peterson, Department of the Air Force, Headquarters United States Air Forces in Europe, Flugplatz Ramstein, Germany; First Lieutenant Jay W. Pyles, Department of the Air Force, 67th Aerospace Rescue and Recovery Squadron (MAC) New York; Gene Queson, Johnson Controls Incorporated, March ARC, California; Rosemary Roth, Australian Defence Headquarters, Canberra, ACT; R. K. Salmon, Air Staff Headquarters, Royal New Zealand Air Force, Wellington, New Zealand; Simon Watson of the Aviation Bookshop, Holloway Road, London, for yet again coming up trumps on all my unusual book needs; Captain Lindajean H. Western, USMC, Headquarters United States Marine Corps, Washington, DC; Nick Williams, AAHS, Waverly, Iowa; Peter Williams, Dowty Aerospace, Staverton. And to good friends Ken and Roma Smith, for their hospitality at their home in Fredericksburg, Virginia, and their enormous enthusiasm for visiting important research sites. Also to Peter Liander, Flygvapnet, Stockholm.

Foreword

There has been an enormous number of books on the C-130 Hercules, and I have consulted most of them (for those who also wish to do so there is a bibliography at the end of the book). So complex has the Hercules family tree become, however, that I found most of these books rather confusing, and not a single one of them contained information about every single variant or proposed design that might not have come to fruition. As I intended my book not to be a repeat of all these, but more a warm tribute to the C-130 in all its many facets, with both facts and photographs, I decided to abandon traditional chapters, which would be just too all-embracing, and instead adopt my own idea: a string of sections. This, I hope, will allow easier access to the multitude of Hercules varieties, and although there is some duplication I feel it is worth it for clarity. Likewise, I consider the c/n number of each aircraft as the anchor on which to base the equally diverse changes and shifts of these long-lived aircraft, and these are therefore always included in any references. Individual aircraft histories are *not* included here, and the reader is strongly recommended to consult the current edition of Lars Olausson's definitive *Lockheed Hercules Production List* for these.

The result is, I hope, a new look at the Herk in all her many faces, and any errors or omissions I would hope to rectify in future editions.

PETER C. SMITH   Riseley, Bedfordshire

Contents

The Worldwide Operators of Hercules – Military

The Worldwide Operators of Hercules – Civilian

Appendices

The Family of Hercules

1 | Origins of the Herky Bird

Aerial transportation came into its own during World War II and has played an ever-increasing role in international warfare ever since. The ability to move troops, military equipment and supplies quickly to trouble-spots around the globe is now a basic requirement for the world's major air forces, rather than a desirable luxury. With the aggressive expansion of communism from its centralised position in the Asian land-mass (the then Soviet Union and China), the free world found itself on the periphery of a giant amoeba that was probing and growing out into south-east Asia (South Korea, Vietnam, Cambodia, Tibet) and eastern Europe (Romania, Czechoslovakia, Bulgaria, Yugoslavia and Poland being swallowed up, and Greece being threatened), while yet further afield the newly independent colonial states of Africa and even the Caribbean were being subverted. In order to respond to many 'brush fire' situations, bearing in mind the statement by an American Civil War General that the winner would usually be 'the firstest with the mostest', speed of response was a growing military requisite. Sea power, an area where the western alliance dominated for the first fifteen years of the Cold War only, would always be necessary for heavy equipment, but to nip situations in the bud, or to try to restore deteriorating war situations, that was when the bulk air lift came into its own.

The situation in the Korean War in the early 1950s brought these facts into sharp focus, and in the United States, which by then had taken over the former duty of the rapidly fading British Empire as the world's policeman, the matter was the subject of hard study. The Korean War had almost been lost before it had begun, when the North suddenly invaded and there were almost no United Nations troops in the area to stem their rapid advance. Only a last-ditch stand in the Pusan perimeter and a subsequent seaborne landing at Inchon in the rear of the Communist lines had saved the day. It took six weeks to get two US Army divisions into line to begin the counter-attack. It had been, as Wellington said of Waterloo, 'a damn close-run thing'. Existing air transport in the United States Air Force was based on the C-124 *Globemaster* and the C-54 *Skymaster*, both strategic air transports but with limited capacity and range, while in Korea aircraft like the old piston-engined C-48, C-47 and the newer C-110 *Flying Boxcar* did their best, but the whole effort was too small, too limited in capacity and scope, and the aircraft were too obsolete to do the job well, so a solution had to be found, and speedily, before the next nasty surprise being concocted in the Kremlin or Beijing. Rapid mobility was the keynote of all subsequent thinking on the issue.

On the last day of July 1950, barely a week after the communist invasion armies had poured over the 38th parallel, Lieutenant-General Gordon Saville called a meeting at USAF HQ in Washington DC to discuss how best to implement the speedy introduction into service of new types of military combat aircraft for which a supplemental research and development (R&D) budget of $105,000,000 had just been assigned. Eventually they got around to discussing transport aircraft needs. Already awed by such a sum the discussion on that hot summer Sunday got bogged down and seemed to be going nowhere until an Air Force Colonel voiced his exasperation by wryly stating that what they needed was 'a medium transport than can land on unimproved ground, be extremely rugged, be primarily for freight transport, with troop-carrying capability, and carry about 30,000 pounds to a range of 1,500 miles!'[1]

The accountant was no flying expert, and did not realise that what was being asked for was far more than anyone had hitherto deemed possible in a transport aircraft, so he did not smile. Instead, as accountants always do, he asked, 'How much would that cost?' The deadlock was broken and a provisional figure of a few million dollars per plane was tossed into the discussion and duly, gravely, recorded. When the entire supplementary budget was finally approved the funding allocated for the transport was retained and preparations for a General Operational Requirement (GOR) put in train. The transport GOR was not finally issued until some months later, 2 February 1951, but the need had not lessened in the intervening period. The aircraft was still urgently required by the Tactical Air Command (TAC), Military Air Transport Service (MATS) and the US Army. As was normal practice, what followed was a Request for Proposal (RFP), which would be sent to

---

[1] Quoted by Mr H. H. Test, Military Officer assigned to USAF HQ, and present at that meeting.

all major aircraft manufacturers for their responses and ideas.

The Air Force's RFP took the original throw-away line and turned it into hard figures, and these proved little less daunting to the manufacturers who received it: Boeing, Douglas, Fairchild and Lockheed, all of whom had high expertise in this particular field of aeronautical design. Basic requirements for the new aircraft were that she be a medium transport (this applying to both payload and range) capable of performing both the tactical and logistic mission as required. The devil was in the detail. As a troop transport they wanted ninety men hauled to any point in the globe in 2,000-mile (3,220km) hops. The same aircraft should be capable of carrying up to 30,000lb (13,600kg) of military hardware (of any type) into unpaved battle-zone air strips. Oh, and she should also have the ability to get off a mud, sand or clay air strip on three engines and be able to make paratroop drops at low speeds, remaining reliable and fully controllable in such scenarios. There was also the need for an 8,000ft (2,438.4m) pressure altitude, not just for the aircrew but for the cargo hold as well, and room for the carriage of seventy-two stretcher cases, as well as an integral ramp and rear door, both capable of in-flight operations. To ensure versatility of loading capability an obstruction-free cargo compartment with the dimensions 41.5ft × 10.3 ft × 9ft (12.6m × 3.1m × 2.7m), with deck level to accommodate existing truck height from the ground had to be built in.

The Lockheed team had already ensured that they knew what the practicalities were by despatching Al Lechner, a design engineer, and Chuck Burns, from the sales team, on an exploratory visit to the Pentagon in Washington DC, to Andrews Air Force Base, Maryland, to the Strategic Air Command (SAC) HQ in Nebraska and to watch a field paratroop drop exercise at Fort Bragg, North Carolina, the US Army Airborne HQ. They learnt a lot, including an estimate from SAC that at least two thousand such aircraft would be required. These were dizzy numbers to the starved post-World War II aircraft manufacturers and well worth putting themselves out for, even if the RFP seemed ambitious, or even, to some, almost unattainable with the then current state of the art. To reinforce the full picture Lockheed also consulted with the Air Force's Air Research and Development Command, the Joint Airborne Troop Board, the Joint Air Transport Board and No.1 Field Forces Board of the Army.

All this input, and much more, was taken on board by the Lockheed Advanced Design Team which was brought together at Burbank, California, under Willis Hawkins to initiate the Model 82, following the signing of the contract for detail design work on 11 July 1951. The team he headed up included his deputy, Eugene Frost, with Robert W. Middlewood, later to become Chief Engineer, Art Flock, as Project Leader, Preliminary Design, E. C. Frank and E. A. Peterman, with Dick Pulver joining in as the programme got rolling. Others heavily involved with their specialist areas included Willard Thossen and Merrill Kelly for the engines, which early on Lockheed decided would have to be (then) revolutionary turbo-props which gave excellent range at high altitude; Jack Lebold concentrated on the new-design tandem-wheel and landing-gear to get this new bird in and out of all the precarious situations envisaged for her by the USAF and Army, while the general arrangements fell to Al Lechner. Thus came about the Lockheed Model L-206 concept. The watchwords became 'Keep it simple' and 'Keep it light but strong'.

Gradually the design came together, with a high-aspect-ratio wing (a 10 aspect ratio, with 132ft (40m) wingspan giving a 1,745 sq ft/162.1m² wing area) adopted to accommodate a low (45in/114.3cm) cargo flooring requirement. Four engines were considered essential to meet the Air Force specification, despite the extra cost this would involve. The 3,750 equivalent shaft horse-power (eshp) Allison YT56-A-1A axial-flow propeller turbine engines had a weight of 1,600lb (725.7kg) and were contained in slim, titanium-built nacelles to lessen drag. Not only did they combine the best features of both propeller and jet propulsion, they were to prove highly efficient in fuel consumption, another important factor. Four of these each drove a three-bladed Curtiss turbo, variable-pitch, constant-speed propeller. The pitch of the propeller was reversible, enabling the wondrously fast stopping distances that the Hercules was to revel in down the years. In an age of sleek jet engines this radical adoption of the turbo-prop, the first for an American aircraft, seemed a retrospective step, yet it proved the making of the design.

The landing arrangement ditched the usual wing-mounted layout for side blister accommodation outside the fuselage itself, so it did restrict capacity, and featured soft, low-pressure, 'doughnut', semi-recessed tyres and smoothed-in fairings for good flotation effect and low structural weight. Anti-skid brakes were also fitted.

New thinking on airframe design flattened out the usual fuselage cross-form from the traditional oval shape. The wings were mounted across the top of the fuselage, well out of the way, and had a 2.5in (6.35cm) dihedral. The in-built ramp gave unrestricted access to both wheeled and tracked heavy vehicles to drive straight in, and when shut smoothed right in the after ventral fuselage, while the huge cargo door had an inward-opening top section so that similar heavy and wide loads could be despatched straight out in air drops without difficulty.

To give this flying boxcar with its ungainly loads maximum stability in all the various mission profiles she was expected to undertake, similar new thinking was applied to the empennage. The after ventral hull was swept up at a high angle to give clearance for loading and culminated in a huge 38ft (11.6m) high 'sail', the vertical stabiliser, yet another truly distinctive Hercules feature, along with a beaver-tail and large, low-mounted horizontal stabilisers to ensure maximum lift and excellent handling at low speeds for such a large airplane.

Finally, in order to maximise visibility for the pilot and aircrew, who had to manoeuvre this bulky flying machine fully laden with freight in and out of tiny and unprepared air strips anywhere from a tropical jungle clearing to a cleared stretch of Antarctic ice, the whole aircraft terminated forward in a blunt, chopped-off nose, almost a straight cliff-like frontage that did little to redeem the overall appearance of the Hercules, which was unique in so many ways. The so-called 'Roman Nose', ugly though it might be, gave the aircrew an unprecedented 20° of down vision, which was to prove invaluable. Further enhancement to the ground steering of this big machine on primitive air strips was the provision of an abnormally large number of windshield windows, some twenty-three in all, with some ventrally mounted for maximum visibility in difficult situations.

Internally, the required pressurisation was achieved, despite the huge rear door, the ramp, the multi-faceted windows of the cockpit, the crew door and two troop doors that pierced the mighty hull in so many places. Bleed air from the engines fed both air conditioning and pressurisation systems. The hydraulics featured a 3,000 psi high-pressure system. Apart from the pumps, every other feature of the system was located inside the fuselage and could be readily accessed by the flight engineer. The electrics were of the high-voltage alternating current (AC) type. Another smart new innovation was the fitting of servo controls to ease the work on the flight deck when operating all this complex equipment.

All this was achieved with around 75,000 component parts, which made for ease of construction of the 54-ton aircraft, in an age when complexity was increasing with each new aircraft design. The designated five-man aircrew consisted of two pilots, a navigator, a systems manager and a loadmaster.

The first flight of the first production Hercules, 53-3129 (c/n 3001) in May 1955. A crowd greets the returning aircraft and congratulates the pilots. This batch featured the original 'Roman Nose', as is clearly seen in the top photograph. Later they were converted to the more usual Herk profile, as can be seen in the lower photograph, which shows the same aircraft at Dukes Field, Florida, many years later. (Lockheed via Audrey Pearcy)

Despite the many different or unusual features the preliminary design and estimated performance figures Lockheed came up with impressed the people who mattered, and on 2 July 1951 they were announced the winners of the RFP. Awarding them the contract, the Air Force required two prototype YC-130s, as the new aircraft was designated. Work on these commenced in Lockheed's C-1 Plant at Burbank, but already Building No. 1 at the new Marietta plant in Georgia, located to the immediate north of the sprawling city of Atlanta, had been earmarked for the full production run. On 19 September 1952, Lockheed was awarded a contract for an initial production run of seven C-130 (Model 182) aircraft (confirmed on 10 February 1953).

The company followed earlier precedent by naming the new aircraft after one of the constellations, and Hercules was certainly the most apt! The name, of course, was a legendary one, being bestowed on the son of Zeus and Alcmene, who was renowned for his physical strength and for his many incredible feats, which included the famous twelve labours he had to perform to appease the gods. Lockheed's product took the name and made an aeronautical legend out of it. The number of labours the latter-day Hercules has performed are almost without number.

The designated production team for Marietta was headed up by Al Brown, with Project Engineer E. A. Peterman, and they were brought across to California to familiarise

A close-up view of the 'Grandmamma of 'em all!' This is The First Lady, *the very first production Herk, AF53-3129 (c/n 3001) a C130A-LM showing her inaugural flight at Marietta on 7th April 1955. (Lockheed-Georgia, Marietta via Audrey Pearcy)*

themselves with the project in readiness. They returned to Marietta and were joined by a 100,000lb (45,359kg) mock-up built of wood which was shipped from the West Coast via the Panama Canal to Savannah, and then via a convoy of low-loader trucks. It was placed in Building B-4.

2 The C-130 Programme

The two YC-130-*LO* (Model 082-44-01) prototypes received the USAF serials 53-3396 (c/n 1001) and 53-3397 (c/n 1002) respectively. They were completed *sans* radar, navigator's station and with the minimum of internal and radio fittings at Burbank in August and September 1955. This partly accounted for the fact that she was 108,000lb (48,988kg) gross weight instead of the 113,000lb (51,257kg) proposed, with an empty weight of 57,500lb (26,082kg), while the designed payload was 25,000lb (11,340kg). This lead aircraft, completed on 26 August, was used for static tests at the Air Research and Development Center at Edwards Air Force Base with the 6515 MAIGP. On 23 March 1956 she joined USAF Logistics Command at Marietta and was transferred to the powerplant manufacturer's plant at Indianapolis that same December so that Allison's engineers could conduct further testing.

The second aircraft made her maiden flight from the Lockheed Air Terminal on 23 August 1954, piloted by Stanley Beltz, the Lockheed Engineering test pilot, with Roy Wimmer, co-pilot, and flight engineers Jack Real and Dick Stanton. She got airborne at 1445 using only 855ft (260.6m) of runway, making a steep 30° ascent, setting many mouths agape, and thus proving her STOL qualities right from the outset. With two chase aircraft, a P-2V with Chief Designer Kelly Johnson aboard (still unhappy and far from impressed with the design as it was) and a B-25 conducting in-flight photographs, the aircraft flew the sixty-one minutes to Edwards AFB in the Mojave desert at 10,000 ft (3,048m) to join her sister. Beltz landed the aircraft within an equally impressive short distance, and later boasted to the base commandant, Brigadier-General Albert Boyd, that, had he wanted to, he could have landed it 'cross-ways of the runway'.

Here, vigorous trials were conducted and the Herk passed most of the tests with flying colours. The aircraft improved on the USAF's own minimum flying requirements in several vital areas, with 20% better average cruising speed; 35% higher normal power, three-engine power ceiling, normal ceiling and rate of climb; and was 55% faster than predicted, with the required take-off distance at maximum power decreased by 25% and landing without reverse thrust by 40%. These figures were very impressive. These two prototypes continued to be used as engine installation test-frames for the rest of their lives, at the Allison plant. In 1959 they were both re-designated as NC-130s and were consigned to Warner Robins AFB, where they were both finally broken up, in October 1969 and April 1962 respectively. They were the only Hercules to be built at Burbank.

The impressive C-130 Hercules line-up at Marietta. (Lockheed via Audrey Pearcy)

3 Original Profile of the Basic C-130

The Air Force was impressed enough to order an additional twenty aircraft for Tactical Air Command in April 1954. All twenty-seven Hercules from the initial orders bore a close resemblance to the prototypes in appearance, with the 'Roman Nose'. They featured the improved T56-A-9 engines and had 15ft (4.57m) three-bladed Curtiss-Wright hollow propellers, and also had provision for a pair of optional 450 US gallon (1,705-litre) externally slung fuel tanks, carried outboard of the engine nacelles, to materially increase range. They had a 3g load factor which enabled her to be pushed hard in the air. This announcement was followed, that September, by another firm Air Force order for no fewer than four dozen more.

All these eighty-five aircraft became the C-130A (Model 182-1A). The first of these aircraft, serial 53-3129 (c/n 3001), was completed at Marietta on 10 March 1955. As she emerged, the Governor of the State of Georgia, one Marvin Griffin, repeatedly tried to break a bottle of Chattahoochee River water on her nose during a christening ceremony. After this debut, she made her maiden flight on 7 April, lifting off after an 800ft (244m) run at 1139 with Bud Martin at the controls, Leo Sullivan as co-pilot and Anthony 'Bob' Brennan, Jack Gilley and Chuck Littlejohn as flight engineers. After undercarriage tests at 5,000ft (1,524m) she was taken to twice that height and put through her paces. Everything went well. Bud Martin was quoted as saying that in all his twenty years of flying he had 'never flown an airplane as easy to handle'.

4 | The C-130A-*LM*

The basic layout of the C-130A formed the general outline for all early Herk development. The fuselage is of a semi-monocoque design, divided into a flight station and a cargo compartment, with seating for each flight station. Full pressurisation maintains a cabin pressure-altitude of 5,000ft (1,524m) at an aircraft altitude of 28,000ft (8,534m). The full cantilever wing contains four integral main fuel tanks and two bladder-type auxiliary tanks. The weight of the fuel gives the Hercules a marked 'wing-droop' when sitting on the ground. The empennage comprises horizontal stabiliser, vertical stabiliser, elevator, rudder, trim tabs and a tail cone, and is also an all-metal full cantilever semi-monocoque structure, bolted to the after fuselage section.

The four Allison turbo-prop engines are attached to the wings, with nacelles that have cowl panels and access doors forward of the vertical fire wall. Clam-shell doors are situated aft of the vertical fire wall and air enters the engine through a scoop assembly at the front of the nacelle. Four independent oil systems provide 12 US gallon (45.4-litre) oil capacity for each engine, with oil serviced through a filler neck located on the upper right engine cowling. The fuel system comprises a modified manifold-flow type which incorporates fuel crossfeed, single-point refuelling (SPR) and defuelling. Later models incorporated fuel dumping and blue fire suppression foam.

The landing gear is of the modified tricycle-type, and consists of dual nose gear wheels and tandem main wheels. The main gear retraction is vertical, into

The Lockheed Georgia plant in full swing in the 1950s, with the B-47 line on the left, rear, and the C-130A 53-3132 (c/n 3004) prominent in the foreground. (Lockheed via Audrey Pearcy)

fuselage fairings, while the nose gear folds forward into the fuselage and has power steering. The brakes are of the hydraulically operated, multiple-disc type, and the system incorporates differential braking and parking brake control with a modulating anti-skid system.

The hydraulic system comprises four engine-driven pumps supplying 3,000 psi pressure to the utility and booster systems, and maintains a constant pressure during zero or negative-g conditions. The 6.6 US gallon (25-litre) liquid oxygen (LOX) type system provides for ninety-six man-hours of oxygen at an altitude of 25,000ft (7,620m). It uses diluter-demand automatic pressure-breathing regulators, and the system pressure is maintained at 300 psi.

The primary flight control system of conventional aileron, elevator and rudder systems has hydraulic power boost. The wing flaps are also conventional, being of the high-lift Lockheed-Fowler type, hydraulically operated but with an emergency hand crank. De-icing is effected by engine bleed air on the wing and empennage leading edges, the radome and engine inlet air ducts. The propellers have electrical heating, as do the windshield and pitot tubes.

The basic figures came out as follows:

Overall length	97ft 9in (29.8m) (with retrofitted radome)
Span	132ft 7in (40.4m)
Overall height	38ft 3in (11.6m)
Horizontal tailplane overall length	52.7in (133.8cm)
Main landing gear overall width	14.3in (36.3cm)
Cabin to ramp cargo length	40.4ft (12.3m)
Cabin to ramp cargo width	123.2in (3.13m) tapering to 120in (3.05m) at rear entrance
Maximum ramp weight	124,200lb (56,337kg)
Maximum landing weight – 5 fps	124,200lb (56,337kg)
Maximum landing weight – 9 fps	96,000lb (43,545kg)
Operating weight	61,842lb (28,051kg)
Empty weight without external tanks	72,231lb (32,763kg)
Maximum payload	35,000lb (15,876kg)
Fuel capacity @ 6.5lb/gal	39,975lb (18,132kg)
internal tanks	5,250 US gallons (19,873 litres)
external tanks	900 US gallons (3,407 litres)
total fuel volume	6,150 US gallons (23,280 litres)

Engine model	4 × Allison turbo-prop, constant-speed T56-A-9; provision for 8 × 1,000lb (454kg) thrust-assisted take-off (ATO) rockets.
Engine take-off power	3,750 eshp
Auxiliary power	1 auxiliary power unit (APU) to provide air during ground engine starting and for air conditioning and electrical power; emergency electrical power during flight up to 20,000ft (6,096m)
Propeller	4 × Aeroproducts electro-hydromatic, constant-speed, full-feathering, reversible-pitch
Number of propeller blades	3
Diameter of propellers	15ft (4.6m)
Outboard propeller/ground clearance	68in (1.73m)
Inboard propeller/ground clearance	60.6in (1.54m)
Inboard propeller/fuselage clearance	28.8in (73.1cm)
Performance:	
maximum speed	383mph (616km/h)
cruise speed	356mph (573km/h)
rate of climb	1,700ft/min (518m/min)
Service ceiling at 100,000lb	34,000ft (10,360m)
Range with maximum payload	1,830 miles (2,945km)
Range with external tanks	3,359 miles (5,390km)
Wing area	1,745 sq ft (162.1m^2)
Wing loading	71.2lb (32.7kg) /sq ft
Wing aspect ratio	10.09
Cargo compartment floor length	41ft (12.5m)
Cargo compartment width	120in (3.05m)
Cargo compartment height	108in (2.74m)
Cargo compartment floor area	533 sq ft (49.5m^2) – including ramp space
Cargo compartment usable volume	4,500 cu ft (127.4m^3)
Wing-tip turning radius	85ft (25.9m)
Nose-gear turning radius	37ft (11.3m)
Wheel base	32.1ft (9.8m)
Main-gear tyre size	20:00–20
Nose-gear tyre size	12:50–16

Oil	8 US gallon (30.3-litre) capacity independent system per engine
Fuel	Modified manifold-flow type incorporating fuel cross-feed, single-point refuelling (SPR) and defuelling
Electrics	4×40-kVa engine-drive DC generators for 28-volt system; 1×20-kVa APU-driven generator; 1×24-volt, 36-ampere-hour battery
Hydraulics	$4 \times$ engine-driven pumps supplying 3,000 psi pressure to utility and booster systems; $1 \times$ compressed air pump supplying pressure to auxiliary system, backed up by hand-pump
Air conditioning & pressurisation	$2 \times$ independent systems for flight deck and cargo compartment, bleed-operated from engine compressors in flight, or APU on ground; each system providing 15,000ft (4,572m) cabin at 35,000ft (10,668m) altitude; maximum pressure differential of 7.5 psi maintains an 8,000ft (2,438m) cabin at the same altitude
Oxygen	Gaseous-type system providing 36 manhours of oxygen at 25,000ft (7,620m) with diluter-demand automatic pressure-breathing regulators; also portable units
Cargo fittings & fixtures	10,000lb (4,536kg) D-ring tiedown floor fittings on a 20in (51cm) centre-on-centre grid pattern; $6 \times 25,000$lb (11,340kg) tiedown rings each side of floor; additional 5,000lb (2,268kg) tiedown rings along fuselage walls and on ramp; interchangeable troop seats/litter racks have special overhead, sidewall and floor fittings, normally stowed
Mechanised loading system	The USAF 463L MLS, with dual-rails, comprising roller conveyors attached to floor with tiedown fittings, with locking devices for cargo restraint and remote-operation release capable of handling both 88in (2.23m) $\times$ 54in (1.37m) and 88in (2.23m) $\times$ 108in (2.74m) pallets

The euphoria that surrounded the maiden flight of the Herk was followed by a near-disastrous in-flight fire which broke out in the No. 2 engine of 53-3129 (c/n 3001) on 14 April 1955, as she was landing at Dobbins AFB. The Lockheed test pilots Leo Sullivan and Art Hansen had been conducting routine aerial engine tests on the aircraft's third flight, under the supervision of Chief Development Test Engineer Lloyd Frisbee and his team. Each engine was, in turn, feathered and then air-started again. The trials went well, but while landing the Royln coupling, which had not been properly locked, came apart and the quick-disconnect fuel line came loose at the fuel tank boost pump. Within seconds JP-4 oil started pumping out from the No. 2 nacelle, and subsequently ignited. Although the aircraft survived, the fire spread and the port wing broke in half on the runway as the crew abandoned the aircraft.

Subsequently repaired, she was later converted into a JC-130A and served a long life in various capacities, including gunship combat duty in Vietnam, surviving a direct hit by a 37mm (1.45in) round. Named *The First Lady*, she ended up in the USAF Armament Museum at Eglin. All that could be salvaged from her was transferred to serial 54-1624 (c/n 3011), which became the new flight test programme aircraft in her stead.

Retro fittings on forty-nine production aircraft included the substitution of the original Curtiss-Wright variable-pitch, electric, three-bladed, hollow-steel propellers for the four-bladed Hamilton Standard type. This followed continuing problems with the former due to the reduction gear system being unable to cope with pitch control changes, resulting in propeller oscillation and numerous defective units. This threatened the whole programme and aircraft serial 53-3134 (c/n 3006) was used to experiment with a different design, the Aeroproducts hydraulically operated propeller, built by General Motors Detroit Diesel Allison Division from 26 November 1955 to July 1956. This led to it being adopted for the C-130A for a time. However, this proved but a temporary expedient, and a second change was made to the Hamilton Standard product, and this

became the standard Hercules powerplant until the C-130J arrived on the scene decades later.

The 3245th Test Group (Bombardment) based at Eglin conducted a series of trials in mid-1956 in conjunction with Continental Army Command Board Five at Fort Bragg and the 3rd Aerial Port Squadron. One C-130A flew from El Centro, California, and made a para-drop of what was then a world record single load of 27,000lb (12,247kg) of iron. This was followed by another Hercules, serial 54-1623 (c/n 3010), which conducted a series of eighty-six sorties from Pope AFB, North Carolina, in which a total of 160 tons of supplies, 485 paratroops and 315 dummies were dropped successfully. The conversion versatility figures were equally impressive, with just twenty minutes being taken to change the configuration of thirty troop-seats to the heavy freight hold and forty minutes to change from a forty-seater to a heavy-freight platform dropper. During trial a 22,235lb (10,086kg) Marine Corps weapons-carrier was dropped, followed immediately by paratroops. During a six-day test period a freight platform was dropped from the ramp, again closely followed by five parachutists.

The USAF in Europe conducted an early loading

The City of Ardmore, *55-0023 (c/n 3050), which was the first C-130A to go on operational duty with the USAF and was still flying regular airlift missions a decade or more later with the Air Force Reserve after a world-wide career that included Purple Heart action in Vietnam. This aircraft was assigned to the 928th Tactical Airlift Group based at O'Hare airport, Chicago and the aircraft is pictured over that city. She was later transferred to the Air National Guard at Nashville, Tennessee.* (Lockheed-Georgia Newsbureau via Audrey Pearcy)

demonstration during which a 13,000lb (5,897kg) *Matador* missile was engorged by a Hercules in less than fifteen minutes. At the US Army Engineer Research and Development Laboratories at McGuire AFB, New Jersey, the Army's Corps of Engineers offloaded Bailey Bridge section-carrying trucks from a Hercules at the rate of one every fifteen seconds and proved capable of airlifting an 18-ton D7 bulldozer, a wheeled asphalt plant, road graders and scrapers, heavy highway rollers and similar road and runway building equipment with ease. They also shifted a

Bell XH-40 helicopter from Fort Worth, Texas, to Edwards AFB, California, along with a test crew of eight in just a few hours.

The 463rd Troop Carrier Wing (TCW) of Tactical Air Command was present at these trials, and assessments were made of spare parts availability, maintenance requirements and crew-training needs. This unit subsequently took delivery of the first four C-130As at Ardmore AFB, California, on 9 December 1956. The first aircraft to arrive, the fiftieth to come off the production line, was 55-0023 (c/n 3050), which was named *City of Ardmore*. She also gave good service, also surviving combat damage in Vietnam, and was preserved at the Texas Museum of Military History (now Linear Air Park at Dyess AFB).

The most significant retrofit of all (from the public perception of the Hercules, if nothing else) was the introduction of the AN/APS-42 and AN/APS-59 search radar sets, which were fitted to the lower half of the blunt front of the fuselage. This transferred the stern 'Roman Nose' appearance of the Hercules into a softer 'Baby Seal' profile, and the Herk took on a whole new image which, if not beautiful, was more enduring.

Between 1958 and 1969 all C-130As were progressively given make-overs, with re-skinning of 30% of the fuselage with thicker panels, making them capable of carrying a 20-ton payload to 35,000ft (10,668m). In

This is a Hercules C-130B, coded 403, making a steady approach. (Martin W. Bowman)

addition, a tandem rudder boost system was installed and electrical systems were redesigned. Provision was also made to carry two 450 US gallon (1,703-litre) underwing pinion fuel tanks outboard of the engines. Propeller speed was reduced, lessening the internal noise level and decreasing vibration, but without any reduction in performance.

5 The C-130B-*LM*

The C-130B-*LM* (Model 282), which first flew on 20 November 1958, had an improved engine, the four-bladed propeller, stronger landing gear and additional in-built centre-wing section fuel tanks, thus doing away with the optional pylon-mounted tanks of the C-130A. The forward cargo door on the port side remained but was sealed, bunks were provided in a deepened cockpit space for the aircrew, and the centre wing section was strengthened. Some had the AN/URT-26 crash position indicator (CPI) in the extended tail cone, and a tactical precision approach system (TPAS).

Overall length	97ft 8in (29.8m)	cruise speed	356mph (573km/h)
Span	132ft 7in (40.4m)	rate of climb	1,700ft/min (518m/min)
Overall height	38ft 3in (11.6m)	Service ceiling at 100,000lb	34,000ft (10,360m)
Horizontal tailplane overall length	52.7in (1.34m)	Range with maximum payload	1,830 miles (2,945km)
Main landing gear overall width	14.3in (36.3cm)	Range with external tanks	3,359 miles (5,390km)
Cabin to ramp cargo length	40.4ft (12.3m)	Wing area	1,745 sq ft (162.1m^2)
Cabin to ramp cargo width	123.2in (3.13m) tapering to 120in (3.05m) at rear entrance	Wing loading	77.4lb (35.1kg) /sq ft
		Wing aspect ratio	10.09
Maximum ramp weight	135,000lb (61,235kg)	Cargo compartment floor length	41ft (12.5m)
Maximum landing weight – 5 fps	135,000lb (61,235kg)	Cargo compartment width	120in (3.05m)
Maximum landing weight – 9 fps	118,000lb (53,524kg)	Cargo compartment height	108in (2.74m)
		Cargo compartment floor area	533 sq ft (49.5m^2) – including ramp space
Operating weight	69,376lb (31,468kg)		
Maximum payload	35,000lb (15,876kg)	Cargo compartment usable volume	4,500 cu ft (127.4m^3)
Fuel capacity @ 6.5lb/gal	45,240lb (20,520kg)	Wing-tip turning radius	85ft (25.9m)
internal tanks	6,960 US gallons (26,346 litres)	Nose-gear turning radius	37ft (11.3m)
		Wheel base	32.1ft (9.8m)
external tanks	Nil	Main-gear tyre size	20:00–20
total fuel volume	6,960 US gallons (26,346 litres)	Nose-gear tyre size	12:50–16
		Oil	12 US gallon (45.4-litre) capacity independent system per engine
Engine model	4 × Allison turbo-prop, constant-speed T56-A-7; provision for 8 × 1,000lb (453.5kg) thrust-assisted take-off (ATO) rockets.	Fuel	Modified manifold-flow type incorporating fuel cross-feed, single-point refuelling (SPR) and defuelling; provision for fuel dumping
Engine take-off power	4,050 eshp		
Auxiliary power	1 auxiliary power unit (APU) to provide air during ground engine starting and for air conditioning and electrical power; emergency electrical power during flight up to 20,000ft (6,096m)	Electrics	4 × 40-kVa engine-drive AC generators for 28-volt system; 1 × 20-kVa APU-driven generator; 1 × 24-volt, 36-ampere-hour battery
		Hydraulics	4 × engine-driven pumps supplying 3,000 psi pressure to utility and booster systems; 1 × electrical motor-driven pump supplying pressure to auxiliary system, backed up by hand-pump
Propeller	4 × Hamilton Standard electro-hydromatic, constant-speed, full-feathering, reversible-pitch		
Number of propeller blades	4		
Diameter of propellers	13.5ft (4.1m)		
Outboard propeller/ground clearance	79in (2m)		
Inboard propeller/ground clearance	69.6in (1.7m)	Air conditioning & pressurisation	2 × independent systems for flight deck and cargo compartment, bleed-operated from engine compressors in flight, or APU on ground; each system providing 15,000ft (4,572m) cabin at 35,000ft
Inboard propeller/fuselage clearance	37.8in (96cm)		
Performance:			
maximum speed	383mph (616km/h)		

Oxygen

Cargo fittings & fixtures

(10,668m) altitude; maximum pressure differential of 7.5 psi maintains an 8,000ft (2,438m) cabin at the same altitude Gaseous-type system providing 40 manhours of oxygen at 25,000ft (7,620m) with diluter-demand automatic pressure-breathing regulators; also portable units 10,000lb (4,536kg) D-ring tiedown floor fittings on a 20in (51cm) centre-on-centre grid pattern; 6 × 25,000lb (11,340kg) tiedown rings each side of floor; additional 5,000lb (2,268kg) tiedown rings along fuselage walls and on ramp; interchangeable troop seats/litter racks have special

Mechanised loading system

overhead, sidewall and floor fittings, normally stowed The USAF 463L MLS, with dual-rails, comprising roller conveyors attached to floor with tiedown fittings, with locking devices for cargo restraint and remote-operation release capable of handling both 88in (2.23m) × 54in (1.37m) and 88in (2.23m) × 108in (2.74m) pallets

Seen over Hickam Field Air Force Base in June 1969 is this C-130B of 11 JDS/355. (Nick Williams AAHS)

A contrast in styles and size at Marietta. In the foreground the XV-4A Hummingbird I prototype, with, behind her, the C-130B-70-LM, No. 62-3492 (c/n 3702), flanked by early JetStar models. (Lockheed via Audrey Pearcy)

While the engines were rated at 300hp above the As, they still revolved at 13,820rpm; 10,000rpm ground operation selection was available. One engine had to be operated at full rpm for the a/c generator operation or the ATM switched on. The B had no provision for any under-wing pinion-mounted tanks.

As just one example of the C-130B's longevity, as late as June 1988 the 731st Tactical Airlift Squadron (AFRES) at Peterson AFB, Colorado was running seventeen Bs, serials 58-0713 (c/n 3508); 58-0723 (c/n 3518); 58-0738 (c/n 3535); 58-0757 (c/n 3558); 59-1526 (c/n 3563); 59-1527 (c/n 3568); 59-1530 (c/n 3576); 59-1531 (c/n 3579); 59-1537 (c/n 3589); 60-0294 (c/n 3593); 60-0295 (c/n 3596); 60-0296 (c/n 3597); 60-0299 (c/n 3603); 60-0300 (c/n 3604); 60-0303 (c/n 3613); 60-0310 (c/n 3622) and 61-0948 (c/n 3624). The airframe

with the highest time at that date was 59-1527 which had 18,194.2 hours on her clock on 24 June 1988.[2]

6 The C-130E-*LM*

On 15 August 1961, the C-130E made her debut, being specifically designed for the Military Airlift Command (MAC) with their longer-range logistic supply role. Fuel bunkerage was accordingly increased, and larger, optional, underwing tanks could be carried, necessarily this time further inboard, being positioned between the two engine nacelles. The large cargo-loading door on port side of the forward fuselage had been found to be virtually redundant in earlier models and was seldom used, and with the C-130E this was done away with completely.

---

[2] Letter from Flight Engineer Eric P. Deylius, 731st TAS, AFRES, Peterson Air Force Base, Colorado, dated 24 June 1988.

Flanked by the Lockheed C-130 production line at the Georgia plant, the then President of the company, Larry Kitchen, makes a Christmas 1970 address to the employees. (Lockheed via Audrey Pearcy)

Showing clearly the vast difference in size, two of the RAF's Hercules fleet, XV223 (c/n 4253) and XV217 (c/n 4244), of different vintages, lined up side-by-side. (Martin W. Bowman)

Overall length	97ft 8in (29.8m)
Span	132ft 7in (40.4m)
Overall height	38ft 3in (11.6m)
Horizontal tailplane overall length	52.7in (1.34m)
Main landing gear overall width	14.3in (36.3cm)
Cabin to ramp cargo length	40.4ft (12.3m)
Cabin to ramp cargo width	123.2in (3.13m) tapering to 120in (3.05m) at rear entrance
Maximum ramp weight	155,000lb (70,307kg)
Maximum landing weight – 5 fps	155,000lb (70,307kg)
Maximum landing weight – 9 fps	130,000lb (58,967kg)
Operating weight	73,563lb (34,275kg)
Maximum payload	45,579lb (20,674kg)
Fuel capacity @ 6.5lb/gal	62,920lb (28,540kg)
internal tanks	6,960 US gallons (26,346 litres)
external tanks	2,720 US gallons (10,296 litres)
total fuel volume	9,680 US gallons (36,643 litres)
Engine model	4 × Allison turbo-prop, constant-speed T56-A-7; provision for 8 × 1,000lb (453.5kg) thrust-assisted take-off (ATO) rockets.

Engine take-off power	4,050 eshp
Auxiliary power	1 auxiliary power unit (APU) to provide air during ground engine starting and for air conditioning and electrical power; emergency electrical power during flight up to 20,000ft (6,096m)
Propeller	4 × Hamilton Standard electro-hydromatic, constant-speed, full-feathering, reversible-pitch
Number of propeller blades	4
Diameter of propellers	13.5ft (4.1m)
Outboard propeller/ground clearance	79in (2m)
Inboard propeller/ground clearance	60.6in (1.54m)
Inboard propeller/fuselage clearance	37.8in (96cm)
Performance:	
maximum speed	384mph (618km/h)
cruise speed	368mph (558km/h)
rate of climb	1,830ft/min (518m/min)
Service ceiling at 100,000lb	23,000ft (7,010m)
Range with maximum payload	2,420 miles (3,895km)
Range with external tanks	4,700 miles (7,560km)
Wing area	1,745 sq ft (162.1m^2)
Wing loading	88.8lb (40.3kg) /sq ft

Wing aspect ratio	10.09
Cargo compartment floor length	41ft (12.5m)
Cargo compartment width	120in (3.05m)
Cargo compartment height	108in (2.74m)
Cargo compartment floor area	533 sq ft (49.5m^2) – including ramp space
Cargo compartment usable volume	4,500 cu ft (127.4m^3)
Wing-tip turning radius	85ft (25.9m)
Nose-gear turning radius	37ft (11.3m)
Wheel base	32.1ft (9.8m)
Main-gear tyre size	20:00–20
Nose-gear tyre size	12:50–16
Oil	12 US gallon (45.4-litre) capacity independent system per engine
Fuel	Modified manifold-flow type incorporating fuel cross-feed, single-point refuelling (SPR) and defuelling; fuel dumping provision
Electrics	4 × 40-kVa engine-drive AC generators for 28-volt system; 1 × 20-kVa APU-driven generator; 1 × 24-volt, 36-ampere-hour battery
Hydraulics	4 × engine-driven pumps supplying 3,000 psi pressure to utility and booster systems; 1 × electrical motor-driven pump supplying pressure to auxiliary system, backed up by hand-pump
Air conditioning & pressurisation	2 × independent systems for flight deck and cargo compartment, bleed-operated from engine compressors in flight, or APU on ground; each system providing 15,000ft (4,572m) cabin at 35,000ft (10,668m) altitude; maximum pressure differential of 7.5 psi maintains an 8,000ft (2,438m) cabin at the same altitude
Oxygen	300 psi liquid-type system providing 96 manhours of oxygen at 25,000ft (7,620m) with diluter-demand automatic pressure-breathing regulators; also portable units
Cargo fittings & fixtures	10,000lb (4,536kg) D-ring tiedown floor fittings on a 20in (51cm) centre-on-centre grid pattern; 6 × 25,000lb (11,340kg) tiedown rings each side of floor; additional 5,000lb (2,268kg) tiedown rings along fuselage walls and on ramp; interchangeable troop seats/litter racks have special overhead, sidewall and floor fittings, normally stowed
Mechanised loading system	The USAF 463L MLS, with dual-rails, comprising roller conveyors attached to floor with tiedown fittings, with locking devices for cargo restraint and remote-operation release capable of handling both 88in (2.23m) × 54in (1.37m) and 88in (2.23m) × 108in (2.74m) pallets

The extra fuel bunkerage enabled the E to haul a 35,000lb (15,876kg) payload 900 nautical miles (1,667km), further than the B and about 1,200 miles (1,931km) further than the A, and greatly extended its value.

In June 1980, Lockheed announced that a USAF C-130E from Pope AFB had been equipped with the experimental two 7ft (2.1m) long 'tail fins', which they termed 'afterbody strakes', along with strain gauges and flight test instrumentation equipment. The strakes consisted of lightweight aluminium/fibreglass fins, 7ft (2.1m) long × 4in (10.16cm) thick and 20in (50.8cm) in height, installed ventrally on the after fuselage. They were designed to smooth the air flow over the rear of the fuselage, reducing the Herk's aerodynamic drag. Although not a new concept at that time, those fitted to the C-130 were the first to be fitted solely with the aim of improving fuel conservation. Mr L. R. Woodward of Lockheed's aerodynamic section went on record claiming that, as a result of tests at the Warner Robins Air Logistic Center, a 3 to 3.5% fuel consumption saving could result, which would save the USAF $9 million annually on J-4 aviation fuel. Each strake fitted to the USAF's 550 Herks would therefore pay for itself within three months. Further air drop trials at Pope confirmed that these strakes did not interfere with routine cargo-handling operations.

In May 1964, a specially prepared C-130E, registration N11390E (c/n 3946), painted red, white and blue, carried out a round-the-world, record-breaking flight covering 50,000 miles (80,462km) and touching down in sixteen different countries, starting with the 11th Annual Italian International Air Show at Turin. The crew was headed by pilot Joe Garrett, with Ira Giles as navigator, Al Barrett as chief flight engineer, Bob Hill as flight engineer and Ralph Evans as co-pilot. Also in 1964, on 20/21 April, this same C-130E, the *One-World* machine, broke the first production flight record with an endurance flight lasting twenty-five hours, one minute and eight seconds.[3] This broke the record formerly held by an HC-130 of the USAF Aerospace Rescue and Recovery Service (ARRS) which had flown 8,790 miles (14,146km) from Taiwan to Scott AFB, Illinois, in twenty-one hours and twelve minutes on 20 February 1962. The E never looked back from then on.

7 The C-130H-*LM*

By far the most prolific of all the Hercules variants to date, the C-130H (Model 382C) first appeared in March 1965 when the Royal New Zealand Air Force (RNZAF) took delivery of the first one, serial NZ 7001 (c/n 4052), having made her first flight on 19 November 1964. Again the engines were improved with the adoption of the 4,910 eshp T56-A-15 (de-rated to 4,508 eshp in service). Opportunity was also taken to make strength improvements to the centre-wing box assembly, and they were fitted with a beefed-up brake system. This 'long life' design-improvement wing box included fatigue-resistant fasteners. The new wing structure was fatigue-tested to 40,000 simulated flight hours and all the US services had their fleets retrofitted with the new centre wing section (but not the As), and the Australian, Brazilian, Colombian, Indonesian, Iranian, New Zealand, Pakistani and Saudi Arabian Herks all followed suit.

In 1972 the C-130's outer wings were given the same fatigue standards with the wing structural aluminium alloy upgraded to stress-corrosion-resistant 7057-T73 material with the latest sulphuric acid anodised surfaces as a base

for a polyurethane protective coating, and these were all incorporated in the later production line aircraft of late marks. The wing boxes were fay-surface sealed on assembly with corrosion-inhibitive polysulphide sealant, and structural fasteners were wet-installed with the same material, while external joins and seams were further protected with environmental 'aerodynamic smoother' sealant. The integral fuel tanks thus formed by the sealed structure were further sealed by fillet-sealing and fastener over-coating techniques. For extra corrosion protection within the integral tanks, and to eliminate the bacteria-promoting 'water bottoms', the new wings were equipped with a water-removal suction system actuated by the fuel boost pumps, which was pioneered on the C-5A.

Overall length	97ft 9in (29.8m)
Span	132ft 7in (40.4m)
Overall height	38ft 3in (11.6m)
Horizontal tailplane overall length	52.7in (1.34m)
Main landing gear overall width	14.3in (36.3cm)
Cabin to ramp cargo length	40.4ft (12.3m)
Cabin to ramp cargo width	123.2in (3.13m) tapering to 120in (3.05m) at rear entrance
Maximum ramp weight	155,000lb (70,307kg)
Maximum landing weight – 5 fps	155,000lb (70,307kg)
Maximum landing weight – 9 fps	130,000lb (58,967kg)
Operating weight	75,381lb (34,192kg)
Empty weight	73,618lb (33,393kg)
Empty weight without external tanks	72,231lb (32,763kg)
Maximum payload	43,761lb (19,850kg)
Fuel capacity @ 6.5lb/gal	62,920lb (28,540kg)
internal tanks	6,960 US gallons (26,346 litres)
external tanks	2,720 US gallons (10,296 litres)
total fuel volume	9,680 US gallons (36,643 litres)
Engine model	4 × Allison turbo-prop, constant-speed T56-A-9; provision for 8 × 1,000lb (453.5kg) thrust-assisted take-off (ATO) rockets
Engine take-off power	4,050 eshp
Auxiliary power	1 auxiliary power unit (APU) to

---

[3] See *Southern Star*, the newspaper of the Lockheed Corporation, April/May 1964 issues.

	provide air during ground engine starting and for air conditioning and electrical power; emergency electrical power during flight up to 20,000ft (6,096m)	Electrics	4 × 40-kVa engine-drive AC generators for 28-volt system; 1 × 20-kVa (40-kVa on some) APU-driven generator; 1 24-volt, 36-ampere-hour battery
Propeller	4 × Hamilton Standard electro-hydromatic, constant-speed, full-feathering, reversible-pitch	Hydraulics	4 × engine-driven pumps supplying 3,000 psi pressure to utility and booster systems; 1 × electrical motor-driven pump supplying pressure to auxiliary system, backed up by hand-pump
Number of propeller blades	4		
Diameter of propellers	13.5ft (4.1m)		
Outboard propeller/ground clearance	79in (2m)		
Inboard propeller/ground clearance	69.6in (1.77m)	Air conditioning & pressurisation	2 × independent systems for flight deck and cargo compartment, bleed-operated from engine compressors in flight, or APU on ground; each system providing 15,000ft (4,572m) cabin at 35,000ft (10,668m) altitude; maximum pressure differential of 7.5 psi maintains an 8,000ft (2,438m) cabin at the same altitude
Inboard propeller/fuselage clearance	37.8in (96cm)		
Performance:			
maximum speed	385mph (620km/h)		
cruise speed	332mph (535km/h)		
rate of climb	1,900ft/min (579m/min)		
Service ceiling at 100,000lb	33,000ft (10,060m)		
Range with maximum payload	2,356 miles (3,791km)		
Range with external tanks	4,894 miles (7,867km)	Oxygen	300 psi liquid-type system providing 96 manhours of oxygen at 25,000ft (7,620m) with diluter-demand automatic pressure-breathing regulators; also portable units
Wing area	1,745 sq ft (162.1m^2)		
Wing loading	88.8lb (40.3kg) /sq ft		
Wing aspect ratio	10.09		
Cargo compartment floor length	41ft (12.5m)		
Cargo compartment width	120in (3.05m)	Cargo fittings & fixtures	10,000lb (4,536kg) D-ring tiedown floor fittings on a 20in (51cm) centre-on-centre grid pattern; 6 × 25,000lb (11,340kg) tiedown rings each side of floor; additional 5,000lb (2,268kg) tiedown rings along fuselage walls and on ramp; interchangeable troop seats/litter racks have special overhead, sidewall and floor fittings, normally stowed
Cargo compartment height	108in (2.74m)		
Cargo compartment floor area	533 sq ft (49.5m^2) – including ramp space		
Cargo compartment usable volume	4,500 cu ft (127.4m^3)		
Wing-tip turning radius	85ft (25.9m)		
Nose-gear turning radius	37ft (11.3m)		
Wheel base	32.1ft (9.8m)		
Main-gear tyre size	20:00–20		
Nose-gear tyre size	39 × 13		
Oil	12 US gallon (45.4-litre) capacity independent system per engine	Mechanised loading system	The USAF 463L MLS, with dual-rails, comprising roller conveyors attached to floor with tiedown fittings, with locking devices for cargo restraint and remote-operation release capable of handling both 88in
Fuel	Modified manifold-flow type incorporating fuel cross-feed, single-point refuelling (SPR) and defuelling; fuel dumping provision		

(2.23m) × 54in (1.37m) and
88in (2.23m)
× 108in (2.74m) pallets

The upgrading of the engines gave standard day operators an increase of about 150 eshp per engine, making for
greatly improved aircraft performance. This increased
potential was particularly noticeable in hot weather conditions (103°F+) when the A-15 engine delivered 24%
greater shaft horse-power. This in turn translated itself into
as much as 500ft (152m) less take-off ground run and
1,000ft (305m) less total distance in order to clear a 50ft
(15m) obstacle, as well as lessening the landing distance.
No mean attributes in the type of environment that the
Herk regularly operates in. Also, the H could cruise some
3,000ft (914m) higher, five knots faster and had 2% greater
range than the E.

8 The C-130J-*LM*

Durable as the Hercules was (by 1999 she had accu-
mulated over twenty million flight hours and was in
use by sixty nations), with airframes that went on
for decades while their internal equipment was revamped
and revamped to keep up to date with half a century of fast
technological advances, there ultimately came a time when
the building of a brand-new aircraft became a more viable,
and in some cases cheaper, option long-term. At that point,
in 1991, the C-130J concept was born.[4] A projected production run of 600 machines was envisaged at that time.

The RAF was particularly anxious to replace its ageing,
twenty-seven-year-old Hercules fleet, but, as always, any
decision was preceded by a whole raft of speculation in the
British media, ranging from the sublime to the ridiculous,
and a hostile attitude from the Treasury, traditionally
opposed to any form of spending on the defence of the
realm. Contenders (real or imaginary) were touted almost
daily, and ranged from the European consortium Future
Large Aircraft (FLA), an updated, upgraded version of the
British HS.681 (which had been killed off by the 1964

C-130J cockpit layout, port side. (Martin W. Bowman)

defence cuts),[5] to the Russian-designed Antonov An-70T
built in Kiev, Ukraine.[6] It seemed that nothing was too
bizarre for the experts to tout as a Hercules replacement.
The scowling Treasury had yet another option: don't buy
any, just refurbish the existing aircraft and keep them going
somehow until the proposed British Aerospace FLA arrives
(a date of 2003 was given for this).[7] Air Chief Marshal Sir

[5] See 'Tailskid', article 'Full Circle', in *Air Pictorial* magazine, October
1993.

[6] See Harvey Elliott, 'RAF could replace its trusted Hercules with
Russian aircraft', article in *The Times*, 29 December 1992.

[7] As early as May 1961, the then British Aircraft Corporation had proposed building the BLC-130 Tactical Transport, which would be known
as the BAC 222, and which was to have been powered by Rolls-Royce
R. Ty 20-15 engines to meet UK Specification O.R.351.

[4] The J suffix had been briefly assigned to the projected design which
became the C-130SS, but was not officially adopted – see appropriate
section.

Patrick Hine, BAe's military adviser, stated that for the FLA to be selected, 'There has got to be a will within government to support this programme, but that will in the MoD is not there'. For the other side, Micky Blackwell, President of Lockheed's Aeronautical Systems company, put it clearly: 'Even the current model Hercules can't go on for ever. Most of the aircraft have been in service between twenty and thirty years.'[8]

In the end the British Government accepted the view (highly predictable for most outside observers, if not the press) that 'only a Hercules can replace a Hercules'. However, currently (2000) the RAF is also looking at the European Airbus A400M as a possible replacement for the rest of the C-130Ks.[9] With the direct British involvement and technological input of major companies like Rolls-Royce, Dowty Aerospace, Lucas Aerospace and GKN Westland, with more than forty others, and spurred by the urgent need to upgrade an obsolescent RAF transport fleet, work pressed ahead. The stated aim of Lockheed-Martin was to produce a state-of-the-art Hercules for the new millennium, a low-cost, low-risk aircraft, one that retained and capitalised on the Herk's name and fame, and even looked superficially the same, but which was a brand-new aircraft. The RAF placed an order for twenty-five of these 'second-generation' Herks in 1995 at a total cost of £1.1 billion, and the C-130J and C-130J-30 were designated the Hercules C4 and C5 respectively.

Even the test team was international in its composition, with test pilots including Lockheed-Martin's Bob Price working with Major Dave Alvin, USAF, Flight Lieutenant Muz Colquhoun, RAF, and Squadron Leader Robyn Williams, RAAF.

The C-130J essentially had much the same dimensions as the C-130E/H, while the stretched J-130J-30 had fifteen extra feet built into her in the form of two extension plugs. The forward extension plug is 100in (2.54m) long and the rear extension plug is 80in (2.03m) long to give a total of 180in (4.57m).

Internally, things are very different. The 'Glass Cockpit' concept prevails with multi-function displays. Each system component has its own computer and everything can be controlled: mission planning, digital mapping,

monitoring and advisory systems, integrated systems diagnostic testing and maintenance data recording and advisory systems. The dual Flight Dynamics (Collins-Kaiser) holographic head-up displays (HUD) each have a wide angle field of view (FOV) of 24° vertical by 30° horizontal and form the primary flight display for the first time ever on a transport aircraft. The HUD gives the pilot the whole control scenario, including altitude, attitude, roll scale, flight path, airspeed, vertical velocity and heading, as well as projecting flight director cues, time displays, reference settings and the like. This system minimises 'head-down' display transitions and maintains full situational awareness during air-drop and in-flight refuelling profiles when maximum up-to-the-second data is essential, as well as simplifying approach and landing operations. The HUD was not only a boon, it had reliability, with a mean time between failure (MTBF) of 5,400 hours. Straight away its introduction reduced the aircrew to just two, plus a loadmaster, with the elimination of the flight engineer and navigator, an enormous saving in personnel and costs.

The four head-down displays (HDD) are colour, multi-functional, liquid-crystal displays (LCDs) and are equally impressive, featuring the Avionic Display Corporation's high-resolution, active matrix, flat-panel LCDs which are able to present twelve alternative formats or pages of data. This LCD also permits overlaying the formats with route of flight (ROF) and colour weather information. This system alone obviates the need for in excess of ninety electromechanical flight deck displays, an enormous simplification. It has durability also, with a MTBF of 8,900 hours. Each internal display is also fully compatible with the night vision imaging system (NVIS), with night vision goggles, with Type 1, Class A or Type II, Class B systems. Both interior and exterior lighting is controlled through the avionics management unit (AMU) of the J and is compatible with this, including the internal light in the cargo compartment with the use of Class B, Types I and II systems. This lighting system supports night formation flying, air-to-air refuelling (both as tanker and receiving aircraft), night take-off, landing operations and night covert ground work. Exterior lights, formation lights and navigation lights all have a normal and a covert option.

The automatic thrust control system (ATCS) was also introduced, which automatically reduces asymmetric engine thrust should there be unexpected outboard engine failure. Power is automatically restored on the good engine as the airspeed increases. The system comprises computer-fed software working with the outboard engine's own computers.

---

[8] See John Davison and Andrew Lorenz, 'Funding row hits Hercules', article in *The Times*, 1993.

[9] See Paul Jackson, 'In the Pipeline?', article in *The Royal Air Force Yearbook 2000*, PRM Aviation, Bristol.

Close-up view of the unique scimitar-bladed D600-series propellers on a C-130J. (Courtesy of Dowty Aerospace Propellers, Gloucester)

Features include all-weather air drop capability (AWADS), one every aircraft to replace the fifty or so C-130E/Hs which had that capability. High-resolution ground-mapping capability with the APN-241 low-power colour radar, coupled with the Honeywell dual embedded INS/GPS and digital mapping systems, makes this possible. The weather/navigation radar is the Westinghouse AN/APN-241, with an enhanced traffic avoidance system (E-TCAS) as well as a ground avoidance system (GCAAS), the advisory caution and warning system (ACAWA) and the SKE-2000 station-keeping equipment, and she has the instrument landing system (ILS). The Alliant Defense AN/AAR-47 missile-warning system uses electro-optic sensors to detect missile exhaust and advanced signal processing algorithms and spectral selection to analyse and prioritise threats through sensors nose-mounted below the

second cockpit window and in the tail cone. The Tracor AN/ALE-47 countermeasures system dispenses chaff and infrared flares in addition to the primed oscillator expendable transponder (POET) and generic expendable (GEN-X) active expendable decoys. The Lockheed-Martin AN/ALQ-157 infrared countermeasures system, mounted at the aft end of the main undercarriage bay fairing, generates a varying IR jamming signal and gives all-round protection. The Northrop Grumman MODAR 4000 colour weather and navigation radar, installed in the

upward-hinged dielectric radome in the nose, has a range of 250 nautical miles (463km) and completes the sophisticated electronics suite.

The powerplant for the aircraft is the Rolls-Royce Allison AE2100D3 turbo-prop, rated at 4,591 eshp (3,424kW). There is automatic thrust control to the fly-by-wire propulsion system with the Lucas Aerospace Full-Authority, Digital Engine-Control (FADEC) system. The propeller that each engine drives is of the Dowty Aerospace, Staverton, Gloucestershire, R391 composite, scimitar-shaped, six-bladed type. They have a diameter of 13ft 6in (411.5cm), and the whole system, including control modules, weighs about 750lb (340kg) as against the C-130H's propellers, which Dowty also service, which weigh about 1,102lb (500kg). These distinctively shaped Series D-6000 propellers, so called because they can generate 6,000 shp, act as one of the J's few external identifying points against earlier models, the other being that the refuelling probe is now mounted on the port side of the aircraft, above the cockpit. These are each housed in a Westland-modified nacelle. Ground feathering of the propeller blades (HOTEL mode) is another built-in option, and this does away with troublesome prop blast while

Close-up detail of the experimental propeller on the RAF Hercules. (Martin W. Bowman)

loading or offloading troops and other personnel. Ease of replacement is another feature, with a change of propeller taking forty-five minutes to complete, compared to eight to ten hours on the C-130E/H.

There is a new and much-improved auxiliary power unit with double the life of the old one, the AiResearch APU. The fuel supply shows an equally impressive simplification, with just a solitary cross-ship manifold with foam installation in dry bays for extra fire safety. The landing gear shares the general upgrading with a new-design nose gear strut and a modular wheel fitting with self-jacking struts incorporated for faster wheel changing. A new automated braking system is installed, married to an anti-skid mechanism, as well as the Mk.IV carbon brakes themselves.

During trials unexpected stall characteristics were experienced and Lockheed developed an enhanced stall warning system with a stick pusher to help in this. The initial audible stall warning indication is given through the

The spacious pilot's cockpit of the C-130-30J. (Martin W. Bowman)

headset while speed is still in excess of 40 knots above stalling speed. When this drops to 7% above stall speed there is also a pilot visual indicator on both sides of the HUD and HDD, in addition to an audible warning. Should these warnings not be acted upon and the aircraft continues to decelerate, the stick pusher activates and automatically puts the aircraft in a nose-down attitude.

The J tankers are equipped with a new boom refuelling option developed by Lockheed-Martin in order to provide them with the capability of refuelling aircraft like the F-15 and F-16, which do not have the drogue and probe system in their build. A pump rate for this boom is 800 US gallons (3,028 litres) per minute. These gave impressive results, with General Walt Kross, commander of USAF Air Mobility Command, lifting off a J from Lockheed-Martin's Aeronautical Systems runway on 4 April 1997 in under 800ft (245m) of rolling length at a speed of 76 knots and a nose-up angle of 20°. Range was also increased to an impressive 3,000 nautical miles (5,556km). As a KC tanker aircraft the offloading rate for each refuelling pod is up to

300 US gallons/2,040 lb (1,137 litres/925kg) per minute simultaneously, with a load of 45,000lb (20,410kg).

As cost-saving was a prime selling point, Lockheed were at pains to point out the estimated advantages of the new C-130J over a revamped C-130E. They gave the following figures: a 50% reduction in maintenance manhours; 50% improved reliability; 46% reduction in total manpower requirements; and 47% savings in operating and support cost.

How some of these savings were achieved becomes clearer when one looks at the enhanced servicing and maintenance facilities of the C-130J over earlier models. For a start, the old maintenance plan based strictly on flying hour totals has been completely done away with. The new concept is for calendar-based servicing. Regardless of major usage, the new aircraft will receive servicing to the following schedule:

Every 30 weeks – primary servicing (two days instead of up to one week)

Every 120 weeks – intermediate minor servicing

Every 480 weeks – major servicing

Making this all possible is the new integrated diagnostic system (IDS) which communicates to all the onboard computers via the MIL-STD-1553 data bus.[10] Into the onboard reader is inserted a PCMCIA[11] card which is written to by the MCs after they have interrogated the onboard systems records. The fully downloaded card is removed and re-inserted into the ground maintenance system (GMS) computer which analyses all the card's data and makes diagnostic fault evaluations. This system will eventually do away with the time-consuming Form 700 aircraft maintenance record.

Of course, the PCMCIA card will also have stored on it the whole sum of each flight's data, including duration, engine hours, fuel usage, system malfunction and so on, and this data will also be downloaded to the GMS to build up a permanent record for each aircraft. As most of the onboard systems are modular in design, replacement is relatively simple and straightforward, with Lockheed-Martin

---

10 MIL-STD-1553 is the military standard bus originally developed to define a communications bus to interconnect different sub-systems which needed to share and exchange information. It evolved to become the predominant, internationally accepted data bus standard for military platforms and was adopted by the air forces, navies, armies and space agencies of nations worldwide. In addition to military aircraft this standard is used on tanks, warships, missiles, satellites and the International Space Station, as well as ground-based support in test equipment, simulators and trainers.

11 PCMCIA (Personal Computer Memory Card International Association) is the international standards body and trade association founded in 1989 to establish standards for integrated circuit (IC) cards and to promote interchangeability among mobile computers. It currently has more than three hundred members and its mission in the twenty-first century is to develop standards for modular peripherals and promote their worldwide adoption.

12 For example, the Lockheed-Martin storage facility for the RAF in the UK is at Cheney Manor Industrial Estate, Swindon, convenient for their main operational base of RAF Lyneham.

establishing warehouses containing most of them at strategic points both in the USA and overseas.[12]

The development of the new technology was difficult, resulting in delays in delivery. The US Federal Aviation Administration did not grant approval until September 1998, some four weeks after the first C-130J had been delivered to the RAF, a delay of twenty-one months. The first in-flight refuelling demonstrations by an RAF C-130J-30 utilising the HUD, with Lockheed-Martin Chief Test Pilot Bob Price and Flight Lieutenant Mark Robinson at the controls, took place from a VC tanker aircraft on 17 and 20 February 2000 at an 18,000ft (5,486m) rendezvous 100 miles (160km) east of Charleston, South Carolina. Some 30,000lb (13,607kg) of fuel was transferred.

At Edwards AFB, Dave Shaw of Lockheed took an RAF C-130J-30 successfully through a fortnight of air and ground propeller blade strain tests to comply with FAA regulations.

The maiden flight of the first of the twelve RAAF C-130J-30s took place on 16 February 2000 with Robyn Williams, RAAF, and Lyle Schaefer, Lockheed test pilot, with James Blagg, RAAF, and Steve Bloodworth, Lockheed-Martin, as flight test engineers, along with Lockheed's Jerry Edwards and Paul Buege. This aircraft is flying a dedicated avionics testing programme in service.

Meanwhile, the USAF, having ordered twenty-eight aircraft, anticipates buying at least 150 at twelve per year commencing in 2006. The first trio of J-30s are to undergo a comprehensive test plan to test the take-off and landing performance and their paratroop drop capabilities before joining their assigned unit, 143 Airlift Wing, Air National Guard, at Quonset State Airport, Rhode Island.

Italian orders for eighteen and Marine Corps for yet five more followed. Marine Corps Brigadier-General Randall L. West, the Legislative Assistant to the Commandant, flew a C-130J on 16 May 1997 in a demonstration which moved sixty fully equipped Marines over 1,200 miles (1,931km) to their forward operating base. Take-off was achieved in under 700ft (213m). Additional Italian orders increased their total take of twelve C-130Js and ten C-130J-30s. Their instrumentation included UHF/VHF combined multi-band radios and a laser warning receiver system. They are operated by the 46th Air Brigade, based at Pisa.

Perhaps one of the greatest boosts to the J's fledgling career came with the award of the National Aeronautic Association's (NAA) 'Most Memorable Record Flights of 1999'. With Lockheed test pilots Lyle Schaefer and Arlen Rens at the helm, an unmodified C-130 took off from

Dobbins AFB, Georgia, with a 22,500lb (10,205kg) payload, up in a distance of 915ft (279m) and then to a 40,386ft (12,309m) altitude in the spring of that year, breaking both the US and the world 10,000kg (22,046lb) payload records. She landed in a distance of 1,224ft (373m). The same flight also saw the breaking or setting of no fewer than fifty other world records in both the C-1.N and STOL categories. These records included speed over both 1,000km (621 miles) and 2,000km (1,242 miles) closed courses with payload; altitude; greatest altitude in horizontal flight, and time-to-climb to 3,000m (9,842ft), 6,000m (19,685ft) and 9,000m (29,527ft) respectively with a payload. By the end of that year the C-130J held a total of fifty-four world records, with an average of one a week being set, *itself* a unique record! By May 2000 orders had built up to ninety-six aircraft, thirty-seven for the US Government (including one Air National Guard EC-130J Psychological Warfare aircraft for 2001 delivery) and fifty-nine internationally.

Overall length	97ft 9in (29.8m)
Span	132ft 7in (40.4m)
Overall height	38ft 3in (11.6m)
Horizontal tailplane overall length	52.7in (1.34m)
Main landing gear overall width	14.3in (36.3cm)
Cabin to ramp cargo length	40.4ft (12.3m)
Cabin to ramp cargo width	123.2in (3.13m) tapering to 120in (3.05m) at rear entrance
Maximum ramp weight	155,000lb (70,307kg)
Maximum landing weight – 5 fps	155,000lb (70,307kg)
Maximum landing weight – 9 fps	96,000lb (43,545kg)
Operating weight	79,090lb (35,875kg)
Empty weight	73,618lb (33,393kg)
Empty weight without external tanks	72,231lb (32,763kg)
Maximum payload	41,043lb (18,617kg)
Fuel capacity @ 6.5lb/gal	39,975lb (18,132kg)
internal tanks	45,900lb (20,820kg) – 43,900lb (20,723kg) with foam
external tanks	18,700lb (8,482kg)
total fuel volume	64,100lb (29,075lb)
Engine model	4 × Allison AE2100D3 two-spool turbo-prop, oil-bath starter and modular gearbox; provision for 8 × 1,000lb

	(453.5kg) thrust-assisted take-off (ATO) rockets.
Engine take-off power	4,591 eshp (3,424kW)
Auxiliary power	1 auxiliary power unit (APU) to provide air during ground engine starting and for air conditioning and electrical power; emergency electrical power during flight up to 20,000ft (6,096m)
Propeller	4 × Dowty Aerospace composite R391 scimitar-shaped unit
Number of propeller blades	6
Diameter of propellers	13.6ft (4.1m)
Performance:	
maximum cruise speed	400mph (645km/h)
rate of climb	1,700ft/min (518m/min)
Service ceiling at 100,000lb	34,000ft (10,360m)
Range with maximum payload	1,830 miles (2,945km)
Range with external tanks	3,359 miles (5,390km)
Wing area	1,745 sq ft (162.1m^2)
Wing loading	71.2lb (32.3kg) /sq ft
Wing aspect ratio	10.09
Cargo compartment floor length	56ft (17.1m)
Cargo compartment width	120in (3.05m)
Cargo compartment height	108in (2.74m)
Cargo compartment floor area	533 sq ft (49.5m^2) – including ramp space
Cargo compartment usable volume	4,500 cu ft (127.4m^3)
Cargo loading:	37,216lb (16,881kg)
Wing-tip turning radius	85ft (25.9m)
Nose-gear turning radius	37ft (11.3m)
Wheel base	32.1ft (9.8m)
Main-gear tyre size	20:00–20
Nose-gear tyre size	12:50–16
Oil	12 US gallon (45.4-litre) capacity independent system per engine
Fuel	Modified manifold-flow type incorporating fuel cross-feed, single-point refuelling (SPR) and defuelling
Electrics	4 × 40-kVa engine-drive DC generators for 28-volt system; 1 × 20-kVa APU-driven generator; 1 24-volt,

Hydraulics	36-ampere-hour battery 4 × engine-driven pumps supplying 3,000 psi pressure to utility and booster systems; 1 × compressed air pump supplying pressure to auxiliary system, backed up by hand-pump	(11,340kg) tiedown rings each side of floor; additional 5,000lb (2,268kg) tiedown rings along fuselage walls and on ramp; interchangeable troop seats/litter racks have special overhead, sidewall and floor fittings, normally stowed
Air conditioning & pressurisation	2 × independent systems for flight deck and cargo compartment, bleed-operated from engine compressors in flight, or APU on ground; each system providing 15,000ft (4,572m) cabin at 40,000ft (12,192m) altitude; maximum pressure differential of 7.5 psi maintains an 8,000ft (2,438m) cabin at the same altitude	Mechanised loading system
Oxygen	Gaseous-type system providing 36 manhours of oxygen at 25,000ft (7,620m) with diluter-demand automatic pressure-breathing regulators; also portable units	
Cargo fittings & fixtures	10,000lb (4,536kg) D-ring tiedown floor fittings on a 20in (51cm) centre-on-centre grid pattern; 6 × 25,000lb	

Mechanised loading system — Integral flip-over roller conveyors and dual row, right/left centreline container delivery system (CDS) centre vertical restraint (CVR) rails; variable speed, electric winch flush-mounted in front cargo compartment floor; Loadmaster console controls electric load-sensing locks on low-profile rails; electric towplate flush-mounted in the ramp or accurate airdrop load extraction; aerial delivery system (ADS) ramp support arms remain connected for all operations; also note cargo ramp and door opening capability for high-speed target ingress/egress

In-flight portrait of C-130J, N130JC (c/n 5413). (Martin W. Bowman)

*Low-level turn seen from above by this RAF Hercules XV190
(c/n 4211) over the English countryside.* (Martin W. Bowman)

Flight deck view and instrument layout. (Martin W. Bowman)

The Hercules head-up display. (Martin W. Bowman)

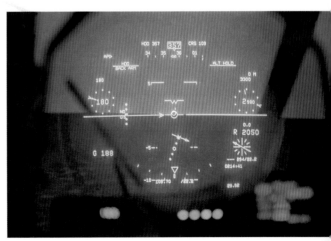

The first C-130-J, N130JA (c/n 5408), which became ZH 865, rollout at Lockheed Martin, pipers and all, on 18 October 1995. The aircraft is a C-130J-30 for the Royal Air Force. (Lockheed Martin Aeronautical Systems Company via Martin W. Bowman)

A magnificent spectacle, the new C-130-30J N130JA (c/n 5408) Hercules, immaculate in RAF colours, climbs from Marietta on her maiden flight. (Martin W. Bowman)

Comparison loading for the C-130J and the C-130J-30

Aircraft	C-130J	C-130J-30	Increase
Cargo Floor	40ft (12.2m)	55ft (16.8m)	37%
463L Cargo Pallets	6	8	34%
Litters	74	97	31%
Container Bundles	16	24	50%
Combat Troops	92	128	39%
Paratroops	64	92	44%

Currently (2000), ninety-eight C-130Js of both types are built or being built:

America Serials 94-3026 (c/n 5413) later civilian N130JC; 94-3027 (c/n 5415) later civilian N130JG; 96-8153 (c/n 5454) former civilian N4099R; 96-8154 (c/n 5455); 97-1351 (c/n 5469); 97-1352 (c/n 5470); 97-1353 (c/n 5471); 98-1355 (c/n 5491); 98-1356 (c/n 5492); 98-1357 (c/n 5493); 98-1358 (c/n 5494); 46-20 (c/n 5495).

Starboard inner firing nicely as RAF Hercules XV181 (c/n 4198) kicks off in her revetment. (Martin W. Bowman)

Comparison in style and design of both the standard and the stretch variants of the C-130J in this excellent aerial study. (Martin W. Bowman)

Great Britain Serials ZH880 (c/n 5478), former civilian N73238; ZH881 (c/n 5479) former civilian N4249Y; ZH882 (c/n 5480) former civilian N4081M; ZH883 (c/n 5481) former civilian N4242N; ZH884 (c/n 5482) former civilian N4249Y; ZH885 (c/n 5483) former civilian N41030; ZH886 (c/n 5484) former civilian N73235; ZH887 (c/n 5485) former civilian N4187W; ZH888 (c/n 5496) former civilian N4187.

Italy – Serials 46-20, later 46-40 (c/n 5495); 46-41 (c/n 5497); 46-42 (c/n 5498); 46-43 (c/n 5503); 46-44 (c/n 5504); 46-45 (c/n 5505); 46-46 (c/n 5510); 46-47 (c/n 5511); 46-48 (c/n 5512); 46-49 (c/n 5513); 46-50 (c/n 5514); 46-51 (c/n 5520). C-130J-30s:- 46-52 (c/n 5521); 46-53 (c/n 5523); 46-54 (c/n 5529); 46-55 (c/n 5530); 46-56 (c/n 5531); 46-57 (c/n 5539); 46-58 (c/n 5540); 46-59 (c/n 5550); 46-60 (c/n 5552).

All the main types, C-130A, C-130B, C-130E, C-130H and C-130J, have spawned a huge number of sub-types and variants with specialised spin-offs from the 'norm', and these are all described in their appropriate sections.

9 The C-130K

First flown on 19 October 1966, the C-130K (Model 382-19B) was the British equivalent for RAF Support Command of the C-130H, but with many components supplied by Scottish Aviation and with UK electronics and instrumentation fitting the responsibility of the Cambridge-based company Marshall Engineering. Some sixty-six of this Variant C.1 were delivered, and were known in the RAF as the Hercules C.Mk I. Six C.1s were modified to tankers as the C.1K – serials XV192 (c/n 4212), XV201 (c/n 4224), XV203 (c/n 4227), XV204 (c/n 4228), XV213 (c/n 4240) and XV296 (c/n 4262) – while twenty-six serials – XV178 (c/n 4188), XV179 (c/n 4195), XV181 (c/n 4198), XV182 (c/n 4199), XV185 (c/n 4203), XV186 (c/n 4204), XV187 (c/n 4205), XV191 (c/n 4211), XV192 (c/n 4212), XV195 (c/n 4216), XV196 (c/n 4217), XV200 (c/n 4223), XV205 (c/n 4230), XV206 (c/n 4231), XV210 (c/n 4236), XV211 (c/n 4237), XV215 (c/n 4242), XV218 (c/n 4245), XV291 (c/n 4256), XV292 (c/n 4257), XV293 (c/n 4258), XV295 (c/n 4261), XV297 (c/n 4263), XV298 (c/n 4264), XV300 (c/n 4267) and XV306 (c/n 4274) – had in-flight refuelling added to become C.1Ps. Subsequently thirty C.1 aircraft – serials XV176 (c/n 4169), XV177 (c/n 4182), XV183 (c/n 4200), XV184 (c/n 4201), XV188 (c/n 4206), XV189 (c/n 4207),

XV190 (c/n 4210), XV193 (c/n 4213), XV197 (c/n 4218), XV199 (c/n 4220), XV202 (c/n 4226), XV207 (c/n 4232), XV209 (c/n 4235), XV212 (c/n 4238), XV214 (c/n 4241), XV217 (c/n 4244), XV219 (c/n 4246), XV220 (c/n 4247), XV221 (c/n 4251), XV222 (c/n 4252), XV223 (c/n 4253), XV290 (c/n 4254), XV294 (c/n 4259), XV299 (c/n 4266), XV301 (c/n 4268), XN302 (c/n 4270), XV303 (c/n 4271), XV304 (c/n 4272), XV305 (c/n 4273) and XV307 (c/n 4275) – were modified with 'stretched' fuselages like the civilian L-100-30s, with a 15ft (4.6m) extension, and these became the Hercules C.3. These then had in-flight refuelling added to become the C.3P.

10 Civilian Use: the Basic L-100

Enormously useful and efficient in military service the world over, Lockheed were obviously not over-looking the huge potential civilian market for such a versatile aircraft. Since she first obtained her FAA type certificate on 16 February 1965, the basic civilian variant, the L-100 series (Models 382 and 382B), which was derived from the C-130E model, has proved just about the most popular bulk hauler there is and has been operated by the full range of users: scheduled airlines, contract carriers, leasing companies and quasi-governmental agencies in the Third World where they double as military transports whenever the need arises. Like their Air Force counterparts these civilian operators have found that the Hercules can get into, and get out of, practically any air strip, from jungle clearing and mountain-hemmed patch to compacted sand.

In the same manner as the C-130 variants, the first L-100, registration N1130E (c/n 3946), which made her maiden twenty-five-hour-and-one-minute flight on 20/21 April 1964, most of it on just two engines, had both fully air-conditioned and fully pressurised cockpit and cargo compartments, both on the ground and in the air. Much of the military fittings were extraneous to commercial operation and were done away with, including the aerial delivery system, troop seating and litter racking; even the navigator's station was redundant, and the underwing fuel tanks were also omitted. Aircrew accommodation was for three men plus one observer, while the 10ft (3.05m) wide × 9ft (2.75m) high cargo compartment gave easy access and wide, straight-in loading, as useful for moving freight as for moving tanks. The 42in (1.07m) high truck-level integral ramp, adjustable to ground level, was just as useful for loading from a freight-dock and gave a further ten feet.

The cargo compartment itself was fitted out with the same 20in (51cm) centre-on-centre grid pattern of 10,000lb (4,536kg) D-ring tiedown floor fittings and 25,000lb (11,340kg) tiedown rings along the sides of the fuselage and on the ramp. Flooring, strengthened with military vehicles and equipment in mind, was therefore quite capable of carrying the heaviest machinery, like oil rig parts and heavy trucks, as well as anything else that could be palletised. The loading system employed on the L-100 was dual rail-roller with removable side restraint rails and rollers on the cargo floor, plus a 9g barrier net at the forward end. The guide rails along the outboard rollers were movable, accommodating either 88in (2.23m), 109in (2.77m) or 118in (2.99m) wide pallets, or 8ft (2.44m) wide containers. The L-100 could therefore swallow with ease either the standard 8ft × 8ft (2.44m × 2.44m) container straight from the haulage vehicle or a selection of palletised loads, including, with length-wise loading, the 88in (2.23m) × 125in pallet, or conventional 88in (2.23m) × 118in (2.99m), 88in (2.23m) × 108in (2.74m) or 88in (2.23m) × 54in (1.37m) half-sized pallets, all of which could be secured by hand-operated 9g restraining locks.

The first airline to operate the L-100 was Alaskan on 8 March 1965, when they leased the lead demonstrator aircraft from Lockheed. Twenty-one Model 382B production aircraft followed. Initial cargoes ranged from supplies for Alaskan bases to copper bars transportation in Africa. Most were subsequently 'stretched' to L-100-20, and some were stretched again to L-100-30 standard.

The figures for the basic L-100 were as follows:

Overall length	97ft 8in (29.8m)
Span	132ft 6in (40.4m)
Overall height	38ft 3in (11.6m)
Horizontal tailplane overall length	52.7in (1.34m)
Main landing gear overall width	14.3in (36.3cm)
Cabin to ramp cargo length	40.4ft (12.3m)
Cabin to ramp cargo width	123.2in (3.13m) tapering to 120in (3.05m) at rear entrance
Maximum ramp weight	155,800lb (70,670kg)
Maximum landing weight – 10 fps	130,000lb (58,967kg)
Operating weight	69,926lb (31,718kg)
Maximum payload	47,990lb (21,768kg)
Fuel capacity @ 6.7lb (3.039kg)/gal	64,668lb (29,333kg)
internal tanks	6,942 US gallons (26,278 litres)
external tanks	2,712 US gallons (10,266 litres)
total fuel volume	9,654 US gallons (36,544 litres)
Engine model	4 × Allison turbo-prop, constant-speed 501-D22
Engine take-off power	4,050 eshp flat-rated (sea level)
Auxiliary power	1 auxiliary power unit (APU) to provide air during ground engine starting and for air conditioning and electrical power; emergency electrical power during flight up to 20,000ft (6,096m)
Propeller	4 × Hamilton Standard electro-hydramatic, constant-speed, full-feathering, reversible-pitch
Number of propeller blades	4
Diameter of propellers	13.5ft (4.1m)
Outboard propeller/ground clearance	79in (2m)
Inboard propeller/ground clearance	69.6in (1.77m)
Inboard propeller/fuselage clearance	37.8in (96cm)
Performance:	
maximum speed	343mph (552km/h)
rate of climb	1,700ft/min (518m/min)
Service ceiling at 100,000lb	34,000ft (10,360m)
Range with maximum payload	1,569 miles (2,526km)
Range with external tanks	5,733 miles (9,227km) – with zero payload
Wing area	1,745 sq ft (162.1m²)
Wing loading	86.2lb (39kg) /sq ft
Wing aspect ratio	10.09
Cargo compartment floor length	49ft (14.9m)
Cargo compartment width	120in (3.05m)
Cargo compartment height	108in (2.74m)
Cargo compartment floor area	533 sq ft (49.5m²) – including ramp space
Cargo compartment usable volume	4,500 cu ft (127.4m³)
Wing-tip turning radius	85ft (25.9m)
Nose-gear turning radius	37ft (11.3m)
Wheel base	32.1ft (9.8m)

Main-gear tyre size	20:00–20	Total volume	4,500 cu ft (127.4m^3)
Nose-gear tyre size	12:50–16	Palletised loading	
Oil	12 US gallon (45.4-litre)	no. pallets	6*
	capacity independent system	Main compartment loading	2,825 cu ft (80m^3)
	per engine	Ramp volume	490 cu ft (13.9m^3)
Fuel	Modified manifold-flow type	Total volume	3,315 cu ft (93.8m^3)
	incorporating fuel cross-feed,	Containerised loading	
	single-point refuelling (SPR)	no. Containers	6** (5 in hold + 1 on ramp)
	and defuelling and fuel	Main compartment volume	2,725 cu ft (77.1m^3)
	dumping	Ramp volume	490 cu ft (13.9m^3)
Electrics	4 × 40-kVa engine-drive AC	Total volume	3,215 cu ft (91m^3)

Main-gear tyre size — 20:00–20
Nose-gear tyre size — 12:50–16
Oil — 12 US gallon (45.4-litre) capacity independent system per engine
Fuel — Modified manifold-flow type incorporating fuel cross-feed, single-point refuelling (SPR) and defuelling and fuel dumping
Electrics — 4 × 40-kVa engine-drive AC generators for 28-volt system; 1 × 20-kVa APU-driven generator; 1 × 24-volt, 36-ampere-hour battery; 4 × 200-ampere transformer-rectifier units convert AC to DC power, both can also be supplied by external power sourcing
Hydraulics — 4 × engine-driven pumps supplying 3,000 psi pressure to utility and booster systems; 1 × electrical motor-driven pump supplying pressure to auxiliary system, backed up by hand-pump
Air conditioning & pressurisation — 2 × independent systems for flight deck and cargo compartment, bleed-operated from engine compressors in flight, or APU on ground; each system providing 15,000ft (4,572m) cabin at 35,000ft (10,668m) altitude; maximum pressure differential of 7 psi maintains an 8,000ft (2,438m) cabin at 32,000ft (9,754m) altitude
Oxygen — Gaseous-type system providing 10 manhours of oxygen at 25,000ft (7,620m) with diluter-demand automatic pressure-breathing regulators; also portable units
Bulk loading
  clear cube volume — 3,670 cu ft (103.9m^3)
  cheek volume — 200 cu ft (5.7m^3)
  ramp volume — 630 cu ft (17.8m^3)

Total volume — 4,500 cu ft (127.4m^3)
Palletised loading
  no. pallets — 6*
Main compartment loading — 2,825 cu ft (80m^3)
Ramp volume — 490 cu ft (13.9m^3)
Total volume — 3,315 cu ft (93.8m^3)
Containerised loading
  no. Containers — 6** (5 in hold + 1 on ramp)
Main compartment volume — 2,725 cu ft (77.1m^3)
Ramp volume — 490 cu ft (13.9m^3)
Total volume — 3,215 cu ft (91m^3)

The L-100s produced, with the first civilian/military registrations, were as follows: (Model 382) N1130E (c/n 3946), Lockheed demonstration aircraft, leased to Alaskan Airlines in March 1965; (Model 382B) N9260R (c/n 4101), N9261R (c/n 4109), 9J-RBW (c/n 4129), N9263R (c/n 4134), 9J-RBX (c/n 4137), AP-AUT (c/n 4144), AP-AUU (c/n 4145), N9267R (c/n 4146), N9268R (c/n 4147), N9258R (c/n 4170), N9259R (c/n 4176), N9269R (c/n 4197), N9227R (c/n 4208), 9J-REZ (c/n 4209), N9248R (c/n 4221), N9254R (c/n 4222), N759AL (c/n 4225), N7999S (c/n 4234), N9262R (c/n 4248) and N9266R (c/n 4250).

11 The L-100-20

U seful and versatile as the standard L-100 proved to be in civilian usage, there soon came calls for a 'stretched' version to cope with the ever-increasing demands of heavy airlifting the world over. Lockheed responded with two such extended variants. The first of these was the L-100-20, which gave an extra 9ft (2.75m) of cargo compartment length to 48.7ft (14.84m). Six containers could be accommodated plus one, contoured, on the

---

* based on standard pallet 118in (2.99m) × 88in (2.23m), loaded 102in (2.59m) high, with a weight of 361lb (163.7kg). With a cargo set-back of 2in (5.1cm) from each pallet edge, volume was 565 cu ft (16m^3).

** based on fibreglass containers in main compartment, 114in (2.9m) wide × 84in (2.13m) long × 101in (2.56m) high, with a weight of 680lb (308.4kg) each. Volume was 545 cu ft (15.4m^3). Plus ramp-mounted, contoured fibreglass container with a weight of 650lb (294.8kg). Volume was 490 c ft (13.9m^3).

ramp. But this was at the cost of external fuel tanks and a shortening of range. Nine L-100s were converted and sixteen built from new to this specification, the first of the type being FAA certified on 4 October 1968 and joining Interior Airways. Most utilised the alternative 4,508 eshp 501-D22A engine, the commercial equivalent of the T56-A-15. Subsequently, eight were extended even further to L-100-30 standard.

Overall length	106ft 7in (32.49m)
Span	132ft 6in (40.4m)
Overall height	38ft 3in (11.6m)
Horizontal tailplane overall length	52.7in (1.34m)
Main landing gear overall width	14.3in (36.3cm)
Cabin to ramp cargo length	48.7ft (14.84m)
Cabin to ramp cargo width	123.2in (3.13m) tapering to 120in (3.05m) at rear entrance
Maximum ramp weight	155,800lb (70,670kg)
Maximum landing weight – 10 fps	130,000lb (58,967kg)
Operating weight	73,236lb (33,219kg)
Maximum payload	46,764lb (21,212kg)
Fuel capacity @ 6.7lb/gal	46,498lb (21,091kg)
internal tanks	6,942 US gallons (26,278 litres)
external tanks	Nil
total fuel volume	6,942 US gallons (26,278 litres)
Engine model	4 × Allison turbo-prop, constant-speed 501-D22A
Engine take-off power	4,508 eshp flat-rated (capable of 4910 eshp)
Auxiliary power	1 auxiliary power unit (APU) to provide air during ground engine starting and for air conditioning and electrical power; emergency electrical power during flight up to 20,000ft (6,096m)
Propeller	4 × Hamilton Standard electro-hydromatic, constant-speed, full-feathering, reversible-pitch
Number of propeller blades	4
Diameter of propellers	13.5ft (4.1m)
Outboard propeller/ground clearance	79in (2m)
Inboard propeller/ground clearance	69.6in (1.77m)
Inboard propeller/fuselage clearance	37.8in (96cm)
Performance:	
maximum speed	363mph (584km/h)
rate of climb	1,700ft/min (518m/min)
Service ceiling at 100,000lb	34,000ft (10,360m)
Range with maximum payload	1,569 miles (2,526km)
Range with external tanks	5,733 miles (9,227km) – with zero payload
Wing area	1,745 sq ft (162.1m^2)

An L-100-30 Hercules demonstrates her capacity for unusual loads by accommodating a Rolls-Royce RB-211 jet engine in her capacious hold in 1979. The Herk could carry three such engines per flight. (Rolls-Royce (1971) Limited)

Wing loading	88.8lb (40.3kg) /sq ft
Wing aspect ratio	10.09
Cargo compartment floor length	49.3ft (15m)
Cargo compartment width	120in (3.05m)
Cargo compartment height	108in (2.74m)
Cargo compartment floor area	602 sq ft (56m^2) – including ramp space
Cargo compartment usable volume	5,307 cu ft (150.2m^3)
Wing-tip turning radius	88ft (26.8m)
Nose-gear turning radius	43ft (13.1m)
Wheel base	37.1ft (11.3m)
Main-gear tyre size	56 × 20:00–20
Nose-gear tyre size	39 × 13
Oil	12 US gallon (45.4-litre) capacity independent system per engine
Fuel	Modified manifold-flow type incorporating fuel cross-feed, single-point refuelling (SPR) and defuelling and fuel dumping
Electrics	4 × 40-kVa engine-drive AC generators for 28-volt system; 1 × 20-kVa (40 kVa on some) APU-driven generator; 1 24-volt, 36-ampere-hour battery; 4 × 200-ampere transformer-rectifier units convert AC to DC power, both can also be supplied by external power sourcing
Hydraulics	4 × engine-driven pumps supplying 3,000 psi pressure to utility and booster systems; 1 × electrical motor-driven pump supplying pressure to auxiliary system, backed up by hand-pump
Air conditioning & pressurisation	2 × independent systems for flight deck and cargo compartment, bleed-operated from engine compressors in flight, or APU on ground; each system providing 15,000ft (4,572m) cabin at 35,000ft (10,668m) altitude; maximum pressure differential of 7 psi maintains an 8,000ft (2,438m) cabin at 32,000ft (9,754m) altitude
Oxygen	Gaseous-type system providing 10 manhours of oxygen at 25,000ft (7,620m) with diluter-demand automatic pressure-breathing regulators; also portable units

Bulk loading	
clear cube volume	5,101 cu ft (144.4m^3)
cheek volume	326 cu ft (9.2m^3)
ramp volume	630 cu ft (17.8m^3)
Total volume	6,057 cu ft (171.4m^3)
Palletised loading	
no. pallets	8
Main compartment loading	3,955 cu ft (111.9m^3)
Ramp volume	490 cu ft (13.9m^3)
Total volume	4,445 cu ft (125.8m^3)
Containerised loading	
no. containers	8 (7 in hold + 1 on ramp)
Main compartment volume	3,815 cu ft (108m^3)
Ramp volume	490 cu ft (13.9m^3)
Total volume	4,305 cu ft (121.8m^3)

The L-100-20s (Model 382E), with their first civilian/military registrations, were: N9232R (c/n 4299), N9265R (c/n 4300), N7951S (c/n 4301), N7952S (c/n 4302), N9237R (c/n 4303), N7957S (c/n 4333), N7954S (c/n 4350), N7960S (c/n 4355), N7985S (c/n 4358), N7982S (c/n 4361), N7984S (c/n 4362), N7986S (c/n 4364), N10ST (c/n 4383), N11ST (c/n 4384), ZS-GSK (c/n 4385), 318 (c/n 4412), OB-R-956 (c/n 4450), N7967S (c/n 4512), RP-C101 (c/n 4593), OB-R-1183 (c/n 4706), 383 (c/n 4708), TR-KKB (c/n 4710), 384 (c/n 4715), N4080M (c/n 4830), N4081M (c/n 4832), N4115M (c/n 4850) and N4119M (c/n 4853).

The solitary Model 382 L-100, registration N1130E (c/n 3946), was extended to a L-100-20 (Model 382E). Similarly modified were six former Model 382Bs, registrations N9268R (c/n 4147), N9258R (c/n 4170), N9259R (c/n 4176), N9248R (c/n 4221), N9254R (c/n 42222) and N759AL (c/n 4225). Two other Model 382Bs were stretched to L-100-20s (Model 382F): N109AK (c/n 4129) and N9266R (c/n 4250).

12 The L-100-30

Even the L-100-20 proved insufficient for some operators, so Lockheed took the basic L-100 Hercules and extended her even further, a full 15ft (4.6m) over the L-100, giving an overall cargo compartment length of 55ft (16.8m). As such she became the L-100-30 Super Hercules. Yet another container could now be embarked, seven in the hold and one, contoured, on the ramp. It also enabled wide-bodied jet engines to be engorged from transatlantic flights from Rolls-Royce in England, and this engine hauling was done by Saturn Airways for Lockheed, among others. Space vehicles were among the new range of cargo this enhancement opened up for the Herk, and civilian L-100-30s came into demand by the US Air Force and Navy, who contracted several for such duties on regular-schedule LOGAIR and QUICKTRANS route systems. This further extension was done to several L-100s and also retrofitted to some L-100-20s, in addition to the fifty-three new-build aircraft of the type.

Overall length	112.7ft (34.35m)
Span	132ft 6in (40.38m)
Overall height	38ft 3in (11.6m)
Horizontal tailplane overall length	52.7in (1.34m)
Main landing gear overall width	14.3in (36.3cm)
Cabin to ramp cargo length	55.4ft (16.8m)
Cabin to ramp cargo width	123.2in (3.13m) tapering to 120in (3.05m) at rear entrance
Maximum ramp weight	155,800lb (70,670kg)
Maximum landing weight – 10 fps	135,000lb (58,967kg)
Operating weight	73,889lb (33,219kg)
Maximum payload	51,111lb (23,184kg)
Fuel capacity @ 6.7lb/gal	46,498lb (21,091kg)
internal tanks	6,942 US gallons (26,278 litres)
external tanks	Nil
total fuel volume	6,942 US gallons (26,278 litres)
Engine model	4 × Allison turbo-prop, constant-speed 501-D22A
Engine take-off power	4,058 eshp flat-rated (capable of 4,910 eshp)
Auxiliary power	1 auxiliary power unit (APU) to provide air during ground engine starting and for air conditioning and electrical power; emergency electrical power during flight up to 20,000ft (6,096m)
Propeller	4 × Hamilton Standard electro-hydromatic, constant-speed, full-feathering, reversible-pitch
Number of propeller blades	4
Diameter of propellers	13.5ft (4.1m)
Outboard propeller/ground clearance	79in (2m)
Inboard propeller/ground clearance	69.6in (1.77m)
Inboard propeller/fuselage clearance	37.8in (96cm)
Performance:	
maximum speed	363mph (583km/h)
rate of climb	1,700ft/min (518m/min)
Service ceiling at 100,000lb	34,000ft (10,360m)
Range with maximum payload	1,569 miles (2,526km)
Range with external tanks	5,733 miles (9,227km) – with zero payload
Wing area	1,745 sq ft (162.1m^2)
Wing loading	88.8lb (40.3kg) /sq ft
Wing aspect ratio	10.09
Cargo compartment floor length	56ft (17m)
Cargo compartment width	120in (3.05m)
Cargo compartment height	108in (2.74m)
Cargo compartment floor area	666 sq ft (61.9m^2) – including ramp space
Cargo compartment usable volume	6,057 cu ft (171.4m^3)
Wing-tip turning radius	90ft (27.4m)
Nose-gear turning radius	46.8ft (14.3m)
Wheel base	40.4ft (12.3m)
Main-gear tyre size	56 × 20:00–20
Nose-gear tyre size	39 × 13
Oil	12 US gallon (45.4-litres) capacity independent system per engine
Fuel	Modified manifold-flow type incorporating fuel cross-feed, single-point refuelling (SPR) and defuelling and fuel dumping
Electrics	4 × 40-kVa engine-drive AC generators for 28-volt system;

1 × 20-kVa (40 kVa on some)
APU-driven generator;
1 × 24-volt, 36-ampere-hour
battery;
4 × 200-ampere transformer-
rectifier units convert AC to DC
power, both can also be
supplied by external power
sourcing

Hydraulics — 4 × engine-driven pumps
supplying 3,000 psi pressure to
utility and booster systems;
1 × electrical motor-driven
pump supplying pressure to
auxiliary system, backed up by
hand-pump

Air conditioning & — 2 × independent systems for
pressurisation — flight deck and cargo
compartment, bleed-operated
from engine compressors in
flight, or APU on ground; each
systems providing 15,000ft
(4,572m) cabin at 35,000ft
(10,668m) altitude; maximum
pressure differential of 7 psi
maintains an 8,000ft (2,438m)
cabin at 32,000ft (9,754m)
altitude

Oxygen — Gaseous-type system providing
10 manhours of oxygen at
25,000ft (7,620m) with diluter-
demand automatic pressure-
breathing regulators; also
portable units

Bulk loading	
clear cube volume	3,670 cu ft (103.9m³)
cheek volume	200 cu ft (5.7m³)
ramp volume	630 cu ft (17.8m³)
Total volume	4,500 cu ft (127.3m³)
Palletised loading	
no. pallets	6
Main compartment loading	2,825 cu ft (79.9m³)
Ramp volume	490 cu ft (13.9m³)
Total volume	3,315 cu ft (93.8m³)
Containerised loading	
no. containers	8 (7 in hold + 1 on ramp)
Main compartment volume	2,725 cu ft (77.1m³)
Ramp volume	490 cu ft (13.9m³)
Total volume	3,215 cu ft (91m³)

The original artist's concept of the stretched 'High Capacity' Herk, the proposed L-100-50 which would have featured an additional 20-foot stretch over the existing L-100-30 Super Hercules, or a total stretch of 35 feet over the standard C-130 or L-100. (Lockheed-Georgia, Marietta via Audrey Pearcy)

The L-100-30s (Model 382G), with the first civilian/military registrations, were: N7988S (c/n 4388), N15ST (c/n 4391), ZS-RSB (c/n 4472), ZS-RSC (c/n 4475), ZS-RSD (c/n 4477), ZS-RSE (c/n 4558), N20ST (c/n 4561), ZS-RSF (c/n 4562), ZS-RSG (c/n 4565), TR-KKA (c/n 4582), N21T (c/n 4586), ZS-RSH (c/n 4590), ZS-RSI (c/n 4600), ZS-RSJ (c/n 4606), N108AK (c/n 4610), ZS-JIV (c/n 4673), ZS-JVL (c/n 4676), ZS-JIW (c/n 4679), ZS-JIX (c/n 4684), ZS-JIY (c/n 4691), ZS-JIZ (c/n 4695), ZS-JJA (c/n 4698), ZS-JVM (c/n 4701), N108AK (c/n 4763), 9Q-CBJ (c/n 4796), N4301M (c/n 4798), C-GHPW (c/n 4799), N4304M (c/n 4800), PK-PLU (c/n 4824), PK-PLV (c/n 4826), PK-PLW (c/n 4828), N4083M (c/n 4833), N4085M (c/n 4834), N4110M (c/n 4839), N4116M (c/n 4851), N4148M (c/n 4880), N4152M (c/n 4883), N4160M (c/n 4886), PK-PLR (c/n 4889), N4170M (c/n 4891), N4175M (c/n 4893), TR-KKD (c/n 4895), N4185M (c/n 4915), PK-PLT (c/n 4923), N4107F (c/n 4949), N4253M (c/n 4950), N4249Y (c/n 4951), N4254M (c/n 4952), N4242N (c/n 4953), HZ-117 (c/n 4954), N4232B (c/n 4955), N4255M (c/n 4956), N4261M (c/n 4957), N4266M (c/n 4960), N4248M (c/n 4992), N4269M (c/n 5000), N4272M (c/n 5022), N4274M (c/n 5024), N4276M (c/n 5025), N4278M (c/n 5027), N4232B (c/n 5029), N4281M (c/n 5032), N82178 (c/n 5048), N8213G (c/n 5055), N8218J (c/n 5056), N4161T (c/n 5225), ET-AKG (c/n 5306), N41030 (c/n 5307) and N4080M (c/n 5320).

Four L-100s were extended to L-100-30s: N24ST (c/n 4101), N16ST (c/n 4134), N18ST (c/n 4208) and N101AK (c/n 4248). Eight L-100-20s were also extended to L-100-30s: N19ST (c/n 4147), N14ST (c/n 4225), N9232R (c/n 4299), N104AK (c/n 4300); N7951S (c/n 4301), N10ST (c/n 4383) N79575 (c/n 4333) and N11ST (c/n 4384).

13 The L-100-50 (GL-207)

This was a proposed commercial Hercules with the addition of a further 20ft (6.1m) section, but nothing came of it. The passenger deck floor was to be raised by 23in (58cm) to give the passenger cabin the full width of the Hercules' widened girth. The proposal for the GL-207 'Super Hercules' had some interesting details in its data, among which were the following:

Powerplant	4 × Allison T-61B7 engines rated at 5,500 eshp
Wingspan	44m (144.3ft)
Length	36.8m (120.7ft)
Height	11.6m (38ft)
Wing area	190 sq m. (623.3ft)
Track	4.75m (15.6ft)
Wheelbase	13.6m (44.6ft)
Capacity	length 19.8m (65ft) × height 2.77m (9ft) × width 3.1m (10.2ft)
Empty weight	41,800 cubic m (1,182.94 cu ft)
Loaded weight	92,000 cubic m (2,603 cu ft)
Fuel capacity	39,000 litres (10,303 US gallons)

The twin-engine design, L-400, in a contemporary artist's impression, 30 November 1977. At this time Lockheed-Martin launched a world-wide marketing drive to sell the new aircraft, offering potential customers firm prices and delivery positions. The L-100 derivative was a medium-size cargo and personnel transport aircraft which featured the same structure and versatility of its progenitor, the four-engined C-130. (Lockheed-Georgia, Marietta via Audrey Pearcy)

Maximum speed	680km/h (423mph)
Maximum cruising speed	640km/h (398mph)
Rate of climb	595m/min (22.2mph)
Service ceiling	13,000m (42,651ft)
Range, maximum	7,200km (4,474 miles)
Useful payload	20,500kg (45,195lb)[13]

To meet the Air Force's advanced civil/military aircraft (ACMA) specification, the proposed Super Hercules had a cabin girth three feet wider than the DC-9, with two-abreast, dual-aisle seating, recessed overhead lighting and luggage compartments, and fully pressurised, air-conditioned ambience. Operating costs were estimated at 25% less than the four-engined C-130/L-100. In May 1980, Lockheed announced that it had awarded a contract to Rohr Industries Incorporated of Chula Vista, California, to build eighteen sets of powerplant nacelles. Despite this, the aircraft never materialised.

14 The L-100-PX

As a cheap airline alternative for Third World nations with limited spending power, Lockheed drew up a proposal for a passenger-carrying variant of the L-100 series. This was a one-hundred-seater aircraft with palleted units, but again, she never materialised.

15 The L-100-30*QC*

Yet another proposal that has so far come to naught was for a convertible airliner/freighter version of the extended L-100-30 which could be readily adapted to either market as the world situation fluctuated. Again a good concept in theory but one which aroused little or no interest, and never happened.

16 The L-400 – Twin Hercules

Lockheed continue to tout new variations of the Herk on the world markets, and this idea, first made public in January 1989, was for a lightweight and more cost-affordable version of the standard commercial aircraft. They proposed a twin-engine design using two of the new Allison 501-D22D engines, rated at 4,910 eshp.

The same airframe and fuselage structure as the standard Hercules was to be used, and the same 10ft wide × 9ft high × 40ft long (3m × 2.7m × 12.5m) cargo bay, with a loading floor height of 3.4ft (1m) above the ground, was to feature. The concept was for a lightweight, in-country airlifter for short-haul work. The L-400 was seen as the natural successor to older types then in the process of being phased out of service, like the DC-3, C-119, C-123 and C-54. The L-400 would carry a 22,500lb (10,206kg) payload over 550 miles (885km) and operate from 3,600ft (1,097m) runways, being able to land and take off from dirt, gravel, sand or snow runways.

The major changes were in the wing, landing gear and powerplant. The L-400 was to have a new centre wing, 22.5ft (6.85m) shorter than the existing L-100, while the span of the outer wings was to be extended by adding 4.5ft (1.37m) wing-tips. The Allison 501-D22A engine was to be emplaced in a strengthened nacelle capable of accommodating the engine's full 4,910 shp. A water-alcohol system was added to retain this power for hot-day take-offs. In order to increase the efficiency of the propellers at the high shp, a new 14ft (4.3m) diameter Hamilton Standard propeller was to be shipped, which was six inches greater than on existing C-130s.

The main landing gear for a predicted take-off weight of 84,000lb (38,102kg) was reduced from four to two wheels. The crew was also reduced to two, with simplified systems and instrumentation plus a raft of easy-maintenance features to enable small operators to keep the machine in the air for maximum usage and turn-round, but many of the parts were to be fully compatible with the larger C-130 as an attraction for larger companies which might wish to operate both types.

Lockheed's marketing organisation canvassed thirty-nine countries and delineated a sizeable potential market of more than 250 aircraft of the Twin Hercules specification. Robert B. Ormsby, Lockheed-Georgia's President at that time, went on record as saying that they expected to go into full-scale production, with first deliveries in 1981.[14] In the event, however, no actual orders were forthcoming, and the concept was finally abandoned for good.

---

[13] See 'Von de Hercules zur Super-Hercules', article *Der Flieger* magazine, issue 10, 1959.

---

[14] See Robert B. Ormsby, 'Lockheed launches world-wide sales drive for its L-400 "Twin-Hercules" transport', Newsbureau, 30 November 1977.

17 Military/Civilian Use – the L-130H-30

F inally the governments of many countries found the versatility of the Hercules, in both military and civilian usage, made her ideal for a wide range of interchangeability possibilities, which for nations strapped for cash proved irresistible. By extending the fuselage of the military C-130H by 15ft (4.6m) in the same way as the L-100-30, an all-round aircraft resulted which, if sales are any indication, proved the ideal solution. These became the L-130H-30 and their versatility is reflected in the many changes of military serial/civilian registration they have undergone. At the time of writing the following nations have taken delivery of this most successful version of the Herk since the first one, A-1317 (c/n 4864), was delivered to Indonesia in September 1980.

Algeria   8 aircraft: 7T-VHN (c/n 4894), 7T-VHO (c/n 4897), 7T-VHM (c/n 4919), 7T-VHP (c/n 4921), 7T-WHD (c/n 4987), 7T-WHL (c/n 4989) former civilian 4989, 7T-WHA (c/n 4997), 7T-WHB (c/n 5224).

Cameroon   1 aircraft: TJX-AE (c/n 4933) former civilian N4206M.

Canada   2 aircraft: 130343 (c/n 5307) former civilian N41030, 130344 (c/n 5320) former civilian N4080M.

Chad   1 aircraft: TT-AAH (c/n 5184).

Dubai   1 aircraft: 312 (c/n 4961).

Egypt   3 aircraft: 1293 (c/n 5187) later civilian SU-BKS, 1294 (c/n 5191) later civilian SU-BKT, 1295 (c/n 5206) later civilian SU-BKU.

France   10 aircraft: 61-PD (c/n 5140) former civilian F-RAPD, 61-PE (c/n 5142) former civilian F-RAPE, 61-PF (c/n 5144) former civilian F-RAPF, 60105 (c/n 5146), 61-PG (c/n 5150) former civilian N4242N and F-RAPG, 61-PH (c/n 5151) former civilian F-RAPH, 61-PI (c/n 5152) formerly civilian F-RAPI, 61-PJ (c/n 5153) former civilian N73235 and F-RAPJ, 61-PK (c/n 5226) former civilian F-RAPK, 61-PL (c/n 5227) former civilian F-RAPL.

Indonesia   7 aircraft: A-1317 (c/n 4864), A-1318 (c/n 4865), A-1319 (c/n 4868), A-1320 (c/n 4869), A-1321 (c/n 4870), A-1321 (c/n 4925), A-1324 (c/n 4927).

Malaysia   6 aircraft: M30-10 (c/n 5268), M30-12 (c/n 5277), M30-11 (c/n 5309), M30-14 (c/n 5311), M30-15 (c/n 5316), M30-16 (c/n 5319).

Netherlands   2 aircraft: G273 (c/n 5273) former civilian N4080M, G275 (c/n 5275) former civilian N4080M.

Nigeria   3 aircraft: NAF916 (c/n 4962) former civilian N4081M, NAF917 (c/n 4963) former civilian N4099R, NAF918 (c/n 5001).

Portugal   1 aircraft: 6806 (c/n 5264).

Saudi Arabia   2 aircraft: HZ-MS8 (c/n 4986) former civilian N4243M, 1622 (c/n 5212).

South Korea   4 aircraft: 5006 (c/n 5006) former civilian N4080M, 5019 (c/n 5019) former civilian N73232, 5030 (c/n 5030) former civilian N4249Y, 5036 (c/n 5036) former civilian N4161T.

Spain   1 aircraft: TL10-01(c/n 5003) former civilian N7323D.

Thailand   5 aircraft: 60104 (c/n 4959), 60106 (c/n 5148), 60107 (c/n 5208), 60111 (c/n 5280), 60112 (c/n 5281).

An impressive line-up of the Herk Herd *with USAF HC-130P 66-0223 (c/n 4185) in the foreground. RAF XV200 (c/n 4223) is beyond her. A total of twenty-two C-130 variants from many operators can be seen. (Lockheed-Georgia, Marietta via Audrey Pearcy)*

The Versatile Hercules

18 Aerial Delivery

The transportation of personnel and all manner of goods, stores and equipment from one base to another is the basic function of the Hercules, but equally important is her ability to precisely deliver the same payloads without touching down, due to inaccessibility, a lack of or total unsuitability of landing sites, combat danger, or required speed of turn-around. Lockheed developed the aerial delivery system (ADS) taking advantage of the Herk's wide, obstruction-free belly, and utilising standardised palleting capable of carrying just about anything and offloading it accurately and safely to the customers below. The inherent stability of the aircraft ensures safe control at all heights and during the sudden transference of weights off the cargo ramp.

For airdrop missions, the basic personnel exit procedure applies to the military aspects of the aircraft, with paratroop dropping as a prime function. With the capacity to

Loading drums into a Herk at a USAF base. This photo affords a good close-up of engines, wings, etc. (Lockheed-Georgia, Marietta via Audrey Pearcy)

embark sixty-four fully equipped paratroopers, the early marks of Hercules could offload these in only thirty seconds via the two paratroop doors located on either side at the after end of the cargo compartment. Alternatively the troops could go out via the lowered ramp. This ensures that the unit stays relatively close together when it hits the ground and can re-form into fighting formation quickly.

For associated military equipment, light vehicles and small tracked vehicles, even 105mm (4.13in) howitzers, could be equally accommodated, the C-130A and C-130Bs being able to cope with single loads of up to 25,000lb (11,340kg), which was increased to 35,000lb (15,876kg) in the C-130H, and offloaded via the ramp. In one test conducted by the USAF a record airdrop for a single palletised discharge was 41,740lb (18,937kg)! Airdrop speeds range between 115 and 150 knots (59 and 77mps), and the normal altitude of the drop (if 'normal' actually exists for the Hercules) is around 1,200ft (366m).

A more precise method of aerial placement was devised, this being the ground proximity extraction system (GPES), which is based on a low-level approach guided from the ground. This sub-system comprises an extraction line, hook and pole assembly in the aircraft itself, a pair of rotary hydraulic energy absorbers (known as 'water twisters' as the retardant vaned rotors turn in a housing filled with water) with their associated ground anchoring equipment, and a steel pendant cable, which have to be pre-set on the landing site. The aircraft has to steer a straight and level course no more than 5ft (1.5m) from the ground, with ramp open and hook fully extended, similar to a carrier-based aircraft's tail-hook approach. When the hook touches the

Tests at Eglin, Florida, included landings in which the Hercules sank more than 20 inches into the soft ground. These trials proved useful in the Vietnam War when USAF Hercules operated from short, dirt strips. (Lockheed via Audrey Pearcy)

ground an audible warning is sounded to the pilot so that he knows he has the right height to hold, and it catches the stretched-out pendant cable held between the two energy absorbers on either side of the air strip. As the cargo comes clear, its forward momentum is slowed by the action of the 'water twisters', and in five seconds the palletised load is dumped safely and the Herk can climb free. Such deliveries require steady hands and a high degree of nerve and skill, but it enables loads of up to 25,000lb (11,340kg) to be delivered into delivery areas only 1,200ft (366m) in length. Naturally this form of low, slow approach is suicidal in combat conditions (but, needless to say, it has been done!)

Dependent as it is upon the ground equipment being set up, which is never always a practical option given the range of missions the Hercules has to cope with worldwide, an alternative aerial delivery system was perfected, the low-altitude parachute extraction system (LAPES). This method employs a ring-slot extraction parachute to pull the palletised cargo via the hatch and bring it quickly to a standstill with minimum impact. Loads to be thus delivered are stacked in either single or multiple platforms and retained in the cargo hold of the C-130, utilising restraining gear on the 463L dual-rail cargo handling system. According to load size and weight, either a single 28ft (8.5m) extraction

parachute or multiple chutes are deployed. The approach is similar to the GPES drop, and once over the pre-designated drop point, which is about 600ft (183m) from the target zone, or about three seconds' flight time, the basic aerial delivery system (ADS) is activated, whereupon the extraction chute (or chutes) is released into the aircraft's slipstream. The extraction force required to move the cargo is 2g and a single chute can extract a load maximum of 12,000lb (544kg); a pair of such chutes is required for loads double this weight, and the maximum load thus delivered by LAPES with multiple chutes deployed is 50,000lb (22,680kg). The cargo slides about 100–200ft (30–60m) on hitting the ground.

A similar method, or refinement of the LAPES method, is the parachute low-altitude delivery system (PLADS). This enables special loads (electronics, medical equipment and the like) to be parachute-dropped from low levels while ensuring that delicate or sensitive cargo reaches the ground safely because the impact shock is minimised. These loads are securely packaged in 2,000lb (907kg) capacity supply containers, which have plywood bases to absorb the impact. Up to sixteen such containers could be embarked in the Herk, and these could be dropped singly or in pairs to within 25ft (7.6m) of the aiming point by this method. While the approach speed at 130 knots (66.8 mps) indicated airspeed (IAS) is similar to LAPES, the height is greater at

Hercules 63-7789 (c/n 3856) of USAF Military Airlift drops into base with other Herks visible on the apron to the right. The aircraft achieved notoriety when she was stolen from Mildenhall on 23 May 1969 and crashed into the sea off Alderney. (Author's collection)

250ft (76m) altitude. The reefed extraction parachute, when deployed, is towed against the container until it reaches the required extraction deployment. When this happens an electrically actuated pyrotechnic cutter slices the reefs, the parachute inflates and the load is pulled clear. Impact speeds are between 70 and 90ft (21 and 27m) per second down a projected trajectory and the horizontal velocity is a predicted zero at point of touchdown of the load.

Another parachute-assisted airdrop system adopted specifically for the accurate delivery of multiple small re-supply loads is the container delivery system (CDS). It lacks the accuracy of the LAPES delivery but can be made from great heights, up to 400ft (122m), and this form of stick release ensures better ground distribution than conventional methods. Each load is securely packed in 52 × 65in (1.32 × 1.65m) A-22 containers, which have a maximum capacity of 2,200lb (998kg). Eighteen such

containers are loaded nine to a side, and can be delivered simultaneously by the Herk in two sticks, totalling 39,600lb (17,962kg). Again the ADS system kicks in at the desired position during the approach and releases the extraction chute, one of which is attached to the first-out container of either stick. As this occurs the Herk's nose is pulled up at an angle of 6° and gravity does the rest. Once clear of the ramp each individual container's parachute is activated in the normal way by static lines.

During famine-relief operations in Ethiopia in 1985, the Belgian Air Force Hercules pilots developed their own unique method of delivery, the very low altitude gravity extraction system (VLAGES), or green light-gate system. Due to appalling Ethiopian Government restrictions which prevented them making parachute drops in case supplies reached the rebels by mistake, many areas full of starving citizens were unable to be supplied. Determined to overcome this awe-inspiring bureaucratic idiocy, the Belgians adopted this method for supply areas like Mehoney.

Under the VLAGES system eight one-and-a-half-tonne pallets of sacked supplies were prepared by Belgian paratroopers, and these were loaded in a single line down the Herk's cargo hold. The whole process of installing the roller conveyors and pallets took almost an hour per load.

A study in power. One C-130E Herk 72-1288 (c/n 4499) revs up to full power as her sister climbs into the sky astern of her during exercises held in 1970. (USAF)

A forward restraining buffer was placed at the cockpit end in case of shifting through turbulence. During the approach the team of three paratroopers took off the main lashings as the seconds were counted off by the navigator, leaving just one restraining strap in place. The main restraining band behind the ramp was fitted with a large knife. A static line followed after each pallet, which had a small amount of slack in it. As the loadmaster activated a handle, located just below the cockpit, this tightened the slack and activated the knife, which severed each pallet's last restraint. Any pallets which jammed, or sacks which fell off the pallets, were dealt with by this team to ensure free-flow over the drop zone.

Again the sudden trim-change called for expert flying. Drop heights were initially trialled at about 30ft (9m), but this resulted in too many split sacks and lost food. Height was gradually increased to 50ft (15m), with a 130 knot (66.8mps) approach speed, and this worked well, increasing the vertical speed and decreasing the horizontal speed making for less spoilage and a failure rate which came down to three or four sacks out of 240 per drop, especially when British polypropylene sacks were superseded by Belgian jute and plastic dual ones which proved far tougher in practice.

19 Aerial Photography and Mapping

T he RC-130 was developed specifically as a long-range, steady aerial photography platform in order to conduct accurate worldwide photogrammetric mapping and electronic geodetic surveying by the USAF.

A prototype RC-130A, serial 54-1632 (c/n 3019) (R for Reconnaissance), was modified from a TC-130A and first flew in this configuration on 8 November 1957. She served with the 1375 Mapping and Charting Squadron for several years, but was subsequently converted back to a standard C-130A.

Fifteen RC-130As were specifically built for the Hiran Electronic Surveying, Hiran Controlled Photography and Mapping Photography missions. Both high-altitude photography and electronic measuring could be simultaneously operated, which made for far more accurate charting and mapping. These aircraft were delivered to the USAF between March and November 1959 for use by the Military Air Transport Service: 57-0510 (c/n 3217), 57-0511 (c/n 3218), 57-0512 (c/n 3219), 57-0513 (c/n 3220), 57-0514 (c/n 3221), 57-0515 (c/n 3222), 57-0516 (c/n 3223), 57-0517 (c/n 3224), 57-0518 (c/n 3225), 57-0519 (c/n 3226), 57-0520 (c/n 3227), 57-0521 (c/n 3228), 57-0522 (c/n 3229), 57-0523 (c/n 3230) and 57-0524 (c/n 3231).

These aircraft showed little exterior differences from their conventional sisters, the addition of a television viewfinder bubble under the nose radome, the large camera windows for the prime vertical cameras (forward) and fixed convergent cameras (aft) and the viewfinders for the precision automatic photogrammetric intervalometer (PAPI) cut into the underside of the main fuselage being about the only give-aways as to their role. The hand-held oblique camera was sited just forward of the rear hatch. Internally, removable provision was made in the cargo hold to house a chief photographer, two Hiran operators and an airborne profile recorder (APR) operator, along with their huge cameras, electronic, photographic and surveying instruments and installations, photographers' racking, dropsonde stowage and a darkroom for developing film. By removing the operators' stations extra cargo capacity was available almost instantly, while with the palletised Hiran apparatus

also taken out, four extra standard recliner passenger seats could be fitted abaft the main leading-gear-wheel well. Alternatively, TAC-type jump seats could accommodate twenty passengers in considerably less comfort. A temperature and humidity probe was mounted on the port side forward of the cabin, and a driftmeter was mounted in a ventral position below the cabin.

The Hiran electronic surveying devices could ensure precise scientific measurements with an accuracy of 1/50,000 (or under one foot in an eight-mile length). The method used was trilateration, whereby the exact distance between two fixed ground points was acquired after the Hercules had flown a 'racetrack crossing path' several times between them, the instruments electronically measuring and recording the data for comparison until the optimum was achieved. The Hiran photographic equipment worked from this precise data, feeding signals to an A-1 straight line indicator. The Hiran instruments ensured a series of parallel runs could be made with a high degree of guaranteed accuracy, with timed photographs of the terrain being photographed to give an overlapping and total picture. In conditions where the Hiran control method could not be operated, the RC-130As used standard mapping photography, using visually referenced flight lines – less accurate and requiring greater overlap.

All served in 1375 Mapping and Charting Squadron, 1370 Photomapping Group, which was based at Turner AFB, Georgia. This outfit later became the 1370 Photomapping Wing in 1960, and was subsequently based at Forbes AFB, Kansas, until it was de-activated in June 1972. Some RC-130As also served with 1 Aerospace Cartographic and Geodetic Squadron and 1866 Facility Checking Squadron, with serial 57-0515 taking part in the US–Ethiopian Aerial Mapping Survey in 1963/4. All were subsequently converted into C-130As in the 1970s, except 57-0523, which became a DC-130A.

A further refinement of the type was the RC-130S, which saw two JC-130As, serials 56-0493 (c/n 3101) and 56-0497(c/n 3105), fitted with searchlight pods for experiments from 1965 onwards, but these were both later converted back to standard C-130As again.

20 Aerial Search and Rescue

T here was no doubting that the Hercules was the optimum aircraft for any number of jobs that required long range, high endurance and fuel economy coupled with the ability to conduct broad-altitude search patterns and carry a wide variety of customised and palletised packages. Search and rescue potential was obvious, and both the USAF and the USN were quick to exploit the C-130s in this direction. They were originally designated as the SC-130B (USAF) or R8V-1G (USN).

In total, twelve such search and rescue conversions were made for both services, and they were allocated those services' respective serials. In September 1962, these designations were combined as the HC-130G, but this was quickly replaced by the designation HC-130B-*LM*, and all twelve aircraft were instead allocated to the US Coast Guard, thus: CG 1339 ex 58-5396 (c/n 3529), CG 1340 ex 58-5397 (c/n 3533), CG 1341 ex 58-6973 (c/n 3542), CG 1342 ex 58-6974 (c/n 3548), CG 1344 ex 60-0311 (c/n 3594), CG 1345 ex 60-0312 (c/n 3595), CG 1346 ex 61-0958 (c/n 3638), CG 1347 ex 61-2082 (c/n3641), CG 1348 ex 61-2083 (c/n 3650), CG 1349 ex 62-3753 (c/n 3745), CG 1350 ex 62-3754 (c/n 3763) and CG 1351 ex 62-3755 (c/n 3773).

These aircraft differed from the standard C-130B in the flight deck and aft observation window layouts. The former was redesigned to accommodate a radio operator and an on-scene commander (OSC) situated where the normal crew rest bunks had been located, in addition to the pilot, co-pilot, flight engineer and navigator. Two clear-vision observer stations were built into the aft cargo compartment to give a wide field of vision via the paratroop door apertures. A manually controlled observation door was emplaced to shield this embrasure during any wave-top-type visual searches as the aircraft were not pressurised at such low altitudes. When in pressurised flight configuration this door was stowed and the paratroop door closed.

Two alternative mission scenarios were catered for, dependent on whether the aircraft was employed as a search platform or as a support aircraft deploying men and equipment out to reinforce a search area. Dependent on the requirement, a removable command/passenger interior module could be shipped, which had fourteen airliner-type seats for use by the OSC and his staff for the co-ordination of large rescue operations, or for the transportation of personnel to the scene of the mission.

In the case of the former requirement the cargo hold could stow droppable rescue kits on ramps. As a support aircraft, disassembled helicopters could be transported to the search area, disembarked, assembled and used in the work. For the latter the cargo compartment behind the control module could accommodate either a further twenty-four airliner-type seats or a forty-four standard troop seater module in addition to the normal C-130B ambulance configuration of seventy-four patients and two

attendants. The shipping of these modules required just simple modifications to the electrical power and air-conditioning equipment.

Far more common in their twenty years of sterling USCG service was patrol duty, in both the Atlantic and Pacific Oceans. The most high-profile missions were the ice patrols, when the northern ice pack and western Greenland area was patrolled daily during the spring and summer months when the glaciers were calving to give continuously updated records on the number, size and direction of the bigger bergs deemed hazardous to shipping.

The 67th Aerospace Rescue and Recovery Squadron (ARRS) equipped with five HC-130s and five HH-53 'Super' Jolly Green Giant helicopters, moved to RAF Woodbridge, Suffolk, from Moron, Spain, in March 1970 in order to provide greater rescue coverage in the North Atlantic. The 67th was then providing rescue coverage from the North to the South Poles and from mid-Atlantic in the west to the Indo-Burmese border in the east, approximately 68,000,000 square miles (176,120km²). The unit had as its primary mission Combat Rescue and Support of Special Operations NATO in Europe, with the secondary role of peacetime search and rescue. The Herks carried a team of pararescue specialists called 'PJs', who could parachute, scuba or mountain climb their way to a survivor and provide him with medical attention as necessary.

21 Aerial Search, Rescue and Recovery

The USAF had for many years utilised the Douglas HC-54 in its air rescue service units, and they had perfected the techniques and equipment suitable for their era. With the increased need for offshore out-of-the-water pick-ups in Vietnam, and the burgeoning aerospace programme also calling for high numbers of water retrievals, the arrival of the Hercules enabled these units to be updated and upgraded and for improved equipment and techniques to be employed.

With the primary mission of searching for, locating and retrieving both personnel and/or material in support of global air and space operations, including those associated with research and development activities, the Aerospace Rescue and Recovery Service (ARRS) was established, and a programme that originally included forty-five specially equipped Hercules was put in train. Known as the *Crown Birds*, eventually only forty-three were completed: 64-14852 (c/n 4036), 64-14853 (c/n 4037), 64-14854 (c/n 4038), 64-14855 (c/n 4055), 64-14856 (c/n 4072), 64-14857 (c/n 4073), 64-14858 (c/n 4081), 64-14859

(c/n 4082), 64-14860 (c/n 4084), 64-14861 (c/n 4088), 64-14862 (c/n 4089), 64-14863 (c/n 4094), 64-14864 (c/n 4097), 64-14865 (c/n 4098), 64-14866 (c/n 4099), 65-0962 (c/n 4102), 65-0963 (c/n 4103), 65-0964 (c/n 4104), 65-0965 (c/n 4106), 65-0966 (c/n 4107), 65-0967 (c/n 4108), 65-0968 (c/n 4110), 65-0969 (c/n 4111), 65-0970 (c/n 4112), 65-0971 (c/n 4116), 65-0972 (c/n 4120), 65-0973 (c/n 4121), 65-0974 (c/n 4123), 65-0975 (c/n 4125), 65-0976 (c/n 4126), 65-0977 (c/n 4127), 65-0978 (c/n 4130), 65-0979 (c/n 4131), 65-0980 (c/n 4132), 65-0981 (c/n 4133), 65-0982 (c/n 4135), 65-0983 (c/n 4138), 65-0984 (c/n 4139), 65-0985 (c/n 4140), 65-0986 (c/n 4141), 65-0987 (c/n 4142), 65-0989 (c/n 4150) and 65-0990 (c/n 4151). These were designated as the HC-130H.

Their specialised equipment included the Fulton surface-to-air recovery system (STAR), which enabled repeated pick-ups, from both land and water, of personnel or material objects with weight loading up to 500lb (227kg), including recoverable gear. The STAR kit comprised a nose-mounted, vee-shaped yoke which folded back on either side of the nose radome when not in use, with fending lines stretched from the nose to both wing-tips. This was not always carried on every mission but could easily be fitted. Also carried in a fairing built atop the aircraft's nose was the Cook AN/ARD-17 electrical

Carrying parachute teams to enter the water to assist with recovery was also a function of the HC-130H Hercules, 64-14859 (c/n 4082) equipped with the Surface-to-Air recovery system, and here a parachutist is seen leaving the after-bay of 14859. (USAF)

aerial tracking system (EATS). It was anticipated at the time that NASA space capsule re-entry would be a large part of the Hercules remit, but, in the event, none of this type of operation ever took place. Scanner windows were built into either side of the fuselage aft of the flight deck, while ten parachute flare/illumination markers/smoke marker, sonar buoy and beacon launching tubes were installed in the rear cargo door.

Increased accommodation totalled five flight deck personnel (with a special radio operator station replacing the crew bunks, which were re-located in the main cargo hold), two loadmasters and two pararescue technicians carried in the cargo compartment. This had two observer window positions with fully swivelling seats, mounted aft of the forward bulkhead. To increase range either one or two cradle-mounted 1,800 US gallon (6,814 litre) fuel tanks could be carried. They were also fitted with overhead delivery system tracking and recovery winches. A range of three palletised MA-1/2 rescue/recovery packages was carried,

each one of which contained cylindrical bundles, two of which held inflatable and three water-proof store containers. All these bundles were linked together by four buoyant 210ft (46m) polyethylene linking straps.

The normal recovery technique was for an initial pass to be made over the target zone, during which a personnel rescue kit was dropped to the group awaiting rescue. The harnessed suits were donned and the inflatable balloon was released on its 500ft (152m) nylon line. Meanwhile the Hercules had gone round again, and made a second pass at under 140 knots (72.6mps) airspeed to facilitate the deploying of the recovery yoke to its full extension. The yoke then snared and trapped the nylon line suspended below the balloon. The hoisted personnel or package was then reeled into the cargo hold from the trail position astern the aircraft, and the subject experienced no more impact than that felt during a normal parachute descent. Two people could be snatched from the ground or the sea at one pass by this method.

The system was first used effectively by the HC-130H on 3 May 1966, when two personnel were plucked from the runway at Edwards AFB, California. This first test was followed by a second on 5 May, when in a simulation of an Apollo space splash-down and pick-up, three volunteers were lifted from the sea by the same method. In continuation of this aspect of the programme a special team was attached to the 6593rd Test Squadron, based at Hickam Field, Hawaii. It comprised six aircraft especially

Converted to JC-130B, fourteen C-130Bs were utilised as aerial recovery vehicles for satellite capsules. Equipment included a radar tracking system mounted in a radome atop the fuselage and a retrieval system mounted from the rear access doors to catch the parachutes as they descended as shown in this photo. Most of these conversions were only temporary. (Author's Collection)

converted to snatch the Apollo capsule crews from above the Pacific; these were re-designated: 64-14858 (c/n 4081) became the solitary JC-130H-*LM*; 64-14854 (c/n 4038) and 64-14857 (c/n 4073) became JHC-130Hs and 65-0979 (c/n 4131) for a while before being re-designated as a DC-130H-*LM*.

The majority of the HC-130Hs found more than adequate employment in the rescue of downed US pilots off the coast of Vietnam during the American involvement in that war. Combat pilots hit over North Vietnam quickly found that they stood a far better chance of survival if they ditched at sea ('feet wet') instead of ashore ('feet dry') in hostile territory (and large parts of South Vietnam were also hostile territory for most of the time). A considerable number of aircrew owe their lives to the Herky Bird in this configuration.

A further twenty-four Hercules for the US Coast Guard

received similar HC-130H modifications, but did not feature the ARD-17 Cook aerial tracker, the HRU pods or the Fulton STAR recovery yoke. These aircraft were produced in two batches: twelve aircraft serials CG 1452 ex 66-13533 (c/n 4255), CG 1453 ex 67-7184 (c/n 4260), CG 1454 ex 67-7185 (c/n 4265), CG 1500 ex 72-1300 (c/n 4501), CG 1501 ex 72-1301 (c/n 4507), CG 1502 ex 72-1302 (c/n 4513), CG 1503 ex 73-0844 (c/n 4528), CG 1504 ex 73-0845 (c/n 4529), CG 1600 ex 77-0320 (c/n 4764), CG 1601 ex 77-0319 (c/n 4762), CG 1602 ex 77-0318 (c/n 4760), CG 1603 ex 77-0317 (c/n 4757), six aircraft serials CG 1710 (c/n 5028), CG 1711 (c/n 5031), CG 1712 (c/n 5033), CG 1713 (c/n 5034), CH 1714 (c/n 5035) and CG 1715 (c/n 5037).

A further eleven US Coast Guard Hercules were produced: CG 1700 (c/n 4947), CG 1701 (c/n 4958), CG 1702 (c/n 4966), CG 1703 (c/n 4967), CG 1704 (c/n 4969), CG 1705 (c/n 4993), CG 1706 (c/n 4996), CG 1707 (c/n 4999), CG 1708 (c/n 5002), CG 1709 (c/n 5005) and CG 1790 (c/n 4931). They were fitted with the side-looking airborne radar (SLAR) and forward-looking infra-red (FLIR). This latter system, intended for use tracking drug-smuggling vessels at sea, also utilised the Lockheed special avionics mission strap-on now system (SAMSON) which coupled the FLIR with an optical data link and a display and recording console to record and register evidence as it came in. They were designated HC-130H-7s.

Later, many of these latter aircraft were given the additional duty of in-flight helicopter refuelling like the

Wheels down as Hercules HC-130P 66-0223 (c/n 4185) of 79 ARRS, Military Air Command, prepares to land at Hickam Field Air Force Base, in Hawaii. (Nick Williams AAHS)

HC-130Ps, and were fitted with wing pods carrying hose-and-drogue gear for this mission. They were also equipped with night vision goggles (NVG), while both cockpit lighting and navigation capability were also upgraded. All these aircraft have served with the USCG from their seven bases in North America, and while some have been reduced to care at the AMARC in Arizona, many others are still working today.

Seventeen C-130Es and one NC-130E were similarly converted to the STAR system by the USAF to rescue downed combat flyers in Vietnam, but were mainly used for clandestine operations behind enemy lines as *Combat Talon I*s. These were serials 62-1843 (c/n 3806), 63-7785 (c/n 3852), 64-0508 (c/n 3992), 64-0523 (c/n 4007), 64-0547 (c/n 4040), 64-0551 (c/n 4046), 64-0555 (c/n 4056), 64-0558 (c/n 4059), 64-0559 (c/n 4062), 64-0561 (c/n 4065), 64-0562 (c/n 4068), 64-0563 (c/n 4071), 64-0564 (c/n 4074), 64-0565 (c/n 4077), 64-0566 (c/n 4080), 64-0567 (c/n 4083), 64-0568 (c/n 4086) and 64-0572 (c/n 4090).

22 Aerial Search, Rescue and Helicopter In-flight Refuelling

The usefulness of the HC-130H type was indisputable, and a further twenty aircraft – (65-0988 (c/n 4143), 65-0991 (c/n 4152), 65-0992 (c/n 4155), 65-0993 (c/n 4156), 65-0994 (c/n 4157), 66-0211 (c/n 4161), 66-0212 (c/n 4162), 66-0213 (c/n 4163), 66-0214 (c/n 4164), 66-0215 (c/n 4165), 66-0216 (c/n 4166), 66-0217 (c/n 4173), 66-0218 (c/n 4174), 66-0219 (c/n 4175), 66-0220 (c/n 4179), 66-0221 (c/n 4183), 66-0222 (c/n 4184), 66-0223 (c/n 4185), 66-0224 (c/n 4186) and 66-0225 (c/n 4187) – were allocated for that role, the first completing in 1966. They still featured the Cook AN/ARD 17 aerial tracking antenna and carried the Fulton STAR recovery equipment as before, but now an additional role was incorporated for this group, that of helicopter in-flight refuelling. These aircraft were designated the HC-130P. They were all assigned to the Aerospace Rescue and Recovery Service (ARSS) initially.

The HC-130Ps were fitted with two underwing refuelling probe-and-drogue pods some 90ft (27.5m) apart beneath the outer wing sections, with the associated plumbing reels containing 85ft (26m) of hose. This helicopter refuelling unit (HRU) equipment enabled them to replenish two turbine-powered helicopters simultaneously.

Two 1,800 US gallon (6,814 litre) cradle-mounted fuel tanks were installed in the cargo compartment, and a pair of reel observer seats were fitted. The fuel carried in the aircraft's wing tanks could be transferred in addition to these fuselage-carried tanks at a maximum pumping rate of 200 US gallons (757 litres) per minute if just one receiving aircraft was being replenished, or 165 US gallons (625 litres) per minute if two helicopters were simultaneously receiving fuel from the mother ship.

The technique normally employed was for the HC-130P to fly at an altitude of between 4,000 and 5,000ft (1,219 and 1,524m), with 70% flaps applied and at an indicated airspeed of between 105 and 120 knots (54 and 61.7mps). The helicopter herself maintained a set course, allowing the Hercules to approach the rendezvous from astern and some 200ft (61m) below. Once the tanker pulled ahead and stabilised her speed, the heli would descend, the probe would engage the drogue and fuelling would commence.

Again the war in Vietnam showed just how important this mission was, with both the big HH-3E 'Jolly Green Giant' and the HH-53B 'Super Stallion' rescue helis having their range and endurance considerably enhanced by this method. These aircraft saw considerable combat service, and two were lost the same night to Viet-Cong ground attacks in the war, 66-0214 and 66-0218, on 29 July 1968 at Tuy Hoa air base, South Vietnam. A third loss was recorded on 2 April 1986, when 66-0211 lost her starboard

A three-quarter rear port view of a USAF HH-3B helicopter being refuelled in flight over the Gulf of Tonkin off the coast of North Vietnam by an HC-130F air tanker on 16 June 1970. (USAF)

A Herk KC130T, 162308 (c/n 4972) of VMGR-234, acts as refueller for two Sikorsky CH-53 Super Stallion helicopters in over-water trials. (Author's Collection)

wing and crashed in a bad-weather incident in the Magdalena area of New Mexico. Subsequently thirteen survivors were re-designated MC-130Ps and assigned to special service units.

A simplified version was produced, designated the HC-130N, which dropped the nose yoke, fending lines and associated recovery equipment toted by the HC-130P, and also did not carry the fuselage tanks, but was otherwise almost identical. Fifteen of these aircraft – 69-5819 (c/n 4363), 69-5820 (c/n 4367), 69-5821 (c/n 4368), 69-5822 (c/n 4370), 69-5823 (c/n 4371), 69-5824 (c/n 4372), 69-5825 (c/n 4374), 69-5826 (c/n 4375), 69-5827 (c/n 4376), 69-5828 (c/n 4377), 69-5829 (c/n 4378), 69-5830 (c/n 4379), 69-5831 (c/n 4380), 69-5832 (c/n 4381) and 69-5833 (c/n 4382) – were produced for the ARRS in the 1970s.

The success of the HC-130P and HC-130N variants led to a further pair of aircraft – 88-2101 (c/n 5202) and 88-2102 (c/n 5210) – being delivered in 1990, with a third, 90-2103 (c/n 5294), in 1992 and three more – 93-2104 (c/n 5381), 93-2105 (c/n 5387) and 93-2106 (c/n 5388) – in 1995. They were basically similar to the HC-130P with the HRU beneath the wings as before, but with updated and upgraded electronics, and they had auxiliary fuel tanks carried within the fuselage. They received the designation HC-130(N). All were allocated to the Air

National Guard (ANG) in Alaska where they perform both rescue and recover missions and helicopter in-flight refuelling duties.

Some twenty-nine former HC-130N/Ps were re-designated MC-130P-*LM* (*Combat Shadows*) in February 1996. They were modified with forward looking infra-red scanners; night vision goggles (NVG) and lighting; a self-contained integrated navigation system (INS) of the ring-laser gyro type; a secure communications suite; global positioning system (GPS); digital scan dual-navigation radar systems; and enhanced ECM capability and incoming missile detection scanners. These aircraft were serials 64-14854 (c/n 4038), 64-14858 (c/n 4081), 65-0971 (c/n 4116), 65-0975 (c/n 4125), 65-0991 (c/n 4152), 65-0992 (c/n 4155), 65-0993 (c/n 4156), 65-0994 (c/n 4157), 66-0212 (c/n 4162), 66-0213 (c/n 4163), 66-0215 (c/n 4165), 66-0216 (c/n 4166), 66-0217 (c/n 4173), 69-6825 (c/n 4174), 66-0219 (c/n 4175), 66-0220 (c/n 4179), 66-0223 (c/n 4185), 66-0225 (c/n 4187), 69-5819 (c/n 4363), 69-5820 (c/n 4367), 69-5821 (c/n 4368), 69-5822 (c/n 4370), 69-5823 (c/n 4371), 69-5825

Naturally the versatile Herk found the air-to-air refuelling mission added to her enormous repertoire. This sequence shows 65-0988 (c/n 4143) refuelling a Sikorsky helicopter during trials. (Sikorsky Aircraft, United Aircraft Corporation)

(c/n 4374), 69-5826 (c/n 4375), 69-5827 (c/n 4376), 69-5828 (c/n 4377), 69-5831 (c/n 4380) and 69-5832 (c/n 4381).

In their new role the MC-130P-LMs act as refuelling hosts for deep-penetration special operations helicopter missions into hostile territory in minimum-risk environments. They are distributed among various SOS units, including 5 Special Operations Wing and 9, 17, 58 and 67 Special Operations Squadrons at bases in Florida, New Mexico, England and Japan.

23   Airborne Drone Launch and Control

Examples of the C-130A, the C-130E and the C-130H were modified into airborne drone launch and control platforms for Air Research Development Command. Modifications for this duty were not very extensive, the chief physical changes being the adoption of underwing pylons for carrying the drones and an extended (30in/76cm) *Pinocchio* nose radome, which in some was later modified to a 'thimble' nose radome which carried the AN/APN-45. Many also carried a ventral chin-mounted microwave guidance system radome. Modular internal changes mounted on portable consoles in the cargo compartment were two launch officer stations, a three-man tracking and control station along with avionics command and control equipment.

The ability of the Hercules to loiter for long periods awaiting the most suitable launch times according to the dictates of weather or other operational parameters, coupled with her ability to cruise at a wide range of speeds to altitudes of 35,000ft (10,668m), made her a particularly appropriate vehicle for these duties.

The drones themselves – or to give them their official designation, remotely piloted vehicles (RPVs), four of which could be carried, or, as an alternative longer-range loading, two on the outer pylons and two external fuel tanks on the internal – were of both subsonic and supersonic varieties, like the Teledyne Ryan BQM-34 Firebee, and could be launched and remotely controlled from the Hercules 'mother ship' to provide more realistic training in detection, interception and defensive action postures against hostile missiles. The extra crew members consisted of two launch control officers and two remote-controllers. As such the modified Hercules were used by both the US Air Force (DC-130A and DC-130E) and the US Navy (DC-130A).

The first pair of USAF C-130As to be adapted were 57-0496 (c/n 3203) and 57-0497 (c/n 3204), which were converted in 1957. They received the official designation GC-130A, as did the succeeding conversions which

Extended nose of USAF Herk 56-0514 (c/n 3122) carrying two BQM-34 Firebee target drones on underwing extensions during trials for the US Navy. (McDonnell Douglas via Audrey Pearcy)

followed during the 1960s: three former C-130As – 56-0491 (c/n 3099), 56-0514 (c/n 3122) and 56-0527 (c/n 3135) – and 56-461 (c/n 3168), along with a former C-130D, 55-0021 (c/n 3048), and a former RL-130A, 57-0523 (c/n 3230). In 1962 they were all re-designated the DC-130A-*LM*s.

Next for conversion were seven of the early production C-130Es: 61-2361 (c/n 3662), 61-2362 (c/n 3663), 61-2363 (c/n 3681), 61-2364 (c/n 3687), 61-2368 (c/n 3713), 61-2369 (c/n 3714) and 61-2371 (c/n 3716). The conversions followed the usual pattern, with these aircraft having the chin (microwave guidance) and the thimble (tracking radar) radomes to become DC-130E-*LM*s. They served with the 408th/100th Strategic Reconnaissance Wing, mainly in the SW Pacific area, before reverting to their former configuration and service in the 314th TAW.

Two former rescue HC-130Hs, 65-971 (c/n 4116) and 65-979 (c/n 4131), were planned to be modified to DC-130Hs in 1977, with four underwing pylons to carry the Ryan BGM-34C multi-mission drones. With the ending of the war in Vietnam, and cutbacks, only one aircraft, 65-979, was actually converted and she became the solitary DC-130H-*LM*. After she was converted they both joined the 6514th Test Squadron, based at Hill AFB, Utah. After some eighteen months' trials the whole RPV programme was summarily abandoned as electronic countermeasures (ECM) advances rendered them increasingly vulnerable. The APVs were scrapped and the bulk of the Hercules mother ships allocated to the MASDC, and the two Hs were subsequently re-converted into an MC-130P

Close-up of the XQ-4B remote-control piloted vehicle carried on the starboard inner pylon Hercules DC-130A-LM, 57-0497 (c/n 3204), one of two modified from C-130As. (Author's Collection)

and an NC-130H respectively.

The US Navy took delivery of first two DC-130As on transfer, as 158228 (c/n 3048), with a normal radome, and 158229 (c/n 3099) in 1969. These were followed by a further three conversion transfers – 560514 (c/n 3122), 570496 (c/n 3203) and 570497 (c/n 3204) – which joined the Navy's Composite Squadron Three (VC-3) in the early 1970s.

Subsequent to their naval service life, the latter three were contract-operated in the same task by civilian companies, initially Lockheed Aircraft Service and subsequently by Avtel Services Inc. working out of Mojave Airport, California.

24 Aircraft Carrier Operation – COD

Experimental trials were conducted by the US Marine Corps and US Navy in 1963, to see whether such a large aircraft as the C-130 Hercules could operate from aircraft carriers. Contrary to what has been written, there was no question of making the Herky Bird a permanent carrier-borne operator, although it was thought that it would be useful during combined operations of the kind the USMC specialised in; the ability to use offshore carriers as

Deck landing and take-off or COD (Carrier Onboard Delivery) trials aboard the aircraft carrier USS Forrestal *(CVA-59) were conducted by this KC-130F 149798 (c/n 3680) named* Look Ma, No Hook, *during October 1963. The refuelling pods were removed from this machine and Hytrol anti-skid brakes were fitted. The nose doors were also modified for the tests. The test commenced at the Naval Air Test Centre, Patuxent River, early in October. Commencing 30 October deck landing and take-offs, with touch-and-go 'bolters' were conducted off the Massachusetts coast. Top: Piloted by Lieutenant James H. Flatley, USN, the KC-130F lifts off over the bows of the* Forrestal *easily. Below: Lined-up on the flight deck, there is no room to spare on either side for any parked aircraft. Both hookless landings and catapultless take-offs were conducted without any hitches at various aircraft loading weights, but the idea was not proceeded with any further.*
(Lockheed-Georgia, Marietta via Audrey Pearcy)

safe bases from time to time during combat and supply operations in hostile territory would be of great value. The vast wingspan of the Hercules would preclude any other of the ship's aircraft complement being able to operate on deck while she was landing or taking off and would have been too big a price to pay for regular usage, even had there been an overriding need.

Accordingly, sea trials were held using the aircraft carrier USS *Forrestal* (CVA 59) and a Marine Corps KC-130F tanker aircraft (149798, c/n 3680) which was adapted for the job by the removal of the in-flight wing pylon-mounted refuelling pods and the 3,600 US gallon (13,644 litre) fuselage tank. This programme was designated Carrier Onboard Delivery (COD) and was organised from the US Navy's Air Testing Centre at Patuxent River. An improved Hytrol anti-skid brake system was fitted, along with a more sensitive speed-sensing system and strengthened nose wheel doors. For these sea trials the USMC markings were temporarily replaced by US Navy markings. The modified aircraft was at Patuxent on 8 October 1963, and initially the trials were conducted on a land simulation of the carrier deck, where some ninety-five take-offs and one hundred and forty-one landings were carried out.

The trials then moved out to sea off the Massachusetts coast for the real thing. Piloted by Lieutenant James H. Flatley, USN (later a Rear-Admiral), a series of fifty-four experimental approaches were made, which included sixteen touch-and-go 'bolters'. This phase was followed by twenty-one unarrested full-stop landings, and the Herk was brought to a halt in distances that ranged from 270ft (82m) to 495ft (151m). Shipborne take-offs were carried out, with the test aircraft configured with various loading weights up to a maximum of 121,000lb (54,340kg). The maximum length of deck required was 745ft (227m). Only normal braking and full-reverse throttle procedures were followed in these trials, all of which were accomplished with no problems whatsoever. In theory these trials showed that the KC-130F could deck-land a load of 25,000lb (11,340kg) with perfect safety. The Hercules remains the largest aircraft ever to have operated from any aircraft carrier.

25 Air Emergency Hospitals

Taking the relief and rescue concept to its final extreme, the Saudi Government had Lockheed Aircraft Services (LAS) at Ontario, California, make a very special conversion of a C-130H, civilian registration N4098M (c/n 4837), to serve as the King's own special flying hospital and surgery aircraft. She was outfitted internally with the full range of medical equipment and necessities for any conceivable emergency, including an operating theatre and an intensive care unit, and staffed with a stand-by medical team of doctors and nurses. Special APUs were built in, contained in underwing pods, and these could provide on-ground power to run all these facilities for up to seventy-two hour's duration. She was delivered in September 1981, and became HZ-MS019, operated by Saudia.

She became the first airborne emergency hospital (AEH). When a major earthquake hit the neighbouring Yemen Arab Republic this aircraft was immediately despatched to give aid and succour. Where the Herk landed instantly became a hospital with examination and operating rooms, while a tent city was established for the injured and the aircraft herself was utilised for surgery and intensive care. The medical team's work was described as ". . . absolutely outstanding . . .". The Saudis then considered the prospects of bringing such fast aerial surgical aid to disaster areas in its remote desert hinterland. They extended the programme and the first AEH was followed by more of the same type, similarly converted by LAS, carrying the special registration letter MS (for medical services). These AEH aircraft were three more conversions from C-130Hs – HZ-116 (c/n 4915), HZ-MS021 (c/n 4918) and HZ-MS7 (c/n 4922) – and six aircraft converted from L-100-30s: – HZ-117 (c/n 4954), HZ-MS05 (c/n 4950), HZ-MS06 (c/n 4952), HZ-MS09 (c/n 4956), HZ-MS10 (c/n 4957) and HZ-MS 14 (c/n 4960). One of these, HZ-MS06 (c/n 4952), was specially equipped as a dental hospital.

These special hospital ships had their own electrical generators and air conditioners built into wing pods, which gave them the ability to function as full emergency hospitals for 72 hours without outside support. The operating theatre was located at the front of the hold, and could perform two surgical operations simultaneously. The central section contained removable seats for the medical personnel and at the rear were located the patient bunk beds where post-operative care could be provided and full monitoring done. Each aircraft was fitted out with a full range of anaesthesia and X-ray facilities. Three L-100s were fitted out as medical evacuation/litter aircraft, accommodating 52 stretchers in addition to a smaller operating room.

No other nation followed the Saudi lead, probably due to the enormous cost and the limited usage to which they were subsequently put.

26 Airplane In-flight Refuelling

A natural assignment for so versatile and adaptable an aircraft as the Hercules was that of an in-flight refuelling aircraft, and adaptations were made to the C-130A, C-130E, C-130H and C-130J variants accordingly, and they became the KC-130F, KC-130R and KC-130J.

The US Marine Corps had an obvious interest in the Hercules' potential for in-flight refuelling (which they dubbed 'bird feeding'). They were traditionally land-based and had been tasked for long over-water deployments, especially in the Pacific. To test the feasibility of such a conversion two C-130As were loaned from the USAF, 55-0046 (c/n 3073) and 55-0048 (c/n 3075). They were initially designated the GV-1.

These were fitted with two 934lb (424kg) pylon-mounted probe-and-drogue refuelling pods which were positioned some 90ft (27.5m) apart under the wings, outboard of the outboard engines. Thus they could refuel two Marine Corps aircraft simultaneously. To facilitate visual contact large observer windows were cut in the aft personnel doors. Each HRU refuelling pod contained a hydraulically operated drogue-and-hose reel, with 91ft (27.7m) of hose and the refuelling basket.

Internal modifications included increased flight deck accommodation for five crew members plus the two refuelling observers positioned at the aft personnel doors. Two 1,800 US gallon (6,814 litre) fuel tanks were cradle-mounted and located in the cargo compartment. All the refuelling appendages were designed for quick removal so that the aircraft could be re-configured back to the pure transport role when required.

Commencing in 1957, the two trial aircraft were evaluated at the Naval Air Test Centre (NATC) at Patuxent River, Maryland, and these trials were declared successful. An ongoing programme of C-130B conversion to produce further such tankers (the US Navy's seven aircraft designated GV-1Us) was therefore initiated, which finally produced no fewer than forty-six tanker/transport aircraft.

The original powerplant for these aircraft was the T56-A-7 engine, which developed 4,050 eshp, but later on they were all converted over to the improved T56-A-16, which was the US Navy's designation of the 4,910 eshp T56-A-15 used on the standard C-130H at the time. (Interestingly, these were flat-rated to 4,508 eshp for take-off in order not to exceed the nacelle/wing structural capability of the aircraft.) They were also re-designated the KC-130F-*LM*. As would be expected in aircraft subjected to a salt-water environment, extensive galvanising was done throughout to protect against corrosion.

They proved most successful in this role. The technique employed was that the in-flight fuel transfer to the receiver aircraft could be made directly from the tanker's six wing tanks, even when the fuselage tank was installed. There was also the ability to transfer fuel from the internal fuselage tank to the tanker's own engines to extend her range if necessary. Once the Marine Corps fighters/attack aircraft had positioned themselves and locked onto the basket, fuel was transferred from the fuselage tank by two internally mounted, electrically driven pumps, whose maximum pumping rate was 300 US gallons (1,136 litres) per minute to each host aircraft. Alternatively, the wing tanks could pump at half that rate to each host aircraft. There was a battery of three coloured lamps: RED – pressure off; YELLOW – ready for transfer; GREEN – fuelling in progress. In an emergency all the fuel could be jettisoned at a rate of 750 US gallons (2,842 litres) per minute.

With the production of the C-130H, Lockheed built on this experience to produce their KC-130H-*LM* tanker aircraft, aimed specifically at foreign air forces, and orders

quickly followed. They utilised the same single or twin 1,800 US gallon (6,814 litre) fuel tanks initially but these were later discontinued and replaced by a single 3,600 US gallon (13,628 litre) fuselage tank. A total of twenty such tankers were built from scratch, while a further six were conversions from C-130Hs.

With the arrival of the KC-130H as a tanker version of the C-130H the US Marine Corps placed orders which resulted in fourteen aircraft of this type being delivered between 1975 and 1978. As expected, the adaptations were basically similar to the KC-130F-*LM* but with increased capacity, and the USMC version was designated the KC-130R-*LM*. Fuel bunkerage went up to 13,320 US gallons (50,420 litres) carried in a single fuselage-mounted tank which replaced the two smaller tanks of the earlier aircraft, whose capacity had totalled 10,623 US gallons (40,212 litres).

The latest tanker version for the US Marine Corps is based on the C-130J and is designated the KC-130J. At the time of writing, orders have been placed for seven such aircraft: 165735 (c/n 5488), 165736 (c/n 5489), 165737 (c/n 5499), 165738 (c/n 5506), 165739 (c/n 5507), 165740 (c/n 5508) and 165741(c/n 5509).

27 Boundary Layer Control Research

The testing of a new system (boundary layer control, BLC) to enhance the short take-off (STOL) performance characteristics of the C-130B from short air strips resulted in a one-off temporary conversion. A single C-130B, serial 58-0712 (c/n 3507), was

Prior to delivery to the US Air Force, this C-130B 58-0712, (c/n 3507) was modified to NC-130B 'Boundary Layer Control' test aircraft for an intended C-130C STOL version. She first flew on 8 February 1969, and is depicted here during flight trials on unprepared ground at Eglin, Florida. (Lockheed-Georgia, Marietta via Audrey Pearcy)

Sequence showing the landing of the Hercules which was a C-130B (58-0712, c/n 3507). Wheels down, the BLC looms over the waiting camera teams. (Lockheed-Georgia, Marietta via Audrey Pearcy)

Very low-level supply drops are a feature of the Hercules, which, despite being a big aircraft, can be handled delicately and with great precision. Here the drag chutes ease the descent of a palletised cargo released very close to terra firma. (Author's Collection)

Final seconds before the touch-down on the rough and ready strip. (Lockheed-Georgia, Marietta)

flight-tested by Lockheed and several US Government agencies and was re-designated the NC-130B-*LM*. The intention was that, if the experiment proved successful, a new variant would result, the C-130-C, specifically for work with the US Army. The augmented air flow would increase STOL ability from close to the battle-front air

strips and allow the supply situation of troops in forward positions to be vastly enhanced.

The BLC system as fitted comprised two T56-A-6 engine load compressors, Allison YT56-A-6 turbojets operating as gas generators, which were pod-mounted (in 'clam shell' fairings) below the aircraft's outer wings and had the associated ducting for the distribution of blown air in the wings, fuselage and empennage. Modifications also included the fitting of single-hinged flaps in place of the Fowler flaps and increased rudder chord. The compressors forced the air out over the whole span of the upper sides of the flaps and ailerons and over each side of both the rudder and the elevator. In order to enhance the total flap area to maximise the effect during the tests, at low speeds the flaps were hinged so that they deflected the flow to a maximum of 90°, while the ailerons were depressed 30°.

The equipment and modifications resulted in slightly increased operational weight of the test aircraft, and also in a small reduction in the aircraft's payload and range. The first flight of the NC-130B took place on 8 February 1960. The US Army had already abandoned its requirement, but the USAF continued the programme for a while, and the aircraft even flew to England, where it was inspected at the Vickers Aircraft Company's airfield at Wisley, Surrey, in the spring of 1961. No British interest resulted, however, and the project was terminated. Having logged some twenty-three flight hours, the aircraft was placed in storage for a while.

28 Cargo Transport

T he basic duty for which the Hercules was built is often so routine and accepted as part of worldwide aerial activity as to be almost forgotten or taken for granted amid the plethora of 'special mission' activities that have grown up around this legendary aircraft. Yet in this simple, basic role the Hercules is unsurpassed and has a record that is as versatile as it is unassailable. Her basic built-in attributes assured this success from the onset of her long career. With design features which featured a wide, encumbrance-free cargo hold; the straight-in, low-level, rear-loading cargo deck easily accessible with the minimum of outside specialised equipment; the large cargo doors for maximum capacity and a fully adjustable ramp able to cope with just about everything, the Hercules gulps down all manner of cargo, military and civilian, without effort. She thus proved able to cope with the diversity of air cargo across the whole spectrum, and even invented a few of her own as the decades rolled by.

Anything that required air shipping from one part of the globe to another with the minimum of fuss and effort and with economy, range and reliability vanished into the Herk's maw and was duly disgorged, safely, at its point of destination, be it military vehicles (from full-size tanks and artillery, through tracked armoured personnel carriers and fuel trucks down to jeeps), military hardware (disassembled aircraft, helicopters, missiles, aircraft engines, lorries, ammunition and stores), civilian heavy equipment (road-building machinery, oil rig assemblies, pipeline sections, mobile workshops and associated equipment and fittings), dangerous bulk fuels, sensitive electronics, emergency medical supplies, equipment and fully fitted laboratories, all manner of bulk livestock in internal pens (fish and animal containers, and not forgetting displaced humans), fresh produce (fruit, grain, general foodstuff, and relief supplies of every conceivable type and size), mail, parcel and packages, timber, metals and other raw materials, palletised or containerised – the list is endless.

In war situations the Herk, from Vietnam to the Gulf, has truly proved herself indispensable. So reliant was the US war effort in Vietnam on the Hercules for supply and myriad other duties that one high-ranking officer stated that

without her the Allied attempts to stem the Communist invasion would have come to a complete stop. From 1972 they flew also with the Vietnamese Air Force (VNAF), the RAAF and the RNZAF. On 22 February 1967 they flew in the largest parachute drop of the war, Operation 'Junction City' at Tay Ninh. They ensured the survival of the Marine garrison at Khe Sanh between 21 January and 8 April 1968, logging 74% of the 1,128 transport missions flown. In many other dangerous supply runs the cost to the 'trash and ass haulers', as the Hercules aircrew wryly dubbed themselves, was enormous, with heavy losses being incurred, from ground fire, missiles and anti-aircraft batteries (see table).

USAF/USMC Hercules losses in the South-east Asia Theatre of War

Serial	C/n	Serial	C/n	Serial	C/n
54-1625	3012	57-0467	3174	62-1814	3776
54-1629	3016	57-0475	3182	62-1815	3777
55-0002	3029	58-0718	3513	62-1840	3803
55-0009	3036	58-0722	3517	62-1843	3806
55-0038	3065	58-0737	3534	62-1853	3817
55-0039	3066	58-0743	3540	62-1854	3818
55-0042	3069	60-0298	3602	62-1861	3825
55-0043	3070	60-0307	3618	62-1865	3829
55-0044	3071	61-0953	3630	63-7772	3838
56-0472	3080	61-0965	3652	63-7780	3846
56-0477	3085	61-0967	3654	63-7798	3864
56-0480	3088	61-0970	3667	63-7827	3904
56-0490	3098	61-0972	3669	64-0508	3992
56-0499	3107	61-2637	3673	64-0511	3995
56-0502	3110	61-2644	3682	64-0522	4006
56-0506	3114	61-2649	3692	64-0547	4040

56-0510	3118	149809	3709	64-0563	4071
56-0521	3129	149813	3719	66-0214	4164
56-0533	3141	62-1785	3730	66-0218	4174
56-0548	3156	62-1797	3748	69-6571	4345
56-0549	3157				

Having 'trash-hauled, air-dropped, flare-dropped, bombed, machine-gunned, fire-suppressed, drone-launched, photo-mapped, missile-tracked, air-evacuated, Fulton-rescued, capsule-recovered, air-refuelled, carrier-landed and ski-lifted everything from food, guns, toilet paper, jeeps, tanks and paratroops to bridges for the Dominican Republic, water for Peruvian earthquake victims, hay bales for starving cattle in North Dakota, wheat to starving Africans in Mali and beer to fighter pilots at Phu Cat'[15] with the TAC, the Herk was eventually phased out of that command. The Tactical Air Command finally turned over the last of their Herks to the Military Airlift Command in December 1974, ending a unique era for the trash and ass haulers. But it was not the end of their military record by a long chalk.

In the Gulf several decades later the Herk logged 11,799 sorties during the defence 'Desert Shield' period, acting both as the prime tactical air lift facilitator and as one of the main struts of the air supply bridge between Europe, CONUS and the war zone. Some 130 C-130E/Hs were directly assigned to Operation 'Desert Storm'. Among their many heavy strategic and tactical air lift operations was the moving of the 82nd Airborne Division from Safwa, Saudi Arabia, to the forward operating location (FOL) as part of Operation 'Desert Sabre'. There was just one war casualty, an AC-130H, serial 69-6567 (c/n 4341), which, on 28 January 1991, courageously remained over the battle zone south of Kuwait City after dawn in order to assist a US Marine Corps unit threatened by a Frog-7 missile site. She took a hit from a hand-held missile and crashed into the sea, killing all fourteen crew members.

---

[15] From Major Joe Tillman, 'Farewell to the Herk', from *TAC ATTACK* magazine, January 1975.

29 Earth Survey Program

A standard C-130B, 58-0712 (c/n 3507) was modified prior to delivery, with blown flaps and control surfaces for boundary layer control work, and given the civilian registration N707NA. Subsequent to this the test machine was re-converted to normal C-130B configuration, with the modified wings and rudder being replaced by a conventional set from a damaged L-100 aircraft (c/n 4109), and, as N929NA, arrived at the Johnson Space Center in July 1968. Purchased by NASA in September 1969, she resumed active duties on Earth Survey work with the NASA Earth Resources Program, initially based at Ellington AFB, Texas.

In 1979, as part of the Airborne Instrumentation Research Program (AIRP) (Earth Survey 2), this aircraft was fitted out with a new nose section from a Lockheed P-3 Orion which held a C-band microwave antenna, along with a four-channel radiometer for remote-sensing in addition to the normal C-130 sensors. Internally, a special camera bay was built into the aircraft's hold, which also contained a unique thermometer, eleven-channel and eight-channel scanners and active microwave scanner. At the rear a further microwave scanner was mounted on an extension to the tail, with three more on the upper rear ramp area, and two more were fitted on extensions which could be flown from the open ramp aperture.

During 1979 this aircraft surveyed the Arctic, covering some 25,000 miles (40,225km) in all. This aircraft was re-designated yet again, in February 1982, N707NA, and is currently still in service with NASA Dryden, flying from Edwards AFB, California.

30 Electronic Reconnaissance and Surveillance

There have been numerous special adaptations, modifications and conversions of standard USAF and other nations Hercules variants to perform highly specialised ECM, ER and ES, electronic intelligence-gathering (ELINT) and communications intelligence (COMINT) missions down the decades. The Herk had the bulk to accommodate the specialist equipment in all its complexity, and room to house the operators, as well as having the range and endurance to be used along the sensitive perimeters of the expanding Communist world and other hotspots, and act as an airborne trip-wire for each new aggression.

The first such were twelve C-130As modified from 1957

onwards into C-130A-IIs specifically as communications intelligence and signals intelligence-gathering (COMINT/SIGINT) aircraft: 54-1637 (c/n 3024), 56-0484 (c/n 3092), 56-0524 (c/n 3132), 56-0525 (c/n 3133), 56-0528 (c/n 3136), 56-0530 (c/n 3138), 56-0534 (c/n 3142), 56-0535 (c/n 3143), 56-0537 (c/n 3145), 56-0538 (c/n 3146), 56-0540 (c/n 3148) and 56-0541 (c/n 3149).

The modification comprised the fitting of direction-finding (D/F) equipment, pulse and signal receivers, recorders and analysers, and accommodation for up to fifteen operatives to work in shifts, with limited sleeping accommodation. They were flown by 7406 Operations Squadron, 7407 Combat Support Wing along the Iron Curtain in Europe, and were based at Rhein-Main Airbase in what was then West Germany, and for southern areas and Middle Eastern missions worked out of Athens airport. It was during one of these flights along the Soviet border that 56-0528 was destroyed by Soviet fighter aircraft near Yerevan, Armenia, on 2 September 1958. All the survivors were re-converted to standard C-130As in 1971 on being replaced by the newer C-130B-II.

In May 1961, the USAF patrols along the demilitarised zone (DMZ) which separated North and South Koreas, which had to be constantly monitored against northern excursions, military build-up and spy penetrations, had their ageing Boeing RB-50Es replaced by thirteen newly built but modified RC-130Bs which were re-designated C-130B-IIs (*Sun Valley IIs*): 58-0711 (c/n 3506), 58-0723 (c/n 3518), 59-1524 (c/n 3560), 59-1525 (c/n 3561), 59-1526 (c/n 3563), 59-1527 (c/n 3568), 59-1528 (c/n 3571), 59-1530 (c/n 3576), 59-1531 (c/n 3579), 59-1532 (c/n 3581), 59-1533 (c/n 3586), 59-1535 (c/n 3585) and 59-1537 (c/n 3589).

These thirteen machines were equipped with long-focal-length (LFL) oblique cameras and other electronic reconnaissance equipment and were flown by 6091 Reconnaissance Squadron, which was based at Yakota Airbase in Japan. From 1 July 1968 they were taken over by 556 Reconnaissance Squadron performing the same role, and later joined 7406 Combat Support Squadron. They were all converted back to standard C-130Bs in the early 1970s by the simple expedient of removing their specialised equipment and the fittings.

A single Coast Guard C130-E, serial 1414 (c/n 4158), was built in 1966 as a long-range navigation (LORAN) A & C calibration aircraft, and was initially designated as EC-130S (for Search), which was later changed to E on delivery. She operated from Elizabeth City, St Petersburg

and Clearwater between August 1966 and July 1983, again re-designated HC-130E. After this she went to the Military Storage and Disposition Center (MASDC) in Arizona, and received the USAF designation CF049 before being sold out to Certified Aircraft Parts, who sold her cockpit to Reflectone, later Asia-Pacific Training & Simulation PTE Ltd. She was finally scrapped in November 1995.

In April 1967 this same designation, EC-130E, was applied to ten C-130E-IIs which had been modified for the Airborne Command & Control Center (ABCCC) role over Vietnam: 62-1791 (c/n 3738), 62-1809 (c/n 3770), 62-1815 (c/n 3777), 62-1818 (c/n 3780), 62-1820 (c/n 3783), 62-1825 (c/n 3788), 62-1832 (c/n 3795), 62-1836 (c/n 3799), 62-1857 (c/n 3821) and 62-1863 (c/n 3827).

They were flown in combat by No. 7 Airborne Command and Control Squadron (ACCS), and one of them, 62-1815 (c/n 3777), was destroyed by enemy action at Da Nang Airbase on 15 July 1967. The survivors soldiered on after the war, and another one, 62-1809 (c/n 3770), became one of the casualties of the ill-fated and botched rescue mission into Tabas, Iran, when she collided with an RH53D at Posht-I-Badam on 24 April 1980. Many of these aircraft were modernised with 4,910 eshp T56-A-15 engines (de-rated to 4,058 eshp) and carried an in-flight refuelling receptacle forward, but retained their (ABCC) status.

The ABCCII capsules carried in Vietnam, which had manual plotting boards and grease pencils, were upgraded in two aircraft to the ABCCIII system, which used secure communications equipment with computer-generated text and graphic displays, satellite communications equipment, and a digital switching system (JTIDS) which could detect hostile ground forces and transfer the data and co-ordinates to aircraft like the A-10A Thunderbolt-II (*Warthog*) anti-tank aircraft for destruction. Equipped with twenty-three fully securable radios, secure teletype and fifteen automatic, fully computerised consoles, they allowed a quick analysis of any battlefield scenario for swift and accurate counter-action to be initiated. Two of these, 62-1791 (c/n 3738) *Grey Ghost* and 1825 (c/n 3788) *War Wizard*, with the 7th ACC Squadron of 28 Air Division, headquartered at Keesler AFB, Mississippi, went out to Saudi Arabia during the Gulf War of 1990/1 and played a leading role in Operation 'Desert Storm'. In the actual aerial assault of the battle, they flew forty combat sorties, totalling 400 hours flying time. They were credited with controlling almost 50% of all aerial attacks and also co-ordinated many of the search and rescue (SAR) operations to get Allied pilots out from behind enemy lines.

Five C-130Es – 63-7783 (c/n 3850), 63-7815 (c/n 3889), 63-7816 (c/n 3894), 63-7828 (c/n 3896) and 63-9816 (c/n 3977) – were modified to EC-130E(CL)s between March and April 1979. These *Comfy Levi/Senior Hunter*s were configured by Lockheed Aircraft Services for both the electronic intelligence acquisition and electronic jamming roles utilising palletised systems.

Three C-130Es – 63-7773 (c/n 3839), 63-7869 (c/n 3939) and 63-9817 (c/n 3978) – were similarly modified to EC-130E(RR)s between April and December 1979. This trio of *Rivet Rider/Volant Scout* electronic surveillance aircraft, along with the EC-130E(CL)s, were flown by 193 Tactical Early Warning Systems (TEWS) Squadron (Pennsylvania Air National Guard), and later by 193rd Electronic Countermeasures (ECS) Squadron, but with their missions directed by Electronic Security Command, USAF and their specialist equipment operated by National Security Agency personnel. From June 1987 all eight aircraft were upgraded with T56-A-15 engines, in-flight refuelling and infra-red countermeasures (IRCM) jammers. In April 1980 one of the CLs, 63-7783 (c/n 3839), was modified to an RR.

Four of the Harrisburg-based aircraft – 63-7773, (c/n 3839), 63-7783 (c/n 3850), 63-7869 (c/n 3939) and 63-9817 (c/n 3978) – were modified to *Volant Solo* standard for psychological operations (PSYOP) duties. Large-blade aerials were fitted on the upper rear fuselage and ventrally on the wings outboard of the engines. They later changed from *Volant Solo II* to *Coronet Solo* aircraft with the movement of the ANG unit from Tactical Air Command into Military Airlift Command. During Operation 'Just Cause' in Panama they flew as substitute radio and television stations, an operation they had also performed in local missions.

Their primary mission was to conduct psychological operations by the use of electromagnetic transmissions which covered commercial AM and FM radio bands, VHF and UHF television bands and VHF, HF and FM military frequencies. The equipment includes pre-recorded audio and video material, live broadcasts from eight aircrew broadcast microphones, using Army-supplied linguists if required, cassette tape, reel-to-reel tape and video playback modulations. They also act as a link to re-transmit ground station signals. They have a five-man crew – two pilots, navigator, flight engineer and loadmaster – plus extra personnel – a third pilot, navigator and flight engineer – on special long-endurance missions, achieved by dropping some of the five communications systems

operators, who are under the command of an electronic warfare officer.

The 193rd Special Operations Squadron, 193 Special Operations Group, deployed four CL and four RR *Volant Solo II*s during the Gulf War with spectacular results. Being stand-off platforms, they did not over-fly enemy-held territory, but their sorties flew eight- to ten-hour missions along the existing front-line with fighter cover at high altitudes. Arabic-speaking linguists were provided by the Army and the Kuwaiti Government in exile. Their broadcasts are credited with inducing thousands of Iraqi soldiers to lay down their arms and surrender without firing a shot. These Herks also flew other, very secret, *Senior Scout*-type missions on behalf of Electronic Security Command.

These four aircraft were further modified to *Commando Solo* status in 1992/3, in the light of the Gulf War experience. A pair of upgraded UHF/VHF antenna for the global capability TV broadcast system was fitted under each wing in 23ft × 6ft (7m × 1.8m) pods. The leading-edge blade aerial on the dorsal fin was removed, and in its place four forward-facing antenna pods are now carried for low-frequency (L/F) TV broadcasts. High-frequency (H/F) broadcasts are by way of a trailing wire antenna and AM broadcasts also by trailing wire antenna fitted with a 500lb (227kg) weight. In addition to their psychological broadcasting capability, this quartet also has huge civilian usage potential as airborne TV relay co-ordinators in times of natural emergencies or disasters.

This system was first put to use during the Haitian crisis when USAF paratroop and ground support units were placed on standby. The fact that the USA had heavy forces imminently poised to invade was broadcast and convinced the ring-leaders that resistance was futile. The President resigned and the whole of Operation 'Uphold Democracy' was made a bloodless episode.

In addition, six *Combat Talon I*s were operational during the Gulf War: 64-0523 (c/n 4007) and 64-0561 (c/n 4065) with 7 Special Operations Squadron from Rhein-Main, Germany; and 64-0551 (c/n 4046), 64-0559 (c/n 4062), 64-0562 (c/n 4068) and 64-0568 (4086) from 8 SOS, Hurlburt Field, Florida. Their main role was inserting and retrieving special forces troops inside Iraq itself, as well as behind enemy lines in occupied territory. They also co-operated with such units as the US Navy SEALS, the Army's Green Berets and the Joint-Service DELTA Force. They also acted as refuelling tankers for the 20 SOS's MH-53J *Pave Low* helicopters working from behind enemy lines.

The Research Flight Facility, US Department of Commerce, was part of the National Oceanic and Atmospheric Administration Environmental Research Laboratories. They later became NOAA's Office of Aircraft Operations at Miami, Florida. In 1975 they were operating a single specially equipped WC-130B Hercules, carrying out atmospheric research world-wide. In addition to the basic instrumentation needed to measure weather elements and position, the Herk carried cloud physics instrumentation for sampling the interiors of clouds. These devices included an infra-red air temperature radiometer, ice-nuclei counter, aerosol detector, liquid water content sensors and a hydrometer foil sampler. In 1974 this aircraft was modified to carry the Airborne Reconnaissance Systems (AWRS), a minicomputer-centred airborne meteorological data system developed for the Air Weather Service by Kaman Aerospace Corporation. The WC-130B, 58-0732 (c/n 3526), which also carried civilian registration N6541C and was named One-Four Charlie, *was also equipped to launch standard drosondes as well as the Omega drosonde, which sensed temperature, humidity, pressure and position (or wind) as it fell from the aircraft to the surface; the position-sensing capability used an Omega-updated inertial navigation system. Side, nose, radar and vertical cameras provided time-lapse photographic coverage of her missions. The C-130 flew numerous missions in support of the National Aeronautics and Space Administration's Skylab earth-sensor experiments, and was extensively used in the development of new remote-sensing techniques developed for use aboard satellites. She was also heavily involved in weather modification experiments. The Herk carried four seeding racks on each side of the fuselage, containing a total of 416 silver-iodide flares. A pushbutton firing mechanism, located at the visiting scientist station on the flight deck and connected to an electrical-sequencer, was used to ignite and launch the flares during cloud penetrations.* (US Department of Commerce, Rockville, MD)

One unusual duty that came the way of the four 8 SOS birds was a mission to blast a path through Iraqi minefields by dropping 15,000lb (6,804kg) BLU-82/B *Big Blue*, Daisy-Cutter, fuel-air blasting bombs. Christened 'The Mother of All Bombs' in sarcastic reference to Saddam Hussein's boasts about the 'The Mother of All Battles' avidly lapped up by the western media, these were placed on pallets in the Herk's cargo hold and, at 17,000ft (5,182m) over the target, simply rolled out down the rear ramp in a similar scenario to that used by the Vietnamese Herks

twenty years earlier. With the spectacular results of five tonnes of their content counter-mining their target zones very obvious, the four Herks were duly dubbed by some wit as 8 Bomb Squadron!

The fourteen MC-130Es – which, in addition to the above, also included 64-0547 (c/n 4040), 64-0555 (c/n 4056), 64-0558 (c/n 4059), 64-0564 (c/n 4074), 64-0565 (c/n 4077), 64-0566 (c/n 4080), 64-0567 (c/n 4083) and 64-0572 (c/n 4090), and which were operated by 1 Special Operations Wing for the clandestine

Combat Talon I missions – were replaced between June 1990 and November 1991 by twenty-four MC-130H *Combat Talon II*s. The new aircraft were 83-1212 (c/n 5004), 86-1699 (c/n 5026) *Merlin's Magic*, 84-0475 (c/n 5041), 86-0476 (c/n 5042) *Hacker*, 85-0011 (c/n 5053), 85-0012 (c/n 5054), 87-0023 (c/n 5091), 87-0024 (c/n 5092), 87-0125 (c/n 5115), 87-0126 (c/n 5117), 87-0127 (c/n 5118), 88-0191 (c/n 5130), 88-0192 (c/n 5131), 88-0193 (c/n 5132), 88-0194 (c/n 5133), 88-0195 (c/n 5134), 88-0264 (c/n 5135), 88-1803 (c/n 5173) *Dead Man's Party*, 89-0280 (c/n 5236), 89-0281 (c/n 5237), 89-0282 (c/n 5243), 89-0283 (c/n 5244), 90-0161 (c/n 5265) and 90-0162 (c/n 5266).

These aircraft were all former C-130Hs modified for the new role with all the tricks of the trade like ground-mapping, terrain-following, terrain avoidance and navigation via the AN/APQ-170, AN/AAQ-15 detector, AN/AAR-44 missile launch warning, ANALQ-172 detector/jammer, AN/ALQ-69 warning and AN/ALQ-8 electronic countermeasure radar packages, internal navigation system (INS) and infra-red jammers with associated flare/chaff dispensers. A system for high-speed, low-level (HSLL) delivery and container release and an automatic computed air-release package were also shipped.

Three further C-130Hs – 74-2139 (c/n 4711), 74-2134 (c/n 4735) and 89-1185 (c/n 5194) – were converted to EC-130H(CL)s for use by the Air National Guard on the highly secretive *Senior Scout* clandestine electronic intelligence-gathering and jamming missions between January 1993 and March 1994.

Sixteen Herks, four EC-130Hs – 64-14859 (c/n 4082), 64-14862 (c/n 4089), 65-0962 (c/n 4102) and 65-0989 (c/n 4150) – and twelve C-130Hs – 73-1580 (c/n 4542), 73-1581 (c/n 4543), 73-1583 (c/n 4545), 73-1584 (c/n 4546), 73-1855 (c/n 4547), 73-1856 (c/n 4548), 73-1857 (c/n 4549), 73-1858 (c/n 4550), 73-1590 (c/n 4554), 73-1592 (c/n 4557), 73-1594 (c/n 4563) and 73-1595 (c/n 4564) – were modified to the command, control and communications countermeasures (CCCCM) mission between 1981 and 1983. These *Compass Call* aircraft are operated by 41, 42 and 43 Electronic Combat Squadrons of the 355 Wing based at Davis-Monthan AFB near Phoenix, with 43 working out of Sembach airfield in Germany. Easily identifiable by their U-shaped antenna array mounted ventrally below the empennage, with streamlined blister fairings midway up the tapering section of the rear fuselage, they were also equipped with additional ram air inlets in the undercarriage bays on either side to improve air cooling for the increased electronic cabinets and displays carried internally.

They also came into their own during the Gulf War when 43 ECS Squadron was deployed to Riyadh King Khalid International Airport in Saudi Arabia, and then moved forward to follow the flow of the battle during 'Desert Storm'. They successfully interrupted Iraq's tactical and strategical military communications and their jamming caused considerable inertia among enemy units. A detachment of EC-130Hs from 43 ECS also operated clandestinely over Iraq during Operation 'Proven Force', working out of Incirlik, Turkey.

Three EC-130Hs – 64-14862 (c/n 4089), 65-0962 (c/n 4102) and 65-0989 (c/n 4150) – still operate with 41 ECS.

Two C-130Es were used as lead aircraft for the electronic special operations support (SOS) aircraft during trials and evaluations at Edwards AFB, California, and Wright-Patterson AFB, Ohio, these being 64-0571 (c/n 4087), used for electronic intelligence-gathering (ELINT) and named *Night Prowler*, and 64-0572 (4090) respectively. They were designated NC-130E-*LM*s, but in 1979 their designations changed to MC-130E-S and MC-130E respectively (see below).

These trials led to the conversion of fifteen Herks into *Combat Talon 1*s. They were re-engined with the T56-A-15, and an in-flight refuelling receptacle was mounted atop the forward fuselage to extend range. The electronics fitted included terrain-following AN/APQ-122(V)8 dual-frequency I/K band radar, an internal navigation system (INS), a special hush-hush communications pinpoint system enabling pinpoint airdrops of special forces units behind enemy lines, and infra-red countermeasure (IRCM) carried in pods, with associated chaff dispensers and flare dispensers. In addition the ten *Rivet Clamp* aircraft were fitted with the Fulton surface-to-air recovery (STAR) system.

These aircraft were in three groups, the first designated MC-130E *Rivet Clamp*, of which ten aircraft were converted: 64-0523 (c/n 4007) *Midnight Creeper*, 64-0551 (c/n 4046), 64-0555 (c/n 4056) *Triple Nickel Ethel*, 64-0559 (c/n 4062), 64-0561 (c/n 4065), 64-0562 (c/n 4068), 64-0566 (c/n 4080), 64-0567 (c/n 4083) and 64-0572 (c/n 4090). As mentioned, one of the trials aircraft became the sole MC130E-S *Rivet Swap* aircraft, 64-0571 (c/n 4087).

Finally, there were four MC-130E-Y *Rivet Yank* aircraft, two of which adopted the serials of crashed Herks and were used in clandestine operations: 62-1843 (c/n 3991) ex 64-0507, 63-7785 (c/n 3991) ex 64-0507, 64-0564 (c/n 4074), which crashed off Tabone Island, Philippines, on 26 February 1981, and 64-0565 (c/n 4077).

In 1981 the Lockheed Corporation put forward their idea of an airborne early-warning aircraft which they classified the EC-130. The US State Department's Office of Munitions Control (OMC) authorised the company to release technical details to any potential overseas customer, and an artist's impression was printed by various magazines.[16] The concept was to incorporate a tail-mounted, updated version of the General Electric APS-125 surveillance radar to provide early detection of approaching airborne threats for both overland and overwater surveillance. Lockheed predicted a demand for such an aircraft and that the Hercules provided the most supportable platform of all the aircraft considered.[17]

The radar antenna would be housed inside a 24ft (7.3m) diameter rotordome mounted atop the vertical stabiliser, which would be cut down in height by 65in (163cm) compared to a standard C-130. The interaction of the rotordome and the stabiliser would continue to provide sufficient directional control despite the shorter tail, it was predicted. An antenna located thus was thought to be capable of providing an almost free-space field of view (FSFV) of 360° in azimuth and 21° in elevation to nominal ranges of 200 nautical miles (370km). In addition to the radar the proposed design would also carry identification friend or foe (IFF) equipment and passive electronic monitoring systems. The overall package would have the capacity to track 300 separate targets simultaneously and would be able to monitor up to 256 electronic threats. It would also be equipped with secure voice and datalink communications for airborne early warning co-ordination.

One early-warning aircraft with rotordome and AN/APAS-14S EC-130V, CG1721 (c/n 5121), was operated by the US Coast Guard for illegal anti-drug importation surveillance duties. She was modified by General Dynamics, Fort Worth, from an HC-130H in 1968 and designated EC-130V. She had the AN/APS-125 radar mounted above the after-fuselage in a similar manner to the smaller Grumman E-2C Hawkeye early-warning aircraft already in use for the same mission. Additionally, various antennae sprouted from fairings around the nose. Three operatives and their associated cabinets, consoles and displays were pallet-mounted in the cargo hold, and in order to give air flow around these additional electronic cabinets and equipment extra cooling vents were cut.

The Coast Guard briefly operated this aircraft from USCGS Clearwater, Florida, between 31 July 1991 and April 1992, then the USAF took an interest in her and her Coast Guard livery was replaced by camouflage and she was placed on the strength of 514 Test Squadron and assigned the serial 87-0157, and in October 1993 was redesignated NC-130H, flying with 418 Test Squadron, before being assigned to the Naval Air Test Center at Patuxent River in November 1998.

31 Forest-Fire Control

The United States has been plagued for decades with large-scale wildfires, fires which are started accidentally or on purpose in areas of thick woodland or shrub-land adjacent to their ever-sprawling city suburbs, and which cause enormous damage running into billions of dollars. Airborne fire-fighting has long been a major weapon in efforts to contain these outbreaks, especially in inaccessible areas, and it was perhaps inevitable that the multi-talented Hercules should have quickly found herself a major contender in this specialised field.

Lockheed worked with the existing services and the USAF in a series of tests in 1971. They developed the modular airborne fire-fighting system (MAFFS), which could be quickly fitted to any standard C-130 with only the minimum modifications. The MAFFS was a modular system which was built around a core of six 500 US gallon (1,893 litre) pressurised air tanks, each tank having a 50lb (22.7kg) per square inch pressure, with their associated plumbing and hardware consisting of dual nozzles and spraying gear located on the main ramp. The total spray cargo a C-130 could dump was therefore 3,000 US gallons (11,356 litres).

The method adopted after trials was for the C-130 to fly straight and steady down to an altitude of only 200ft (61m), and at a speed of 130 knots (66.87 mps). The fire-retardant content of the tanks is forced out down the nozzles at a rate of 400 US gallons (1,514 litres) per second to lay a comprehensive field over the target zone. The tanks can be fired off as individual units or all six can be fired simultaneously to give a blanket cover. A C-130 spray pattern covered a rectangle some 2,000ft (610m) long by 150ft (46m) wide in about six seconds.

---

16 See, for example, 'Lockheed Surveillance Concept Gains Favor', article in *Aviation Week & Space Technology*, 25 May 1981 issue.

17 Other contenders were the C-130, Lockheed P-3 Orion and Boeing 737.

No.	Owner/Operator	Type	Registration	Load (lb)	Volume (US gal)
30	Intl. Air Response	C-130A	116TG	27,000	3,000
31	Intl. Air Response	C-130A	117TG	27,000	3,000
32	Intl. Air Response	C-130A	118TG	27,000	3,000
63	TBM Inc.	C-130A	473TM	27,000	3,000
64	TBM Inc.	C-130A	466TM	27,000	3,000
67	TBM Inc.	C-130A	531BA	27,000	3,000
81	Hemet Valley	C-130A	131FF	27,000	3,000
83	Hemet Valley	C-130A	132FF	27,000	3,000
88	Hemet Valley	C-130A	138FF	27,000	3,000
130	H & P Aviation	C-130A	130HP	27,000	3,000
131	H & P Aviation	C-130A	131HP	27,000	3,000
133	H & P Aviation	C-130A	133HP	27,000	3,000

The retardant used is not only designed to be safe for any humans or plants accidentally caught in the spray, but also acts as a fertiliser to regenerate vegetation in the burn area. C-130 FireShips did not have to wait long to prove their value, and a series of major wildfires in 1973 and 1974 saw them in action in states as far apart as California, Idaho, Montana and New Mexico. By 1975 the USAF Reserve and the Air National Guard units flying the Hercules had established no fewer than eight MAFFS units around the USA, available when called upon, and in the quarter of a century since that date the C-130 has performed frequently in this role. The USAF took over the job from the ANG and Reserves, but repeated cutbacks have today reduced their capability to just one unit, the 910th Airlift Wing (ALW), 773rd Airlift Squadron (ALS), which is a section of 22 Air Force (Air Mobility Command) based at Youngstown Warren Regional Airport in Ohio, flying C-130Hs.

The demands on the pilots of such C-130s are high, with long hours, dangerous flying conditions and much strain involved. The US Forest Service (USFS), based at Sacramento, California, maintained strict minimum requirements on their fire-fighting pilots, including a 1,500 hours of command pilot time which had to include 500 hours multi-engine work with an instrument rating. Experience in low-level agricultural flying, air attack or co-pilot experience on air tankers was highly desirable for recruits. They put a block on the over-35 age group also. Those exclusively flying the Herk had even more stringent qualification to demonstrate according to the Boise

Interagency Fire Center (BIFC). PICs (Captains) had to have an instrument rating, type rating for the tanker involved and a Class II physical. The Forest Service demanded at least 200 hours flight time in the Herk herself, 100 hours at night, 200 hours of typical terrain and landing facilities – mountains and low level, a minimum of 50 hours actual instrument time and 100 hours in the preceding twelve month period.[18]

In order to qualify for an initial attack pilot, captains of fire-fighting Herks had to have 75 hours of fire-fighting time in the preceding three years, twenty-five hours of which were as captain in command, and must have flown twenty-five completed missions and be recommended by two qualified observers, one of whom had to be a USFS-approved pilot inspector. Air tanker co-pilots' qualifications were only slightly less stringent and included at least eight hundred hours of PIC, a multi-engine commercial licence, etc. Co-pilots were only authorised to fly the C-130 over actual fire zones if they had an air tanker pilot card and were authorised by the air attack supervisor to do so. As added incentive any reckless flying, ineffective work or inability to adapt to field living conditions meant they were replaced. Any loads they accidentally or carelessly dropped outside the target were not paid for by the Government Agency. Despite these restrictions, this

---

[18] See Don Dowe, 'Fire-fighting – it's a job for a sharp pilot', article in *Private Pilot* magazine, October 1990.

dangerous job continues to attract top-class pilots looking for out-of-routine missions and initiative.

However, the United States Forestry Service itself operated no fewer than twenty-two Hercules fire aircraft via both the USAF and private companies: N1171TG (c/n 3018), 54-1639 (c/n 3026), N473TM (c/n 3081), N116TG (c/n 3086), N137FF (c/n 3092), N6585H (c/n 3095), N9724V (c/n 3099), N134FF (c/n 3104), N8055R (c/n 3115), N132FF (c/n 3119), N131FF (c/n 3138), N531BA (c/n 3139), N132FF (c/n 3142), N133FF (c/n 3143), N130RR (c/n 3145), N134FF (c/n 3146), N135FF (c/n 3148), N136FF (c/n 3149), N135HP (c/n 3166), N466TM (c/n 3173), 57-0479 (c/n 3186) and N8026J (c/n 1389). The private company Aero Firefighting Services operated a further five machines: N134FF (c/n 3104), N132FF (c/n 3119), N131FF (c/n 3138), N135FF (c/n 3148) and N138FF (c/n 3227) (see appropriate section).

With the unchecked sprawl of American cities into the countryside, the increase in temperatures and lack of rainfall due to global warming and increased pollution, the growth of the wildfire risk rises with each succeeding year,

The AC-130A gunship carried a mean offensive strafing armament that included two 40mm Bofors cannon mounted amidships on the port side of the cabin, in addition to two 7.62mm miniguns and 20mm cannon. These guns were controlled and directed at ground targets by way of fire-control radar and sensor devices to deliver a lethal hail of shells onto Viet-Minh concentrations in the jungles of South-East Asia. (Author's Collection)

and never has the demand been higher for air tanker services, with 2000 seeing unprecedented disasters all over the western United States. The August 2000 Airtanker Register of Fire & Aviation Management lists a number of Hercules still in service as part of the aerial combat teams desperately trying to contain such infernos (see table opposite).

The 115th Airlift Squadron, based at Port Hueneme, California, was the USAF firefighting unit at the forefront of the battle. Forward deployed to Fresno from 24 July 2000, this outfit flew round-the-clock sorties under the direction of United States Forest Service and California Department of Forestry experts, who supplied the retardant and led the

aircraft to the fires, and they were a key part of the Modular
Airlift Fire-Fighting System from the Air National Guard
Channel Island Station.

*Carrying the markings of the Military Airlift Command, this is
63-9814 (c/n 3975) of the 438th Marine Air Wing revving up on
the deck at Hickam Field Air Force Base, Hawaii, in 1968.*
(Nick Williams AAHS)

32 Gunships

T he aerial gunship concept was already well established in the USAF, but the arrival of the Hercules
gave added scope and firepower to the type and it
has been steadily developed ever since.

On 6 June 1967, under Operation 'Gunboat', the
Aeronautical Systems Division, Air Force Systems
Command, based at Wright Field, Ohio, produced the prototype of the AC-130A-*LM Pave Pronto & Pave Pronto Plus*
aircraft, a conversion from a standard C-130A,
54-1626 (c/n 3013) *Plain Jane*. She was equipped with the
Stella Scope, night vision device (NVD), side-looking radar
(SLR), a beacon-tracking device, direction-finding homer,
FM band radio transceiver, semi-automatic flare dispenser
and, on the after ramp, an AN/AVQ-8 steerable searchlight
with an infra-red (IR) and an ultra-violet (UV) Xenon arc
light. She was thus well equipped to find ground targets,
but she was equally well armed in order to deal with the
same targets once located and pinpointed. She had no fewer
than four 20mm (0.79in) General Electric M061 cannon
emplaced, firing obliquely downwards from a special
gunport along her port fuselage. These had a fully comput-

erised fire-control system. She also had an inert tank
system.

Plain Jane was given two periods of combat experience
in Vietnam, the first between October and December 1967,
and the second between February and November of the following year. From her experience in the field the USAF
decided that the experiment was highly successful and further Herk gunships were an obvious requirement. The systems fit was modified in the light of these missions with the
fitting of an AN/AWG-13 analogue computer to upgrade
information faster, an AN/APQ-136 moving target indicator
(MTI) sensor and an AN/AAD-4 side-looking infra-red
(SLIR) sensor.

Seven more conversions from JC-130As were carried out
to this specification by LTV Electrosystems at Greenville,
Texas, and these were completed between August and
December 1968. These seven all saw intense action at
night against the infiltrating North Vietnamese and guerrilla armies invading South Vietnam, attacking their supply
columns and vehicular traffic. They were later brought up
to *Pave Pronto* standard. They were serials 53-3128

(c/n 3001) *First Lady*, which survived battle damage to end her days in the USAF Armament Museum at Eglin, Florida; 54-1623 (c/n 3010) *Ghost Rider*; 54-1625 (c/n 3012) *War Lord*, which was destroyed by enemy action over the Ho Chi Minh Trail on 21 April 1970; 54-1627 (c/n 3014) *Gomer Grinder*; 54-1628 (c/n 3015) *The Exterminator*, which ended her days in Celebrity Row at the AMARC In Arizona; 54-1629 (c/n 3016), which was lost through enemy action and burnt out at Ubon Royal Thai Air Force Base on 25 May 1969; and 54-1630 (c/n 3017) *Azrael*, which ended up at the USAF Museum, Wright-Patterson AFB, Ohio.

A further experimental aircraft was modified in November 1970 for all-weather capability, *Pave Pronto*, and with yet greater firepower. Produced under the *Super Chicken/Surprise Package* programmes, this aircraft was a conversion from C-130A, serial 55-0011 (c/n 3038), later named *Night Stalker*. Her box of tricks included an AN/ASQ-24A stabilised tracker which incorporated ASQ-145 low-light-level television (LLLTV) and a Motorola AN/APQ-133 beacon-tracking radar (BTR). Added punch was provided by a pair of 7.62mm (0.3in) MXU-470 Miniguns, two clip-fed 40mm (1.57in) Bofors mounted aft, and two 20mm (0.79in) Vulcan cannon emplaced forward.

She led to nine further *Pave Pronto* aircraft conversions from C-130As, which carried yet further embellishments: the AN/ASQ-24A stabilised tracker with an AN/AVQ-18 laser designator/rangefinder package with a bomb damage assessment camera built in. They also featured for the first time the *Black Crow* truck ignition sensor (TIS) and had dual AN/ALQ-87 electronic countermeasure (ECM) pods under each wing, as well as SUU-42 flare ejectors. These nine aircraft suffered heavy casualties in Vietnam, so much so that they were nicknamed 'Mortar-Magnets' by their long-suffering aircrews. They were intensively employed, not only in their own right but as target markers for short-range aircraft like the McDonnell F-4 Phantom. They were serials 55-014 (c/n 3041) *Jaws of Death*, which ended up in the Robins AFB Museum; 55-029 (c/n 3056) *Midnight Express*; 55-040 (c/n 3067), 55-043 (c/n 3070), which was destroyed by an enemy SA-7 missile south-west of Hue on 18 June 1972; 55-044 (c/n 3071) *Prometheus*, destroyed by a SA-2 missile south-east of Sepone, Laos, on 28 March 1972; 55-046 (c/n 3073) *Proud Warrior*; 56-469 (c/n 3077) *Grim Reaper*; 56-490 (c/n 3098) *Thor*, lost to enemy action north-east of Pakse, Laos, on 21 December 1972; and 56-509 (c/n 3117) *Raids Kill Um Dead*, which ended up at Hurlburt Field Memorial Air Park.

The next development followed in April 1970 and resulted in the AC-130E-*LM* (*Pave Spectre I*). These two aircraft were prototype conversions from C-130Es which offered a greater payload, endurance and stability to the gunship role. Both serials, 69-6576 (c/n 4351) and 69-6577 (c/n 4352), were therefore taken in hand by Warner-Robbins Air Material Area (WRAMA) and their initial armament was a pair of 7.62mm (0.3in) MXU-470 Miniguns, two 40mm (1.57in) Bofors and a pair of 20mm (0.79in) M-61 cannon.

Subsequently they were re-armed with the *Pave Aegis* with one fewer 40mm (1.57in) Bofors and a huge 105mm (4.13in) howitzer firing obliquely downwards from the port side instead for maximum impact on the target. This weapon, impressive though it was, was the downfall of 69-6576, for when operating from Mombasa during the Somalia confrontation on 14 March 1994, a practice firing saw a premature detonation and the resultant explosion set fire to the port engines, the aircraft crashing into the sea south of Malindi on the Kenyan coast.

Six AC-130As took part in Operation 'Proven Force', working out of Turkey from February 1991, with 711 Special Operations Squadron, 919 Special Operations Group (headquarters at Duke Field, Florida): 54-1623, 54-1630, 55-0011, 55-0014 which flew twenty combat missions, 55-0029 and 56-0509.

Nine further aircraft, conversions from C-130Es, were ordered in February 1971, and incorporated the latest state-of-the-art electronics, and they became *Pave Spectre Is*. An impressive array of equipment followed generally that of the earlier gunships, but much improved, with cockpit head-up display (HUD), nose-mounted AN/APN-59B navigation radar and MTI, AN/ASQ-150 beacon-tracking radar, a stabilised AN/ASQ-24A tracking radar with laser illuminator and rangefinder, AN/ASQ-5 *Black Crow* TIS, the AN/AAD-7 forward-looking infra-red (FLIR), AN/ALQ-87 ECM pods, an AN-AVQ-17 searchlight and SUU-42A/A chaff and flare dispensers.

These aircraft went into action in south-east Asia (Vietnam, Laos, Cambodia) from the spring of 1972 onwards, by which time their targets were no longer just supply and ammunition trucks, but fully fledged North Vietnamese armoured regiments with Soviet-supplied heavy tanks. They were serials 69-6567 (c/n 4341), 69-6568 (c/n 4342), 69-6569 (c/n 4343), 69-6570 (c/n 4344), 69-6571 (c/n 4345), 69-6572 (c/n 4346), 69-6573 (c/n 4347), 69-6574 (c/n 4348) and 69-6575 (c/n 4349). One, 69-6571 (c/n 4345), was lost to enemy action in March 1972 at An Loc, Vietnam. The remainder were progressively upgraded from 1973 to the AC-130H configuration.

The AC-130H-*LM* upgrade was carried out on ten aircraft from June 1973, converted from surviving AC-130E-*LMs* by replacing their engines with the T56-A-15 4,508 eshp engines: 69-6567 (c/n 4341), 69-6568 (c/n 4342), 69-6569 (c/n 4343), 69-6570 (c/n 4344), 69-6572 (c/n 4346), 69-6573 (c/n 4347), 69-6574 (c/n 4348), 69-6575 (c/n 4349), 69-6576 (c/n 4351) and 69-6577 (c/n 4352).

Subsequently, all were given in-flight refuelling ability with a boom receptacle mounted atop the mid-section, and progressively upgrades have been made with the adoption of a digital fire control computer (DFCC) system, FLIR, LLLTV, ECM and navigation replacements, and by the time of the Gulf War they were fully upgraded. Five AC-130Hs were deployed for the war by 16 Special Operations Squadron: 69-6567, 69-6569, 69-6570, 69-6572 and 65-6576. Considered vulnerable to modern air defence systems, they operated by night over enemy lines considered to be low-threat zones, but despite this caution 69-6567 fell victim to enemy defences on 31 January 1991 while attacking an enemy Frog-7 site which was threatening a US Marine force. The aircraft crashed into the sea off Kuwait, killing all fourteen crew members.

Since then, these aircraft have seen action in the world's trouble-spots like Liberia, Bosnia and Somalia, and eight are still in service with 16 SOS. Under the designation Special Operations Force Improvement (SOFI), one aircraft, 69-6568 (c/n 4342), became the prototype aircraft MC-130P in October 1990 (see appropriate section).

In July 1988, the first of thirteen AC-130Us (*Spectre*), serial 87-0128 (c/n 5139), based on C-130H, was delivered to North America Aircraft Operations Division at Palmdale, California, part of the Rockwell International Corporation, for conversion. Not until January 1991 did the finished gunship arrive at the Air Force Flight Test Center at Edwards AFB for evaluation by 6510 Test Wing. She became known as the *U-Boat* by her crews, and this nickname was also applied to her successors.

She featured yet a further advance of the concept incorporating a battle management centre (BMC) whereby all her updated sensors feed into an IBM IP-102 computer system for input evaluation and decision-making data subjection. This has made both beacon-tracking radar and *Black Crow* indicator seem irrelevant. Firepower also saw the replacement of the 20mm (0.79in) Vulcan guns with a fully

trainable 25mm (0.98in) General Electric GAU-12/U Gatling, a single 105mm (4.13in) howitzer and a single 40mm (1.57in) Bofors. Adverse weather conditions pose no problems with the choice of electronically slaved gunnery from these weapons linked to the Hughes AN/APQ-180 digital fire-control radar; the forward-looking infra-red AN/AAQ-117, emplaced on the port side of the aircraft's nose, or the Bell Aerospace all-light-level television (ALLTV) system. There are also special observer stations inbuilt on the starboard forward fuselage and at the rear ramp area. Target location is guaranteed by the Navstar GPS, and she carries combined INS and cockpit HUD.

Nor has the increasing risk posed to such aircraft by modern defence systems been overlooked. Following combat experience and losses, every attempt has been made to decrease the aircraft's vulnerability to ground fire. The AC-130U incorporates an ITT avionics AN/ALQ-172 jamming system, the Texas Instruments AN/ALQ-117 forward-looking infra-red countermeasures system, and decoy equipment with MJU-7 or M296 IR flares and chaff bundles being released by three dispensers located ventrally on the main fuselage. The ability to absorb punishment is provided by a casing of Spectra ceramic armour over areas most at risk.

The first *Spectre* gunship was followed by twelve more which have joined 4 Special Operations Squadron, 16 Special Operations Wing, at Hurlburt Field, Florida: 89-0509 (c/n 5228), 89-0510 (c/n 5229), 89-0511 (c/n 5230), 89-0512 (c/n 5231), 89-0513 (c/n 5232) and 89-0514 (c/n 5233) which arrived between December 1990 and February 1991, and 90-0163 (c/n 5256), 90-0164 (c/n 5257), 90-0165 (c/n 5259), 90-0166 (c/n 5261), 90-0167 (c/n 5262) and 92-0253 (c/n 5279) which were received between August 1991 and March 1992.

The *Spectre* force has served in Operation 'Urgent Fury' in Grenada, Operation 'Just Cause' in Panama and Operation 'United Shield' in Somalia.

33 High-Technology Test Bed (HTTB)

An L-100-20, N4174M (c/n 4412), originally sold to Kuwait in April 1971, was re-purchased in May 1982 and re-registered N130X. She became the famous high-technology test bed (HTTB) aircraft, 23491 (c/n 3701), for accumulation of STOL information for use on the C-130J projection.

The tests were in three phases from June 1984 onwards. She had extensions forward from horizontal and vertical stabilisers ('horsals'), as well as an extension to the dorsal fin, and she was painted overall in high-gloss black. In Phase II the leading edges of the wings were 'drooped' to change air flow, and double-slotted flaps were fitted along with spoilers. Extended chord ailerons and rudder were fitted and she had a special high-sink-rate undercarriage. The final phase saw her fitted with a FLIR outfit in a turret and laser rangefinder equipment. She later utilised the new T56A-1-1 series IV 5,250 shp prop-turbine engines, and established several climbing records. In February 1992 she was also tested with electro-hydrostatic aileron servo. Trials included a forty-hour programme of flutter tests, position-error evaluation and general air-worthiness which were followed by an assesment of a triple-redundant digital flight-control system. The HTTB was also utilised for Head-Up Display presenting images from forward-looking infra-red and from nose-mounted laser ranging sensors, with the HUD having a rastered image overlay. Also tested was the sensor for assessing landing-strip roughness during a preliminary over-flight prior to touch-down, with a discrimination as low as 9 inches.

During a high-speed ground test on 3 February 1993, she crashed on take-off and was a total write-off. She was practising touch-and-go landings all morning and was taking off on her eighth run from west to east along the main runway when she suddenly veered off course in a steep 60° to 70° bank. She reached an altitude of about 300ft (91m) then 'nosed-down steeply' according to one eyewitness.[19] The aircraft crashed within yards of the Navy Dispensary building and then exploded, killing all seven crew members.[20] Julius Alexander for Lockheed explained that the L-100-20 had been 'extensively modified to be a test vehicle for avionics and flight control systems. It was not an ordinary Hercules by any stretch of the imagination. It was an extraordinary airplane.'[21]

---

[19] See Bill Torpy, 'Doomed plane's takeoff unplanned', article in *The Atlanta Constitution*, 5 February 1993.

[20] The aircrew that fatal day were Olin L. 'Oakie' Bankhead Jr, pilot; Troy Cleveland Castona, flight engineer; Malcolm Jesse Davis, flight engineer; Alan J. McLeroy, engineer; George Dennis Mitchell, engineering test pilot; Veda Ruiz, flight engineer; and William Boyd Southerland, specialist engineer.

[21] See Ron Martz, 'Plane "extensively modified" by Lockheed for test flights', article in *The Atlanta Journal*, 4 February 1993.

34 Hurricane Hunters

Perhaps not surprisingly it is the WC-130's most spectacular missions that have gained the most publicity down the decades, as the famous 53rd Weather Reconnaissance Squadron, known as the Hurricane Hunters. The 53rd became the first squadron to deliberately fly its aircraft into a hurricane when a B-17 made such a penetration in September 1945. Since that date this has become their prime mission, and they have melded into the US Weather Bureau's around-the-clock hurricane warning service, first established on 16 June 1947. Reactivated at Bermuda on 21 February 1951, the first WC-130 Hercules came on strength in 1963. As an airborne early-warning system they had few equals and their timely information saved millions of dollars' worth of property and prevented incalculable loss of life.

When not thus engaged the WC-130s performed a wide variety of useful functions, including cloud-seeding using silver iodide crystals to induce rainfall over drought areas, cold fog dispersal operations adjacent to US military airfields in Alaska, Europe and Asia, and patrol work locating and tracking winter storms of exceptional violence.

The 53rd was joined by the 815th WRS, AFRES, the 'Storm Trackers', in 1975 and the two units shared the role until the heavy defence cuts of 1991 obliterated the original Air Force 53rd for ever. The 815th then became the sole unit doing the job, and had to divide itself between this duty and its traditional tactical air lift (cargo) role. This rapidly proved impractical, however, and just two years later the unit split into two squadrons, the 815th reverting fully as the 815th TAS Flying Jennies, while the weather squadron was resurrected as the 53rd Weather Reconnaissance Squadron, AFRES, still based at Keesler, currently with ten WC-130s as part of the 403rd Wing. The proud nickname was reinstated.

The first WC-130J was delivered to the USAF at Wright-Patterson AFB on 12 October 1999 and was assigned to the 53rd. She was followed by six more of the same type and a further three in 2000. The $62.9 million upgrades, including the installation and integration of special avionics and weather sensors, in addition to the structural modifications required, was built in by the DSO's original order in September 1998. The sensors mounted on the outside of the WC-130Js provide real-time temperature, humidity, barometric pressure, radar-measured altitude, wind speed and direction. This data is used to calculate a complete weather observation every thirty seconds of flight. The WC-130J also deploys dropsondes, which are instruments ejected from the aircraft and deployed by parachute through storm areas to the sea. As they fall these gather real-time weather data which is relayed back to the aircraft's computers. Once processed the information is relayed by satellite directly to the National Hurricane Center for input into the national weather data networks.

Another modified C-130B served with the Research Flight of the US National Oceanic and Atmospheric Administration (NOAA). As an aerial laboratory for performing atmospheric and oceanic research missions the Hercules proved invaluable, and she also doubled in her more usual logistic support role in supply and maintenance of far-flung weather research stations.

35 Maritime Patrol

The Hercules had long seemed a natural candidate for the role of maritime patrol aircraft, combining as she did long range, long endurance, broad-altitude range of operations, superb low-speed handling ability and ample room in a converted cargo compartment for the stowage of specialist equipment. With the US Coast Guard featuring the HC-130H since 1977, most successfully, a more specialised variant was expected to be in high demand.

In the 1970s it became common for nations to extend their exclusive economic zones (EEZs) over which they claimed jurisdiction out to 200 miles (322km) from their shoreline, in order to protect their fishing rights, seabed mining and oil drilling, for smuggling prevention, unauthorised shipping entry and pollution monitoring. But claiming these waters was one thing and protecting them against incursion or intrusion was quite another. What was required was an economical aircraft with long range and endurance, able to sweep large areas both frequently and quickly. Strangely enough the concept never really took off as it was expected to, but Lockheed did introduce a specialised variant designed specifically for this mission, the PC-130H.

Included in the offshore zone patrol and sea-search package four observer stations were built into the fuselage forward and aft on a ramp pallet, with scanner seats and observer doors, those forward having large pressurised windows for high-altitude surveillance. Special USCG-type three-window observation doors were located at each side of the rear of the cargo compartment. High-intensity searchlights, with a 1,000 watt bulb providing 800,000 candle power, were carried on the leading edge of the wing, with an infra-red (IR) scanner, a passive microwave imag-

er, both search and Doppler navigation radar, a low-light-level television, ten flare launch tubes installed on the aft ramp and five paradrop rescue medic kits which were pallet-mounted and featured inflatables in their package.

To photograph the targets by day or night, they were equipped with a Hasselblad camera installed in the floor of the forward cargo compartment, which worked automatically with the Hercules' navigation equipment. Information was relayed and analysed by the aircraft's onboard computer and a resulting matrix gave a perfect positional fix and time which was superimposed on each frame of film exposed. This provided essential evidence when perusing oil spillage or other pollution issues, disputed fishing-ground infringements and the like.

Optional extras included an improved sea-search radar (APS-128) carried in the nose which had a dual search/weather radar. The aircraft could ship a rest module for relief crews, a ramp pallet with a rescue kit, flare launchers and loudspeakers and a rear-looking observation station. The aircraft were extensively galvanised against salt corrosion throughout.

A full crew for the PC-130H was eight men: pilot, co-pilot, flight engineer, navigator and four observers. The flight station and cargo hold were completely pressurised and air-conditioned both in flight and on the ground. To give adequate R&R facilities to crews on long endurance patrols, there was a seating area and a rest area built into the hull with slide-in modules for crew rest, featuring two lavatories, five bunks and a galley. A loudspeaker system was inbuilt.

To increase the range and endurance that maritime patrol entails, they were powered by four 4,509 eshp Allison propjet T56-A-15 lean burn engines, while the fuel bunkerage was increased with a 1,800 US gallon (6,813 litre) tank in the fuselage. This gave the PC-130H a maximum range of 5,640 nautical miles (10,445km), based on 5% of initial fuel plus thirty minutes' reserve. The scenario was that the PC-130H could use all four engines to get out into the patrol area fast and then idle around on just two engines. Thus, on a mission of 1,000-mile (1,609km) radius with the same reserves, the maritime Hercules could loiter on just two engines at a 5,000ft (1,524m) altitude for a maximum time of fifteen hours on station. With a maximum mission range of 2,517 nautical miles (4,661 km), a search time of two and a half hours gave a mission radius of 1,800 nautical miles (3,334km). Search time increased as the mission radius was reduced, of course; thus sixteen hours of search time could be obtained at a range of 200 nautical miles (371km). Re-designated the

A dummy mine is loaded into a USAF C-130H, 74-1661 (c/n 4596) during early tests to utilise the Herk as a minelayer under the CAML system. Initial gravity drop tests were conducted by Lockheed and the US Navy at Eglin, Florida, and full powered tests were carried out in 1981. (Lockheed via Audrey Pearcy)

C-130H-MP, such an aircraft seemed ideal also for submarine-hunting, ships and fleet surveillance or search and rescue missions.

The first customer of what was expected to be many was the Malaysian Republic, with its myriad islands, the whole of the South China Sea and parts of the Indian Ocean as part of its defence responsibility. Three C-130H-MPs were ordered in 1980: FM2451 (c/n 4847), FM2452 (c/n 4849) former civilian N4123M, and FM2453 (c/n 4866). The next customer was Malaysia's rival to the south-east. Indonesia, with 13,000 islands to patrol, ordered one aircraft, AI-1322 (c/n 4898), which was delivered in late 1981. However, no further orders came.

36 | Minelaying

In the summer of 1981, Lockheed, in conjunction with the US Navy, began a series of experiments to test the practicability of aerial minelaying being conducted from the Hercules. The concept was designated the Cargo Aircraft Minelayer System (CAML). The Navy contracted Lockheed to build a 180ft (54.9m) long × 25ft (7.6m) high ground test stand, and the object of the ten-week test programme, initiated on 1 June, was to functionally evaluate hydraulically powered rapid sequence deployment of mines. The CAML programme manager, Joe D. Stites, explained that the test stand would simulate the system's drive and restraint conditions, and would enable engineers to develop the optimum sequence for firing.

The Navy's existing minelaying aircraft at that time included the P-3 patrol bomber and the A6 and A-7 fighter bombers (the latter with very limited capacity), while the Air Force's B-52 bombers could also be adapted for this role. All had limited payload and range, however, and furthermore had greater priorities for their usage.

The Lockheed system had three major components: the

mine-bearing pallets, the control/power pallet and the ejector module. Each was designed to fit easily into the C-130's cargo compartment. The actual mines were loaded in stacks three deep and then rolled into the hold of the Hercules, whereupon the pallets were locked into place using the conventional cargo restraints. At the rear of the loaded mine pallets, the ejector module was inserted on the C-130's cargo ramp, linked by the same hydraulic drive system as these pallets. Ahead of the foremost mine pallet was the control/power pallet, which also housed the launch operator's control station.

A year prior to this the Hercules had been used at Eglin, Florida, in a series of experimental mine gravity drop tests to examine just how feasible it was to utilise rear-loading aircraft for aerial minelaying operations. This was part of a twenty-two-month development programme conducted for the Naval Surface Weapons Center located at Silver Spring, Maryland. Some twenty-nine dummy mines were dropped in four sorties from altitudes that varied from 1,000ft to 2,000ft (305m to 610m), with the Hercules flying at a slightly nose-up attitude to simulate the hydraulic-powered thrust. The trials were considered effective and the mines

HC-130H 64-14852 (c/n 4036) on 12 August 1964 is rigged for Satellite capsule recovery and has twelve such missions logged on her forward fuselage. (Lockheed-Georgia, Marietta via Audrey Pearcy)

dropped remained stable when thus seeded.

In the event, although the trials were relatively successful, the concept was abandoned as far as Hercules participation was concerned.

37 Missile and Satellite Tracking and Recovery

In order to track and monitor the behaviour and flight patterns of guided missiles during testing over the Atlantic range, a total of sixteen aircraft – 53-3129 (c/n 3001), 53-3130 (c/n 3002), 53-3131 (c/n 3003), 53-3132 (c/n 3004), 53-3133 (c/n 3005), 53-3134 (c/n 3006), 53-3135 (c/n 3007), 54-1625 (c/n 3012), 54-1627 (c/n 3014), 54-1628 (c/n 3015), 54-1629 (c/n 3016), 54-1630 (c/n 3017), 54-1639 (c/n 3026), 56-0490 (c/n 3098), 56-0493 (c/n 3101) and 56-0497 (c/n 3105) – were modified between 1958 and 1963 from C-130As for Missile Tracking Atlantic with removable test equipment. They carried extra sensor gear and a large radome atop the fuselage. Many were employed by the US Navy during the Polaris submarine-launched IBM launch firing programme to collect telemetry data. These aircraft were designated the JC-130A-*LM*. They were mainly based at Patrick AFB, Florida, for these duties, and later most were re-converted to other duties.

Similar conversions were carried out to fourteen C-130Bs – 57-0525 (c/n 3501), 57-0526 (c/n 3502), 57-0527 (c/n 3503), 57-0528 (c/n 3504), 57-0529 (c/n 3505), 58-0713 (c/n 3508), 58-0714 (c/n 3509), 58-0715 (c/n 3510), 58-0716 (c/n 3511), 58-0717 (c/n 3512), 58-0750 (c/n 3549), 58-0756 (c/n 3557), 61-0962 (c/n 3647) and 61-0963 (c/n 3648) – in connection with the location and aerial recovery of satellite capsules on their parachute descent to the oceans, and these aircraft were designated as JC-130B-*LM*s. They were utilised by the USAF Space Systems Division in both the Pacific (by 6593rd Test Squadron at Hickam AFB, Hawaii, for the recovery of Discovery military satellite ejected capsules) and in the Atlantic on the missile ranges. They carried a package of instruments in a radome atop the fuselage for electronic direction finding and tracking, telemetry reception and recording equipment.

For recovery of the capsules they were fitted with the All-American Engineering Company's aerial recovery system (ARS) which enabled the Hercules to snare its prey in mid-air. This retrieval system comprised a 3,000lb (1,360kg) capacity winch, an outer dolly and transfer boom, an energy-absorber, an inner dolly, a vehicle carriage, recovery poles and loop and tacks, all for guiding the dollies' and recovery poles' movements from within the cargo compartment. A control panel was provided at the winch operator's station.

The technique employed for aerial capsule retrieval was that, once positive lock-on of the target had been made, the Hercules positioned herself at not more than 15,000ft (4,572m) altitude and adopted a recovery speed of about 125 knots (64.305 mps). Then the two recovery poles which held the loop in position were extended behind and below the open rear cargo ramp in order to snare the descending parachutes. Once it had snagged a parachute, the winch furnished the braking and lifting forces required to arrest the whole package so it could be reeled into the after cargo hold like a fisherman landing his catch.

Hercules Paradrop. A fisheye camera catches a paratrooper as he jumps from the rear of a Lockheed C-130 Hercules during manoeuvres. Sixty-four paratroopers could be carried by the original Herk, and they were able to exit the aircraft via paratroop doors on either side of the plane, or via the rear cargo door as shown here. (Lockheed-Georgia Newsbureau via Audrey Pearcy)

A further seven HC-130Hs – 64-14852 (c/n 4036), 64-14853 (c/n 4037), 64-14854 (c/n 4038), 64-14855 (c/n 4055), 64-14856 (c/n 4072), 64-14857 (c/n 4073) and 64-14858 (c/n 4081) – were modified in 1965/6. In 1986/7 most were re-designated HC-130H.

38 Personnel Transport

Troop movements by air are an essential part of any modern combat scenario, and right from the beginning the Hercules was designed to maximise her potential in this field. With the main cargo compartment both fully pressurised (a first) and air-conditioned, the Herk could be fitted out to accommodate passenger variations that ranged from sixty-four paratroops and ninety-two combat-laden infantrymen to, in a casualty evacuation mode, seventy-four litter cases, stacked five high, along with two medics. Fold-down seating arrangements, which could be stowed between such missions, gave the Herk great versatility, and these also enabled various combinations of the three basic loadings to be made to accommodate all eventualities.

As cargo, heavy weapons and equipment were fully palletised according to type and need, so too various passenger-carrying modules were brought into service to fit the ever-changing mission profile of the Hercules. A seat conversion kit capable of seating seventy-five civilians or hospital staff in standard airline-type seats was one refinement. The seats, being mounted on a standard 9g integral seat track, could be mounted on standard cargo pallets, with an all-steel base and fitted with castors to ease loading and unloading during turn-rounds. Separate toilet and galley modules could also be accommodated with three seats on either side of a centre aisle, in the same manner. Again, these standard pallets were designed to be interchangeable and flexible, and different loadings could be adopted with the minimum of delay or work involved. Even more luxurious accommodation modules were designed for the conveyance in some comfort of high-ranking VIPs or military top brass and staff, and these featured recliner

Australian troops of the International Peace-Keeping Force embark aboard an RAAF C-130E Hercules transport at Darwin RAAF base to take part in Operation 'Stabilise' in East Timor, following the Indonesian military atrocities that occurred after the independence referendum in September 1999. (Australian Defence Headquarters, Canberra)

seats with separate modules for conference rooms, sleeping and rest rooms as well. Known as the Staff-Pak, each of these modular containers measured $44 \times 88 \times 88$in (111.7 $\times$ 223.5 $\times$ 223.5cm) and there was also the Lounge-Pak, another totally self-contained unit which housed twenty personnel with seats, tables, bunks and a galley and which had $10 \times 30 \times 9$ft (3.05 $\times$ 9.14 $\times$ 2.74m) dimensions. These modules could be mounted in any combination straight from the truck and quickly connected up for use.

The record for the number of personnel transported in a Hercules was set up in tragic circumstances during the fall of South Vietnam, abandoned by its democratic allies, to the Communist northern armies in 1975. In the final days of the collapse, on 29 April, one South Vietnamese C-130A somehow managed to cram 452 desperate refugees aboard for the last flight from Tan Son Nhut AB to the safety of Utapao, Thailand. The pilot who achieved this incredible feat commented, 'I counted the people again as we disembarked. It is true – 452 people.'[22]

---

22 See Newsbureau press release, 'The Versatile Hercules', Lockheed-Georgia, Marietta, 1 January 1976.

39 Pollution Control

A lthough the only specialised Hercules which featured pollution control as one of their main functions were the PC-130Hs, which never really took off as a concept, the US Coast Guard has this as one of its mission capabilities.

Early experiments into the feasibility of the Hercules in this role were carried out in the 1970s. One of their C-130Bs, CG 1350 ex 62-3754 (c/n 3763), was loaded with a pair of modules which held anti-pollution equipment and a fuel container bladder made from rubberised nylon. A simulated wrecked tanker with a large simulated oil slick was provided as the 'target' and the modules were dropped from an altitude of 800ft (244m).

Standby Coast Guard ships enabled the equipment to be retrieved and assembled, and then connected to the derelict's fuel tanks, and the simulated oil was then pumped out before it could leak into the sea. At a pumping rate of 1,300 US gallons (4,921 litres) per minute, the bladder siphoned off some 95,000 US gallons (360,050 litres) of the simulated oil in an hour and a half. This, it was estimated, would enable about 4,800 tons of oil to be safely leached from any damaged or stranded tanker within a twenty-four-hour period.

Wheels down as Hercules 63-7829 (c/n 3897) of the 438 MAW, Military Airlift Command, makes her final approach to Hickam Field AFB in 1967. (Nick Williams AAHS)

A C-130E Hercules, A97-172 (c/n 41720) of 37 Squadron RAAF, at Dili airfield unloads medical equipment following the Indonesian military atrocities following the independence referendum in September 1999. (Australian Defence Headquarters, Canberra)

Another trouble spot erupts. The Congo, 20 July 1960. Following the Security Council resolution of 14 July 1960, authorising UN military assistance to the Republic of the Congo, soldiers from a number of nations were sent in to help restore law and order and impose calm on the rioting country. As part and parcel of the United Nations force, no fewer than nineteen medical and health teams were provided by Red Cross and Red Crescent societies or by governments. The Government of India provided the equipment and personnel necessary for the setting up of a 400-bed hospital in the Congo. In this photograph the members of the Indian Armed Forces Medical Corps are seen boarding USAF C-130, 57-0456 (3165) at Palam Airport on 8 September 1969, en route to the Congo. (United Nations Photo)

40 Rescue and Relief Operations

I n the wake of both man-made and natural disasters all around the globe, from flood and famine to earthquake, war refugees and displaced populations, it has become an axiom that among the relief and rescue operations the Hercules is bound to appear. Indeed, in terms of easing suffering around this troubled old globe, the ubiquitous Herky Bird would easily prove more enduring than that older, equally welcome feathered friend the Dove of Peace, the latter having been sadly lacking in most places over the last six decades.

A comprehensive list of every operation in which the Hercules brought succour and some comfort in dire situations worldwide would require more pages than this book can encompass, but here are just a few representative cases down the decades. Others will be found among the illustrations.

- Congo – 1960
- Agadir Earthquake Relief, Morocco – 1960
- Mendoza, Peru, road-building equipment supplies – 1965
- Kampuchea – 1966
- South-west Africa drought animal rescue – 1970s
- Nepal – 1973
- Operation 'Thunderball', Israeli rescue of hijacked hostages from Entebbe, Uganda, with four C-130s and 245 commando troops – 1976
- The disastrous American attempt to rescue hostages held at Tabas, Iran, during which one Hercules, 62-1809 (c/n 3770), was lost – 1980
- Search for Mark Thatcher, lost in the Algerian desert – 1982
- Ethiopia famine relief – 1984/85
- Comic Aid, Africa – 1988
- Sudan – 1991
- Operation 'Provide Comfort', Northern Iraq – 1990–92
- Operation 'Provide Hope', Soviet Union – 1991
- Operation 'Provide Comfort II', Southern Iraq – 1992–5
- Sierra Leone – 1992
- Angola – 1992
- Operation 'Provide Hope II', Soviet Union – 1992
- Operation 'Provide Promise', Bosnia – 1992–4
- Operation 'Provide Relief', Somalia – 1992/3
- Operation 'Restore Relief', Somalia – 1992/3
- Operation 'Stabilise', East Timor – 1999

Another mercy mission, this RAF C-130, XV184 (c/n 4201), unloads her supplies. (Martin W. Bowman)

Parachute drop from a C-130E, 64-0572 (c/n 4090). The Herk could drop sixty fully armed paratroops in a relatively small space with great precision. (Lockheed-Georgia, Marietta via Audrey Pearcy)

Many others are recorded in these pages, and elsewhere.[23] Areas of rescue and relief operations are widespread: Jordan and Turkey; earthquake succour in Iran, Italy, Morocco, Nicaragua, Peru and Venezuela; famine relief from the Bay of Bengal to Chile; typhoon aftermath flights in Guam and Japan; hurricane relief flights to Harrisburg and Wilkes-Barre, Pennsylvania, Richmond, Virginia, Terre Haute, Indiana, and Moline, Illinois, in the wake of Hurricane Agnes, and to Biloxi and Gulfport, Mississippi after Hurricane Camile the same year; plus cholera epidemics and food famine relief flights all over Africa (Congo and Chad) and in Nepal. They even helped save the roan antelope from extinction in southern Africa, airlifting tranquillised animals from the desert sands to protected areas. These missions could also be very

Equipped with the Tracor ALE-40 flare and chaff defence as part of the 'snowstorm' system developed by Lockheed for UN flights over Bosnia, a C-130 gives a full defensive display. (Swedish Air Force Official)

dangerous. In the paranoid world of politics, bringing relief to civilians who are starving due to civil war or military uprising is often viewed by Marxist or extreme Right-wing nationalists and terror groups as 'military intervention', and many Hercules have been shot down or at least threatened by such attacks in such places as Angola, Bosnia and Somalia.

In order to bring some relief to hard-pressed Herky-Bird crews threatened by increasingly sophisticated anti-aircraft hardware, including hand-held infra-red-guided, shoulder-launched missiles, Lockheed introduced in an Airborne Self-Protection System (ASPS) for at least ten C-130Hs operated by both UN and NATO nations in such dangerous skies. The operating nations concerned gave their defensive requirements to the US State Department,

---

[23] See, for typical examples, 'Lockheed's Hercules – The goodwill aircraft', article in *Interavia* magazine, June 1972, and Earl and Miriam Selby, 'Hercules – Work-horse of the Air', article in *Reader's Digest*, 1983.

which passed them on to the Defense Security Assistance Agency for review, and the USAF contracted Lockheed Aircraft Services at Ontario, California, to undertake the work. The programme began in October, 1993 and the first three aircraft received their packages from November onward, each system taking up to three months to install and test, each nation's requirements being slightly different.

Great secrecy was maintained about this programme. Most of the nations involved did not want their UN missions advertised in case it made them targets for yet further terrorist activity or reprisal, and while many used American systems, others insisted on their own packages being installed. Lockheed manufactured moulds for fibreglass housings and machined out cavities to install chaff and flare dispensers, as well as building racks to hold the various 'black boxes' and installing the required electrical cabling and connections. In addition to ten aircraft initially protected, Lockheed despatched a further eleven ASPSs in kit form to air forces for them to install locally.[24]

Similarly, secrecy was intense about the exact nature of

A JATO bottle-assisted take-off by USMC C-130B, 149804 (c/n 3695) of VMGR-352, Miramar MCAS, from the McDonnell test field at Lakeside, California in 1973 (McDonnell Douglas via Audrey Pearcy)

the specific systems employed, but all were officially said to have included a form of missile warning system, like the Lockheed Sanders ALQ-156 and the Tracor ALE-40 flare and chaff dispensing systems. Some C-130s were equipped with a radar warning system. Some six of the Herks operators also required special lightweight composite armoured kits to protect their aircrew from small-arms fire.

Despite the dangers, the odds are high that, even as you read these words, somewhere in the world a Herky Bird is bringing hope and help to a despairing people. It is her finest legacy.

41 Short Take-off and Landing (STOL) and Jet-Assisted Take-off (JATO)

Coupled with the unpaved runway capability (see appropriate section), the ease with which the Hercules could get airborne from primitive landing fields with heavy burdens was another factor in making this aircraft legendary. The short take-off and landing (STOL)

---

24 See John D. Morrocco, 'Self-Protection Systems added to Relief C-130s', article in *Aviation Week & Space Technology*, July 1993.

Low-level pass. C-130H, 37SON, a Hercules of the Royal Australian Air Force, is seen overflying the RAAF Curtin Portable/Mobile control tower after delivering troops and equipment in the wind-up to Exercise K89. (Royal Australian Air Force Photo)

requirement was built into the original design and was continually refined in subsequent models.

Lockheed had a multi-level approach to the subject of STOL and many different configurations which changed the aerodynamics of the wing and tail surfaces in order to facilitate lower take-off and landing speeds, coupled with better control. Double-slotted wing flaps with roll-control spoilers were fitted, a longer-chord rudder and a larger dorsal fin were trialled along with new horsal fins, and anti-skid brake gear was fitted.

Both the high-technology test bed (HTTB) and the boundary layer control experiments were offshoots of this facet of the Hercules' operational profile (see appropriate sections). The C-130SS, the stretch/STOL and the C-130 'Option II-A' proposals were all Lockheed ideas to tackle

and improve on the same area and meet the USAF AMST requirement to operate in and out of 2,000ft (610m) unimproved strips with 27,000lb (12,247kg) of payload.

The fitting of Aerojet 15KS-1000 jet-assisted take-off (JATO) bottles (in two sets of four strapped either side of the rear fuselage), which developed 1,000lb (454kg) of thrust for additional boost during take-offs, was trialled with a modified C-130E-I, serial 64-0558 (c/n 4059), by 2 Detachment, 1 Special Operations Squadron, between 1967 and 1969, and later by the 318 Special Operations Squadron between 1971 and 1972, before this particular aircraft was lost in a collision with an F-102A over Myrtle Beach, South Carolina on 5 December 1972. Each unit burns for just fifteen seconds before abruptly cutting off. Use of this method reduced the length of the take-off from 1,000ft (305m) to 790ft (240m) at the designed weight of 108,000lb (48,988kg). This fitment became standard provision for all C-130As.

The US Marines VMGR-352 also employed this method with a KC-130F, serial 149805 (c/n 3695), and the *Blue Arrows* TC-130-G serial 151891 (c/n 3878) support aircraft also employed the system to add to the spectacle. This method was used extensively, especially in Antarctica, but was inherently dangerous – witness the loss of an LC-130F, serial 148321 ex 59-5925 (c/n 3567), on 4 December 1971, when one JATO bottle separated from its mounting and struck the aircraft, causing the take-off from Carrefour D59 landing ground to be aborted, and a crash-landing followed. She then lay ice-bound for fifteen years before being recovered.

Numerous examples of incredible landings and take-offs by the Hercules have been recorded down the decades. On 31 December 1966 a US Coast Guard HC-130B piloted by Lieutenant Commander Clyde Robbins and Lieutenant Chester Wawrzynski was brought down safely on the 2,500ft (762m) gravel strip at Baja, Mexico, on a mission to pick up an injured seaman. The recorded stopping distance was 1,300ft (396m), lots of reverse thrust helped, *and* they also got safely off again with their patient. The same pilot also got down on the 2,380ft (725m) strip at Bridgewater, California, at an altitude of 7,000ft (2,134m) and hemmed in by the Sweetwater Mountains. Using JATO he got her safely up and out again.

42 Ski Operations

In order to extend the useful area of operations of the versatile and indispensable Hercules to cover the snow- and ice-bound regions of the globe, a

US Navy LC-130F (marked up as C-130BL) ski-equipped Hercules 148318 (c/n 3652) turns gracefully away from the camera aircraft with the Antarctic sunlight glinting off her fuselage, in readiness to land at the Annual Ice Runway, Williams Field. (Author's collection)

proposal was made as early as 1956 for the fitting of skis on this large aircraft. In particular the supply and support of the distant early warning (DEW) line of radar stations, constructed across Alaska and Greenland to give maximum warning of an incoming Soviet missile strike across the North Pole, was considered essential. A feasibility study was undertaken, and one C-130A, 55-021 (c/n 3048), was modified accordingly, emerging in her new configuration on 29 January 1957. She retained her normal wheeled undercarriage and had a special nose and two main skis fitted over them.

These skis could only be raised or lowered with the undercarriage in the down position. Before the normal landing gear retracted, the ski automatically moved to the lowered position; as the gear retracted, the skis were drawn up against a fairing on the fuselage. The landing gear doors were therefore omitted. Two 'skegs' were fitted to the after-ends of the nose skis, which made the normal nose-wheel steering system effective for directional control. Under normal conditions a utility hydraulic pressure system operated the skis, but, should this fail, an emergency hydraulic system supplied pressure directly to the actuators via shuttle valves, which brought the skis from their lowered position to the raised position only. Ski unlocks and downlocks were by way of blocking hydraulic fluid in the actuators. The aircraft pneumatic system was altered to allow for a hot bleed air flow to melt snow and ice from the external ports, while an air hose could be plugged into the regular external air supply coupling, positioned above the GTC exhaust, and a check valve over-ride control (with control located inside a small door aft of the GTC exhaust above the main wheel wells) permitted the overboard flow of bleed air from the engine bleed air manifold.

Thus equipped, and with JATO bottles to help with lift-off, this aircraft undertook a series of practical trials in Minnesota and Greenland. The outcome of these tests proved quite satisfactory and she was re-configured to a normal C-130A on conclusion of the programme.

A series run of twelve ski-equipped Hercules was initiated with late production line C-130As (airframes and engines) being completed as C-130Ds: 57-0484 (c/n 3191), 57-0485 (c/n 3192), 57-0486 (c/n 3193), 57-0487 (c/n 3194), 57-0488 (c/n 3195), 57-0489 (c/n 3196), 57-0490 (c/n 3197), 57-0491 (c/n 3198), 57-0492 (c/n 3199), 57-0493 (c/n 3200), 57-0494 (c/n 3201) and 57-0495 (c/n 3202). All these aircraft were allocated to the USAF Troop Carrier Squadrons (TCS) from January 1959 onwards.

In 1962/63, six of these aircraft – 57-0484 (c/n 3191), 57-0485 (c/n 3192), 57-0486 (c/n 3193), 57-0487 (c/n 3194), 57-0488 (c/n 3195) and 57-0489 (c/n 3196) – had their skis removed once more and were re-designated C-130D-6s. One aircraft, 57-0495 (c/n 3202), which carried the name *Frozen Assets* in the 1960s and *The Harker* in the 1970s, stalled and overshot at the Dye III landing strip east of Søndrestrøm on 5 June 1972 and was written off. In 1975 the survivors were allocated to the 139th TAS, New York Air National Guard (ANG), and continued in operation until they were replaced by the LC-130Hs, the last retiring in April 1985.

Further examples of the type were requested and two standard C-130As, 57-0473 (c/n 3180) and 57-0474 (c/n 3181), were duly modified and served for a brief period under the designation C-130D, before re-converting to C-130As once more.

The US Navy also had use for ski-equipped Hercules aircraft, and in a similar manner four such aircraft – 148318 ex 59-5922 (c/n 3562), 148319 ex 59-5923 (c/n 3564), 148320 ex 59-5924 (c/n 3565) and 148321 ex 59-5925 (c/n 3567) – were ordered by the USAF as the C-130BL on behalf of the Navy. On delivery the Navy re-designated them the UV-1L and they served as such until September 1962, when they received a new designation, becoming the LC-130F-*LM*.

They were operated by the US Navy's VX-6 unit (later re-designated VXE-6 and christened *Penguin Airline*) as a key part of the 1960 Operation 'Deep Freeze', the supply and logistical support of the US Antarctic Survey programme, in conjunction with the National Science Foundation (NSF). The ski-fitted Hercules replaced the Douglas R4Ds hitherto used in that role. The four aircraft were all given names – 148313 *City of Christchurch*, 148319 *Penguin Express*, 148320 *The Emperor* and 148321 *The Crown* – and all suffered accidents during their careers, but only the first was totally destroyed. In order to conduct a radar strip chart recording of the earth's

Over a decade and a half after an aborted take-off, the abandoned Lockheed LC-130F, serial 148321 (c/n 3567), had been covered by ice and snow save for the top three feet of the plane's 38-foot high vertical stabiliser. Lockheed and Navy engineers who examined the aircraft found her structurally sound and fit, requiring just six weeks of preliminary repair before she could be flown out. The NSF was hopeful that this could be done and that the aircraft could be placed back in service. Dr Peter Wilkniss, director of the NSF Polar Programs Division in 1987, called the recovery 'a major feat'. The aircraft herself, with just 14,000 flight hours, he described as, '. . . slightly used . . . and rested for 15 years'. The LC-130 ski-equipped Hercules revolutionised the scientific exploration of Antarctica. The US Navy operated seven or eight such aircraft, which, during the 'off season', were based at Pt. Magau, California. (Lockheed via Audrey Pearcy)

surface beneath the Greenland ice cap as part of the National Science Foundation Greenland Ice Sheet Project, one Navy LC-130, 77-0320 (c/n 4764), carrying the unique tail-marking letters JD, was modified with the installation of antenna arrays that operated on 60 and 300Mc. The dipole antennae were horizontally polarised and were built with a balsa core, fibreglass outer skin and aluminium covering. The four 300Mc antennae were carried under the port wing and were easily replaceable. The VHF radars were developed by the Technical University of Denmark for this work. In addition to the

Rocket-assisted take-off for this ski-equipped USAF Herk, coded 21. (Martin W. Bowman)

surface recordings the installations simultaneously recorded ice cap surface contours and variations in sub-surface
strata layers in the ice. The aircraft flew from Søndrestrøm
Airbase in Greenland. The surviving three aircraft were
retired when VXE-6 was disbanded in 1999.

To replace the USAF's ageing ski-equipped C-130Ds, in
1985 four C-130Hs – 83-0490 (c/n 5007) *Pride of Clifton
Park*, 83-0491 (c/n 5010) *Pride of Albany*,
83-0492 (c/n 5013) *City of Amsterdam* and 83-0493
(c/n 5016) *Pride of Scotia* – suitably equipped, were
delivered to the 139th TAS, New York ANG. Another three

*Main emergency access steps on this US Navy LC-130R, 155917
(c/n 4305), duly adorned with symbols of her allies, (note the Kiwi
5s and RAAF roundel) as well as the New Zealand symbol with
Ao-Tea-Roa, seen in September 1969. She later crashed at the
Amundsen-Scott South Pole Station on 28 January 1973.* (Nick
Williams AAHS)

ski-equipped aircraft were due to be delivered to the 139th TAS late in 1995: 92-1094 (c/n 5402), 92-1095 (c/n 5405) and 93-1096 (c/n 5410). Two of this trio also received names, 92-1094 becoming *Pride of Grenville* and 92-1096 given the now traditional name of *City of Christchurch NZ*. All these aircraft carry the designation LC-130H.

In a similar manner the NSF replaced its ski-equipped fleet with six special aircraft: 155917 (c/n 4305), 159129 ex 73-0839 (c/n 4508), 159130 ex 73-0840 (c/n 4516), 159131 ex 73-0841 (c/n 4522), 160740 ex 76-0491 (c/n 4725) and 160741 ex 76-0492 (c/n 4731). These received the designation LC-130R-*LM* and were, as before, operated for the NSF by US Navy squadron VC-6/VXE-6. As expected in such a hostile element, there were accidents, 155917 being involved in no fewer than three of them in 1975 and 1987 before finally being terminally damaged and written off charge. Serial 160740 crashed at Starshot Glacier, Antarctica, in December 1984 and lay in the snow for fourteen years until it was repaired in 1998. The NSF's Polar Programs Division's Dr Peter Wilkniss jested that she was, after all, 'only slightly used' and that she had merely 'rested for fifteen years'! She was returned into service with the 139th AS, 109th AW, ANG and based at Schenectady County Airport, New York State, along with 160741.

All these aircraft received similar modifications to the standard models to enable them to operate within the Arctic, Antarctic, Alaska and Greenland. The ski installations were the largest ever to be incorporated on an aircraft and were designed to allow either wheeled or ski operation without further modification. By attaching the ski adaptations to the conventional landing equipment and making it so that it could be raised or lowered when the landing gear was in the lowered position, the resultant mechanism was extremely versatile.

The main ski 'shoes' fitted around the landing gear are made of aluminium with the bottom surfaces coated with Teflon plastic, which ensures completely free sliding in both snow and slush. The Teflon has the added advantage of minimising the freeze-down rate when the aircraft is parked. They are 20.5ft (6.25m) long and 5.5ft (1.68m) wide and weigh about 2,100lb (953kg). The solitary nose ski is 10.3ft (3.14m) long and the same width as the main gear. Both the main skis and the nose ski have 8° nose-up and 15° nose-down pitch to enable them to coast over uneven terrain. The combined total weight of the ski gear and associated plumbing is 5,600lb (2,540kg). The equivalent reduction in the maximum payload of both the

C-130D and the LC-130F was the penalty on ski or wheels, while for the LC-130R it was for wheels only. However, the LC-130R could not utilise its higher payload capability due to the fact that skis were not uprated to cope with the increased structural design weight of the C-130H.

The powerplant on all was the same as for the standard C-130 equivalents, but although the LC-130F original used the T56-A-7 these were subsequently changed for the T56-A-16 engine, flat-rated to 4,508 eshp for take-off, for higher performance. The turning radii for skis came out at 122ft (37m) for the wing-tip turning radius and 64.5ft (19.5m) for the nose gear turning radius.

The *Fuerza Aérea Argentina* also used about half-a-dozen Hercules to supply their bases in Antarctica, and some were fitted with RATOG and flew on skis. In 1974, an Argentine C-130 made a record first flight from Buenos Aires across Antarctica to Australia and New Zealand.

Other tasks have included the airlifting of machinery, vehicles, fruit, meat and other products all over South America and to African destinations, while the importation of 35 tons of soya beans from the USA was conducted by their C-130Bs.

43 | Special Concepts and Conversions

Diverse and numerous as the speciality Herk designations became, some aircraft merit special attention as 'one-offs' which either acted as pioneers for variants to come or were the answer to a specific mission profile and were never repeated. Among them were the following:

C-130BLC Serial 58-0712 (c/n 3507), which became the STOL test aircraft involved in the boundary layer control experiments.

C-130J This designation was originally briefly assigned to an advance assault Hercules concept, a modified version of the C-130E which incorporated the assault landing gear. A new main gear oleo strut allowed 25in (63.5cm) of wheel travel in order to dissipate the heavy shock and jarring received in rough-field operations. Nose gear was re-designed and strengthened for the same reason and enabled operations to take place on air strips with up to 10in (25cm) long protruding obstacles and depressions. A new and larger main gear fairing was deemed essential to house the main gear, and the lower forward fuselage and radome were adapted for the new landing gear.

The rudder chord was to have been increased by 40%,

giving increased directional control and lower engine minimum control speed. The aileron chord increased by 30% to increase the low-speed rolling capability, while the flaps were modified to increase the maximum deflection to 50° and the elevator re-indexed to provide 5° additional down elevator deflection. Both rudder and aileron controls systems were actuated by fully powered servo systems. The A-15 engine replaced the A-7 and the propeller gearbox ratio was changed to 12.49:1, and this, combined with the additional rudder control, permitted the A-15 to be operated at the maximum rating of 4,591 shp. The fuel tanks were given small-arms fire protection, and there was an improved rate-of-sink indicator as well as an integrated instrument system.

This designation was soon abandoned and became the C-130SS (see following).

C-130SS Another concept featuring both stretch and enhanced STOL performance, this aircraft would have featured double-slotted flaps and roll-control spoilers and was Lockheed's reply to the Boeing YC-14 and McDonnell Douglas YC-15 projects. At a projected cost of $7.4 million per aircraft, including the development and production costs, this would have been a fraction of the unit cost visualised for these two fanjet models being prototyped for the AMST programme in 1976.

Based on the basic C-130 airframe, the C-130SS would have featured a 100in (2.54m) fuselage stretch, a strengthened wing, a longer-chord rudder, a larger dorsal fin, new horsal fins, a higher-strength landing gear and a new

Close-up detail of the front of the ski fixture on US Navy LC-130F, serial 148321 (c/n 3567). This aircraft belonged to VXE-6 and is seen at NAS Barbers Point, June 1969. (Nick Williams AAHS)

anti-skid braking system. Low-speed control would also be enhanced.

The strengthened wing would allow the aircraft to carry a 30,000lb (13,608kg) payload in a 3g flight manoeuvre on tactical or assault missions, and the designed landing gear

Starboard close-up detail of the front of the ski fixture on US Navy LC-130F, serial 148321 (c/n 3567). This aircraft belonged to VXE-6 and is seen at NAS Barbers Point, June 1969. (Nick Williams AAHS)

On April 20 1964, a world first-flight endurance record was established by Hercules, N1130E, (c/n 3946), which remained aloft for over twenty-five hours. (Arthur Pearcy via Audrey Pearcy)

structural strength would be increased to permit the same payload at a design sink rate of 15ft (4.5m) per second. The penalty would be to increase the aircraft's empty weight by 8,300lb (3,765kg), although Lockheed were to claim that 'this additional weight would increase structural strength, permitting significant increases in gross weight on strategic or routine air lift missions'.[25] The stretch was achieved by a 60in (1.52m) plug section forward of the wing and a 40in (1.02m) plug aft of the wing, which increased the cargo compartment length from 40.4ft to 48.7ft (12.3 to 14.8m), giving room for one additional 463L pallet. This was an increase of 85 sq ft (7.9m²) of floor area, to a total of 501.6 sq ft (46.6m²). Clear cube volume was to be increased by 769 cu ft (21.7m³) to a total of 4,514 cu ft (127.7m³). The new Hercules' palletised payload would increase from five to six pallets, or from 25,000lb to 30,000lb (11,340 to 13,608kg) of cargo at an average of 5,000lb (2,268kg) per pallet.

The C-130SS would, it was claimed, carry a high percentage of US Army vehicles of the four types of divisions: 99.4% of airborne vehicles, 93.5% of infantry vehicles, 88% of mechanised vehicles and 87% of armoured division vehicles. Even those vehicles which would not fit into the Hercules, such as tanks and helicopters, would not fit the proposed replacements either, it was stated.

Two thousand hours of wind-tunnel testing on the C-130SS was supplemented by STOL experience from the boundary layer control aircraft tests. Lockheed further claimed that the new design could meet a mid-point 2,000ft (610m) assault runway requirement with a 3g payload of

[25] See 'The C-130SS – Lockheed Offers new Stretch/STOL Hercules at a fraction of the unit cost of the AMST', Lockheed Newsbureau, G-52176-1303N, 1976.

A view of the Lockheed HTTB experimental aircraft, N130X, seen at Shannon airport on 11 June 1985. (Sean O'Brien)

30,000lb (13,608kg) for 400 nautical miles (741km) on a tactical mission.

They also pointed out the turbo-prop versus fanjet advantages, in that they considered the propeller more efficient for generation of take-off thrust and lift, with the propeller acting upon a greater mass of air than the fan, but also that the slipstream affected the entire flap span, giving maximum lift effectiveness. By contrast, it was claimed, 'the propulsive lift of the fanjet engines, in which the fan exhaust is concentrated over a smaller part of the flap span, had to be attained by the addition of heavy, expensive and complicated equipment, such as ducting, valves or variable-geometry nozzles'.[26] It was also stated that a modern high by-pass ratio fan engine burnt about half again as much fuel per pound of take-off thrust as the C-130 turbo-prop, and that this was particularly significant on STOL aircraft. They claimed at that time that a fanjet-powered aircraft of similar size to the Hercules would require, on average, almost twice as much fuel to perform a typical 400 nautical mile (741km) radius mission than the C-130 with an identical payload. Thus a fanjet would be twice as

expensive to buy and operate, yet, while faster, the mission time required was only a few minutes less than that of the C-130 on short-range tactical assault missions.

It was conceded by Lockheed that the fanjet design was superior on two counts: the fuselage size could be made wider using C-5 philosophy and the fan engines could provide some minutes of speed advantage. Lockheed proposed to the Air Force that two current-production C-130Hs be modified to the C-130SS configuration for comparison trials. This offer was not taken up.

EC-130E Serial CG1414 (c/n 4158), a US Coast Guard aircraft which became the LORAN A&C calibration test bed.

EC-130V Serial CG1721 (c/n 5121), which was a US Coast Guard HC-130H modified and fitted with an AN/APS-125 in a large rotordome for early-warning and detection usage.

HOW This acronym ('Hercules-On-Water') described the test-bed flying-boat version of the Hercules with an elongated nose, re-shaped ventral hull, wing-mounted

---

26 *Ibid.*

floats and a hydro-ski, with US Navy needs in mind. As for combat freight loading, HOW indeed!

HTTB　Serial N130X(c/n 4412), which became Lockheed's high-technology test bed aircraft and conducted vital research in the development of the C-130J programme.

JHC-130P　Serial 65-0987 (c/n 4143), which was modified from a HC-130P for the ARRS for tests.

RC-130A　Serial 54-1632 (c/n 3019), a proposed Hercules training aircraft variant prototype modified from a standard C-130A. She was later re-built for the ATS as a photo-reconnaissance (PR) prototype, before again reverting to C-130A status.

TC-130A　Serial 54-1632 (c/n 3019), which was both a prototype for the proposed TC-130A training aircraft and for the RC-130A.

VC-130B　Serial 58-0715 (c/n 3510), a JC-130B especially modified as a VIP transport. She later once more reverted to C-130B status.

W.2　Serial XV208 (c/n 4233), one of the most extraordinary (and ugly) aircraft ever to fly. It was a Marshalls of Cambridge modification of an RAF standard C.1 with an elongated nose probe and scientific instrument suites (internally displacing the radar scanner to an underwing pod) for meteorological research duties. The 26ft (7.9m) long proboscis, painted with red-and-white stripes, had a laser projector and camera to take three-dimensional pictures of cloud samples.

The twenty-six foot long nose boom being fitted to the converted former RAF Far East Air Force Hercules XV208 (c/n 4233) at Marshalls of Cambridge as part of her conversion to the W.2. (Arthur Pearcy Archives courtesy of Audrey Pearcy)

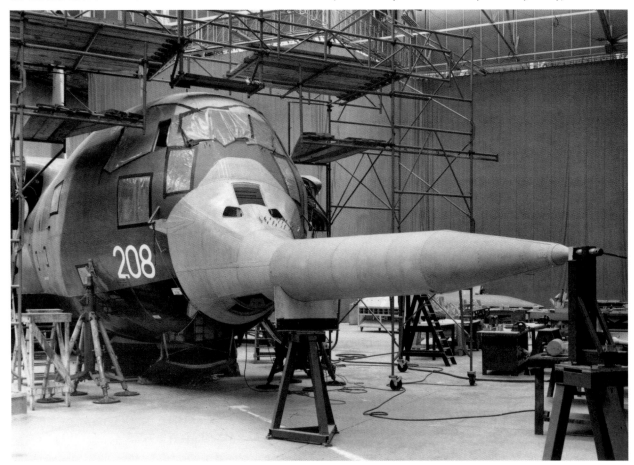

The W.2 operated from 31 March 1973 for the A&AEE at RAE Farnborough, and then by DERA from Boscombe Down. She is nicknamed *Snoopy*.

44 Training

Currently the bulk of USAF C-130 aircrew training is conducted by the 314th Airlift Wing based at Little Rock AFB, Arkansas. This wing is part of Air Education and Training Command, and has the largest C-130 training fleet in the world at its disposal. Its multiple squadrons and forty-four C-130s train not only the USAF pilots but all the aircrew for the Department of Defense, US Coast Guard and twenty-seven foreign operators as well. The wing also hosts the 463rd Air Mobility Command (AMC) group and the 189th Airlift Wing (Arkansas Air National Guard) which provides global tactical air lift capability. The 314th Wing has four groups – operations, logistics, support and medical – plus the HQ element. The 'Schoolhouse' is made up of two air lift squadrons, 53rd AS and 62nd AS, and the 314th Operations Support Squadron, along with the flight simulator contractor. The 189th Airlift Wing assists in the C-130 training programme in times of peace. The 463rd Airlift Group with the 50th and 61st Airlift Squadrons carries out operational air lift missions worldwide, while the AMWC Combat Aerial Delivery School provides aircrews with graduate-level instruction in C-130 tactical employment.

Lockheed at Marietta is in itself a major training facility, with the conversion training of thousands of foreign pilots, flight engineers, navigators and loadmasters from

more than fifty nations to the C-130, conducted down the decades. Courses varied from customer to customer. A typical scenario, for the Royal Thai Air Force, was an

The Herk's flight deck, shown here on 30 September 1980 with C-130 flight training under way. Wing Commander Udomsuk Mahavasu (left) of the Royal Thai Air Force, learns about the C-130 overhead instrument panel from Lockheed pilot instructor Bob Hill. Looking on is Captain Surawit Khemananta. Over the decades Lockheed pilots have taught thousands of pilots from all over the world how to handle the 'jet-age gooney bird'. (Lockheed-Georgia, Marietta via Audrey Pearcy)

Flight-deck simulator at RAF Lyneham, Wiltshire, May 1979. Potential crews were given a thorough grounding here before taking the aircraft aloft. (RAF Official)

Hercules main instrument panel for training at RAF Lyneham. (RAF Official)

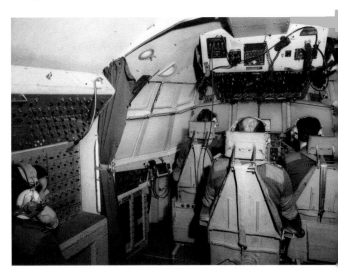

	C-130A	C-130B	C-130-E	C130-H
Gross Weight (lb/kg))	124,200/56,336	135,000/61,235	155,000/70,307	155,000/70,307
Main Gear Load (lb/kg)	117,800/53,433	128,300/58,196	147,400/66,859	147,400/66,859
Single Wheel Load (lb/kg)	29,450/13,358	32,075/14,549	36,800/16,692	36,800/16,692
Normal Tyre Deflection (%)	35	35	35	35
Inflation pressure (psi)	72	80	95	95
Contact Area (sq in/m^2)	409/0.263	400/0.258	386/0.249	386/0.249
Maximum Tyre Deflection (%)	45	45	45	45
Inflation Pressure (psi)	50	55	67	67
Contact Area (sq in/m^2)	589/0.379	582/0.375	459/0.296	549/0.354
Normal Tyre Deflection (in/cm)	29/73.7	29/73.7	29/73.7	29/73.7
Maximum Tyre Deflection (in/cm)	24/61	24/61	24/61	24/61

eight-week ground school instruction which included a study of aircraft systems performance standards, weight and balance information, emergency and normal operational procedure theory. Next came four weeks' flight training, with the emphasis on landing and take-off, instrument approach, stalls, day and night flying, emergency procedures including engine-out landings, engine failure on take-off and short-field landings and take-offs, with flights conducted over northern Georgia, and instrument and visual landings at Dobbins AFB and municipal airports at Chattanooga, Tennessee, Huntsville, Alabama, and Augusta, Georgia. The final phase was in-country operational training which included long-range navigation operations on high-density traffic routes and short-field take-off and landing from unpaved airstrips.

45 Unpaved Airfield Operation

From the earliest conception of the Hercules the ability to work out of primitive air strips in areas far distant from civilisation has always been a priority. The subsequent history of the Herk over five decades of peace and war enshrined this versatility into its design and ensured that whatever the situation on the ground, if any large transport could get in and out of dirt, mud, gravel, grass, asphalt or ice, the C-130 was usually the one to do so.

A great deal of study into the surface hardness and bearing strengths of differing types of unpaved landing sites the world over had already been made. The standard measuring methods to estimate these factors were the modulus of soil reaction, known simply as the K-factor, and the California bearing ration (CBR), which grades surfaces on a scale of 1 to 10 CBR according to materials and the amount of moisture contained at a given time. With this measure the hardness and resistance to various types of aircraft and load displacements can be worked out and performance measured against it. The degree with which an aircraft can operate from such surfaces depends not only on the total weight of the aircraft and its loading, but on the spread of the load across the main undercarriage and the manoeuvrability and steerability of the aircraft to enable it to both touch down safely and 'unstick' from semiboggy morasses or shifting sand-strips.

With her dual wheel nose layout, combined with the reverse thrust of her engines, the Hercules came out well in the tests on the latter, with the wide distribution of load across the tricycle landing gear with its single tandem wheels fitted with big-diameter, wide, low-pressure tyres. These factors give the C-130 an excellent flotation ability, and any doubts on the soundness of the many tests and experiments have been borne out in hard practice time and time again down the years, and the luxury of hard concrete or asphalt airfields has been a distinct rarity in Herk relief and combat operations.

The table above shows the flotation characteristics of early model C-130s.

46 Weather Tracking and Research

Commencing on 7 August 1944, with the 3rd Weather Reconnaissance Squadron, Air Route, Medium, the weather-tracking tradition is firmly established in the USAF.

One RAF Hercules W.Mk 2, XV 208 (c/n 4233), was converted by Marshalls of Cambridge into a flying testbed for the Meteorological Flight of the Royal Aircraft Establishment at Farnborough. She presented a truly unique profile, as this photograph shows. (A P Publications)

In 1962 the USAF placed an order with Lockheed for five specially modified C-130Bs – 62-3492 (c/n 3702), 62-3493 (c/n 3707), 62-3494 (3703), 62-3495 (c/n 3721) and 62-3406 (c/n 3722) – to replace existing Boeing WB-50D aircraft in conducting detailed weather reconnaissance, monitoring and research missions under the auspices of the MATS Weather Reconnaissance Squadron, then based at Ramey AFB, Puerto Rico, with 55th Weather Reconnaissance Squadron. These modified machines were re-designated WC-130B-*LM* Weatherbirds. The first WC-130B (62-3492) was utilised as a flying test aircraft for the Kaman Airborne Weather Reconnaissance System, and following successful trials this became standard fitting to Weatherbird machines.

When Ramey AFB was shut down the 55th re-located to Keesler AFB, near Biloxi, Mississippi. A further twelve aircraft – 58-0725 (c/n 3520), 58-0726 (c/n 3521), 58-0729 (c/n 3524), 58-0731 (c/n 3526) *NOAA's Ark*, 58-0733 (c/n 3528), 58-0734 (c/n 3530), 58-0740 (c/n 3537), 58-0741 (c/n 3538), 58-0742 (c/n 3539), 58-0747 (c/n 3545), 57-0752 (c/n 3551) and 58-0758 (c/n 3559) – nine of them surplus when 463rd Tactical Airlift Wing at Clark AB in the Philippines disbanded in 1970, were subsequently also converted to WC-130Bs and joined their sisters. Their numbers were gradually reduced as they were replaced by later conversions. Surplus aircraft were re-configured as C-130Bs and subsequently served in Air Force Reserve (AFRES) or Air National Guard (ANG) units. One of the 53rd's WC-130Bs (58-0731) was transferred out to the US Government's Department of Commerce's National Oceanic and Atmosphere Administration (NOAA), based at Miami, Florida, receiving the civilian registration N8037, which was later changed to N6541C.

Three modified C-130Es – 64-0552 (c/n 4047), 64-0553 (c/n 4048) and 64-554 (c/n 4049) – were ordered by MATS Air Weather Services in 1964, while a further three serving C-130Es – 61-2360 (c/n 3659), 61-2365 (c/n 3688) and 61-2366 (c/n 3706) – were similarly modified and fitted with the Kaman AWR. These aircraft served throughout the 1960s with the 53rd and also with the 54th WRS based at Andersen AFB on Guam in the Pacific and the 55th WRS based at McClellan AFB, California. In due course these were phased out and, although not re-converted, were utilised by the 815th TAS between 1989 and 1991 as logistic transports, before being retired to the Aerospace Maintenance and Regeneration Center (AMARC) at Davis-Monthan AFB, Arizona.

The 53rd and 54th WRS of 9 WRW also operated in Europe, working from Bitburg, Hahn, Mildenhall, Ramstein, Rhein-Main, Spandahlem, Wiesbaden and

Zweibrucken airfields. They called themselves Fog Floggers Ltd as they had earlier carried out Operation 'Cold Cowl' from Elmendorf AFB in Alaska in the winters of 1967/8 and 1968/9, before they came to gloomy European skies to conduct similar flights for Operation 'Cold Crystal'.

The biggest increase came with the conversion of no fewer than fifteen HC-130H and C-130Hs in 1957: 64-14861 (c/n 4088), 64-14866 (c/n 4099), 65-0963 (c/n 4103), 65-0964 (c/n 4104), 65-0965 (c/n 4106), 65-0966 (c/n 4107), 65-0967 (c/n 4108), 65-0968 (c/n 4110), 65-0969 (c/n 4111), 65-0972 (c/n 4120), 65-0976 (c/n 4126), 65-0977 (c/n 4127), 65-0980 (c/n 4132), 65-0984 (c/n 4139) and 65-0985 (c/n 4140). The Fulton STAR recovery equipment was removed, except for the radome, and replaced by the Kaman system and a range of weather-monitoring systems. As well as the three WRS units these machines also served with the 920th WRG (AFRES) based at Keesler AFB.

Four other aircraft completed as HC-130Hs were modified by the Lockheed Aircraft Service Company, at Ontario, California, to EC-130Hs *circa* 1985 – 64-14859 (c/n 4082), 64-14862 (c/n 4089), 65-0962 (c/n 4102) and 65-0989 (c/n 4150) – and served with 41 ECS. In 1996 the first of these reverted to C-130H's standard with 16 Special Operations Wing working out of Hurlbury, while

Aerial head view of USAF C-130E, 61-2359 (c/n 3651), a Weatherbird which flew global missions for the Air Weather Services, seen on 26 November 1962. (Lockheed-Georgia, Marietta via Audrey Pearcy)

the remaining trio continue to operate as before.

Just how hazardous these missions could be was shown by the loss of 65-965 over the Taiwan Straits on 13 October 1974. The remainder had a long service life, being utilised after 'retirement' by AFRES units, and a few are still currently active with the 53rd WRS and the 403rd AW at Keesler AFB, but are due to be replaced by the WC-130J. The remainder were steadily transferred to the AMARC from December 1997 onwards.

The new-generation WC-130Js first appeared with the introduction of three such machines – 96-5300 (c/n 5451), 96-5301 (c/n 5452) and 96-5302 (c/n 5453) – which joined AFRES units. These were followed by a further four – 97-5303 (c/n 5469), 97-5304 (c/n 5470), 97-5305 (c/n 5471) and 97-5306 (c/n 5472) – with at least one more, 99-5309 (c/n 5501), joining them.

47 US Navy – Communications Platform

The US Navy's airborne fleet broadcast system gave the Commander-in-Chief, Pacific a mobile communications system in support of the Pacific Fleet's strategic forces. This obviated the need for fixed, land-based stations which needed to be located in friendly or protected territory, an increasingly rare option for America as formerly friendly nations like the Philippines and Okinawa turned against it. In 1962 the Defense Department charged the Director of Naval Communications with investigating and developing a highly reliable, mobile, very low frequency communications system, and studies showed that an airborne VLF communications platform would best fulfil that requirement. The order was given 'take charge and move out' and the acronym TACAMO followed and stuck. The new communications system necessitated the formation of a new squadron especially designed for the system, Fleet Air Reconnaissance Squadron 3 (VQ-3).

Originally, trials of the new system were held with two EC-130G aircraft assigned to VR-21 at Hawaii, both machines moving to Airborne Early Warning Squadron 1 (VW-1) in 1966 and working out of Naval Air Station Agana, Guam. They continued the test and evaluation of the system, and at the end of two and a half years of research VQ-3 was commissioned at Agana on 1 July 1968. By June 1969 the unit had accepted the fourth EC-130Q aircraft.

The four EC-130Gs were received between December 1963 and January 1964, and were modified from C-130Gs for *TACAMO III* nuclear submarine communications work; the upgraded system gave increased communications flexibility, much improved in-flight maintenance and a crew rest area. The aircraft were: 151888 (c/n 3849), later modified to a TC-130G and later received civilian registration N93849 with Airplane Sales International; 151889 (c/n 3858), re-designated TC-130G and scrapped in 1994; 151890 (c/n 3871), scrapped after in-flight fire damage in January 1971; and 151891 (c/n 3878), which was later used as a test bed for EC-130Q installations in May 1990 before being re-designated a TC-130G and working for the Blue Angels aerial demonstration team as their supply aircraft, based at Naval Air Station Pensacola, Florida, later carrying the name *Fat Albert Airlines*.

For the *TACAMO III* system of nuclear submarine fleet VLF aerial communications relay aircraft, the US Navy replaced the EC-130Gs with some eighteen EC-130 Q-*LM*s: 156170 (c/n 4239), 156171 (c/n 4249), 156172

(c/n 4269), 156173 (c/n 4277), 156174 (c/n 4278), 156175 (c/n 4279), 165176 (c/n 4280) which subsequently crashed into the sea off Wake Island on 21 June 1977, 156177 (c/n 4281), 159469 (c/n 4595), 159348 (c/n 4601), 160608 (c/n 4781), 161223 (c/n 4867), 161494 (4896), 161495 (c/n 4901), 161496 (c/n 4904), 161531 (c/n 4932), 162312 (c/n 4984) and 162313 (c/n 4988).

These were basically standard C-130Hs powered by the T56-A-16 engine which was rated at 4,910 eshp. The ESM pods carrying the electronic and communications systems had dual trailing antennae, one dropped vertically from the tail cone which had a length of 26,000ft (7.9km), and the second, also paid out ventrally, of 5,000ft (1.5km) length, from the rear ramp. Each of these was fitted with a stabilising cone for deployment, and this gear was steadily improved as time went on. To shield against electro-magnetic pulse (EMP) interference, such as would be encountered in the aftermath of a nuclear missile exchange, equipment hardening was improved. By October 1976, VQ-3 had converted all aircraft to the *TACAMO IV* upgrading.

These aircraft served with the US Navy's VQ-3 based at Naval Air Station Agana on Guam and, from 1 August 1981, back at Barber's Point, Hawaii, in the Pacific, serving the Pacific Fleet's nuclear submarines. The Atlantic Fleet were catered for by those serving with VQ-4, based at Naval Air Station Patuxent River, Maryland, until the surviving aircraft were replaced by Boeing E-6As and had their *TACAMO* removed, following which most of them were taken off charge.

A trio of these veterans – 156170 (c/n 4239), 159348 (c/n 4601) and 159469 (c/n 4595) – saw renewed service usage as TC-13Q training aircraft and transports. One aircraft, 159348 (c/n 4601), after service in VXE-6, ended her days at the static park of Tinker AFB, while 156170 (c/n 4239) and 159469 (c/n 4595) were bought by Airplane Sales International from AMARC in June 1996, becoming civilian registrations N15674 and N54595 respectively (see appropriate section).

48 US Navy – Ski Aircraft

There were four ski-equipped LC-130Fs: 148318 (c/n 3562) *City of Christchurch*, which crashed at McMurdo on 15 February 1975, 148319 (c/n 3564) July 1960, *Penguin Express*, then *Pride of McMurdo* and later *Betty*, which was struck off charge in 1999; 148320 (c/n 3565) July 1960, *The Emperor* and later

Pete, struck off charge in 1999; and 148321 (c/n 3567) August 1960, *The Crown*, which crashed in ice on 1 December 1971 and was finally re-claimed and put back into service fifteen years later, aptly named *Phoenix*, but struck off charge in 1999.

49 US Navy – Transport/Tanker

Four C-130Fs: 149787 (c/n 3636) December 1961, which was sold to South Africa in 1996; 149790 (c/n 3645) March 1962, *GoGo Airlines Naples*, struck off in 1992; 149793 (c/n 3660) March 1962, which was sold to South Africa in 1996; and 149794 (c/n 3661) *Sky Pig*, written off after hurricane damage at Guam in 1992.

Twenty C-130Ts, which were C-130H transports fitted with T56A-16 engines and carried refuelling packages, were received between August 1991 and October 1996: 164762 (c/n 5255) *Dixie Belle*, 164763 (c/n 5258), 164993 (c/n 5298), 164994 (c/n 5299), 164995 (c/n 5300), 164996 (c/n 5301), 164997 (c/n 5304), 164998 (c/n 5305), 165158 (c/n 5341), 165159 (c/n 5342), 165160 (c/n 5344), 165161 (c/n 5345), 165313 (c/n 5383) *Town of Townsham*, 165314 (c/n 5384) *City of Abington*, 165348 (c/n 5404), 165349 (c/n 5406), 165350 (c/n 5407), 165351 (c/n 5409), 165378 (c/n 5429) and 165379 (c/n 5430). They are operated by United States Naval Reserve squadrons: VR-53, from Andrews AFB, Naval Airfield Washington DC,

VR-54, from Naval Air Station New Orleans, Louisiana; VR-55, from Naval Air Station Santa Clara, California; and VR-62, from Naval Air Station New Brunswick, Minnesota.

50 US Marine Corps – Tanker

The US Marine Corps experimented with in-flight refuelling with two C-130As which were loaned from the USAF, 55-0046 (c/n 3073) and 55-0048 (c/n 3075). They were initially designated the GV-1. C-130B conversions, designated GV-1Us, followed, resulting in forty-six KC-130F tanker/transport aircraft in three batches.

Many of these saw extremely hard combat service, VMGR-152, Marine Air Group 36, Marine Air Wing 1, working from Marine Corps Air Station Futenma, on Okinawa, supporting the Marines on the ground in Vietnam, supplying and air-dropping deep over enemy-held territory to surrounded garrisons like Khe San, and not surprisingly suffering some casualties. They later moved out to Iwakuni airfield on Honshu, Japan. Several more of the type were lost in accidents, as recorded.

The United States Marines' Hercules KC-130F, 149816 (c/n 3725), of VMGR-353, tail-coded QB, is featured at Naval Air Station Atsugi. (Nick Williams AAHS)

Other units to employ this variant were VMGR-252 and VMGR-253, MAG-14 and MAW-2 based at MCAS Cherry Point, North Carolina, and VMGR-352, MAG-11 and MAW-3 based at MCAS Miramar, California.

The first seven arrived between March 1960 and February 1961: 147572 (c/n 3554), 147573 (c/n 3555), 148246 (c/n 3566), 148247 (c/n 3573), 148248 (c/n 3574), 148249 (c/n 3577) and 148890 (c/n 3592). The second batch of twenty-one were purchased between April 1961 and June 1962: 148891 (c/n 3605), 148892 (c/n 3606), 148893 (c/n 3607), which served for a spell as the Blue Angels support aircraft, 148894 (c/n 3608), 148895 (c/n 3619), 148896 (c/n 3623), 148897 (c/n 3627), 148898 (c/n 3631), 148899 (c/n 3632), 149788 (c/n 3640), 149789 (c/n 3644), 149791 (c/n 3657), 149792 (c/n 3658), 149795 (c/n 3664), 149796 (c/n 3665), 149798 (c/n 3680), which carried the name *Look Ma, No Hook* during her deck trials aboard the USS *Forrestal* in 1963 (see appropriate section), 149799 (c/n 3684), 149800 (c/n 3685), 149802 (c/n 3693), which crashed at Hong Kong on 24 August 1965, 149803 (c/n 3694) and 149804 (c/n 3695).

Finally, another eighteen arrived on USMC strength between July and November 1962: 149806 (c/n 3703), which became the Blue Angels support aircraft, before going to Naval Air Station Adak, Alaska, in the logistic

Underside view of a KC-130F, USMC's 150684 (c/n 3727) of VMG-152, out of MCAS Futenma, Okinawa, with tail code QD, as she turns low over Hickam Field, Hawaii. (Nick Williams AAHS)

Nice aerial view of this US Marine Corps KV-130F, serial 149800 (c/n 36875), carrying out the simultaneous refuelling of two US Marine Corps Phantoms. (Martin W. Bowman)

US Marines' KC-130F, 150689 (c/n 3741), of VNGR-352 out of MCAS Miramar, California, with tail code QB, fires up her two inboard engines. (Nick Williams, AAHS)

support mission and then to the Naval Air Warfare Center, Patuxent River, from June 1994; 149807 (c/n 3704), written off after engine problems in 1997; 149808 (c/n 3705), 149809 (c/n 3709), destroyed by enemy action off Dong Hoi, Vietnam, 1 February 1966; 149810 (c/n 3710), which was destroyed by fire at Lake City, Florida, on 15 January 1972; 149811 (c/n 3711), 149812 (c/n 3718), 149813 (c/n 3719), which was destroyed by enemy action at Khe Sanh, Vietnam, 10 February 1968; 149814 (c/n 3723), destroyed in mid-air collision with F-4B over Vietnam on 18 May 1969; 149815 (c/n 3725), 149816 (c/n 3726), 150684 (c/n 3727), which was finally struck off charge in 1994; 150685 (c/n 3728), which crashed at El Toro, California, in July 1970; 150686 (c/n 3733), 150687 (c/n 3734), 150688 (c/n 3740); 150689 (c/n 3741) and 150690 (c/n 3742), also utilised as the Blue Angels support aircraft in the 1970s.

With the arrival of the KC-130R as a tanker version of the C-130H, the US Marine Corps placed orders which resulted in fourteen aircraft of this type, powered by the T56-A-16 engine rated at 4,910 eshp. They had a 13,320 US gallon (50,420 litre) fuel capacity. These aircraft were delivered between 1975 and 1978; the first batch of eight aircraft arrived between September 1975 and October 1976 – 160013 (c/n 4615), 160014 (c/n 4626), 160015 (c/n 4629), 160016 (c/n 4635), 160017 (c/n 4677),

160018 (c/n 4683), 160019 (c/n 4689) and 160020 (c/n 4696) – and these were followed by six more of the same type between November 1976 and May 1978: 160021 (c/n 4702), 160240 (c/n 4712), 160625 (c/n 4768), 160626 (c/n 4770), 160627 (c/n 4773) and 160628 (c/n 4776). This variant served with three units: VMGR-152, VMGR-252 and VMGR-352.

The further refinement, as tankers able to refuel both aircraft and helicopters, followed, this being the KC-130T. A total of twenty-six such aircraft were allocated to the US Marine Corps in five allotments, the first four between October and November 1983: 162308 (c/n 4972), 162309 (c/n 4974), 162310 (c/n 4978) and 162311 (c/n 4981). The initial quartet was followed by six more between September 1984 and November 1986: 162785 (c/n 5009), 162786 (c/n 5011), 163022 (c/n 5040), 163023 (c/n 5045), 163310 (c/n 5085) which worked as a Blue Angels support aircraft, and 163311 (c/n 5087) whose completion marked the 1,800th Hercules built.

US Marines Blue Angels *support aircraft, 149806 (c/n 3703) boosted by JATO bottles.* (Jeffrey Wood via Audrey Pearcy)

Between September 1988 and October 1989 a third batch of another six of the same type was received: 163591 (c/n 5143), 163592 (c/n 5145), 164105 (c/n 5147), 164106 (c/n 5149), 164180 (c/n 5174) and 164181 (c/n 5176). Another pair was purchased from Lockheed's stock in October and November 1990: 164441 (c/n 5219) and 164442 (c/n 5222). Next, another batch of six arrived between November 1991 and February 1992: 164999 (c/n 5302), 165000 (c/n 5303), 165162 (c/n 5339), 165163 (c/n 5340), 165315 (c/n 5385) and 165316 (c/n 5386). Finally, a last duo was received in October 1995 and February 1996 respectively: 165352 (c/n 5411) and 165353 (c/n 5412).

A further pair of 'stretched' KC-130Ts were added, these being designated the KC-130T-30: 164597 (c/n 5260) and 164598 (c/n 5263). The KC130-T saw service with VMGR-234, MAG-41 and MAW-4 flying from Naval Air Station Fort Worth, Texas, and VMGR-452, MAG-49 and MAW-4 based at Stewart International Airport, New York State.

The latest tanker version for the US Marine Corps is based on the C-130J and is designated the KC-130J. At the time of writing orders have been placed for nine such aircraft: 165735 (c/n 5488), 165736 (c/n 5489), 165737 (c/n 5499), 165738 (c/n 5506), 165739 (c/n 5507),

165740 (c/n 5508), 165741 (c/n 5509), 165742 (c/n 5515) and 165743 (c/n 5516). Early deliveries have joined the VMGR-252 at NAS Cherry Point.

51 US Coast Guard – Navigation/Electronics Platform

Twenty-four US Coast Guard HC-130Hs, which did not feature the ARD-17 Cook aerial tracker, the HRU pods or the Fulton STAR recovery yoke, were obtained between 1966 and 1985. A single EC-130E was obtained in August 1966, CG 1414 (c/n 4158), her designation later changed to HC-130E, and she was struck off charge in 1983, going to the MASDC via the USAF and being sold to Certified Air Parts for breaking up, the cockpit ending up at Reflectone and later Asia-Pacific Training & Simulation PTE Ltd, until finally scrapped in November 1995.

More of these HC-130H aircraft were obtained in two batches: twelve aircraft between March 1968 and October

The colourful display of the US Coast Guard Herk, serial 1342 (c/n 1341), named Elizabeth City, *as seen on 26 April 1968.* (Nick Williams, AAHS)

1977 – CG 1452 ex 66-13533 (c/n 4255), CG 1453 ex 67-7184 (c/n 4260), CG 1454 ex 677185 (c/n 4265), CG 1500 ex 72-1300 (c/n 4501), CG 1501 ex 72-1301 (c/n 4507), CG 1502 ex 72-1302 (c/n 4513), CG 1503 ex 73-0844 (c/n 4528), CG 1504 ex 73-0845 (c/n 4529), CG 1600 ex 77-0320 (c/n 4764), CG 1601 ex 77-0319 (c/n 4762), CG 1602 ex 77-0318 (c/n 4760) and CG 1603 ex 77-0317 (c/n 4757), which crashed near Attu, Aleutian Islands, on 30 July 1982 – and six aircraft between August and November 1985 – CG 1710 (c/n 5028), CG 1711 (c/n 5031), CG 1712 (c/n 5055), CG 1713 (c/n 5034), CG 1714 (c/n 5035) and CG 1715 (c/n 5037).

A further eleven US Coast Guard Hercules were produced as HC-130H-7s between May 1983 and December 1984: CG 1700 (c/n 4947), CG 1701 (c/n 4958), CG 1702 (c/n 4966), CG 1703 (c/n 4967), CG 1704 (c/n 4969), CG 1705 (c/n 4993), CG 1706 (c/n 4996), CG 1707

(c/n 4999), CG 1708 (c/n 5002), CG 1709 (c/n 5005) and CG 1790 (c/n 4931). These were fitted with the side-looking airborne radar (SLAR) and forward-looking infra-red (FLIR). This latter system, intended for use in tracking drug-smuggling vessels at sea, also utilised the Lockheed special avionics mission strap-on now system (SAMSON) which coupled the FLIR with an optical datalink and a display and recording console to record and register evidence as it came in.

Some of these latter aircraft were given the additional duty of in-flight helicopter refuelling like the HC-130Ps, and were fitted with wing pods carrying hose-and-drogue gear for this mission. They were also equipped with night vision goggles (NVG), while both cockpit lighting and navigation capability had also been upgraded. All these aircraft have served with the USCG from their seven bases in North America, and while some have been reduced to care at the AMARC in Arizona, many others are still working today.

Further HC-130Hs were taken on strength between August 1985 and May 1988, and served at Coast Guard Stations Clearwater, Barbers Point, Borinquen, Kodiak and Pemco: CG 1710 (c/n 5028), CG1711 (c/n 5031), CG1712 (c/n 5033), CG1713 (c/n 5034), CG 1714 (c/n 5035),

CG 1715 (c/n 5037), the former Lockheed N4272M (c/n 5023) built in January 1985 and sold to the Coast Guard in April 1986 becoming their serial CG 1716, CG1717 (c/n 5104), CG 1718 (c/n 5106), CG1719 (c/n 5107), CG1720 (c/n 5120) and CG1721 (c/n 5121), which was modified to an EC-130V with an AN/APS-125 rotordome installation and passed to the USAF's 514 Test Squadron, taking their serial 87-0157. In October 1993 she was again re-designated, this time an NC-130H, before ending up at the US Navy Test Center at Patuxent River in November 1998.

52 US Coast Guard – Search and Rescue

Twelve Hercules HC-130B-L aircraft (which were originally designated R8V-1G, and later SC-130B, then HC-130F, before finally becoming HC-130B-Ls) were fitted for the search and rescue role and allocated to the US Coast Guard between December 1959 and February 1963: CG 1339 ex 58-5396 (c/n 3529), CG 1340 ex 58-5397 (c/n 3533), CG 1341 ex 58-6973 (c/n 3542), CG 1342 ex 58-6974 (c/n 3548), CG 1344 ex 60-0311 (c/n 3594), CG 1345 ex 60-0312 (c/n 3595), CG 1346 ex 61-0958 (c/n 3638), CG 1347 ex 61-2082 (c/n 3641), CG 1348 ex 61-2083 (c/n 3650), CG 1349 ex 62-3753 (c/n 3745), CG 1350 ex 62-3754 (c/n 3763) and CG 1351 ex 62-3755 (c/n 3773). They were fitted with aerial retrieval and transport (ART) systems. After good service, all were struck off charge between October 1983 and January 1987 and broken up for parts and scrap.

In general the US Coast Guard air forces are part of the armed forces set-up and work with the US Navy in times of war under the Maritime Defense Zone (MARDEZ) arrangement, which includes search and rescue, anti-submarine work, aerial harbour defence missions, along with major port security and limited surveillance interdiction, and the aircraft are funded via the Navy. In peacetime they are mainly responsible for the bulk of the North Atlantic ice patrol work, anti-drug running operations in the Caribbean (Operation 'Opbat'), offshore oil installation pollution monitoring and illegal immigration patrols. Bases include Barbers Point, Hawaii; Borinquen, Puerto Rico; Clearwater, Florida; Elizabeth City, North Carolina; Kodiak, Alaska; McClellan AFB, Sacramento, California; and St. John's, Newfoundland.

* Updates

On 27 March 2001, the first Hercules, now called the 'Airlifter' by Lockheed, equipped with the new 'Block 5.3' software upgrade, flew to Edwards AFB for qualification testing. This new configuration is being fitted to all C-130J and C-130J-30 aircraft retrospectively and incorporates the Co-ordinated Aircraft Positioning System (CAPS). As well as being used on US aircraft, including those of the Air National Guard, Air Force Reserve Command Marine Corps and Coast Guard units, the Block 5.3 is also to be deployed on Royal Air Force, Royal Australian Air Force, Italian Air Force and Danish Air Force aircraft.

For advanced C-130J training an Avionics System Management Trainer is being installed at Little Rock, Arkansas and C-130J Weapon System Trainers at both Little Rock AFB and Keesler AFB, Mississippi.

The Multi-roles of the American Hercules

53 AC-130A-*LM*

One aircraft prototype conversion from C-130A, 54-1626 (c/n 3013). Seven aircraft conversions from C-130As, serials 53-3128 (c/n 3001), 54-1623 (c/n 3010), 54-1625 (c/n 3012), 54-1627 (c/n 3014), 54-1628 (c/n 3015), 54-1629 (c/n 3016) and 54-1630 (c/n 3017). One aircraft conversion from C-130A, serial 55-0011 (c/n 3038). Nine aircraft conversions from C-130A, serials 55-0014 (c/n 3041), 55-0029 (c/n 3056), 55-0040 (c/n 3067), 55-0043 (c/n 3070); 55-0044 (c/n 3071), 55-0046 (c/n 3073), 56-0469 (c/n 3077), 56-0490 (c/n 3095) and 56-0509 (c/n 3117).

54 AC-130E-LM *Pave Spectre I*

Two aircraft prototype conversions from C-130Es, serials 69-6576 (c/n 4351) and 69-65777 (c/n 4352). Nine aircraft conversions from

The Thunderbirds' *crew plane, Hercules C130-A, 55-0026 (c/n 3053), serving with the 317 Tactical Control Wing, pictured at Cedar Rapids, Iowa, in October 1964.* (Nick Williams, AAHS)

C-130Es, serials 69-6567 (c/n 4341), 69-6568 (c/n 4342), 69-6569 (c/n 4343), 69-6570 (c/n 4344), 69-6571 (c/n 4345), 69-6572 (c/n 4346), 69-6573 (c/n 4347), 69-6574 (c/n 4348) and 69-6575 (c/n 4349). One, serial 69-6571 (c/n 4345), was lost to enemy action March 1972 at An Loc, Vietnam, while the rest were subsequently modified to AC-130H.

55 AC-130H-*LM*

Ten aircraft converted from surviving AC-130E-LMs, serials 69-6567 (c/n 4341), 69-6568 (c/n 4342), 69-6569 (c/n 4343), 69-6570 (c/n 4344), 69-6572 (c/n 4346), 69-6573 (c/n 4347), 69-6574 (c/n 4348), 69-6575 (c/n 4349), 69-6576 (c/n 4351) and 69-6577 (c/n 4352).

56 AC-130U *Spectre*

Thirteen aircraft based on C-130H, serials 87-0128 (c/n 5139), 89-0509 (c/n 5228), 89-0510 (c/n 5229), 89-0511 (c/n 5230); 89-0512 (c/n 5231), 89-0513 (c/n 5232), 89-0514 (c/n 5233), 90-0163 (c/n 5256), 90-0164 (c/n 5257), 90-0165 (c/n 5259), 90-0166 (c/n 5261), 90-0167 (c/n 5262) and 92-0253 (c/n 5279).

57 C-130A-*LM*

One hundred and ninety-two aircraft for USAF Tactical Air Command, as table.

Serial	C/n	Serial	C/n	Serial	C/n
53-3129	3001	55-0039	3066	56-0523	3131
53-3130	3002	55-0040	3067	56-0524	3132
53-3131	3003	55-0041	3068	56-0525	3133
53-3132	3004	55-0042	3069	56-0526	3134
53-3133	3005	55-0043	3070	56-0527	3135
53-3134	3006	55-0044	3071	56-0528	3136
53-3135	3007	55-0045	3072	56-0529	3137
54-1621	3008	55-0046	3073	56-0530	3138
54-1622	3009	55-0047	3074	56-0531	3139
54-1623	3010	55-0048	3075	56-0532	3140
54-1624	3011	56-0468	3076	56-0533	3141
54-1625	3012	56-0469	3077	56-0534	3142
54-1626	3013	56-0470	3078	56-0535	3143
54-1627	3014	56-0471	3079	56-0536	3144

Serial	C/n	Serial	C/n	Serial	C/n
54-1628	3015	56-0472	3080	56-0537	3145
54-1629	3016	56-0473	3081	56-0538	3146
54-1630	3017	56-0474	3082	56-0539	3147
54-1631	3018	56-0475	3083	56-0540	3148
54-1632	3019	56-0476	3084	56-0541	3149
54-1633	3020	56-0477	3085	56-0542	3150
54-1634	3021	56-0478	3086	56-0543	3151
54-1635	3022	56-0479	3087		
54-1636	3023	56-0480	3088	56-0544	3152
54-1737	3024	56-0481	3089	56-0545	3153
54-1638	3025	56-0482	3090	56-0546	3154
54-1639	3026	56-0483	3091	56-0547	3155
54-1640	3027	56-0484	3092	56-0548	3156
55-0001	3028	56-0485	3093	56-0549	3157
55-0002	3029	56-0486	3094	56-0550	3158
55-0003	3030	56-0487	3095	56-0551	3159
55-0004	3031	56-0488	3096	57-0453	3160
55-0005	3032	56-0489	3097	57-0454	3161
55-0006	3033	56-0490	3098	57-0455	3162
55-0007	3034	56-0491	3099	57-0456	3163
55-0008	3035	56-0492	3100	57-0457	3164
55-0009	3036	56-0493	3101	57-0458	3165
55-0010	3037	56-0494	3102	57-0459	3166

Serial	C/n	Serial	C/n	Serial	C/n
55-0011	3038	56-0495	3103	57-0460	3167
55-0012	3039	56-0496	3104	57-0461	3168
55-0013	3040	56-0497	3105	57-0462	3169
55-0014	3041	56-0498	3106	57-0463	3170
55-0015	3042	56-0499	3107	57-0464	3171
55-0016	3043	56-0500	3108	57-0465	3172
55-0017	3044	56-0501	3109	57-0466	3173
55-0018	3045	56-0502	3110	57-0467	3174
55-0019	3046	56-0503	3111	57-0468	3175
55-0020	3047	56-0504	3112	57-0469	3176
55-0021	3048	56-0505	3113	57-0470	3177
55-0022	3049	56-0506	3114	57-0471	3178
55-0023	3050	56-0507	3115	57-0472	3179
55-0024	3051	56-0508	3116	57-0473	3180
55-0025	3052	56-0509	3117	57-0474	3181
55-0026	3053	56-0510	3118	57-0475	3182
55-0027	3054	56-0511	3119	57-0476	3183
55-0028	3055	56-0512	3120	57-0477	3184
55-0029	3056	56-0513	3121	57-0478	3185
55-0030	3057	56-0514	3122	57-0479	3186
55-0031	3058	56-0515	3123	57-0480	3187
55-0032	3059	56-0516	3124	57-0481	3188
55-0033	3060	56-0517	3125	57-0482	3189
55-0034	3061	56-0518	3126	57-0483	3190

Serial	C/n	Serial	C/n	Serial	C/n
55-0035	3062	56-0519	3127	57-0496	3203
55-0036	3063	56-0520	3128	57-0497	3204
55-0037	3064	56-0521	3129		
55-0038	3065	56-0522	3130		

Twelve aircraft for RAAF, as table.

Serial	C/n	Serial	C/n	Serial	C/n
A97-205	3205	A97-209	3209	A97-213	3213
A97-206	3206	A97-210	3210	A97-214	3214
A97-207	3207	A97-211	3211	A97-215	3215
A97-208	3208	A97-212	3212	A97-216	3216

Fourteen aircraft, former RC-130As, as table.

Serial	C/n	Serial	C/n	Serial	C/n
57-0510	3217	57-0515	3222	57-0520	3227
57-0511	3218	57-0516	3223	57-0521	3228
57-0512	3219	57-0517	3224	57-0522	3229
57-0513	3220	57-0518	3225	57-0524	3231
57-0514	3221	57-0519	3226		

58 C-130A-II-*LM*

Twelve aircraft, C-130As modified for COMINT/SIGINT work from 1957, serials 54-1637 (c/n 3024), 56-0484 (c/n 3092), 56-0524 (c/n 3132), 56-0525 (c/n 3133), 56-0528 (c/n 3136), 56-0530 (c/n 3138), 56-0534 (c/n 3142), 56-0535 (c/n 3143), 56-0537 (c/n 3145), 56-0538 (c/n 3146), 56-0540 (c/n 3148) and 56-0541(c/n 3149).

Hercules C-130B, 61-0962 (c/n 3647) of 4686 ARRS, USAF operating from Hickam Field, Hawaii. (Nick Williams AAHS)

 C-130B-*LM*

O ne hundred and thirty-two aircraft for USAF Tactical Air Command, as table.

Serial	C/n	Serial	C/n	Serial	C/n	Serial	C/n	Serial	C/n	Serial	C/n
57-0525	3501	58-0751	3550	61-0950	3626	58-0716	3511	59-1526	3563	61-0960	3643
57-0526	3502	58-0752	3551	61-0951	3628	58-0717	3512	59-1527	3568	61-0961	3646
57-0527	3503	58-0753	3552	61-0952	3629	58-0718	3513	59-1529	3569	61-0962	3647
57-0528	3504	58-0754	3553	61-0953	3630	58-0719	3514	59-1534	3570	61-0963	3648
57-0529	3505	58-0755	3556	61-0954	3633	58-0720	3515	59-1528	3571	61-0964	3649
58-0711	3506	58-0756	3557	61-0955	3634	58-0721	3516	59-1530	3576	61-0965	3652
58-0712	3507	58-0757	3558	61-0956	3635	58-0722	3517	59-1531	3579	61-0966	3653
58-0713	3508	58-0758	3559	61-0957	3637	58-0723	3518	59-1532	3581	61-0967	3654
58-0714	3509	59-1524	3560	61-0958	3639	58-0724	3519	59-5857	3584	61-0968	3655
58-0715	3510	59-1525	3561	61-0959	3642	58-0725	3520	59-1535	3585	61-0969	3656

Serial	C/n	Serial	C/n	Serial	C/n
58-0726	3521	59-1533	3586	61-0970	3667
58-0727	3522	59-1536	3588	61-0971	3668
58-0728	3523	59-1537	3589	61-0972	3669
58-0729	3524	60-0293	3591	61-2634	3670
58-0730	3525	60-0294	3593	61-2635	3671
58-0731	3526	60-0295	3596	61-2636	3672
58-0732	3527	60-0296	3597	61-2337	3673
58-0733	3528	60-0297	3600	61-2638	3674
58-0734	3530	60-0298	3602	61-2639	3675
58-0735	3531	60-0299	3603	61-2640	3676
58-0736	3532	60-0300	3604	61-2641	3677
58-0737	3534	61-2358	3609	61-2642	3678
58-0738	3535	60-0301	3610	61-2643	3679
58-0739	3536	60-0302	3611	61-2644	3682
58-0740	3537	60-0304	3612	61-2645	3683

Coming in to land at Yokota Air Base, Japan, is Hercules 59-1532 (c/n 3581). (Nick Williams AAHS)

Serial	C/n	Serial	C/n	Serial	C/n
58-0741	3538	60-0303	3613	61-2646	3689
58-0742	3539	60-0305	3614	61-2647	3690
58-0743	3540	60-0306	3617	61-2648	3691
58-0744	3541	60-0307	3618	61-2649	3692
58-0745	3543	60-0308	3620	62-3487	3697
58-0746	3544	60-0309	3621	62-3488	3698
58-0747	3545	60-0310	3622	62-3489	3699
58-0749	3547	61-0948	3624	62-3490	3700
58-0750	3549	61-0949	3625	62-3491	3701

In addition, five former WC-130Bs were modified to C-130Bs between 1976 and 1979: serials 62-3492 (c/n 3702), 62-3493 (c/n 3707), 62-3494 (c/n 3708), 62-3495 (c/n 3721) and 62-3496 (c/n 3722).

Many others were produced for the Canadian, South African, Indonesian, Jordanian, Pakistani and Iranian air forces (see appropriate sections).

60 C-130B-II

Thirteen aircraft, C-130Bs modified as *Sun Valley II* electronics reconnaissance aircraft, serials 58-0711 (c/n 3506), 58-0723 (c/n 3518), 59-1524 (c/n 3560), 59-1525 (c/n 3561), 59-1526 (c/n 3563), 59-1527 (c/n 3568), 59-1528 (c/n 3571), 59-1530 (c/n 3576), 59-1531 (c/n 3579), 59-1532 (c/n 3581), 59-1533 (c/n 3586), 59-1535 (c/n 3585) and 59-1537 (c/n 3589).

61 C-130BL

Four aircraft, ski-equipped for the US Navy, were ordered by the USAF as the C-130BL on behalf of the Navy, serials 148318 ex 59-5922 (c/n 3562), 148319 ex 59-5923 (c/n 3564), 148320 ex 59-5924 (c/n 3565), 148321 ex 59-5925 (c/n 3567). On delivery the Navy re-designated them the UV-1L. In September 1962 they became LC-130F-*LM*s.

62 C-130C-*LM*

This designation was assigned to a proposed US Army-operated STOL aircraft, the prototype for which was the NC-130B-*LM*, serial 58-0712 (c/n 3507), but the concept was never realised.

63 C-130D-*LM*

Twelve aircraft, serials 57-0484 (c/n 3191), 57-0485 (c/n 3192), 57-0486 (c/n 3193), 57-0487 (c/n 3194), 57-0488 (c/n 3195), 57-0489 (c/n 3196), 57-0490 (c/n 3197), 57-0491 (c/n 3198), 57-0492 (c/n 3199), 57-0493 (c/n 3200), 57-0494 (c/n 3201) and 57-0495 (c/n 3202).

64 C-130D-6

Two aircraft, standard C-130As, temporary conversions, serials 57-0473 (c/n 3180) and 57-0474 (c/n 3181).

65 C-130E-*LM*

Three hundred and ninety aircraft for USAF Tactical Air Command and Military Airlift Command from 15 August 1961 to March 1974, as table.

Serial	C/n	Serial	C/n	Serial	C/n
61-2358	3609	63-7797	3863	63-9813	3974
61-2359	3651	63-7798	3864	64-0513	3997
61-2360	3659	63-7799	3865	64-0514	3998
61-2361	3662	63-7800	3866	64-0515	3999
61-2362	3663	63-7801	3867	64-0516	4000
61-2363	3681	63-7802	3868	64-0517	4001
61-2364	3687	63-7803	3869	64-0518	4002
61-2365	3688	63-7804	3870	64-0519	4003
61-2366	3706	63-7793	3872	64-0520	4004
61-2367	3712	63-7794	3873	64-0521	4005
61-2368	3713	63-7805	3874	64-0522	4006
61-2369	3714	63-7806	3875	64-0523	4007
61-2370	3715	63-7807	3876	64-0524	4008
61-2371	3716	63-7808	3877	64-0525	4009
61-2372	3717	63-7809	3879	64-0526	4010
61-2373	3720	63-7810	3880	64-0527	4013
62-1784	3729	63-7811	3881	64-0528	4014
62-1785	3730	63-7812	3882	64-0529	4017
62-1786	3731	63-7813	3883	64-0530	4018
62-1787	3732	63-7818	3884	64-0531	4019
62-1788	3735	63-7819	3885	64-0532	4021
62-1789	3736	63-7821	3886	64-0533	4022
62-1790	3737	63-7821	3887	64-0534	4023
62-1791	3738	63-7815	3888	64-0535	4024

Serial	C/n	Serial	C/n	Serial	C/n	Serial	C/n	Serial	C/n	Serial	C/n
62-1792	3739	63-7815	3889	64-0536	4025	62-1816	3778	63-7843	3913	64-0560	4063
62-1793	3743	63-7822	3890	64-0537	4027	62-1817	3779	63-7844	3914	64-17680	4064
62-1794	3744	63-7823	3891	64-0538	4028	62-1818	3780	63-7845	3915	64-0561	4065
62-1795	3746	63-7824	3892	64-0539	4029	62-1819	3782	63-7846	3916	64-0562	4068
62-1796	3747	63-7825	3893	64-0540	4030	62-1820	3783	63-7847	3917	64-17681	4069
62-1797	3748	63-7816	3894	64-0541	4031	62-1821	3784	63-7848	3918	64-0563	4071
62-1798	3752	63-7817	3895	64-0542	4032	62-1822	3785	63-7849	3919	64-0564	4074
62-1799	3753	63-7828	3896	64-0543	4033	62-1823	3786	63-7850	3920	64-0565	4077
62-1800	3754	63-7829	3897	64-0544	4034	62-1824	3787	63-7851	3921	64-0569	4079
62-1801	3755	63-7830	3898	64-0545	4035	62-1825	3788	63-7852	3922	64-0566	4080
62-1802	3756	63-7831	3899	64-0546	4039	62-1826	3789	63-7853	3923	64-0567	4083
62-1803	3757	63-7832	3900	64-0547	4040	62-1827	3790	63-7854	3924	64-0570	4085
62-1804	3758	63-7833	3901	64-0548	4043	62-1828	3791	63-7855	3925	64-0568	4086
62-1805	3759	63-7834	3902	64-0549	4044	62-1829	3792	63-7856	3926	64-0571	4087
62-1806	3760	63-7826	3903	64-0550	4045	62-1830	3793	63-7857	3927	64-0572	4090
62-1807	3761	63-7827	3904	64-0551	4046	62-1831	3794	63-7858	3928	64-18240	4105
62-1808	3762	63-7835	3905	64-0552	4047	62-1832	3795	63-7859	3929	68-10934	4314
62-1809	3770	63-7836	3906	64-0553	4048	62-1833	3796	63-7860	3930	68-10935	4315
62-1810	3771	63-8737	3907	64-0554	4049	62-1834	3797	63-7861	3931	68-10936	4316
62-1811	3772	63-7838	3908	64-0555	4056	62-1835	3798	63-7862	3932	68-10937	4317
62-1812	3774	63-7839	3909	64-0556	4057	62-1836	3799	63-7863	3933	68-10938	4318
62-1813	3775	63-7840	3910	64-0557	4058	62-1837	3800	63-7864	3934	68-10939	4319
62-1814	3776	63-7841	3911	64-0558	4059	62-1838	3801	63-7865	3935	68-10940	4320
62-1815	3777	63-7842	3912	64-0559	4062	62-1839	3802	63-7866	3936	68-10941	4321

Serial	C/n	Serial	C/n	Serial	C/n	Serial	C/n	Serial	C/n	Serial	C/n
62-1840	3803	63-7867	3937	68-10942	4322	62-1863	3827	63-7891	3962	69-6580	4356
62-1841	3804	63-7868	3938	68-10943	4323	62-1864	3828	63-7892	3963	69-6581	4357
62-1842	3805	63-7869	3939	68-10944	4324	62-1865	3829	63-7893	3964	69-6582	4359
62-1843	3806	63-7870	3940	68-10945	4325	62-1866	3830	63-7894	3965	69-6583	4360
62-1844	3807	63-7871	3941	68-10946	4326	63-7765	3831	63-7895	3966	70-1259	4404
62-1845	3808	63-7872	3942	68-10947	4327	63-7766	3832	63-7896	3967	70-1260	4410
62-1846	3809	63-7873	3943	68-10948	4328	63-7767	3833	63-7897	3968	70-1261	4413
62-1847	3810	63-7874	3944	68-10949	4329	63-7768	3834	63-7898	3969	70-1262	4414
62-1848	3811	63-7875	3945	68-10950	4330	63-7769	3835	63-7899	3970	70-1263	4415
62-1849	3812	63-7876	3947	68-10951	4331	63-7770	3836	63-9810	3971	70-1264	4417
63-7764	3813	63-7877	3948	69-6566	4340	63-7771	3837	63-9811	3972	70-1265	4418
62-1850	3814	63-7878	3949	69-6567	4341	63-7772	3838	63-9812	3973	70-1266	4419
62-1851	3815	63-7879	3950	69-6568	4342	63-7773	3839	63-9814	3975	70-1267	4420
62-1852	3816	63-7880	3951	69-6659	4343	63-7774	3840	63-9815	3976	70-1268	4421
62-1853	3817	63-7881	3952	69-6570	4344	63-7775	3841	63-9816	3977	70-1269	4423
62-1854	3818	63-7882	3953	69-6571	4345	63-7776	3842	63-9817	3978	70-1270	4424
62-1855	3819	63-7883	3954	69-6572	4346	63-7777	3843	64-0495	3979	70-1271	4425
62-1856	3820	63-7884	3955	69-6573	4347	63-7778	3844	64-0496	3980	70-1272	4426
62-1857	3821	63-7885	3956	69-6574	4348	63-7779	3845	64-0497	3981	70-1273	4428
62-1858	3822	63-7886	3957	69-6575	4349	63-7780	3846	64-0498	3982	70-1274	4429
62-1859	3823	63-7887	3958	69-6576	4351	63-7781	3847	64-0499	3983	70-1275	4434
62-1860	3824	63-7888	3959	69-6577	4352	63-7782	3848	64-0500	3984	70-1276	4435
62-1861	3825	63-7889	3960	69-6578	4353	63-7783	3850	64-0501	3985	72-1288	4499
62-1862	3826	63-7890	3961	69-6579	4354	63-7784	3851	64-0502	3986	72-1289	4500

Serial	C/n	Serial	C/n	Serial	C/n
63-7785	3852	64-0503	3987	72-1290	4502
63-7786	3853	64-0504	3988	72-1291	4504
63-7787	3854	64-0505	3989	72-1292	4505
63-7788	3855	64-0506	3990	72-1293	4506
63-7789	3856	64-0507	3991	72-1294	4509
63-7790	3857	64-0508	3992	72-1295	4510
63-7791	3859	64-0509	3993	72-1296	4517
63-7792	3860	64-0510	3994	72-1297	4519
63-7795	3861	64-0511	3995	72-1298	4521
63-7796	3862	64-0512	3996	72-1299	4527

Seen at Hickam Field AFB, Hawaii, in May 1968, is this Military Air Command Hercules C-130E, 63-7831 (c/n 3899) of the 439th Marine Air Wing. (Nick Williams AAHS)

(c/n 4062), 64-0561 (c/n 4065), 64-0562 (c/n 4068), 64-0563 (c/n 4071), 64-0564 (c/n 4074), 64-0565 (c/n 4077), 64-0566 (c/n 4080), 64-0567 (c/n 4083) and 64-0568 (c/n 4086). One aircraft modified from an NC-130E, serial 64-0572 (c/n 4090).

There were also four built for the US Navy, four for the US Coast Guard and 109 more for Australia, Brazil, Canada, Iran, Saudi Arabia, Sweden and Turkey (see appropriate sections).

66 C-130E-I

Seventeen *Combat Talon* aircraft, modified from C-130Es, serials 62-1843 (c/n 3806), 63-7785 (c/n 3852), 64-0508 (c/n 3992), 64-0523 (c/n 4007), 64-0547 (c/n 4040), 64-0551 (c/n 4046), 64-0555 (c/n 4056), 64-0558 (c/n 4059), 64-0559

This United States Navy C-130F of VR-21, serial 149787 (c/n 3636), tail coded RZ, is seen at Naval Air Station, Atsugi in 1967. (Nick Williams AAHS)

1 September 1987. As part of the flight test demonstration programme for the 'Super Hercules' C-130H-30 to show off the increased volume capacity, at Fort Bragg, North Carolina, an Army 'Gamma Goat' is one of three pallets dropped on a single pass along with an eight-man crew. (Lockheed via Audrey Pearcy)

67 C-130E-II

Ten aircraft, C-130E conversions into ABCC aircraft, serials 62-1791 (c/n 3738), 62-1809 (c/n 3770), 62-1815 (c/n 3777), 62-1818 (c/n 3780), 62-1820 (c/n 3783), 62-1825 (c/n 3788), 62-1832 (c/n 3795), 62-1836 (c/n 3799), 62-1857 (c/n 3821) and 62-1863 (c/n 3827). In April 1967 they were re-designated EC-130s.

68 C-130F-*LM*

Seven aircraft, US Navy Transport GV-1U aircraft, re-designated in September 1962, serials 149787 (c/n 3636), 149790 (c/n 3645), 149793 (c/n 3660), 149794 (c/n 3661), 149797 (c/n 3666), 149801 (c/n 3686) and 149805 (c/n 3696).

69 C-130H-*LM*

Three hundred and six aircraft for USAF Tactical Air Command, Air National Guard, Air Force Reserves, Air Combat Command, from June 1974 to December 1996, as table.

Serial	C/n	Serial	C/n	Serial	C/n
73-1580	4542	82-0061	4982	90-1795	5248
73-1581	4543	83-0486	5008	90-1796	5249
73-1582	4544	83-0491	5010	90-1797	5250
73-1583	4545	83-0487	5012	90-1798	5251
73-1584	4546	83-0488	5014	91-1231	5278
73-1585	4547	83-0489	5018	91-1232	5282
73-1586	4548	84-0204	5038	91-1233	5283

Serial	C/n	Serial	C/n	Serial	C/n	Serial	C/n	Serial	C/n	Serial	C/n
73-1587	4549	84-0205	5039	91-1234	5284	74-1674	4631	85-1368	5084	92-1532	5328
73-1588	4550	84-0475	5041	91-1235	5285	74-1675	4640	85-0041	5086	92-1452	5329
73-1590	4554	84-0476	5042	91-1236	5286	74-1676	4641	85-0042	5089	92-1453	5330
73-1592	4557	84-0206	5043	91-1237	5287	74-1677	4643	86-1391	5093	92-3281	5331
73-1594	4563	84-0207	5044	91-1238	5288	74-2061	4644	86-0410	5094	92-0547	5332
73-1595	4564	84-0208	5046	91-1239	5289	74-1678	4645	86-1392	5095	92-1454	5333
73-1597	4571	84-0209	5047	91-1651	5290	74-1679	4646	86-1393	5096	92-3282	5334
73-1598	4573	84-0210	5049	91-1652	5291	74-2062	4647	86-0411	5097	92-0548	5335
74-1658	4579	84-0211	5050	91-1653	5292	74-1680	4651	86-0412	5098	92-3283	5336
74-1659	4585	84-0212	5051	91-9141	5293	74-2063	4655	86-1394	5099	92-0549	5337
74-1660	4592	84-0213	5052	91-9142	5295	74-1682	4657	86-0413	5100	92-3284	5338
74-1661	4596	85-1361	5071	91-9143	5296	74-1683	4658	86-1395	5101	92-0551	5346
74-1662	4597	85-1362	5072	91-9144	5297	74-2064	4659	86-0414	5102	92-3285	5347
74-1663	4598	85-0035	5073	92-3021	5312	74-1684	4663	86-1396	5103	92-0552	5348
74-1664	4603	85-0036	5074	92-3022	5313	74-1685	4666	86-0415	5105	92-3286	5349
74-1665	4604	85-1363	5075	92-3023	5314	74-2065	4667	86-0418	5110	92-0553	5350
74-1666	4611	85-1364	5076	92-3024	5315	74-1686	4669	86-1397	5111	92-3287	5351
74-1667	4613	85-0037	5077	92-0550	5321	74-1687	4670	86-1398	5112	92-0554	5352
74-1668	4616	85-1365	5078	92-1533	5322	74-2066	4671	86-0419	5113	92-3288	5353
74-1669	4617	85-0038	5079	92-1534	5323	74-1688	4675	87-9281	5122	93-1455	5360
74-1670	4620	85-0039	5080	92-1535	5324	74-2067	4678	87-9282	5123	93-1456	5361
74-1671	4621	85-1366	5081	92-1536	5325	74-1689	4681	87-9283	5124	93-1457	5362
74-1672	4623	85-1367	5082	92-1537	5326	74-1690	4682	87-9284	5125	93-1458	5363
74-1673	4627	85-0040	5083	92-1538	5327	74-1691	4687	87-9285	5126	93-1459	5364

Serial	C/n	Serial	C/n	Serial	C/n	Serial	C/n	Serial	C/n	Serial	C/n
74-1692	4688	87-9286	5127	93-1561	5365	79-0479	4859	89-1186	5195	94-7310	5396
74-1693	4693	87-9287	5128	93-1562	5366	79-0480	4860	89-1187	5196	94-6705	5397
74-2068	4694	87-9288	5129	93-1563	5367	80-0320	4900	89-1188	5197	94-6706	5398
74-2069	4699	88-4401	5154	93-1036	5368	80-0321	4902	89-1051	5198	94-6707	5399
74-2070	4700	88-4402	5155	93-1037	5369	80-0322	4903	89-1052	5199	94-6708	5400
74-2071	4703	88-4403	5156	93-2041	5370	80-0323	4905	89-1053	5201	94-7320	5401
74-2072	4705	88-4404	5157	93-2042	5371	80-0324	4906	89-1054	5203	94-7321	5403
74-2131	4718	88-4405	5158	93-1038	5372	80-0325	4908	89-1055	5204	95-6709	5417
74-2132	4722	88-4406	5159	93-1039	5373	80-0326	4910	89-1056	5205	95-6710	5418
74-2133	4730	88-4407	5160	93-7311	5374	81-0626	4939	89-9101	5216	95-6711	5419
74-2134	4735	88-4408	5161	93-1040	5375	81-0627	4941	89-9102	5217	95-6712	5420
78-0806	4815	88-1301	5162	93-1041	5376	81-0628	4942	89-9103	5218	95-1001	5421
78-0807	4817	88-1302	5163	93-7312	5377	80-0332	4943	89-9104	5220	95-1002	5422
78-0808	4818	88-1303	5164	94-6701	5378	81-0629	4944	89-9105	5221	96-1003	5423
78-0809	4819	88-1304	5165	93-7313	5379	81-0630	4945	89-9106	5223	96-1004	5424
78-0810	4820	88-1305	5166	93-7314	5380	81-0631	4946	90-9107	5238	96-1005	5425
78-0811	4821	88-1306	5167	94-6702	5382	82-0054	4968	90-9108	5239	96-1006	5426
78-0812	4822	88-1307	5168	94-7315	5389	82-0055	4970	90-1057	5240	96-1007	5427
78-0813	4823	88-1308	5169	94-7316	5390	82-0056	4971	90-1058	5241	96-1008	5428
79-0474	4854	89-1181	5188	94-7317	5391	82-0057	4973	90-1791	5242	96-7322	5431
79-0475	4855	89-1182	5190	94-7318	5392	82-0058	4975	90-1792	5245	96-7323	5432
79-0476	4856	89-1183	5192	94-6703	5393	82-0059	4977	90-1793	5246	96-7324	5433
79-0477	4857	89-1184	5193	94-6704	5394	82-0060	4979	90-1794	5247	96-7325	5434
79-0478	4858	89-1185	5194	94-7319	5395						

In addition, eight USAF Hercules were converted to C-130H standard for the USAF: one NC-130H, serial 64-14854 (c/n 4038), in April 1986, six WC-130Hs, serials 65-0964 (c/n 4104), 65-0969 (c/n 4111), 65-0972 (c/n 4120), 65-0976 (c/n 4126), 65-0977 (c/n 4127) and 65-0985 (c/n 4140) between July 1990 and March 1992, and one EC-130H, serial 64-14859 (c/n 4082), in June 1993.

The C-130H was the most widely used variant and additionally served with the US Navy, US Coast Guard and fifty foreign air forces (see appropriate sections).

70 C-130H-(CT)

E leven aircraft, C-130E-I *Combat Talon* aircraft, serials 64-0523 (c/n 4007), 64-0551 (c/n 4046), 64-0555 (c/n 4056), 64-0559 (c/n 4062), 64-0561 (c/n 4065), 64-0562 (c/n 4068), 64-0566 (c/n 4080), 64-0567 (c/n 4083) 64-0568 (c/n 4086), 64-0571 (c/n 4087) and 64-0572 (c/n 4090). Nine were subsequently re-designated MC-130Es and two MC-130Es.

71 C-130H-(S)

F our aircraft, C-130Hs, 'stretched' 15ft (4.6m) to L-100-30 standards for the air forces of Canada and Portugal, and fifty-six new-builds to the same specification of twelve more air forces. These were subsequently re-designated C-130H-30s.

72 C-130H-30

F our aircraft, C-130Hs, 'stretched' 15ft (4.6m) to L-100-30 standards for the air forces of Canada and Portugal, serials 6801 (c/n 4749), 6802 (c/n 4753), 130343 (c/n 5307) former civilian N41030 and 130344 (c/n 5320) former civilian N4080M.

Fifty-six aircraft, new-builds to the same specification of twelve more air forces, serials A-1317 (c/n 4864), A-1318 (c/n 4865), A-1319 (c/n 4868), A-1320 (c/n 4869), A-1321 (c/n 4870), 7T-VHN (c/n 4894), 7T-VHO (c/n 4897), 7T-VHM (c/n 4919), 7T-VHP (c/n 4921), A-1321 (c/n 4925), A-1324 (c/n 4927), TJX-AE (c/n 4933) former civilian N4206M, 60104 (c/n 4959), 312 (c/n 4961), NAF916 (c/n 4962) former civilian N4081M; NAF917 (c/n 4963) former civilian N4099R; HZ-MS8 (c/n 4986) former civilian N4243M; 7T-WHD (c/n 4987), 7T-WHL (c/n 4989) former civilian 4989; 7T-WHA (c/n 4997), NAF918 (c/n 5001), TL10-01

(c/n 5003) former civilian N7323D; 5006 (c/n 5006) former civilian N4080M; 5019 (c/n 5019) former civilian N73232; 5050 (c/n 5030) former civilian N4249Y; 5036 (c/n 5036) former civilian N4161T; 61-PD (c/n 5140) former civilian F-RAPD; 61-PE (c/n 5142) former civilian F-RAPE; 61-PF (c/n 5144 former civilian F-RAPF; 60105 (c/n 5146), 60106 (c/n 5148), 61-PG (c/n 5150) former civilian N4242N and F-RAPG; 61-PH (c/n 5151) former civilian F-RAPH; 61-PI (c/n 5152) former civilian F-RAPI; 61-PJ (c/n 5153) former civilian N73235 and F-RAPJ; TT-AAH (c/n 5184), 1293 (c/n 5187) later civilian SU-BKS; 1294 (c/n 5191) later civilian SU-BKT; 1295 (c/n 5206) later civilian SU-BKU; 60107 (c/n 5208), 471 (c/n 5211), 1622 (c/n 5212), 7T-WHB (c/n 5224), 61-PK (c/n 5226) former civilian F-RAPK; 61-PL (c/n 5227) former civilian F-RAPL; 6806 (c/n 5264), M30-10 (c/n 5268), G273 (c/n 5273) former civilian N4080M; G275 (c/n 5275) former civilian N4080M; M30-12 (c/n 5277), 60111 (c/n 5280), 60112 (c/n 5281), M30-11 (c/n 5309), M30-14 (c/n 5311), M30-15 (c/n 5316) and M30-16 (c/n 5319).

73 C-130H(AEH)

F our aircraft converted from C-130Hs, serials HZ-MS019 (c/n 4837), HZ-116 (c/n 4915), HZ-MS021 (c/n 4918) and HZ-MS7 (c/n 4922).

Six aircraft converted from L-100-30s, serials HZ-117 (c/n 4954), HZ-MS05 (c/n 4950), HZ-MS06 (c/n 4952), HZ-MS09 (c/n 4956), HZ-MS10 (c/n 4957) and HZ-MS 14 (c/n 4960).

74 C-130H-MP

T hree aircraft – serials FM2451 (c/n 4847), FM2452 (c/n 4849) and FM2453(c/n 4866) – were produced for the Malaysian Air Force in 1980. They were later modified to aerial tankers and re-registered M30-7, M30-08 and M30-09 respectively. One aircraft, *Tantara Nasional Indonesia-Angkatan Udare* serial AI 1322 (c/n 4989), was built for the Indonesian Air Force in November 1981. This machine was lost on 21 November 1985 when she crashed into the Sibyak volcano.

75 | C-130J

T hirty-four-plus aircraft. At the time of writing thirty-four standard C-130Js are built or being built for the British, American (ANG) and Italian air forces, serials 94-3026 (c/n 5413) later civilian N130JC; 94-3027 (c/n 5415) later civilian N130JG; 96-8153 (c/n 5454) former civilian N4099R; 96-8154 (c/n 5455), 97-1351 (c/n 5469), 97-1352 (c/n 5470), 97-1353 (c/n 5471), ZH880 (c/n 5478), former civilian N73238; ZH881 (c/n 5479) former civilian N4249Y; ZH882 (c/n 5480) former civilian N4081M; ZH883 (c/n 5481) former civilian N4242N; ZH884 (c/n 5482) former civilian N4249Y; ZH885 (c/n 5483) former civilian N41030; ZH886 (c/n 5484) former civilian N73235; ZH887 (c/n 5485) former civilian N4187W; 98-1355 (c/n 5491), 98-1356 (c/n 5492), 98-1357 (c/n 5493),98-1358 (c/n 5494), 46-40 (c/n 5495), ZH888 (c/n 5496) former civilian N4187; 46-41 (c/n 5497), 46-42 (c/n 5498), ZH889 (c/n 5500), 46-43 (c/n 5503), 46-44 (c/n 5504), 46-45 (c/n 5505), 46-46 (c/n 5510), 46-47 (c/n 5511), 46-48 (c/n 5512), 46-49 (c/n 5513), 46-50 (c/n 5514), 46-51 (c/n 5520).

A Hercules DC-130A-LM, 57-0497 (c/n 3204), one of two modified from a C-130A, carrying an XQ-4B remote-control piloted vehicle in 1976. A chin radome featured on these aircraft as well as four pylons for the RCPVs. Internally a host of specialised guidance systems was packed within their fuselages. (Author's Collection)

76 | C-130J-30

N inety-eight aircraft, stretched C-130Js, thirty-seven for the USAF, twenty-five for the RAF, twelve for the RAAF, twenty for the Italian Air Force and four for the Kuwaiti Air Force. Known serials include ZH865 (c/n 5408) former civilian N130JA; ZH866 (c/n 5414) former civilian N130JE; ZH867 (c/n 5416) former civilian N130JJ; A97-440 (c/n 5440) former civilian N130JQ; A97-441 (c/n 5441), A97-442 (c/n 5442) former civilian N130JR; ZH868 (c/n 5443) former civilian N130JN; ZH869 (c/n 5444) former civilian N130JV; ZH870 (c/n 5445) former civilian N73235; ZH871 (c/n 5446) former civilian N73238; A97-447 (c/n 5447) former civilian

N73232; A97-448 (c/n 5448) former civilian N73230; A97-449 (c/n 5449) former civilian N73233; A97-450 (c/n 5450) former civilian N4187W; ZH872 (c/n 5456) former civilian N4249Y; ZH873 (c/n 5457) former civilian N4242N; ZH874 (c/n 5458) former civilian N41030; ZH875 (c/n 5459) former civilian N4099R; ZH876 (c/n 5460) former civilian N4080M; ZH877 (c/n 5461) former civilian N4081M; ZH878 (c/n 5462) former civilian N73232; ZH879 (c/n 5463), A97-464 (c/n 5464), A97-465 (c/n 5465), A97-466 (c/n 5466), A97-467 (c/n 5467), A97-468 (c/n 5468), 99-1431 (c/n 5517), 99-1432 (c/n 5518) and 99-1433 (c/n 5519). (C/ns 5521 5523, 5529, 5530, 5531, 5539, 5540, 5550, 5551, and 5552 are destined for the Italian Air Force.)

77 C-130K-*LM*

S ixty-six aircraft, British equivalents of the C-130H, and known as the Hercules C. Mk 1 in RAF service, serials XV176 (c/n 4169), XV177 (c/n 4182), XV178 (c/n 4188), XV179 (c/n 4195), XV180 (c/n 4196), XV181 (c/n 4198), XV182 (c/n 4199), XV183 (c/n 4200), XV184 (c/n 4201), XV185 (c/n 4203), XV186 (c/n 4204), XV187 (c/n 4205), XV188 (c/n 4206), XV189 (c/n 4207), XV190 (c/n 4210), XV191 (c/n 4211), XV192 (c/n 4212), XV193 (c/n 4213), XV194 (c/n 4214), XV195 (c/n 4216), XV196 (c/n 4217), XV197 (c/n 4218), XV198 (c/n 4219), XV199 (c/n 4220), XV200 (c/n 4223), XV201 (c/n 4224),

A United States Navy VC-3 (DC-130A), 158228 (c/n 3048) on the mat, displays her stunning paint scheme at Davis-Monthan AFB in July 1979. (Bruce Stewart via Nick Williams AAHS)

XV202 (c/n 4226), XV203 (c/n 4227), XV204 (c/n 4228), XV205 (c/n 4230), XV206 (c/n 4231), XV207 (c/n 4232), XV208 (c/n 4233), XV209 (c/n 4235), XV210 (c/n 4236), XV211 (c/n 4237), XV212 (c/n 4238), XV213 (c/n 4240), XV214 (c/n 4241), XV215 (c/n 4242), XV216 (c/n 4243), XV217 (c/n 4244), XV218 (c/n 4245), XV219 (c/n 4246), XV220 (c/n 4247), XV221 (c/n 4251), XV222 (c/n 4252), XV223 (c/n 4253), XV290 (c/n 4254), XV291 (c/n 4256), XV292 (c/n 4257), XV293 (c/n 4258), XV294 (c/n 4259), XV295 (c/n 4261), XV296 (c/n 4262), XV297 (c/n 4263), XV298 (c/n 4264), XV299 (c/n 4266), XV300 (c/n 4267), XV301 (c/n 4268), XV302 (c/n 4270), XV303 (c/n 4271), XV304 (c/n 4272), XV305 (c/n 4273), XV306 (c/n 4274) and XV307 (c/n 4275).

78 C-130T

T wenty aircraft, C-130Ts, which were C-130H transports fitted with T56A-16 engines and carried refuelling packages, serials 164762 (c/n 5255), 164763 (c/n 5258), 164993 (c/n 5298), 164994

(c/n 5299), 164995 (c/n 5300), 164996 (c/n 5301), 164997 (c/n 5304), 164998 (c/n 5305), 165158 (c/n 5341), 165159 (c/n 5342), 165160 (c/n 5344), 165161 (c/n 5345), 165313 (c/n 5383), 165314 (c/n 5384), 165348 (c/n 5404), 165349 (c/n 5406), 165350 (c/n 5407), 165351 (c/n 5409), 165378 (c/n 5429) and 165379 (c/n 5430).

79 CG-130G-*LM*

Four aircraft, C-130Es with T56-A-16 engines and Navy radio suites, received this US Navy designation, serials 151888 (c/n 3849), 151889 (c/n 3858), 151890 (c/n 3871) and 151891 (c/n 3878). They were subsequently re-designated EC-130G *TACAMO* aircraft.

80 DC-130A-*LM*

Two aircraft, serials 57-0496 (c/n 3203) and 57-0497 (c/n 3204), which were converted in 1957. Four more aircraft of the type were former C-130As: 56-0491 (c/n 3099), 56-0514 (c/n 3122), 56-0527 (c/n 3135) and 56-461 (c/n 3168). One aircraft the former C-130D, 55-0021 (c/n 3048). One aircraft the former RL-130A, 57-0523 (c/n 3230).

A DC-130A Herk, No 56-0491 (c/n 3099), cruises past the 12,395ft Mount Fujiyama, in central Japan, on 7 February 1958. She was working with Pacific Air Command and working from Ashiya Air Force Base. (Lockheed via Audrey Pearcy)

81 DC-130E-*LM*

Seven aircraft, former C-130Es, serials 61-2361 (c/n 3662), 61-2362 (c/n 3663), 61-2363 (c/n 3681), 61-2364 (c/n 3687), 61-2368 (c/n 3713), 61-2369 (c/n 3714) and 61-2371 (c/n 3716).

82 DC-130H-*LM*

One aircraft, serial 65-979 (c/n 4131).

83 EC-130E

One aircraft, a former EC-130S, was re-designated thus on delivery in 1966, serial CG1414 (c/n 4158). Ten aircraft, former C-130E-IIs, serials

62-1791 (c/n 3738), 62-1809 (c/n 3770), 62-1815 (c/n 3777), 62-1818 (c/n 3780), 62-1820 (c/n 3783), 62-1825 (c/n 3788); 62-1832 (c/n 3795), 62-1836 (c/n 3799), 62-1857 (c/n 3821) and 62-1863 (c/n 3827).

84 EC-130E (CL)

Five aircraft, former C-130Es, were modified by Lockheed to *Comfy Levi/Senior Hunter* aircraft, serials 63-7783 (c/n 3850), 63-7815 (c/n 3889), 63-7816 (c/n 3894), 63-7828 (c/n 3896) and 63-9816 (c/n 3977).

85 EC-130E(RR)

Three aircraft, former C-130Es, modified to EC-130E(RR) *Rivet Rider/Volant Scout* electronic surveillance aircraft, serials 63-7773 (c/n 3839), 63-7869 (c/n 3939) and 63-9817 (c/n 3978).

86 EC-130G

Four aircraft, former CG-130G-*LM* aircraft, serials 151888 (c/n 3849), 151889 (c/n 3858), 151890 (c/n 3871) and 151891 (c/n 3878). They were subsequently re-designated EC-130G *TACAMO* aircraft.

An unnumbered United States Navy EC-130Q, displaying that unit's crest (and the Playboy Bunny), is seen at Naval Air Station BP. (Nick Williams AAHS)

87 EC-130H(CCCCM)

Four aircraft, former EC-130Hs, serials 64-14859 (c/n 4082), 64-14862 (c/n 4089), 65-0962 (c/n 4102) and 65-0989 (c/n 4150). Twelve aircraft, former C-130Hs, serials 73-1580 (c/n 4542), 73-1581 (c/n 4543), 73-1583 (c/n 4545), 73-1584 (c/n 4546), 73-1855 (c/n 4547), 73-1856 (c/n 4548), 73-1857 (c/n 4549), 73-1858 (c/n 4550), 73-1590 (c/n 4554), 73-1592 (c/n 4557), 73-1594 (c/n 4563) and 73-1595 (c/n 4564).

Modified for command, control and communications control (CCCC) *Compass Call* aircraft under this designation.

88 EC-130H(CL)

Three aircraft, former C-130Hs, converted to EC-130H(CL)s for *Senior Scout* clandestine electronic intelligence-gathering and jamming missions, serials 74-2139 (c/n 4711), 74-2134 (c/n 4735) and 89-1185 (c/n 5194).

89 EC-130J

F our aircraft for ECM work with the Air National Guard, serials 97-1931 (c/n 5477), 98-1932 (c/n 5490) 99-1933 (c/n 5502) and 00-1934 (c/n 5527).

90 EC-130Q-*LM*

E ighteen aircraft, C-130Hs powered by the T56-A-16 engine for *TACAMO* duties, serials 156170 (c/n 4239), 156171 (c/n 4249), 156172 (c/n 4269), 156173 (c/n 4277), 156174 (c/n 4278), 156175 (c/n 4279), 165176 (c/n 4280), 156177 (c/n 4281), 159469 (c/n 4595), 159348 (c/n 4601), 160608 (c/n 4781), 161223 (c/n 4867), 161494 (c/n 4896), 161495 (c/n 4901), 161496 (c/n 4904), 161531 (c/n 4932), 162312 (c/n 4984) and 162313 (c/n 4988).

91 EC-130V

O ne aircraft fitted out for the US Coast Guard as an early-warning aircraft with rotordome and AN/APAS-14S EC-130V, serial CG1721 (c/n 5121).

92 GC-130A-*LM*

T his designation was allocated to what later became the DC-130A. Later still, it was applied to all Hercules aircraft that were permanently grounded as instructional airframes. The first to be so designated was serial 54-1621 (c/n 3008) (see also next entry).

The following additional Hercules served in the ground training role in various capacities, and *some*, but by no means all, received this designation at some period. Serials 53-3131 (c/n 3003) ground trainer; 54-1634 (c/n 3021) fire trainer; 54-1637 (c/n 3024), 54-1640 (c/n 3027) ground trainer; 55-0018 (c/n 3045) loadmaster trainer; 55-0019 (c/n 3046) ground loading trainer; 55-0047 (c/n 3074) paratroop ground trainer; 55-0048 (c/n 3075) evacuation trainer; 56-0469 (c/n 3077) ground and gun trainer; 56-0492 (c/n 3100) paratroop trainer; 56-0498 (c/n 3106) ground trainer; 56-0513 (c/n 3121) loadmaster trainer; 56-0520 (c/n 3218) instructional airframe; 56-0524 (c/n 3132) instructional airframe; 56-0525 (c/n 3133) ECM test bed; 56-0539 (c/n 3147) loadmaster trainer; 56-0550 (c/n 3158) loadmaster trainer; 57-0462 (c/n 3169) fuel loading trainer; 57-0464 (c/n 3171) loading trainer; 57-0469 (c/n 3176) ground trainer; 57-0471 (c/n 3178) maintenance, electrical and air-conditioning trainer; 57-0472 (c/n 3179) paratroop trainer; 57-0477 (c/n 3184) repair trainer; 57-0478 (c/n 3185) aircraft battle damage trainer; 57-0483 (c/n 3190) ground and loading trainer; 57-0486 (c/n 3193) instructional airframe; 57-0489 (c/n 3196) instructional airframe; 57-0490 (c/n 3197) ground trainer; 57-0524 (c/n 3231) battle damage repair trainer; 57-0528 (c/n 3504) loadmaster trainer; 58-0740 (c/n 3537) ground and loader trainer; 58-6973 (c/n 3542) loadmaster trainer; 61-2081 (c/n 3638) loadmaster trainer; 61-2083 (c/n 3650) loadmaster trainer; 61-2362 (c/n 3663) maintenance trainer; 61-2364 (c/n 3687) crew chief trainer; 61-2368 (c/n 3713) loadmaster trainer; 62-1794 (c/n 3744) crew chief trainer; 62-1807 (c/n 3761) crew chief trainer; 62-1830 (c/n 3793) non-flying crew trainer; 62-1860 (c/n 3824) ground trainer; 63-7779 (c/n 3845) engine maintenance trainer; 63-7795 (c/n 3861) maintenance trainer; 63-7801

The white radar 'hump' is matched by the leading edges of fin and horizontal tail surfaces on USAF 61-0962 (c/n 3647) of 4686 ARRS. (Nick Williams AAHS)

(c/n 3867) paratroop trainer; 63-7820 (c/n 3886) loadmaster trainer; 64-0500 (c/n 3984) ground trainer; 64-0524 (c/n 4008) loadmaster trainer; 64-0556 (c/n 4057) maintenance trainer; 64-0566 (c/n 4079) ground trainer; 68-10949 (c/n 4239) loadmaster trainer; 69-6579 (c/n 4354) ground maintenance trainer; 72-1298 (c/n 4521) crew chief trainer; and 74-1693 (c/n 4693) loadmaster trainer.

93 GC-130D/GC-130D-6

Confusingly, both these designations have also been applied to permanently grounded Hercules airframes down the years.

94 GVI

Two aircraft, the original US Marine Corps designation applied to the first aerial tanker on loan from the USAF, serials 55-0046 (c/n 3073) and 55-0048 (c/n 3075).

See KC-130F-*LM* section.

95 GVI-U

Seven US Navy tanker aircraft, serials 149787 (c/n 3636), 149790 (c/n 3645), 149793 (c/n 3660), 149794 (c/n 3661), 149797 (c/n 3666), 149801 (c/n 3686) and 149805 (c/n 3696).

See C-130F section.

Magnificent view of Hercules HC-130H, 65-0985 (c/n 4140), Rescue, of the 79 ARRS, Military Air Command, climbing from Hickam Field Air Force Base, Hawaii, June 1964. (Nick Williams AAHS)

96 HC-130B-*LM*

Twelve aircraft, serials CG 1339 ex 58-5396 (c/n 3529), CG 1340 ex 58-5397 (c/n 3533), CG 1341 ex 58-6973 (c/n 3542), CG 1342 ex 58-6974 (c/n 3548), CG 1344 ex 60-0311 (c/n 3594), CG 1345 ex 60-0312 (c/n 3595), CG 1346 ex 61-0958 (c/n 3638), CG 1347 ex 61-2082 (c/n 3641), CG 1348 ex 61-2083 (c/n 3650), CG 1349 ex 62-3753 (c/n 3745), CG 1350 ex 62-3754 (c/n 3763) and CG 1351 ex 62-3755 (c/n 3773). They were variously based at Elizabeth City, Barber's Point, Clearwater and Sacramento during their twenty years of service and the bulk were finally retired to MASDC from 1982. Eleven of them still survived in the AMARC Park as it was re-designated in 1985, but were due to depart to various CFs that October.

97 HC-130E-*LM*

One aircraft, a former Coast Guard EC-130E, built as a long-range navigation (LORAN) A & C calibration aircraft, serial 1414 (c/n 4158).

An aerial view of a Hercules HC-130H, 64-14861 (c/n 4088) of USAF which first saw service with 57 Aerospace Rescue and Recovery Squadron, (ARRS). She was later modified to a WC-130H and served with 54 WRS. (Author's Collection)

98 HC-130G

Twelve aircraft, serials CG 1339 ex 58-5396 (c/n 3529), CG 1340 ex 58-5397 (c/n 3533), CG 1341 ex 58-6973 (c/n 3542), CG 1342 ex 58-6974 (c/n 3548), CG 1344 ex 60-0311 (c/n 3594), CG 1345 ex 60-0312 (c/n 3595), CG 1346 ex 61-0958 (c/n 3638), CG 1347 ex 61-2082 (c/n 3641), CG 1348 ex 61-2083 (c/n 3650), CG 1349 ex 62-3753 (c/n 3745), CG 1350 ex 62-3754 (c/n 3763) and CG 1351 ex 62-3755 (c/n 3773). All were re-designated HC-130B-*LM*s early on.

99 HC-130H

Forty-three aircraft for ARRS, fitted with AN/ARD-17 Cook aerial tracker, Fulton STAR recovery yoke and HRU pods. Serials 64-14852 (c/n 4036), 64-14853 (c/n 4037), 64-14854 (c/n 4038), 64-14855 (c/n 4055), 64-14856 (c/n 4072), 64-14857 (c/n 4073), 64-14858 (c/n 4081), 64-14859 (c/n 4082), 64-14860 (c/n 4084), 64-14861 (c/n 4088), 64-14862 (c/n 4089), 64-14863 (c/n 4094), 64-14864 (c/n 4097), 64-14865 (c/n 4098), 64-14866 (c/n 4099), 65-0962

(c/n 4102), 65-0963 (c/n 4103), 65-0964 (c/n 4104), 65-0965 (c/n 4106), 65-0966 (c/n 4107), 65-0967 (c/n 4108), 65-0968 (c/n 4110), 65-0969 (c/n 4111), 65-0970 (c/n 4112), 65-0971 (c/n 4116), 65-0972 (c/n 4120), 65-0973 (c/n 4121), 65-0974 (c/n 4123), 65-0975 (c/n 4125), 65-0976 (c/n 4126), 65-0977 (c/n 4127), 65-0978 (c/n 4130), 65-0979 (c/n 4131), 65-0980 (c/n 4132), 65-0981 (c/n 4133), 65-0982 (c/n 4135), 65-0983 (c/n 4138), 65-0984 (c/n 4139), 65-0985 (c/n 4140), 65-0986 (c/n 4141), 65-0987 (c/n 4142), 65-0989 (c/n 4150) and 65-0990 (c/n 4151).

Twenty-four aircraft for USCG, serials CG 1452 ex 66-13533 (c/n 4255), CG 1453 ex 67-7184 (c/n 4260), CG 1454 ex 677185 (c/n 4265), CG 1500 ex 72-1300 (c/n 4501), CG 1501 ex 72-1301 (c/n 4507), CG 1502 ex 72-1302 (c/n 4513), CG 1503 ex 73-0844 (c/n 4528), CG 1504 ex 73-0845 (c/n 4529), CG 1600 ex 77-0320 (c/n 4764), CG 1601 ex 77-0319 (c/n 4762), CG 1602 ex 77-0318 (c/n 4760), CG 1603 ex 77-0317 (c/n 4757), CG 1710 (c/n 5028), CG 1711 (c/n 5031), CG 1712 (c/n 5033), CG 1713 (c/n 5034), CG 1714 (c/n 5035), CG 1716 (c/n 5023), CG 1717 (c/n 5104), CG 1718 (c/n 5106), CG 1719 (c/n 5107), CG 1720 (c/n 5120), CG 1721 (c/n 5121) and CG 1715 (c/n 5037).

100 HC-130H-7

Eleven aircraft for the USCG with SLAR and FLIR pods, serials CG 1700 (c/n 4947), CG 1701 (c/n 4958), CG 1702 (c/n 4966), CG 1703 (c/n 4967), CG 1704 (c/n 4969), CG 1705 (c/n 4993), CG 1706 (c/n 4996), CG 1707 (c/n 4999), CG 1708 (c/n 5002), CG 1709 (c/n 5005) and CG 1790 (c/n 4931).

101 HC-130H(N)

Six aircraft – serials 88-2101 (c/n 5202), 88-2102 (c/n 5210), 90-2103 (c/n 5294), 93-2104 (c/n 5381), 93-2105 (c/n 5387) and 93-2106 (c/n 5388) – produced for the Air National Guard, Alaska, in the 1990s.

102 HC-130N-*LM*

Fifteen aircraft – serials 69-5819 (c/n 4363), 69-5820 (c/n 4367), 69-5821 (c/n 4368), 69-5822 (c/n 4370), 69-5823 (c/n 4371), 69-5824 (c/n 4372), 69-5825 (c/n 4374), 69-5826 (c/n 4375), 69-5827 (c/n 4376), 69-5828 (c/n 4377), 69-5829

The KC-130F, 149806 (c/n 3706), the USMC Blue Angels *support aircraft with her brood of A-4F Skyhawk fighter-bombers makes a striking picture over the Florida Keys.* (McDonnell Douglas via Audrey Pearcy)

(c/n 4378), 69-5830 (c/n 4379), 69-5831 (c/n 4380), 69-5832 (c/n 4381) and 69-5833 (c/n 4382) – produced for the AFRS in the 1970s.

103 HC-130P-*LM*

Twenty aircraft, serials 65-0988 (c/n 4143), 65-0991 (c/n 4152), 65-0992 (c/n 4155), 65-0993 (c/n 4156), 65-0994 (c/n 4157), 66-0211 (c/n 4161), 66-0212 (c/n 4162), 66-0213 (c/n 4163), 66-0214 (c/n 4164), 66-0215 (c/n 4165), 66-0216 (c/n 4166), 66-0217 (c/n 4173), 66-0218 (c/n 4174), 66-0219 (c/n 4175), 66-0220 (c/n 4179), 66-0221 (c/n 4183), 66-0222 (c/n 4184), 66-0223 (c/n 4185), 66-0224 (c/n 4186) and 66-0225 (c/n 4187).

104 JC-130A-*LM*

Sixteen aircraft, serials 53-3129 (c/n 3001), 53-3130 (c/n 3002), 53-3131 (c/n 3003), 53-3132 (c/n 3004), 53-3133 (c/n 3005), 53-3134 (c/n 3006), 53-3135 (c/n 3007), 54-1625 (c/n 3012), 54-1627 (c/n 3014), 54-1628 (c/n 3015), 54-1629 (c/n 3016), 54-1630 (c/n 3017), 54-1639 (c/n 3026), 56-0490 (c/n 3098), 56-0493 (c/n 3101) and 56-0497 (c/n 3105). Modified from C-130As for missile tracking over the Atlantic with removable test equipment.

105 JC-130B-*LM*

Fourteen aircraft, serials 57-0525 (c/n 3501), 57-0526 (c/n 3502), 57-0527 (c/n 3503), 57-0528 (c/n 3504), 57-0529 (c/n 3505); 58-0713 (c/n 3508), 58-0714 (c/n 3509), 58-0715 (c/n 3510), 58-0716 (c/n 3511), 58-0717 (c/n 3512), 58-0750 (c/n 3549), 58-0756 (c/n 3557), 61-0962 (c/n 3647) and 61-0963 (c/n 3648). Modified from C-130Bs for satellite tracking.

106 JC-130E-*LM*

One aircraft, 61-2358 (c/n 3609). Completed as a trials aircraft 1964, converted to standard C-130E 1972.

107 JC-130H-*LM*

One aircraft, serial 64-14858 (c/n 4081). An HC-130H with 6593rd Test Squadron, Hickam AFB, Hawaii. Subsequently re-designated HC-130P.

108 JHC-130H-*LM*

Seven aircraft, modified HC-130Hs, serials 64-14852 (c/n 4036), 64-14853 (c/n 4037), 64-14854 (c/n 4038), 64-14855 (c/n 4055), 64-14856 (c/n 4072), 64-14857 (c/n 4073) and 64-14858 (c/n 4081). Modified in 1965/6, re-designated HC-130H 1986/7.

109 JHC-130P

One aircraft, serial 65-0987 (c/n 4143), which was modified from an HC-130P for the US Aerospace Rescue and Recovery Service (ARRS) for tests. On 20 February 1972 this aircraft, commanded by Lieutenant Commander Edgar Allison Jr, with a representative of the *Fédération Internationale Aéronautique* (FIN) aboard, flew 8,790 miles (14,146km) from Taiwan to Scott AFB, Illinois, at heights of between 37,000 and 39,000ft (11,277 and 11,887m) and set a new long-distance flight record for a turbo-prop aircraft. Taking advantage of 70mph (112km/h) tail winds, the aircraft landed with 4,500lb (2,041kg) of reserve fuel.

110 KC-130B-*LM*

Six aircraft, C-130Bs modified as tankers for the Indonesian and Singaporean Governments, serials A-1309 (c/n 3615), A-1310 (c/n 3616), 720 (c/n 3519), 721 (c/n 3557), 724 (c/n 3611) and 725 (c/n 3620).

111 KC-130F-*LM*

Two C-130A aircraft on loan from USAF for US Navy, serials 55-0046 (c/n 3073) and 55-0048 (c/n 3075), formerly designated GVIs. Forty-six aircraft, former C-130Bs, as table.

BuNo	C/n	BuNo	C/n	BuNo	C/n	BuNo	C/n
147572	3554	148896	3623	149800	3685	159814	3723
147573	3555	148897	3627	149802	3693	149815	3725
148246	3566	148898	3631	149803	3694	149816	3726
148247	3573	148899	3632	149804	3695	150684	3727
148248	3574	149788	3640	149806	3703	150685	3728
148249	3577	149789	3644	149807	3704	150686	3733
148890	3592	149791	3657	149808	3705	150687	3734
148891	3605	149792	3658	149809	3709	150688	3740
148892	3606	149795	3664	149810	3710	150689	3741
148893	3607	149796	3665	149811	3711	150690	3742
148894	3608	149798	3680	149812	3718		
148895	3619	149799	3684	149813	3719		

112 KC-130H-*LM*

Twenty-two aircraft, as table.

Customer	Registration	C/n	Customer	Registration	C/n
Israeli AF	75-0540	4660	Spanish AF	TK10-7	4652
Israeli AF	75-0541	4664	Brazilian AF	2461	4625
Argentine AF	TC-69	4814	Brazilian AF	2462	4636
Argentine AF	TC-70	4816			

On 26 October 1968, at Williams Field, Antarctica, a propeller change is underway on an LC-130F Hercules cargo transport on the parking strip. The bleak vastness stretches out to infinity in all directions, but the Herk made herself at home even in this environment. (Naval Photograph Center, Washington DC)

Customer	Registration	C/n	Customer	Registration	C/n
Saudi AF	N79925	4503	Moroccan AF	CNA-OR	4907
Saudi AF	457	4511	Singapore	734	4940
Saudi AF	458	4532	RSAF	1620	4872
Saudi AF	459	4539	RSAF	1621	4873
Saudi AF	1616	4746	Spanish AF	TK 10-11	4871
Saudi AF	1617	4750	Spanish AF	TK 10-12	4874
Spanish AF	TK10-5	4642	Moroccan AF	CNA-OS	4909
Spanish AF	TK10-6	4648			

Excellent close-up view showing a US Navy LC-130F of VXE-6 having a bent propeller replaced in December, 1970. The prop was damaged when the aircraft was blown off the runway as she touched down. Men from VXE-6 flew in from McMurdo Station with a new engine and propeller. (Navy Photograph Center, Washington DC)

Salvage work in the Antarctic in 1977. The US Navy's 'Penguin Airlines' supports the National Science Foundation scientific research programs, relying heavily on the ski-fitted LC-130 Hercules. Naturally, accidents occurred from time to time in such extreme conditions, but in many cases, as illustrated here, salvage work was done which resulted in badly damaged aircraft being brought back into service. Bottom photo shows the damaged aircraft prior to repair. The Herk crashed while taking off from the treacherous Ice Dome, a two-mile high plateau, in January 1975 carrying an International Antarctic glaciological research team from their base. In order to repair the aircraft, the centre and starboard outer wing sections and two engines had to be replaced, not an easy task in a field camp setting. Despite average temperatures of minus 22 degrees at an altitude of 10,548 feet, the combined US Navy/Lockheed team completed the salvage operation in 45 days; 30 days ahead of schedule. Top photo shows the repaired Herk, flying with VXE-6 and piloted by Commander D. A. Desko, lifting off safely from the Ice Dome. This was the third aircraft rescued from Dome Charlie over the previous two years by the same Navy/Lockheed team. The US Navy stated that the three aircraft, valued at approximately US $27 million, were salvaged at a cost of around $2.5 million.
(Lockheed-Georgia, Marietta via Audrey Pearcy)

113 KC-130J

Seven aircraft, serials 165735 (c/n 5488), 165736 (c/n 5489), 165739 (c/n 5507), 165740 (c/n 5508), 165741 (c/n 5509), 165742 (c/n 5515) and 165743 (c/n 5516). All for the US Marine Corps.

114 KC-130R-*LM*

Fourteen aircraft for USMC, as table.

BuNo	C/n	BuNo	C/n	BuNo	C/n
160013	4615	160018	4683	160625	4768
160014	4626	160019	4689	160626	4770
160015	4629	160020	4696	160627	4773
160016	4635	160021	4702	160628	4776
160017	4677	160240	4712		

115 KC-130T

Twenty-six aircraft refuelling for the US Marine Corps, serials 162308 (c/n 4972), 162309 (c/n 4974), 162310 (c/n 4978), 162311 (c/n 4981), 162785 (c/n 5009), 162786 (c/n 5011), 163022 (c/n 5040), 163023 (c/n 5045), 163310 (c/n 5085), 163311 (c/n 5087), 163591 (c/n 5143), 163592 (c/n 5145), 164105 (c/n 5147), 164106 (c/n 5149), 164180 (c/n 5174), 164181 (c/n 5176), 164441 (c/n 5219), 164442 (c/n 5222), 164999 (c/n 5302), 165000 (c/n 5303), 165162 (c/n 5339), 165163 (c/n 5340), 165315 (c/n 5385) and 165316 (c/n 5386), 165352 (c/n 5411) and 165353 (c/n 5412).

116 KC-130T-30

Two aircraft, 'stretched' versions of the KC-130T, serials 164597 (c/n 5260) and 164598 (c/n 5263).

117 LC-130F-*LM*

Four aircraft (ex C130BL, ex UV-1L), serials 148318 ex 59-5922 (c/n 3562), 148319 ex 59-5923 (c/n 3564), 148320 ex 59-5924 (c/n 3565) and 148321 ex 59-5925 (c/n 3567).

118 LC-130H

Seven aircraft, USAF's ski-equipped C-130Ds and C-130Hs, were thus re-designated, serials 83-0490 (c/n 5007), 83-0491 (c/n 5010), 83-0492 (c/n 5013), 83-0493 (c/n 5016), 92-1094 (c/n 5402), 92-1095 (c/n 5405) and 93-1096 (c/n 5410).

119 LC-130R-*LM*

Six aircraft, serials 155917 (c/n 4305), 59129 ex 73-0839 (c/n 4508), 159130 ex 73-0840 (c/n 4516), 159131 ex 73-0841 (c/n 4522), 160740 ex 76-0491 (c/n 4725) and 160741 ex 76-0492 (c/n 4731).

120 MC-130E-C

Ten aircraft, converted for the Special Operations role (*Rivet Clamp*), serials 64-0523 (c/n 4007), 64-0551 (c/n 4046), 64-0555 (c/n 4056), 64-0559 (c/n 4062), 64-0561 (c/n 4065), 64-0562 (c/n 4068), 64-0566 (c/n 4080), 64-0567 (c/n 4083) 64-0568 (c/n 4086) and 64-0572 (c/n 4090).

121 MC-130E-S

One aircraft, *Rivet Swap*, serial 64-0571 (c/n 4087).

122 MC-130E-Y

Four aircraft, *Rivet Yank*, two of which adopted the serials of crashed Herks and were used in clandestine operations, serials 62-1843 (c/n 3991) ex 64-0507, 63-7785 (c/n 3991) ex 64-0507, 64-0564 (c/n 4074) and 64-0565 (c/n 4077).

123 MC-130H-*LM*

Twenty-four aircraft for *Combat Talon II* operations, serials 83-1212 (c/n 5004), 86-1699 (c/n 5026), 84-0475 (c/n 5041), 86-0476 (c/n 5042), 85-0011 (c/n 5053), 85-0012 (c/n 5054), 87-0023 (c/n 5091), 87-0024 (c/n 5092), 87-0125 (c/n 5115), 87-0126 (c/n 5117), 87-0127 (c/n 5118), 88-0191 (c/n 5130), 88-0192 (c/n 5131), 88-0193 (c/n 5132), 88-0194 (c/n 5133), 88-0195 (c/n 5134), 88-0264 (c/n 5135), 88-1803 (c/n 5173), 89-0280 (c/n 5236), 89-0281 (c/n 5237), 89-0282 (c/n 5243), 89-0283 (c/n 5244), 90-0161 (c/n 5265) and 90-0162 (c/n 5266).

124 MC-130P-*LM*

Twenty-eight aircraft, former HC-130N/Ps, were re-designated MC-130P-*LM Combat Shadows*, serials 64-14854 (c/n 4038), 64-14858 (c/n 4081), 65-0971 (c/n 4116), 65-0975 (c/n 4125), 65-0991 (c/n 4152), 65-0992 (c/n 4155), 65-0993 (c/n 4156), 65-0994 (c/n 4157), 66-0212 (c/n 4162), 66-0213 (c/n 4163), 66-0215 (c/n 4165), 66-0216 (c/n 4166), 66-0217 (c/n 4173), 66-0219 (c/n 4175), 66-0220 (c/n 4179), 66-0223 (c/n 4185), 66-0225 (c/n 4187), 69-5819 (c/n 4363), 69-5820 (c/n 4367), 69-5821 (c/n 4368), 69-5822 (c/n 4370), 69-5823 (c/n 4371), 69-5825 (c/n 4374), 69-5826 (c/n 4375), 69-5827 (c/n 4376), 69-5828 (c/n 4377), 69-5831 (c/n 4380) and 69-5832 (c/n 4381).

125 NC-130

Two aircraft. The original prototypes, YC-130-LOs, serials 53-3396 (c/n 1001) and 53-3397 (c/n 1002), were both re-designated NC-130s in 1959, having come to the end of their useful test-bed lives. Both were scrapped at Warner Robins AFB in October 1969 and April 1962 respectively.

126 NC-130A-*LM*

Six aircraft, temporarily re-designated C-130As and JC-130As while being utilised as the Air Force Special Weapons Center test vehicles at Kirtland AFB, New Mexico. Also applied to those Hercules used in the airborne seeker evaluation test system (ASSETS). Serials 53-3133 (c/n 3005), 54-1622 (c/n 3009), 54-1635

(c/n 3022), 55-0022 (c/n 3049), 55-0023 (c/n 3050) and 55-0024 (c/n 3051).

127 NC-130B-*LM*

Four aircraft. One aircraft, serial 58-0712 (c/n 3507), used in STOL experimentation with BLC; later employed in NASA Earth Survey Program and Airborne Instrumentation Research Program. One aircraft, 58-0717 (c/n 3512), used as a special testing machine with the 6593rd Test Squadron; another, 58-0716 (c/n 3511), used by the 514th Test Squadron, and one former JC-130B, serial 61-0962 (c/n 3647).

128 NC-130E-*LM*

Two aircraft, former C-130Es, were used as lead aircraft for the electronic special operations support (SOS) aircraft. Serials 64-0571 (c/n 4087), used for electronic intelligence-gathering (ELINT), and 64-0572 (4090). In 1979 their designations changed to MC-130E-S and MC-130E respectively.

129 NC-130H-*LM*

Five aircraft, modified HC-130Hs for test usage, serials 64-14854 (c/n 4038), 64-14857 (c/n 4073) with 6593rd Test Squadron; 65-0971 (c/n 4116), 65-0979 (c/n 4131) with 514th Test Squadron; and 87-0157(c/n 5121) with 418th Test Squadron. The designation was later changed to JHC-130H.

130 PC-130H

Four aircraft built as maritime patrol aircraft, three for Malaysia and one for Indonesia, serials FM2451 (c/n 4847), FM2452 (c/n 4849), FM2453 (c/n 4866) and AI-1322 (c/n 4898). The designation was changed to C-130H-MP before delivery.
See C-130H-MP section.

131 RC-130A-*LM*

One aircraft was trial-converted to an RC-130A (R for Reconnaissance), serial 54-1632 (c/n 3019), from a TC-130A. She was subsequently converted back to a standard C-130A. Fifteen aircraft, new-build RC-130As, were specifically built for the Hiran

Line-up of Hercules of the Belgian Air Force C-130Hs.
(Jean-Charles Boreux via Nick Williams AAHS)

electronic surveying, Hiran controlled photography and mapping photography missions, serials 57-0510 (c/n 3217), 57-0511 (c/n 3218), 57-0512 (c/n 3219), 57-0513 (c/n 3220), 57-0514 (c/n 3221), 57-0515 (c/n 3222), 57-0516 (c/n 3223), 57-0517 (c/n 3224), 57-0518 (c/n 3225), 57-0519 (c/n 3226), 57-0520 (c/n 3227), 57-0521 (c/n 3228), 57-0522 (c/n 3229), 57-0523 (c/n 3230) and 57-0524 (c/n 3231).

132 RC-130B-*LM*

Thirteen new-build but modified RC-130Bs, serials 58-0711 (c/n 3506), 58-0723 (c/n 3518), 59-1524 (c/n 3560), 59-1525 (c/n 3561), 59-1526 (c/n 3563), 59-1527 (c/n 3568), 59-1528 (c/n 3571), 59-1530 (c/n 3576), 59-1531 (c/n 3579), 59-1532 (c/n 3581), 59-1533 (c/n 3586), 59-1535 (c/n 3585) and 59-1537 (c/n 3589). All were re-designated C-130B-II *Sun Valley II*s.

133 RC-130S

Two aircraft, JC-130As, modified under the Shed Light programme to illuminate the Ho Chi Minh trail in Vietnam as *Bias Hunters*, serials 56-0493 (c/n 3101) and 56-0497 (c/n 3105), but both were later re-converted to standard C-130As again. Two others were to be so converted but this was not done.

134 R8V-1G

Twelve aircraft converted for search and rescue missions as either the SC-130B (USAF) or R8V-1G (USN), serials CG 1339 ex 58-5396 (c/n 3529), CG 1340 ex 58-5397 (c/n 3533), CG 1341 ex 58-6973 (c/n 3542), CG 1342 ex 58-6974 (c/n 3548), CG 1344 ex 60-0311 (c/n 3594), CG 1345 ex 60-0312 (c/n 3595), CG 1346 ex 61-0958 (c/n 3638), CG 1347 ex 61-2082 (c/n 3641), CG 1348 ex 61-2083 (c/n 3650), CG 1349 ex 62-3753 (c/n 3745), CG 1350 ex 62-3754 (c/n 3763) and CG 1351 ex 62-3755 (c/n 3773). These designations were changed when they joined the US Coast Guard to HC-130B-*LM*s.

135 SC-130B-*LM*

Twelve aircraft, as R8V-1Gs above.

136 TC-130A-*LM*

One aircraft, the prototype RC-130A (R for Reconnaissance), serial 54-1632 (c/n 3019), modified from a TC-130A. She was subsequently converted back to a standard C-130A.

137 TC-130G

Three aircraft, retired from the *TACAMO* mission, were allocated this designation as trainer/utility aircraft, serials 151888 (c/n 3849), 151889 (c/n 3858) and 151891 (c/n 3878). In the event only the first two received this designation before being struck from charge, while the latter became a support aircraft for the Blue Angels formation team.

138 TC-130Q

Four aircraft, former US Navy EC-130Qs, were thus re-designated for use as trainers and utility transports, serials 156170 (c/n 4239), 156174 (c/n 4278), 159469 (c/n 4595) and 159348 (c/n 4601).

139 UV-1L

Four aircraft, ski-equipped for the US Navy (ordered by the USAF as the C-130BL on behalf of the Navy), serials 148318 ex 59-5922 (c/n 3562), 148319 ex 59-5923 (c/n 3564), 148320 ex 59-5924 (c/n 3565) and 148321 ex 59-5925 (c/n 3567). On delivery the Navy re-designated them UV-1L. In September 1962 they became LC-130F-*LM*s.

140 VC-130B-*LM*

One aircraft, former JC-130B, modified as a staff transport under this designation, serial 58-714 (c/n 3510). Later re-modified to a C-130B.

141 VC-130H-*LM*

Seven aircraft, modified C-130Hs as VIP aircraft with larger, squared windows in the main fuselage, first-class seating accommodation, deeper sound-proofing and a built-in service galley and toilet module. Built for the Government of Egypt (two) and the Government (two) and Royal Family (three) of Saudi Arabia between July 1975 and 1984. Registrations SU-BAM (c/n 4803) and SU-BAV (c/n 4811); serials 102 (c/n 4605) and 112 (c/n 4737); registrations HZ-115 (c/n 4845), HZ-114 (c/n 4843) and HZ-116 (c/n 4915).

142 WC-130A

Three aircraft, modified from C-130As for weather experimentation services, including the Operation 'Popeye' rain-inducement trials in December 1970, serials 56-0519 (c/n 3127), 56-0522 (c/n 3130) and 56-0537 (c/n 3145).

143 WC-130B-*LM*

Five aircraft, modified C-130Bs, serials 62-3492 (c/n 3702), 62-3493 (c/n 3707), 62-3494 (c/n 3708), 62-3495 (c/n 3721) and 62-3496 (c/n 3722).

144 WC-130E-*LM*

Three aircraft, modified C-130Es, serials 64-0552 (c/n 4047), 64-0553 (c/n 4048) and 64-0554 (c/n 4049). Three aircraft, former serving C-130Es, serials 61-2360 (c/n 3659), 61-2365 (c/n 3688) and 61-2366 (c/n 3706).

145 WC-130H-*LM*

Fifteen aircraft, former HC-130H and C-130Hs in 1957, serials 64-14861 (c/n 4088), 64-14866 (c/n 4099), 65-0963 (c/n 4103), 65-0964 (c/n 4104), 65-0965 (c/n 4106), 65-0966 (c/n 4107), 65-0967 (c/n 4108), 65-0968 (c/n 4110), 65-0969 (c/n 4111), 65-0972 (c/n 4120), 65-0976 (c/n 4126), 65-0977 (c/n 4127), 65-0980 (c/n 4132), 65-0984 (c/n 4139) and 65-0985 (c/n 4140). One aircraft (65-0965) lost over the Taiwan Straits on 13 October 1974.

146 WC-130J

hree aircraft – serials 96-5300 (c/n 5451), 96-5301 (c/n 5452) and 96-5302 (c/n 5453) – which joined AFRES units. Seven aircraft – serials 97-5303 (c/n 5473), 97-5304 (c/n 5474), 97-5305 (c/n 5475), 97-5306 (c/n 5476), 98-5307 (c/n 5486), 98-5308 (c/n 5486) and 99-5309 (c/n 5501) – all with 53rd AFRES.

147 YC-130-*LO*

wo aircraft, the original prototype YC-130-*LO*s (Model 082-44-01), USAF serials 53-3396 (c/n 1001) and 53-3397 (c/n 1002), completed in 1955. They were re-designated NC-130s in 1959.

148 YMC-130H-*LM*

hree aircraft, modified C-130Hs with DC-130 radome, in-flight refuelling and ventral activating retro-rockets in 1980, as proposed rescue aircraft for US citizens illegally held in Iran (Operation 'Eagle Claw'). Those modified were designated YMC-130H-LMs *Credible Support*, serials 74-1683 (c/n 4658), 74-1686 (c/n 4667) and 74-2065 (c/n 4669). Of these, 74-1683 (c/n 4658) was lost in an accident at Duke Field on 29 October 1980 due to premature use of retros, and in November 1984 the two survivors reverted to C-130H status, 74-1686 (c/n 4667) ending her days in the Air Museum at Warner-Robins AFB.

The Worldwide Operators of Hercules – Military

149 Abu Dhabi and Dubai (*United Arab Emirates Air Force*)

Two C-130Hs, 382C-40D, registrations 1211 (c/n 4580) and 1212 (c/n 4584), were purchased for Abu Dhabi and Dubai (the former Trucial States of the Arabian Gulf) in March 1975. They served for seven years and in September 1982 were sold back to Lockheed as part exchange for two replacement aircraft, C-130Hs, 382-54E, registrations N4161T (c/n 4983) and N4249Y (c/n 4985), which took over their registration numbers.

In 1976, following a state visit two years earlier by President Habib Bourguiba of Tunisia, Sheikh Zayed Bin Sultan Al Nahyan used the Hercules to fulfil his dream of making his tiny city-state green by turning it into an oasis of trees and flowers. The Tunisian leader offered to help by gifting date palm trees of the Tunisian variety, the hardiest there were and secretly cultivated, to the Gulf – one of the most unusual cargoes hauled by the C-130, each Hercules carrying approximately 2,000 of the 4ft (1.2m) high, 20lb (9kg) date palms each journey. Under mission commander Major Nasseer Saadeh, each date palm was dug up, the roots carefully packed in wooden boxes, and the delicate fronds sprayed just prior to take-off to keep the moisture level satisfactory for the long haul. On arrival in Abu Dhabi the military precision of the operation continued, with twenty trucks shuttling the precious cargo to special nurseries.

Two more C-130Hs, 382C-14E, registrations N4140M (c/n 4879) and N4147M (c/n 4882), were purchased in February 1981 and took the registrations 1213 and 1214 respectively.

150 Algerian Air Force (*Al Quwwat al Jawwiya al Jaza'eriya*)

The then *Force Aérienne Algérienne* took delivery of two *Combat Talon* C-130H-30s, 7T-VHN 8112 (c/n 4894) delivered in July and 7T-VHO 8112 (c/n 4897) in August 1981.

A total of eleven C-130Hs were delivered between April and September 1982: 7T-WHT (c/n 4911), 7T-WHS (c/n 4912), 7T-WHY (c/n 4913), 7T-WHZ (c/n 4914), 7T-VHM (c/n 4919) later re-registered as 7T-WHM, 7T-VHP (c/n 4921) later re-registered as 7T-WHP, 7T-WHR (c/n 4924), 7T-WHQ (c/n 4926), 7T-WHJ (c/n 4928), 7T-WHI (c/n 4930) and 7T-WHF (c/n 4934). They were supplemented by four further C-130H-30 *Combat Talons* – 7T-WHE (c/n 4935), 7T-WHD (c/n 4987), 7T-WHL (c/n 4989) and 7T-WHA (c/n 4997) – which arrived between September 1982 and June 1984. Finally, a fifth aircraft of this type, 7T-WHB (c/n 5224), was not delivered until November 1990.

One of their first missions was a search for the son of British Prime Minister Margaret Thatcher, who lost himself in the Sahara near the border with Mali during a car race. One of the Herks, with a joint Algerian trainee crew/Lockheed instructional crew, found him at noon on 14 January 1982. After pinpointing Mark Thatcher's position using the Herk's inertial navigation system (INS), they called up a ground rescue team before refuelling at Tamanrasset. Later that same day they flew the lost rally driver's father and the British Ambassador, Benjamin Strachan, and vectored a Land Rover rescue team to his location.

The survivors are operated by *Escadrilles* 31, 32, 33 and 35.

151 Argentine Air Force (*Fuerza Aérea Argentina*)

Three former USAF C-130Bs were delivered to Argentina: ex 58-0720 (c/n 3515) in January 1994, which became TC-56, ex 58-0741 (c/n 3538) in November 1992, which became TC-58, ex 59-1526 (c/n 3563) in November 1994, which became TC-57.

Three C-130Es were delivered in 1968: TC-61 (c/n 4308), modified in 1977 to a C-130H, TC-62 (c/n 4309), destroyed in a bomb explosion at Tucuman airfield on 28 August 1975, and TC-63 (c/n 4310), destroyed in combat by a Sea Harrier during the Falklands War on 1 June 1982.

Five C-130Hs arrived fresh from the Lockheed factory between December 1971 and March 1976: TC-64

This Belgian Air Force C-130A, serial CH-01 (c/n 4455), makes a port wing-over for the camera. (Martin W. Bowman)

(c/n 4436), TC-66 (c/n 4437), TC-66 (c/n 4464), TC-67 (c/n 4576) and TC-68 (c/n 4578), the latter made over into a makeshift bomber during the Falklands War of 1982.

A solitary KC-130H was delivered in April 1974, TC-60 (c/n 4814). Most of these aircraft were flown by *1 Esquadron de Transporte, Grupo 1 de Transporte Aero* based at El Plomar.

Finally, a single Lockheed L-100-30 demonstration aircraft, N4248M (c/n 4891), was purchased by *Fuerza Aérea Argentina* in December 1982. Re-registered as LV-APW in February 1982, she was operated by the LADE company.

152 Bangladesh

The Bangladeshi Government took delivery of four former USAF C-130Bs in the late 1990s: ex 58-0754 (c/n 3553), ex 59-1537 (c/n 3589), ex 61-0962 (c/n 3647) and ex 61-2640 (c/n 3676).

153 Belgian Air Force (*Force Aérienne Belge*)

Twelve C-130Hs were delivered to Belgium between June 1972 and 1973, and formed *20 Amaldeel*, *Groupement de Transporte*, with 15 Wing, based at Melsbroek airfield near Brussels. Operated by *Force Aérienne Belge*, they have been widely utilised in humanitarian and relief roles for the United Nations. Serial CH-01 (c/n 4455), CH-02 (c/n 4460), CH-03 (c/n 4461), CH-04 (c/n 4467), CH-05 (c/n 4470), CH-06 (c/n 4473), CH-07 (c/n 4476), CH-08 (c/n 4478), CH-09 (c/n 4479), CH-10 (c/n 4481), CH-11 (c/n 4482) and CH-12 (c/n 4483).

154 Bolivian Air Force (*Fuerza Aérea Boliviana*)

The following aircraft were on the strength of the *Fuerza Aérea Boliviana* at various times, but mainly operated by the peacetime civilian arm, the *Transporte Aéro Bolivano* or TAB (see appropriate section), and painted in airline colours performing commercial as well as civil air lift missions, operated from the world's highest commercial airport, the 14,100ft (4,298m) high La Paz International. This made Bolivia the eighth South American nation to fly the C-130.

Seven former USAF C-130As: TAM64 (c/n 3023), TAM65 (c/n 3034), TAM66 (c/n 3144) which became CP-2187 in 1996, TAM61 (c/n 3181), TAM62 (c/n 3187), TAM63 (c/n 3188) and TAM69 (c/n 3228) which became CP-2184. Four former USAF C-130Bs: TAM60 (c/n 3559), TAM66 (c/n 3560), TAM67 (c/n 3581) and TAM68

The Belgian Air Force, the Force Aérienne Belge *received the first of twelve C-130H Hercules in 1972. They formed 20 Squadron (Smaldeel) of the* Groupement de Transport, *which operated under 15 Wing at Melsbroek airfield near Brussels. They were widely used for United Nations work in Africa. CH-01, seen here arriving, wears the standard camouflage pattern which was later changed to white overall. (Lockheed-Georgia, Marietta via Audrey Pearcy)*

(c/n 3655). TAM67 was lost at Trinidad Airport, Bolivia, on 31 December 1994, and TAM60 crashed on take-off from Chimorre airfield, Bolivia, on 14 January 2000, while the rest were ultimately placed in storage.

Two C-130Hs, TAM90 (c/n 4744) and TAM91 (c/n 4759), were directly purchased in 1977.

Finally, the Bolivian Government purchased a single L-100-30 from Lockheed in October 1979, the former N4083M (c/n 4833), for the *Fuerza Aérea Boliviana* which became their TAM92 and was leased and operated for them by TAB as CP-1564.

155 Botswana Air Force

Three former USAF C-130 and B-IIs – the ex 58-0711 (c/n 3506) in November 1996, the ex 58-0742 (c/n 3539) in October 1999 and the ex 58-0746 (c/n 3544) in February 1997 – were made available to the Botswana Government. They were re-registered OM-1, OM-3 and OM-2 respectively.

156 Brazilian Air Force (*Forca Aérea Brasileira*)

The *Forca Aérea Brasileira* took delivery of eight brand-new C-130Es: 2450 (c/n 4091) delivered in November 1965, 2451 (c/n 4092), 2452 (c/n 4093) which crash-landed on 26 October 1966, 2453 (c/n 4113) delivered in December 1965, which served for the United Nations in Angola in 1999, 2454 (c/n 4114), 2455 (c/n 4202) delivered in March 1967, 2456 (c/n 4287) delivered in July 1968, and 2457 (c/n 4290) delivered in August 1968, which crashed in fog near Santa Maria Airbase on 24 June 1985.

Three further C-130Es, but which featured three-windowed paratroop doors, were also received: 2458 (c/n 4291) delivered November 1968, 2459 (c/n 4292), and 2460 (c/n 4293) which was burnt out at Formosa airfield, Brazil, on 14 October 1994.

Four C-130Hs arrived between March and November 1975 – 2463 (c/n 4570), 2464 (c/n 4602), 2465 (c/n 4630) and 2462 (c/n 4636) – and were joined by a solitary KC-130H, registration 2461 (c/n 4625), in October 1975. They were joined by three later C-130H acquisitions from the Lockheed pool: 2466 (c/n 4990) in February 1984, 2467 (c/n 4991) in October 1988 and 2468 (c/n 4998) in January 1987, the last of which crashed into the sea off Fernando de Noronha on 14 December 1987.

They all mainly served with *1⁰ Esquadrão of 1 Gruppo*, based at Galeaoa near Rio de Janeiro, as paratroop carriers, but some were fitted with skis and had a stint with the *2⁰ Esquadrão* running down to Antarctica before reverting again. Like most South American nations, the Herks were widely used in governmental commercial projects, like aiding the construction of the Trans-Amazon Highway.

In March 2001, Lockheed sold ten refurbished C-130Hs to Brazil for $76 million, with deliveries due between May 2001 and November 2002. All were former Italian aircraft.

157 Cameroon Air Force (*L'Armée de l'Air de Cameroun*)

A pair of C-130Hs were obtained in August and September 1977, which operated services from Douala to other Cameroon cities with Cameroon Airlines. One, TJX-AC (c/n 4747), crashed at Marseilles airport in December 1989 and was subsequently re-built at Bordeaux. The other was TJX-AD (c/n 4752). These two were joined by a single C-130H, TJX-AE (c/n 4933), in June 1982, which was later registered TJX-CE.

Although carrying civilian registrations and being used as President Omar Bongo's official aircraft, the Herks were frequently used in the passenger/freight role. Their routine was to pick up transferred imported air cargo from Douala and haul it to Yaounde, Garoua, Marou and Ngounder in the Cameroon, Libreville in Gabon, Bangui in the Central African Republic and Malabo in Equatorial Guinea. They also made twelve flights to transport 1,104 pilgrims, ninety-two at a time, from Douala to Mecca, Saudi Arabia, and football teams to Nairobi in Kenya, Accra in Ghana and Lagos in Nigeria. These Herks also performed in the counter-insurgency war role, working out of Batouri, Garoua and Yaounde airfields.

158 Chad Air Force (*Force Aérienne Tchadienne*)

Seven Hercules have served with the *Force Aérienne Tchadienne* since 1963, including four former USAF C-130As: the ex 54-1634 (c/n 3020) in August 1984, registered as TT-PAB, which subsequently crashed on take-off on 7 March 1986; the ex 55-0010 (c/n 3037), re-registered TT-PAE, impounded by the Portuguese Government in 1990 and subsequently sold for spare parts; the ex 56-0550 (c/n 3159), re-registered TT-PAC, which crash-landed on 16 November 1987; and the ex 57-0473 (c/n 3180), re-registered TT-PAD, also impounded and then sold off by the Portuguese Government.

One further C-130A was obtained in November 1983 by the French *Securité Civile* for the Chad Government, the former Australian 57-0501/A97-208 (c/n 3208), which became TT-PAA.

More recently, two brand-new Herks were obtained: a C-130H, N73238 (c/n 5141), in 1988 from GELAC, re-registered TT-PAF; and a C-130H-30 (c/n 5184) in 1989, which became TT-AAH.

Colombian Air Force's first Herk, FAC1001 (c/n 3512), at Merino Benitez Airfield near Santiago in 1972. (Lockheed-Georgia, Marietta via Audrey Pearcy)

159 Chilean Air Force (*Fuerza Aérea de Chile*)

T wo C-130Hs were purchased in 1972, the 995 (c/n 4453) and the 996 (c/n 4496). This pair has been supplemented in the *10 Grupo de Aviacion* by four former USAF C-130Bs obtained in 1992: the ex 58-0752 (c/n 3551) which became 997; the ex 61-0310 (c/n 3622) becoming 994; the ex 61-09567 (c/n 3637) becoming 993; and the ex 61-2647 (c/n 3690) re-registered 998. They are all based at Merino Benitz Airbase near Santiago.

160 Colombian Air Force (*Fuerza Aérea Colombiana*)

T o operate with the Air Force's *Escuadron de Transporte* from Eldorado airfield near Bogotá, the *Fuerza Aérea Colombiana* initially obtained three former RCAF C-130Bs from Lockheed in 1968: the ex RCAF 10301/Lockheed N4652 (c/n 3572) which became FAC 1003 in 1969, and ran out of fuel due to navigation error and was lost in the sea off Cape May, New Jersey, on 16 October 1982; the ex RCAF 10302/Lockheed N4653 (c/n 3575) which became FAC 1001 in 1968; and the ex-RCAF 10303/Lockheed N4654 (c/n 3587) which became the FAC 1002, but crash-landed and burned at Bogotá on 26 August 1969.

Eight further USAF surplus C-130Bs were acquired on loan to the Colombian Government from 1990 to help with anti-drug-running operations: the ex USAF 58-0717 (c/n 3512) which became FAC 1006, the ex USAF 59-0726 (c/n 3521), the ex-58-0735 (c/n 3531) which was subsequently lost in a crash-landing in July 1995, the ex USAF 58-0757 (c/n 3558), the ex 59-1535 (c/n 3585) which became FAC 1011, the ex 61-0956 (c/n 3635) which became FAC 1012, the ex 61-2639 (c/n 3675) and the ex 62-3487(c/n 3697) which became the FAC 1009.

Finally, two brand-new C-130Hs were obtained in 1983, FAC 1004 (c/n 4964) and FAC 1005 (c/n 4965).

161 Dubai Air Force

Two L-100-30s – 311 (c/n 4834), the former Lockheed stock N4085M, in January 1981, and the new-build 312 (c/n 4961) in April 1984 – were purchased by Dubai and work as part of the United Emirates Air Forces.

162 Ecuador Air Force
(*Fuerza Aérea Ecuatoriana*)

A quartet of former USAF C-130Bs: 57-0525 (c/n 3501) was purchased in 1992, becoming their number 894; 57-0529 (c/n 3505) was purchased in 1993, becoming 895; 58-0733 (c/n 3528) became 896 in 1992; and 61-2645 (c/n 3683) became 897. All were utilised by the Government of Ecuador. The *Fuerza Aérea Ecuatoriana* also purchased three new, C-130Hs between 1977 and 1979: HC-BEF (c/n 4743) as 743, number 748 (c/n 4748) and HC-BGO (c/n 4812) as number 892.

A solitary L-100-30, N4175M (c/n 4893), was purchased from Lockheed and became FAE893. She was damaged in an accident at Guayaquil in June 1992.

163 Egyptian Air Force
(*Al Quwwat Ali Jawwiya Ilmisriya*)

Six C-130Hs were allocated to Egypt from the 1976 USAF schedule and delivered between December 1976 and April 1977: SU-BAA (c/n 4707) later re-registered 1270, which was burnt at Larnaca, Cyprus, during an anti-terrorist operation, SU-BAB (c/n 4709) re-registered as 1271, SU-BAC (c/n 4714) re-registered as 1272, SU-BAD (c/n 4719) re-registered as 1273, SU-BAE (c/n 4721) re-registered as 1274 and SU-BAF (c/n 4728), re-registered as 1275.

They were followed into service by a further four C-130Hs delivered in October/November 1978: SU-BAH (c/n 4792) later re-registered as 1276, which crashed on take-off from Cairo West Airport on 29 May 1981, SU-BAI (c/n 4794) re-registered as 1277, SU-BAJ (c/n 4795) re-registered as 1278, and SU-BAK (c/n 4797) which became 1279.

Between January and March 1979 a further nine brand-new C-130Hs were delivered: SU-BAL (c/n 4802) which became 1280, SU-BAM (c/n 4803) later 1281, SU-BAN (c/n 4804) later 1282, SU-BAP (c/n 4805) later 1283, SU-BAQ (c/n 4806) later 1284, SU-BAR (c/n 4807) later 1285, SU-BAS (c/n 4808) later 1286, SU-BAT (c/n 4809)

later 1287, and SU-BAU (c/n 4810) later 1288. They were based at Cairo East airfield, near Heliopolis. A tenth C-130H, SU-BAV (c/n 4811), was also delivered in March 1979, but was modified to a VC-130H for VIP use. She was later re-registered 1289.

Yet a third batch of three new C-130Hs arrived in September/October 1982: SU-BEW (c/n 4936) later re-registered as 1290, SU-BEX (c/n 4937) later 1291, and SU-BEX (c/n 4938) later 1292. The last two have been converted to conduct ECM/ELINT duties, while the remainder are utilised as conventional transports.

A second stretched version C-130-H arrived in June 1990, also for use as a VIP aircraft; this was SU-BKS (c/n 5187), which took the number 1293. A third of the same type, SU-BKT (c/n 5191), later 1294, arrived in August of the same year but was lost in an accident near Dover, Delaware, in May 1999. The fourth and final C-130-H, SU-BKU (c/n 5206), was delivered in August 1990 and took the number 1295.

164 Ethiopian Air Force

Four former USAF C-130Bs were operated by the Ethiopian Air Force for a decade from 1998, after purchase from store: 61-0954 (c/n 3633) as their 1561, 61-2635 (c/n 3671) which became 1562, 61-2636 (c/n 3672) which became 1563, and 61-2638 (c/n 3674) which became 1564.

165 French Air Force (*L'Armée de l'Air*)

Despite a strong nationalistic policy of using only home-built aircraft, the versatile Hercules proved irresistible and finally featured in the *L'Armée de l'Air* inventory with the arrival of two confiscated Zaire Air Force C-130Hs, which were impounded at Malpensa airfield, Milan, in February 1982, and later used to equip the *Escadron de Transport 2/61*, based at Bricy airfield near Orleans. These were the former 9T-TCF (c/n 4588) and 9T-TCC (c/n 4589), which were initially given the French registrations 61-PM and 61-PN, and later became F-RAPM and F-RAPN respectively.

Three more brand-new C-130Hs – F-RAPA (c/n 5114) later 61-PA, F-RAPB (c/n 5116) later 61-PB, and F-RAPC (c/n 5119) later 61-PC – joined them in December 1987.

To further increase the unit's capability, three stretched-version C-130H-30s were purchased in August/September 1988: F-RAPD (c/n 5140) later 61-PD, F-RAPE (c/n 5142) later 61-PE, and F-RAPF (c/n 5144) later 61-PF.

A further batch of four L-130H-30s was purchased in March 1989: the former Lockheed N4242N (c/n 5150) which became F-RAPG, later 61-PG, F-RAPH (c/n 5151) later 61-PH, F-RAPI (c/n 5152) later 61-PI, and the former Lockheed N73235 (c/n 5153) which became F-RAP, later 61-PJ.

Finally, another brace of C-130H-30s arrived in March 1991: F-RAPK (c/n 5226) later 61-PK, and F-RAPL (c/n 5227) later 61-PL.

166 French *Securité Civile*

Two C-130As, the former USAF 54-1631 (c/n 3018) and the former USAF 56-0478 (c/n 3086), both of which had been modified as water tankers and were flying with T&G Aviation as N117TG and N116TG, were used by the French Government's *Securité Civile* in that role in Corsica between 1992 and 1995, but there are claims that the organisation is the French equivalent of the CIA[27] and also conducted covert operations with them in Chad for two years. At one time they carried the names *Iron Butterfly* and *City of Phoenix* respectively, and they later reverted to T&G once more.

Two more C-130As, the former USAF 56-0530 (c/n 3138) and 56-0540 (c/n 3148), similarly converted to water bombers and registered with Aero Firefighting Service as N131FF and N135FF respectively. They were sub-leased to the French Government from Hemet in 1993, taking the numbers 81 and 82, before reverting once more.

The *Securité Civile* also acted as a broker for the Chad Government in 1983 by obtaining two further C-130As, the former USAF 57-0501 (c/n 3208) and 57-0512 (c/n 3219), modified as water bombers and registered with Ford & Vlahos as N4445V, and T&G as N118TG respectively, the latter for spares.

167 Gabon Air Force (*Force Aérienne Gabonaise*)

The West African state of Gabon operated two L-100s commercially and in 1977 ordered a further single C-130H, TR-KKC (c/n 4765), which was delivered in February 1978 and was still flying in 1998.

An L-100-20, TR-KKB (c/n 4710), was purchased from Lockheed in December 1976 and, despite a ground accident and being placed on sale, was still flying as late as 1997.

The Gabonese Government utilised their Hercules as flying trucks to support country-building projects like the construction of the Trans-Gabon Railway and the airlifting of people and products into and out of interior communities not served by a good surface transportation system. They also flew them on cargo hauling to and from Europe. They were also flown as passenger aircraft, with the quick-change pallet system being employed to roll on seating for ninety-one passengers, with a double toilet and a hot and cold galley. They also had a decorative ceiling and extra sound-proofing, with an overhead stereo system. One strange cargo, strange even by the Herk's catholic standards, was the transference of a whole supermarket complex from Libreville to a provincial town.

Two L-100-30s, TR-KKA (c/n 4582), April 1975, and TR-KKD (c/n 4895), September 1981, were purchased from Lockheed, the latter, *N'tem*, for use as the presidential aircraft. They served with the *Escadrille de Transport* from Leon M'Ba Airport near Libreville until 1989 and July 1988 respectively, when the former was sold to Pegasus Aviation and the latter was leased to Schreiner Airways.

168 Honduras Air Force (*Fuerza Aérea Hondurena*)

Four C-130As – the former USAF numbers 54-1635 (c/n 3022) which became FAH560, 55-0003 (c/n 3030) which became FAH557, 55-0015 (c/n 3042) which became FAH558, and 57-0476 (c/n 3183) which became FAH559 – were obtained between 1986 and 1989 and operated by the *Escadrilla de Transporte* from Tocontin Airport at Tegucigalpa for many years.

A solitary C-130D, the former USAF 57-0487 (c/n 3194), was purchased in 1986 and became FAH556, but she crashed at Wampusirpi on 14 August 1986.

169 Imperial Iranian Air Force (*Nirou Haval Shahanshahiye Iran*)

While the pro-Western Shah was still in power in Iran, he took the greatest pride in building up the *Nirou Haval Shahanshahiye Iran*, along with Iran's other armed forces, with the latest technology, and large orders were placed which included the Hercules, and

Iran's Herk force was at one time one of the strongest outside the USA, only ranking below that of the RAF.

The first order, in June 1962, was for a quartet of new C-130Bs obtained through the US Government's Military Assistance Program, and these aircraft were initially assigned USAF serials: 62-3488 (c/n 3698) which became Iran's 5-101, 62-3489 (c/n 3699) which became 5-102, 62-3490 (c/n 3700) which became 5-103, and 62-3491 (c/n 3701) which became 5-104. In use with 5 Air Transport Squadron based at Mehrabad International Airport near Tehran, these were all soon sold off to Pakistan (see appropriate section).

Four brand-new C-130Es followed, from December 1965 to January 1966: 5-105 (c/n 4115) subsequently re-numbered 5-101 and then 5-850, 5-106 (c/n 4117) later 5-102 and sold to Pakistan as 10687, 5-107 (c/n 4118) which was struck by lightning and burnt out on 18 April 1967, and 5-108 (c/n 4119) later 5-103, then sold to Pakistan as 10689.

A second batch of four more C-130Es followed in June/July 1966: 5-109 (c/n 4148) later 5-104, then sold to Pakistan as their 64310, 5-110 (c/n 4149) later 5-105, then 5-8502, 5-111 (c/n 4153) later 5-106 and sold to Pakistan

Like Libya before Gadaffi, Iran under the Shah was staunchly pro-western in outlook and the Imperial Iranian Air Force (Nirou haval Shahanshahiye Iran, IIAF) had no trouble in obtaining a large fleet of Hercules between 1962 and 1975. No less than sixty-four Herks served with the Shah's forces, comprising four C-130Bs, twenty-eight C-130Es and thirty-two C-130Hs which made Iran's fleet third largest (after the USA and UK) in the Herk fleets of the 1960s. (Lockheed-Georgia, Marietta via Audrey Pearcy)

as their 64312, and 5-112 (c/n 4154) later 5-112, which crashed at Shiraz during engine trials on 7 April 1969.

Nine more C-130Hs formed the third order, between May and October 1968: 5-113 (c/n 4276) later 5-107, then 5-8503, 5-114 (c/n 4282) later 5-108, and sold to Pakistan as their 14727, 5-115 (c/n 4283) later 5-109, then 5-8504, 5-116 (c/n 4284) later 5-110, then 5-8505, 5-117 (c/n 4294) later 5-111, then 5-8506, sold to Pakistan as their 97706, 5-118 (c/n 4295) later 5-112, then 5-8507, 5-119 (c/n 4296) later 5-113, then 5-8508, 5-120 (c/n 4297) later 5-114, then 5-8509, and 5-121 (c/n 4298) later 5-115, then 5-8510.

A fourth and final order for eleven more C-130Es followed between January 1970 and January 1971: 5-122 (c/n 4365) later becoming 5-116, then 5-8511, 5-123 (c/n 4386) later 5-117, then 5-8512, 5-124 (c/n 4387) later 5-118, then 5-8513, 5-125 (c/n 4389) later 5-119, then 5-8514, the former Lockheed demonstrator N7927S (c/n 4390) which became 5-126, then 5-120 and later 5-8515, 5-127 (c/n 4392) September 1970, later 5-121, 5-128 (c/n 4393) September 1970, later 5-122, which crashed near Mehrabad on 28 February 1974, 5-129 (c/n 4394) October 1970, later 5-123, then 5-8517, 5-130 (c/n 4398) November 1970, later 5-124, then 5-8518, 5-131 (c/n 4399) December 1970, later 5-125, then 5-8519, and 5-132 (c/n 4402) January 1971, later 5-126, then 5-8520, which crashed at Shiraz on 19 June 1979.

With the arrival of the C-130H, even larger orders were placed by the *Nirou Haval Shahanshahiye Iran*, the first batch of thirty such aircraft being delivered between November 1971 and April 1973: 5-133 (c/n 4432), later re-registered 5-127, then 5-8521, which was destroyed by Armenian guerrillas at Stepanakert, Nagorno-Karabach, on 17 March 1994; 5-134 (c/n 4433), later 5-128, then 5-8522; 5-135 (c/n 4438), later 5-129, then 5-8523; 5-136 (c/n 4439), later 5-130, then 5-8524; 5-137 (c/n 4440), later 5-131, then 5-8525; 5-138 (c/n 4442), later 5-132, then 5-8526; 5-139 (c/n 4444), later 5-133, then 5-8527; 5-140 (c/n 4445), later 5-134, then 5-8528; 5-141 (c/n 4448), later 5-135, then 5-8529; 5-142 (c/n 4454), later 5-136, then 5-8530; 5-143 (c/n 4456), later 5-137, then 5-8531; 5-144 (c/n 4457), later 5-138, then 5-8532; 5-145 (c/n 4458), later 5-139, then 5-8533; 5-146 (c/n 4459), later 5-140, then 5-8534; 5-147 (c/n 4462), later 5-141, then 5-8535; 5-148 (c/n 4463), later 5-142, then 5-8536; 5-149 (c/n 4465), later 5-143, then 5-8537; 5-150 (c/n 4466), later 5-144, then 5-8538; 5-151 (c/n 4468), later 5-145, then 5-8539; 5-152 (c/n 4469), later 5-146, then 5-8540; 5-153 (c/n 4471), later 5-147, then 5-8541; 5-154 (c/n 4474), later 5-148, then 5-8542; 5-155 (c/n 4480), later 5-140, then 5-8543; 5-156 (c/n 4484), later 5-150, then 5-8544; 5-157 (c/n 4485), later 5-151, then 5-8545; 5-158 (c/n 4486), later 5-152, then 5-8546; 5-159 (c/n 4487), later 5-153, then 5-8547; 5-160 (c/n 4488), later 5-154, then 5-8548; 5-161 (c/n 4489), later 5-155, then 5-8549; and 5-162 (c/n 4490), later 5-156, then 5-8550.

Two final C-130Hs reached Iran in May 1975, ordered before the overthrow of the Government and before the violently anti-Western Ayatollahs took over, serials 5-157 (c/n 4591) later 5-8551, and 5-158 (c/n 4594) later 5-8552, the latter of which crashed at Kahrisak on 29 September 1981 with the Defence Minister aboard.

Most of these aircraft initially served with transport units based at Shirah, but four have been converted to perform the ELINT intelligence-gathering role. Since the overthrow of the Shah seven have been lost in accidents, while many of the remainder, some of which served through the Iran/Iraq conflict, have been grounded through lack of maintenance and spares, and only a few remain operational.

170 Indonesian Air Force (*Angkatan Udara Republik Indonesia*)

As with so many Third World nations, there was much blurring of the edges with regard to the Hercules in their use as military or civilian aircraft; often aircraft switched roles frequently, which led to much confusion. Also, the official naming of the Air Force was changed almost as often.

With regard to the *Angkatan Udara Republik Indonesia* proper, three new C-130Bs were delivered between January and November 1960: T-1301 (c/n 3546), which later carried the civilian registration PK-VHD in 1978 as part of the Pelita Air Services fleet, before reverting in 1982 to A-1301; T-1302 (c/n 3578), later re-numbered A-1302; and in October 1960 the former Lockheed demonstrator N9298R (c/n 3580), which became T-1303 and was later re-serialled A-1303. All three served with 31 Squadron at Halim airfield, near Djakarta, on the island of Java.

Four more C-130Bs were purchased in 1960: T-1304 (c/n 3582), T-1305 (c/n 3583), T-1306 (c/n 3598) and T-1307 (c/n 3599). During the confrontation with Britain in defence of Malaysia in 1964/5 the latter two were lost. The former two were later re-registered A-1304 and A-1305 respectively.

One brand-new C-130B, T-1308 (c/n 3601), arrived in March 1961 and was subsequently leased to Pelita Air Services in 1969 as PK-VHA, and returned and re-registered as A-1308.

C-130B, former USAF serial 60-0305 (c/n 3614), was received in 1975 and given the serial T-1311, being later re-registered as A-1311. Two new C-130Bs, T-1309 (c/n 3615) and T-1310 (c/n 3616), were modified to KC-130Bs and re-registered A-1309 and A-1310 respectively. Two further former USAF C-130Bs, 60-0306 (c/n 3617) and 60-0309 (c/n 3621), were also received in 1975, and took the serials T-1312 and T-1313, later re-numbered as A-1312 and A-1313 respectively.

Seen aloft on 25 September 1979 is a Lockheed Super Hercules PK-PLV (c/n 4826) People Hauler, an L-100-30 acquired by the Indonesian Government for their 'transmigration' programme to shift the population around the crowded islands of that nation. (Lockheed-Georgia, Marietta via Audrey Pearcy)

Three L-100-30s were to be purchased at a cost in excess of $40 million, including spares, training and technical support in 1979, and all three were to be delivered in July, August and September. The planned use was by Pelita Air Services to airlift families from Java to Sumatra. A Lockheed demonstrator had carried out a series of thirteen twice-daily demonstration flights in mid-1978 which proved the feasibility of such an internal migration, in which 1,300 people were transported the 600 miles (966km) from Jakarta to Padanag and Jambi, Sumatra.

An L-100-30, A-1314 (c/n 4800), was purchased from Lockheed in December 1978. Another, A-1315 (c/n 4838), was purchased in December 1979, and A-1316 (c/n 4840)

The 1600th Hercules, TNI-AU, A-1321 (c/n 4870), pictured in flight at Marietta on 15 December 1980. This aircraft was delivered to the Indonesian Air Force that month, making the Hercules the most popular medium-sized propjet in aviation history. (Lockheed-Georgia, Marietta via Audrey Pearcy)

in January 1980. (Two further L-100-30s, PK-PLU (c/n 4824) and PK-PLKW (c/n 4828), were not *Angkatan Udara Republik Indonesia* aircraft as such but were leased from Mitsui Corporation at various times between 1979 and 1991, but see also Pelita Air Services section.)

The first ever stretched C-130H-30, A-1317 (c/n 4864), was soon joined by eight more: A-1318 (c/n 4865), A-1319 (c/n 4868), A-1320 (c/n 4869), A-1321 (c/n 4870), A-1322 (c/n 4898), A-1323 (c/n 4899). (Similarly, the last two C-130H-30s, PK-PLS (c/n 4917) and PK-PLT (c/n 4923), were not *Angkatan Udara Republik Indonesia* aircraft at all, but were purchased by the Indonesian Government and leased to Pelita between 1982 and 1992. Two more C-130H-30 aircraft which *did* belong to the *Tantara Nasional Indonesia–Angkatan Udara* were A-1324 (c/n 4925) and A-1325 (c/n 4927), but the latter crashed at Halim-Perdanakasuma near Jakarta on 5 October 1991.

Dropping down to land is Italian Air Force MM 62001 (c/n 4498) code 46-15, which was originally delivered in May 1973. (F. Ballista)

171 Israeli Air Force (*Heyl Ha'Avir*)

Twelve former USAF Tactical Air Wing C-130Es were obtained by the *Heyl Ha'Avir* in the period 1971/72, but to fool international observers who did not look too hard, they were given both civilian and military serials; these were the former USAF serials 62-1796 (c/n 3747), which became the civilian 4X-FBE, but was the military number 304; 63-7774 (c/n 3840), becoming the dual 4X-FBF/301; 63-7810 (c/n 3880), 4X-FBG/310; 63-7843 (c/n 3913), 4X-FBH/305; 63-7844 (c/n 3914), 4X-FBI/314; 63-7855 (c/n 3925), 4X-FBK/318; 63-7862 (c/n 3932), 4X-FBL/313; 63-7870 (c/n 3940), 4X-FBM/316; 63-7873 (c/n 3943), 4X-FBN/307; 64-0509 (c/n 3993), 4X-FBO/203; 64-0516 (c/n 4000), 4X-FBP/208; and 64-0528 (c/n 4014), 4X-FBQ/311, which was re-registered 4X-FBD.

Twelve additional brand-new C-130Hs were delivered in 1976/7 to serve with 131 Squadron based at Lod airfield, Tel Aviv, and their registrations/serials were treated in the same way, the dual serials being 4X-JUA/102 (c/n 4430) later re-registered as 4X-FBA; 4X-JUB/106 (c/n 4431), later 4X-FBB, then 4X-EBB; 4X-FBC/109 (c/n 4530); 4X-FBD/011 (c/n 4533), which crashed on

Gebel Halai on 25 November 1975; 4X-FBQ/420 (c/n 4653), which was converted into a KC-130H in November 1989; 4X-FBY/522 (c/n 4660); 4X-FBS/427 (c/n 4662); 4X-FBZ/545 (c/n 4664); 4X-FBT/435 (c/n 4668); 4X-FBU/448 (c/n 4680); 4X-FBW/436 (c/n 4686) which was converted into a KC-130H; and 4X-FBX/428 (c/n 4692).

The majority of these aircraft are now in storage in Israel.

172 Italian Air Force (*Aeronautica Militare Italiana*)

S even C-130Hs were delivered to the *Aeronautica Militare Italiana* between March and May 1972: MM 61988 (c/n 4441), MM61989 (c/n 4443), MM61990 (c/n 4446), MM61991 (c/n 4447), MM61992 (c/n 4449), which was later adapted as a fire bomber; MM61993 (c/n 4451); and MM61994 (c/n 4452).

They were followed by a second batch of seven more of the same type, delivered between April and June 1973: MM61995 (c/n 4491), scrapped in 1976 but re-built and later used for Antarctic supply work in 1989; MM61996 (c/n 4492), which crashed on Monte Serra near Pisa on 3 March 1977; MM61997 (c/n 4493), which was converted to a fire bomber and later used in Antarctica; MM61998 (c/n 4494); MM61999 (c/n 4495); MM6200 (c/n 4497),

Seen at Treviso Airport in 1980 is Matricola Militare (MM) 61997 *(coded 46-11). She was a C-130H (c/n 4493) and carried the name 'Portobello'. Her tail marking shows she belonged to MAFFS (Modular Airborne Fire Fighting System), and she was one of two such examples used by 46*[a] Aerobrigata *for fire-fighting duties from June 1978 onward.* (F. Ballista)

At rest at Treviso Airport in 1986 is Italian Hercules MM 61990 (c/n 4446) coded 46-04, which had originally been delivered on 30 March 1972. (F. Ballista)

converted to a fire bomber but scrapped after a ground accident on 23 January 1979; and MM62001 (c/n 4498).

These fourteen aircraft served with the *50⁰ Gruppo, 46ᵃ Aerobrigata*, based at San Giusto airfield near Pisa. They were replaced from March 2000 onward by a batch of nine C-130Js: 46-20 (c/n 5495), 46-21 (c/n 5597), 46-22 (c/n 5598), 46-23 (c/n 5503), 46-24 (c/n 5504), 46-25 (c/n 5505), 46-29 (c/n 5514), 46-30 (c/n 5520) and 46-34 (c/n 5535).

In addition there are seven of the stretched C-130J-30s: 46-26 (c/n 5510), 46-27 (c/n 5511), 46-28 (c/n 5512), 46-28 (c/n 5513), 46-31 (c/n 5514), 46-32 (c/n 5521) and 46-33 (c/n 5522).

A total of twenty-two C-130J/C-130J-30s are currently envisaged (2001).

Dropping down at the UK Air Tattoo of 1983 is Italian Hercules MM 61995 (c/n 4491) coded 46-09. She carried the MAFFS fire-fighting system in 1978–9. (F. Ballista)

BELOW LEFT: Seen here at Istrana airport in 1999 is this Italian Hercules MM 61992 (c/n 4449), carrying the new low-visibility codes 46-06. She had taken part in the Italian Everest expedition in 1973. (F. Ballista)

Revving up all four engines at Villafranca airfield in 1991 is Italian Hercules MM 61991 (c/n 4447). She is wearing the new livery which was introduced from 8 February 1985. The red titles behind the cockpit read: 'Best Maint. Best Pre-Flight earned at Airlift Rodeo in 1982 and 1984'. (F. Ballista)

Port bow aerial view of three C-130Hs, 75-1076 (c/n 5090), 75-1077 (c/n 5108) and 75-1082 (c/n 5171) of 401 Squadron JASDF, stacked up in close formation over their home base of Komaki AB prior to their deployment to Thimol. (Hayakawa, JASDF)

173 Japanese Air Self-Defence Force (*Koku Jietai*)

T he Japanese Self-Defence Force Air section, the *Koku Jietai*, received a total of sixteen C-130Hs in a number of batches, with which it equipped its

401st Hikotai, which belonged to *1 Kokutai* at Komaki Airbase near Nagoya. The first pair of these Japanese Herks were 82-0051 (c/n 4976) and 82-0052 (c/n 4980) which arrived in December 1983. They were followed by a second pair, 45-1073 (c/n 5015) and 45-1074 (c/n 5017), which arrived in October and November 1984 respectively. A further duo, 75-1075 (c/n 5088) and 75-1076 (c/n 5090), reached them in November and December 1986 and two more, 75-1077 (c/n 5108) and 75-1078 (c/n 5109), in July 1987. Another two, 85-1079 (c/n 5136) and 85-1080 (c/n 5138), reached them in June and July 1988, while three more were purchased from GELAC in 1989 arriving the following year: 95-1081 (c/n 5170), 95-1082 (c/n 5171) and 95-1083 (c/n 5172). Another pair, 05-1084 (c/n 5213) and 05-1085 (c/n 5214), arrived in September 1990, and the sixteenth, and last, C-130H to enter Japanese service, 85-1086 (c/n 5435), was a former Lockheed aircraft which was not delivered until March 1998.

The JASDF have modified some of these aircraft locally for the aerial minelaying role, while 85-1079 and 95-1083 have been used for United Nations relief work.

The *401st Hikotai* provided the following data on their Hercules fleet in 2000.

Type	Const. No.	JASDF Serial	Delivery Date	Serial No.
382C-27E	4976	35-1071	12-12-1983	82-0051
328C-27E	4980	35-1072	12-12-1983	82-0052
382C-44E	5015	45-1073	12-1984	83-0001
382C-44E	5017	45-1074	12-1984	83-0002
382C-68E	5088	75-1075	1987	85-0025
382C-68E	5090	75-1076	1987	85-0026
382C-75E	5108	75-1077	1987	86-0372
382C-75E	5109	75-1078	1987	86-0373
382C-82E	5136	85-1079	1988	87-0137
382C-82E	5138	85-1080	1988	87-0138
382C-90E	5170	95-1081	1989	88-1800
382C-90E	5171	95-1082	1989	88-1801
382C-90E	5172	95-1083	1989	88-1802
382C-02F	5213	05-1084	1990	88-0118
382C-02F	5214	05-1085	1990	89-0119
382C-60F	5435	85-1086	3-1998	75-1086

174 Kuwaiti Air Force

The Air Force flew two L-100-20s from 1970, the former N7954S, which became their 317 (c/n 4350), and 318 (c/n 4412). The first aircraft served a decade before crashing near Montelimar on 5 September 1980 after being hit by lightning. The second survived to be sold back to Lockheed in May 1982 and became the HTTB (see appropriate section).

The Kuwait Government acquired four L-100-30s from Lockheed in 1983: the former N4107F, which became their number 322 (c/n 4949); former N4349Y, which became 323 (c/n 4951), former N4242N, which became 324 (c/n 4953), and former N4232B, which became 325 (c/n 4955). In the Iraq invasion the first aircraft was damaged at Kuwait City Airport and taken over by the Iraqis, who flew her back to Baghdad as loot. She was again damaged by a bomb there, and although subsequently returned to Kuwait, was only fit for scrap. The other three were hastily flown to safety in Saudi Arabia and survived. They now fly with N.41 Squadron based at Kuwait International Airport itself. The Kuwaiti Air Force currently has four more on order.

175 Liberian Air Force

The former RAAF/Bob Geldof C-130A, N22FV (c/n 3207), was briefly registered in Liberia as EL-AJM in April 1986 during her varied and frequent changes of ownership, carrying the name *Wizard of Oz*.

176 Libyan Arab Republic Air Force

Prior to September 1969 this moderate and pro-Western nation purchased many Hercules aircraft, but following the installation of a rabid left-wing revolutionary dictatorship clandestine means have been used to keep them operational. The nation's civilian operators, Jamahiriya Air Transport and Libyan Air Cargo, both based at Tripoli Airport, utilised many of these former Air Force Hercules.

Eight brand-new C-130Hs were lawfully delivered in 1970 (the first six) and 1971 before relations with the West were severed: LAAF 111 (c/n 4366), LAAF 112 (c/n 4369), LAAF 113 (c/n 4373), LAAF 114 (c/n 4395), LAAF 115 (c/n 4400), LAAF 116 (c/n 4401), LAAF 117 (c/n 4403), and LAAF 118 (c/n 4405). Following the severing of relations, the following new C-130Hs on order and completed in 1973/74 were refused an export licence and not delivered, and are still stored under embargo at GELAC (Lockheed-Georgia Company, Marietta, Georgia): LAAF 119 (c/n 4515), LAAF 120 (c/n 4518), LAAF 121 (c/n 4523), LAAF 122 (c/n 4525), LAAF 123 (c/n 4536), LAAF 124 (c/n 4538), LAAF 125 (c/n 4540), and LAAF 126 (c/n 4541).

Two L-100-30 stretched Hercules, N4248M (c/n 4992) which became 5A-DOM and N4269M (c/n 5000) delivered in May 1985, were obtained by Armoflex from the West German company POP, it was said for 'oil exploration in Benin, Nigeria'. In fact they were both destined for Libya, and with Libyan aircrews aboard they duly successfully evaded the US ban on sales to that country. They were operated by Jamahiriya Air Transport from 1985.

177 **Mexican Air Force (*Fuerza Aérea Mexicana*)**

I n July 1987 the *Fuerza Aérea Mexicana* took delivery of two of the oldest former USAF Hercules, the ex 53-3130 (c/n 3004) and ex 53-3135 (c/n 3007), and although these ladies had been round the block more than a few times they became FAM 10601 and FAM 10602 respectively. They were operated by *302 Escuadron Aereo Transporte Pesada*, based at Santa Lucia airfield.

They were joined in 1988 by a further seven elderly ladies of the same type and vintage: ex 54-1638 (c/n 3025) in 1988, which became FAM 10603; ex 55-0027 (c/n 3054), 1988, which was delivered as a source of spare parts for the rest; ex 55-0028 (c/n 3055), 1988, which became FAM 10604; ex 55-0031 (c/n 3058), 1988, which became FAM 10605; ex 55-0035 (c/n 3062), 1988,

The Libyan Air Force, back in the days of the old Kingdom, was a friend of the West and there were no problems in delivering the first eight of sixteen C-130Hs ordered by the old regime from 1970 onward. With the arrival of the new revolutionary Government an embargo was placed on the final eight in 1973 and they were put into storage at Marietta. This is C-130H (c/n 4401), which served for eight years before being at Entebbe airfield, Uganda, during a raid mounted by the Israeli forces on 8 April 1979, to free hostages. (Lockheed-Georgia, Marietta via Audrey Pearcy)

which was also delivered as a source of spare parts for the rest; ex 56-0479 (c/n 3087), 1988, after being fully refurbished by Warner Robins at the Air Logistics Center for presidential flight duties – her FAM serial 10606 was changed to TP-300 and she also received the civilian registration XC-UTP for these duties; and the ex 56-0508 (c/n 3116), 1988, which became FAM 10607.

Finally, a single RC-130A, the former USAF 57-0510 (c/n 3217), was acquired the same year for use with the presidential flight as support aircraft. She received the FAM serial 10610, but crashed north-east of Mexico City on 17 September 1999.

The *Fuerza Aérea Mexicana* also took over the former Pemex L-100-30 in April 1993 as their 10611 (c/n 4851).

178 Niger Air Force (*Force Aérienne Niger*)

T wo brand-new C-130Hs were obtained by the *Force Aérienne Niger* in September and October 1979 respectively, 5U-MBD (c/n 4829) and 5U-MBH (c/n 4831). Both served with the *Escadrille Nationale du Niger* based at Niamey, and were used for governmental heavy-lifting cargo duties as well as presidential transport for President Seyni Kountche from time to time. One, 5U-MBD, was placed in storage at Oberpfaffenhoven, Germany, in 1986. She crashed at Sorei, near Niamey, on 16 April 1997 after two engines caught fire. 5U-MBH was similarly placed in storage, at Brussels Airport, in 1996 before returning to Niamey two years later.

179 Nigerian Air Force (*Federal Nigerian Air Force*)

T he Nigerian Air Force purchased six brand-new C-130Hs, commencing with serial NAF910 (c/n 4619) in September 1975, which was later re-numbered AT619, and serial NAF911 (c/n 4624) in October 1975, which was re-numbered AT624 and which crashed at Lagos Airport on 26 September 1992 after three engines failed due to contaminated fuel. Four more quickly joined the first pair between December 1975 and February 1976: NAF 912 (c/n 4638), which became AT744, then AT638 and later NAF913 again; NAF 913 (c/n 4639), which became AT639 and then NAF913 again; NAF914 (c/n 4649), which became AT649, and then reverted to NAF914 again; and NAF915 (c/n 4650), which became AT450, then AT650 before reverting back to NAF915 again. These Herks worked out of Murtala Muhammed airfield near Lagos.

In 1984 the Air Force acquired two former Lockheed C-130H-30s, N4081M (c/n 4962) which became NAF916 and N4099R (c/n 4963) which became NAF917. This pair was joined by a third of the same type, the new NAF918 (c/n 5001), in June 1986.

180 Pakistan Air Force (*Pakistan Fiza'ya*)

T he first Herks on the force's books were four new C-130Bs delivered between January and March 1963: PAF 24140 (c/n 3751), PAF 24141 (c/n 3766), PAF 24142 (c/n 3768); and PAF 24143 (c/n 3781). They were operated by No. 6 Squadron from Chaklala Airport, near Rawalpindi, west Pakistan. One,

24142 (3768), was shot down while conducting a bombing run during the Indo-Pakistan War in July 1966, while another, with civilian registration AS-HFO, was destroyed in a ground collision with 23491 (c/n 3701) at Chaklala on 10 September 1998.

In 1964, the *Pakistan Fiza'ya* acquired five former USAF C-130Bs to supplement these aircraft and equip No. 6 Tactical Support Squadron, 35 (Composite) Transport Wing, based at Chaklala Airbase. These were former USAF serials ex 58-0739 (c/n 3536), which became PAF58739; ex 61-2646 (c/n 3689), which became PAF12646, later receiving the civilian registration AK-MOB; ex 62-2648 (c/n 3691), December 1964, which became PAF 12648, and crash-landed on 18 August 1965; ex 62-3492 (c/n 3702), which became PAF 23492; and ex 62-3494 (c/n 3708), which became PAF 23494, and crashed near Bahawalpur with President Zia-ul-Haq and his retinue aboard, suspected sabotage, on 17 August 1988.

There were also four former *Nirou Haval Shahanshahiye Iran* C-130Bs serving in the same unit: ex 5101 (c/n 3698), which became PAF 23488 and was involved in a ground accident in March 1979 and scrapped; ex 5-102 (c/n 3699), which became PAF 23489 and was scrapped in March 1970; ex 5-103 (c/n 3700), which became PAF 23490, burnt out at Islamabad on 8 July 1969; and ex 5-104 (c/n 3701), which became PAF 23491, burnt in a collision with PAF 10687 at Rawalpindi on 10 September 1998.

In 1975 more modern replacements arrived in the shape of five former *Nirou Haval Shahanshahiye Iran* C-130Es: ex 5-102 (c/n 4117), 1975, which became PAF 10687 and subsequently collided with PAF 23488 in March 1979 and was scrapped; ex 5-103 (c/n 4119), 1975, became PAF 10689; ex 5-104 (c/n 4148), became PAF 64310; ex 5-106 (c/n 4153), became PAF 64312; and ex 5-108 (c/n 4282), which became PAF 1427.

In addition there were two L-100s bought in October 1966 by the Pakistani Government for PIA but, confusingly, operated by the *Pakistan Fiza'ya*: AP-AUT (c/n 4144), but operated as PAF 64144, and AP-AUU (c/n 4145), but operated as PAF 64145, and crashed near Chaklala on 30 April 1968.

181 Peruvian Air Force (*Fuerza Aérea Perunana*)

F ive (originally six) former USAF C-130As were obtained in 1988 and operated by *841 Escuadron, 8 Grupo Aéreo de Transporte* based at Jorge Chavez

Airport, Lima. These were the former USAF serials ex 55-0025 (c/n 3052), which became FAP381, later disposed of to Lester Sumrail Evangelistic Association and received the civilian registration N226LS in November 1990, carrying the names *Mercy Ship Zoe* and *Feed the Hungry* (see appropriate section); ex 55-0030 (c/n 3057), which became FAP394, and in 1996 converted to an aerial tanker aircraft; ex 56-0483 (c/n 3091); ex 57-0455 (c/n 3162), which became FAP393 and was also converted to an aerial tanker in October 1995; and ex 57-0470 (c/n 3177), which became FAP395. The sixth C-130A, the ex 56-0522 (c/n 3130), was part of the original sale in 1988, but the deal fell through due to lack of payment for this aircraft, and so instead she went to the AMARC in Arizona before being utilised as a static loading trainer at Kelly Air Force Base.

The *Fuerza Aérea Perunana* also obtained two former USAF C-130Ds in 1986: ex 57-0484 (c/n 3191), which became FAP383, and ex 57-0491 (c/n 3198), which became FAP399. Both aircraft were scrapped in August 1993.

Eight L-100-20s were flown by the Peruvian Air Force's *41 Grupo Aéreo de Transporte*. Two former Lockheed demonstrators were purchased in October 1970. N7985S (c/n 4358) became FAP394 but crash-landed at Lima on 24 November 1992 and went to the *Comercial Proveedorn del Oriente SA* as OB-1376 in 1994, before reverting to the *Fuerza Aérea Perunana* under her old serial number once more. N7986S (c/n 4364) became FAP 395 and was leased to SATCO as OB-R-1004 before reverting to the *Fuerza Aérea Perunana*, but crashed at Tarapoto on 19 February 1978. A third L-100-20 was purchased new in April 1972, FAP396 (c/n 4450). She was also leased to SATCO as OB-R-956 and returned in 1976. She survived take-off damage from Iquitas in June 1973, but was lost on 24 October 1981 in an emergency night landing due to lack of fuel close to San Juan.

The *Fuerza Aérea Perunana* also operated three further L-100-20s: FAP382 (c/n 4706), civilian registration OB-1374; FAP383 (c/n 4708), which crashed at Puerto Maldonado on 9 June 1983; and FAP384 (c/n 4715), civilian OB-1375. Finally, there were two further former Lockheed demonstrators: N4115M (c/n 4850), which became FAP397, civilian OB-1377, OB-1355, OB-1375 etc; and N4119M (c/n 4853), which became FAP 398, civilian registration OB-1378.

Cargoes varied enormously. One L-100-20 flew eight bulls from Mexico City to Lima for a bullfight; others transported twenty-six steel barges to Pacullpa which were to be used as transports between there and Iquitos on the Amazon. Much of the Peruvian Herks' work was in trans-Andes flights to develop oilfields in the Amazonian headwaters, as well as the transport of livestock cattle and bulk cargoes of frozen fish from Lima to Aycucho in the interior across the Andes barrier. The early completion of the *Carra Terra Marginal* national highway was credited by President Belaunde 'almost entirely to this aircraft'. But persistent reports also claim that clandestine missions were also conducted to Colombia.

Mention should also be made of a single C-130A which was to be purchased as a VIP aircraft for the Peruvian Navy. This was the former USAF serial 55-0008 (c/n 3035) which in February 1987 was flown to Aero Corporation at Lake City, Florida, to be modernised. As payment was never received for this she was subsequently sold in 1993 to Snow Aviation and became the civilian N130SA.

182 Philippines Air Force

In 1991 the Philippines Air Force obtained one C-130A, the former RAAF A97-213, 57-0506 (c/n 3213) and seven former USAF C-130Bs, and equipped their 222 Heavy Airlift Squadron with them, based at Mactan airfield. The Bs were ex 58-0725 (c/n 3520), which became 0725; ex 58-0738 (c/n 3535), which became 0738; ex 58-0747 (c/n 3545), which became 3545; ex 58-0749 (c/n 3547), which became 0749; ex 58-0753 (c/n 3552), which became 3552; ex 60-0294 (c/n 3593), which became 0294 and was grounded in 1996; and ex 61-0961 (c/n 3646), which became 0961 and was grounded in 1996. An eighth C-130B obtained by the Philippines Government was the former USAF/RAAF serial 57-0504/A97-211 (c/n 3211), which was registered to Aboitiz at Manila in May 1988 as NRP-R3211 and which in March 1991 re-registered as RP-C3211, and finally bought from storage at Manila in 1998 by Total Aerospace of Miami for spare parts.

In August 1973 the Philippines Government also purchased two L-100-20s from Saturn, N30FW (c/n 4302) which became P199 and N150FW (c/n 4303), which became P198. They were leased to the Philippines Air Force as 4302 and to Phil Aero Transport as RP-C98 respectively. Both were disposed of, the former to UAA in 1982 and the latter to James Bay Energy Corporation in 1973.

Two additional L-100-20s were obtained in October 1973 and May 1975 respectively, these being the former Lockheed N7967S (c/n 4512) and the new RP-C101 (c/n 4593). They were both leased to Philippine Aero Transport, the former in 1973, which was then sold to PADC and she became Philippines Air Force serial 4512 in 1983, being retired from service in 1991 and used for spares. The latter became Philippines Air Force serial 4593 in July 1983.

Three new C-130Hs joined 222 Squadron in November 1976 and August 1977 respectively: 4704 (c/n 4704), 4726 (c/n 4726) and 4761 (c/n 4761) followed in November that year.

183 Portuguese Air Force
(Forca Aérea Portuguesa)

The Portuguese Government became the forty-first to take delivery of the Hercules when the first of five C-130Hs, acquired by the *Forca Aérea Portuguesa* between August 1977 and June 1978, arrived in October 1977. One of a batch of five of that variant, she was received during a ceremony in Lisbon by the Director of Materiel Services of the Air Force, while the commander of *501 Esquadra de Transporte*, Lieutenant-Colonel Manuel Alvarenga, and his crews completed their training at Marietta. These four aircraft worked out of the Montijo Airbase both on NATO duties and on patrols to maintain the 200-mile (320km) economic zone and supply runs to the Azores.

The original five were 6801 (c/n 4749), stretched to a C-130H-30 in 1992 and used for United Nations work in Angola; 6802 (c/n 4753), stretched to a C-130H-30 in 1995; 6803 (c/n 4772), 6804 (c/n 4777); and 6805 (c/n 4778). In addition, a third factory-fresh C-130H-30 was obtained from GELAC in October 1991, 6810 (c/n 5264).

184 Romanian Air Force
(Fortele Aderiene Romaniei)

The Lockheed-Martin Aeronautical Systems Support Company at Marietta, Georgia, was awarded a $6,358,170 firm fixed-price contract to provide contractor logistic support for four C-130Bs, with completion by September 1998. The company provided the necessary replenishment spares, component overhaul, technical service representatives and simulator training, as well as technical publications and a scheduled maintenance programme and continuous airworthiness inspection programme. Twenty-nine firms were solicited in May 1996, and three proposals were received. The

contracting activity took place at Warner Robins Air Logistic Center at Robins Air Force Base, Georgia. The Aircraft & Logistics Centers, based at Greenville, South Carolina, promised to engage local Romanian companies in support of the programme with a certain amount of locally produced parts, saving the long air journey back to the States for overhauls.

The four former USAF C-130Bs were subsequently delivered from Ogden Air Logistics Center to the *Fortele Aderiene Romaniei* as follows: 59-1527 (c/n 3568) in October 1996, which became 5927; ex 59-1530 (c/n 3576) in November 1996, which became 5930; ex 61-0950 (c/n 3626) in October 1996, which became 6150; and 61-0966 (c/n 3653) in December 1996, which became 6166.

185 Royal Air Force

The British version of the C-130H, originally ordered in 1965, featured the T56-A-15 engine which developed 4,508 eshp, as well as special electronics and other equipment manufactured in the United Kingdom to RAF specifications, and this variant was known as the C-130K. They were all allocated US serial numbers for bureaucratic reasons and were known as the Hercules C.Mk.1 under the archaic RAF system. The lead aircraft, US serial 65-13021 (c/n 4169), received the RAF serial XV176***+ and made her maiden flight at Marietta on 19 October 1966, joining No 27 Operational Conversion Unit 27 based at Thorney Island the following April.

She was the precursor of a fleet of a further sixty-five machines of basically the same configuration, delivered in several batches, as follows: 65-13022 (c/n 4182) became XV177***+; 65-13023 (c/n 4188), XV178*; 65-13024 (c/n 4195), XV179*; 65-13025 (c/n 4196), XV180, which crashed at Fairford on 24 March 1969; 65-13026 (c/n 4198), XV181*; 65-13027 (c/n 4199), XV182*; 65-130028 (c/n 4200) Hector; XV183***+; 65-13029 (c/n 4201), XV184***+; 65-13030 (c/n 4203), XV185*; 65-13031 (c/n 4204), XV186*; 65-13032 (c/n 4205), XV187*; 65-13033 (c/n 4206), XV188***+; 65-13034 (c/n 4207), XV189***+; 65-13935 (c/n 4210), XV190***+; 65-13036 (c/n 4211), XV191*; 65-13037 (c/n 4212), XV192**; 65-13038 (c/n 4213) Horatius, XV193***+, which crashed 3,000ft (915m) up in a 'very inaccessible' mountain area near Beinn A'Ghlo, north-east of Blair Atholl, Perthshire, Scotland, on 27 May 1993, killing the nine-man crew; 65-13037 (c/n 4214), XV194, lost in a ground accident at Tromsö, Norway, on

12 September 1972; 65-13040 (c/n 4216), XV195*; 65-13041 (c/n 4217), XV196*; 65-13042 (c/n 4218), XV197***+; 65-13043 (c/n 4219), XV190, which crashed at Colerne on 10 September 1973; 65-13044 (c/n 4220), XV199***+; 66-8559 (c/n 4223), XV200*; 65-8551(c/n 4224), XV201**; 66-8552 (c/n 4226), XV202***+; 66-8553 (c/n 4227), XV203**; 66-8554 (c/n 4228), XV204**; 66-8555 (c/n 4230), XV205; 66-8556 (c/n 4231), XV206*; 66-8557 (c/n 4232), XV207***+; 66-8558 (c/n 4233), XV208; 66-8559 (c/n 4235), XV209***+; 66-8560 (c/n 4236), XV210*; 66-8561 (c/n 4237), XV211*; 66-8562 (c/n 4238), XV212***+; 66-8563 (c/n 4240), XV213**; 66-8564 (c/n 4241), XV214***+; 66-8565 (c/n 4242), XV215*; 66-8566 (c/n 4243), XV216, which crashed off Melovia, Italy, on 9 November 1971; 66-8567 (c/n 4244), XV217***+; 66-8568 (c/n 4245), XV218*; 66-8569 (c/n 4246), XV219***+; 66-8570 (c/n 4247), XV220***+; 66-8571 (c/n 4251), XV221***+; 66-8572 (c/n 4252), XV222***+; 66-8573 (c/n 4253), XV223***+; 66-13533 (c/n 4254), XV290***+; 66-13534 (c/n 4256), XV291*; 65-13534 (c/n 4257), XV292*; 65-13536 (c/n 4258), XV293*; 65-13537 (c/n 4259), XV294***+; 65-13538 (c/n 4261), XV295*, Hephaestos; 65-13539 (c/n 4262), XV296**; 65-13540 (c/n 4263), XV297*; 65-13541 (c/n 4264), XV298*; 65-13542 (c/n 4266), XV299***+; 65-13543 (c/n 4267), XV300*, Homer; 65-13544 (c/n 4268), XV301***+; 65-13545 (c/n 4270), XV302***+; 65-13546 (c/n 4271), XV303***+; 65-13547 (c/n 4272), XV304***+; 65-13548 (c/n 4273), XV305***+;

Touch-down of first RAF Herk XV176 (c/n 4169) to arrive at a UK airfield from Marietta in August 1967. (Author's Collection)

65-13549 (c/n 4274), XV306*, Hyperion; and 65-13550 (c/n 4275), XV307***+.

Those marked * were subsequently fitted with in-flight refuelling probes and equipment in the light of the Falklands campaign by Marshalls Engineering of Cambridge, and became C.Mk.1Ps. This followed the fitting of an ex-Vulcan probe above the flight deck on one RAF Hercules in 1982. Thus modified she was able to make a contribution to Operation 'Corporate', and even set the world endurance record for a Hercules of twenty-eight hours and four minutes' flight time. Those marked ** were modified with air-refuelling coupled with palletised drum/hose equipment and became C. Mk.1Ks. Those marked *** were stretched by 15ft (4.6m). The prototype, XV223 (c/n 4253), by Lockheed first flew thus on 3 December 1979, and twenty-nine others were also modified by Marshalls. They could thus accommodate ninety-two paratroops against sixty-four and 129 infantry as opposed to ninety-two only. These became the C.Mk.3 Hercules, and thirty of them marked + were subsequently converted to C.Mk.3Ps. The following year AN/ALQ 157 infra-red jammers and chaff and flare ECM dispensing gear was fitted to both C.Mk.1Ps and Ks. Some were also equipped with the Racal Orange Blossom wing-tip ECM pods.

The RAF pilots copied the US Marine Corps, who had nicknamed their tanker aircraft Fat Albert after the American comic-book character. Adopting it also, the name has stuck with British aircrew ever since. The RAF C-130Ks were as fully extended as their American counterparts, flying missions all over the globe, with relief and rapid reinforcement operations in Aden, Anguilla, Belize, Cambodia, Cyprus, Egypt, Ethiopia, Lebanon, supplying the Kurds in northern Iraq, India and Pakistan, as well as supporting Commonwealth peace-keeping operations in Rhodesia (Zimbabwe).

Perhaps one of the most bizarre cargoes ever carried by an RAF Hercules, XV297 (c/n 4264), was the delivery to Bavaria of the body of Rudolf Hess, the former deputy leader of the Nazi party under Hitler, who died in suspicious circumstances at Spandau prison in Berlin on 17 August 1987. The body was transferred from the British Military Hospital to RAF Gatow and then flown to the USAF base at Grafenwohr, the nearest airfield to the Hess family home at Wunsiedel, and the coffin was unloaded amid strict security for burial in the family plot.[28]

RAF Hercules XV179 (c/n 4196) seen at a Cambridge airfield in a dazzling colour scheme. (Marshall of Cambridge Aerospace Ltd via Martin W. Bowman)

RAF Hercules C-130K XV193 (c/n 4213) being towed down the runway at Lyneham in May 1979. (RAF Official)

---

[28] See John England, 'Security veils Hess's last journey to small Bavarian town', article in *The Times*, 21 August 1987.

Concentrated at RAF Lyneham, near Chippenham, Wiltshire, the RAF Hercules force was part of No. 2 Group within RAF Strike Command, and comprised 24, 30, 47, 70 (LXX) and 57 (Reserve) Squadrons, all equipped with the C.1/C.3, with a solitary C.1 of 1312 Flight based in the Falkland Islands. All units operate in the air transport profile, carrying freight and passengers around the world, but 47 and 70 Squadrons specialise in the tactical support role, dropping paratroops and supplies, while 57 (Reserve) Squadron was the Hercules Operational Conversion Unit and provided conversion and refresher training for aircrew. Here also are the UK Mobile Air Movement Squadron (UKMAMS) which processes all freight and passengers while also deploying mobile teams at various bases around the world to load/unload Hercules; and 47 (Air Despatch) Squadron, Royal Logistics Corps, which is responsible for the preparation, loading and despatch of all air-dropped stores. The Hercules Engineering Development and Investigation Team (H-EDIT) is also based at Lyneham and undertakes engineering development and investigations resulting from any changes in tactics, role or application.

In the aftermath of the Gulf War, when retreating Iraqi troops had set fire to all the Kuwaiti oil wells in a wanton fit of vandalism, there was great concern about the worldwide spread of pollution from the enormous blazes and columns of smoke. The result was that acid rain, black snow and similar fallout began to pollute the skies over Iran, southern Turkey and even as far afield as Afghanistan. In March, *Snoopy* was flown from RAE Farnborough into the area and criss-crossed the zone during fifty-five hours of daylight sorties, made at altitudes of up to 25,000ft

A pristine Hercules, XV177, the first RAF C Mk 1 XV177 (c/n 4182) as the inscription shows, seen on the mat at Marietta prior to her delivery to the RAF. The policy at the time was for the aircraft to be delivered in natural metal finish and without some 80% of the standard Lockheed equipment, so that both camouflage and internal fitting could be done in the UK to the required standard. (Lockheed-Georgia, Marietta via Audrey Pearcy)

(7,620m). Measurements were taken up to 62 miles (100km) distant from the fires, which revealed that the maximum concentration of smoke particles were layered at 6,000ft (1,830m). Concentrations were found of 30,000 smoke particles per cubic centimetre, which fell to about 3,000 to 5,000 particles per cubic centimetre some 125 miles (200km) downwind.

In the late 1990s a replacement programme of extended-length C-130J-30s was initiated, following successful trials with the Lockheed prototypes: N130JA (c/n 5408) became ZH865, N130JE (c/n 5414) became ZH866 and N130JJ (c/n 5416) became ZH867. This trio was followed by a further thirteen of the same type: ZH868 (c/n 5443), ZH869 (c/n 5444), ZH870 (c/n 5445), ZH871 (c/n 5446), ZH872 (c/n 5456), ZH873 (c/n 5457), ZH874 (c/n 5458), ZH875 (c/n 5459), ZH876 (c/n 5460), ZH877 (c/n 5461), ZH878 (c/n 5462), ZH879 (c/n 5463), and ZH889 (c/n 5503). They were followed by a programme of standard C-130Js: ZH880 (c/n 5478), ZH881 (c/n 5479), ZH882 (c/n 5480), ZH883 (c/n 5481), ZH884 (c/n 5482), ZH885 (c/n 5483), ZH886 (c/n 5484), ZH887 (c/n 5485), and ZH888 (c/n 5500).

In-flight refuelling study as RAF ZD960 feeds a C-130,
tail-coded 20. (Marshall of Cambridge Aerospace Ltd)

The British Ministry of Defence (MoD) took delivery of the first aircraft, ZH865 (c/n 5408), which was handed over to the Defence Evaluation and Research Agency (DERA) at Boscombe Down on 26 August 1998 and was later joined by ZH871 (c/n 5446) on 30 November 1998 and ZH880 (c/n 5478) on 22 April 1999. The first of the C-130Js, ZH875 (c/n 5459), was officially received by the RAF's Transport Wing at RAF Lyneham, Wiltshire, on 23 November 1999 by Air Vice Marshal Philip Sturley, AOC 38 Group, Strike Command, more than two years behind schedule. According to some press reports so many late penalty points had been racked up by this delay that Lockheed were forced to present the RAF with a 'free' aircraft![29] The first squadrons to re-equip with the new Hercules were No. 57 (R), followed by No. 24.

A purpose-built training facility for conversion of air- and ground crew to the new aircraft (known as The School House) has been built at Lyneham, with eight classrooms and eight computer terminals linked to a central server and a cockpit simulator with a digital moving map linked to the radar. No. 57(R) Squadron was designated the Hercules Operational Conversion Unit, with nine aircrew courses per year, with three crews per course.[30]

Another record went on 7 December 1999 when an RAF Hercules, ZH866 (c/n 5416), made the 4,127.73-mile (6,641.52km) journey from Marietta to the UK in nine hours, fifty-eight minutes and fourteen seconds, averaging a speed of 414.054mph (666.213km/h), the fastest flown by an aircraft of this class without refuelling. Although there is great enthusiasm for the C-130J throughout the RAF, what has not yet been revealed by the MoD is whether stories of weaker jacking points and resultant damage to the new aircraft are rumour or fact.

---

[29] See Peter Almond, 'RAF's new Hercules arrives 2 years late', article in *Daily Telegraph*, 25 November 1999.

[30] See Bob Archer, 'Hercules joins the RAF', article in *The Royal Air Force Yearbook 2000*, PRM Aviation, Bristol.

186 | Royal Australian Air Force

The first overseas customer to purchase the Hercules was the RAAF, for whom, on 8 November 1958, the Menzies Government commissioned twelve C-130A-50-LMs to take over the duties of the existing DC-3 Dakotas of No. 36 Squadron, based at Richmond, NSW. These aircraft were delivered between December 1958 and March 1959: the former USAF serial 57-0498 (c/n 3205), which became A97-205, and later civilian registration N205FA with Fowler Aeronautical Service; 57-0499 (c/n 3206), which became A97-C3206, and later civilian registration RP-C3206 with Aboitiz Air Transport; 57-0500 (c/n 3207), which became A97-207, and later civilian N22FV with Ford & Vlahos; the former 57-0501 (c/n 3208), which became A97-208 and later civilian registration N12FV with Ford & Vlahos; 57-0502 (c/n 3209), which became A97-209, and later civilian registration N4445V with Ford & Vlahos; 57-0503 (c/n 3210), which became A97-210, 57-0504 (c/n 3211), which became A97-211, and later civilian registration N5394L with Ford & Vlahos; 57-0505 (c/n 3212), which became A97-212,

and later civilian registration N13FV with Ford & Vlahos; 57-0506 (c/n 3213), which became A97-213, and later RP-R3213 with Aboitiz; 57-0507 (c/n 3214), which became A97-214, and ended up in the RAAF Museum, Point Cook; 57-0508 (c/n 3215), which became A97-215, and later civilian N4469P with Ford & Vlahos; and 57-0509 (c/n 3216), which became A97-216, and later civilian HK-3017X for Aviaco. All served with 36 and 27 Squadrons RAAF, based at Richmond airfield, New South Wales.

No. 36 Squadron RAAF notched up 100,000 accident-free hours' flying time with their C-130As in 1972, and they were not finally retired until the late 1970s. They were given civilian registrations as they were sold or leased out, and many had very varied subsequent careers (see appropriate sections). One, minus wings and engines, was retained (A97-0219) at Richmond as a ground trainer for

An RAAF C-130 takes departure from Dili airfield, East Timor, 30 September 1999, during the troubles following the referendum there. (Australian Defence Headquarters, Canberra)

cargo loading techniques. The other eleven had more eventful and turbulent careers.

Parmax-Global Jet, an American company, made an offer to buy all eleven aircraft and appointed Mr Peter Hocking as their contact. However, not a single aircraft was pre-sold by Parmax-Global Jet, and in April 1980 the Department of Administrative Services called for tenders for the sale of the eleven. An Australian consortium under Jack Ellis tendered for the disposal, but failed, even though they apparently had buyers lined up for them all: eight for the Mexican Government and three for the World Health Organisation (WHO). Instead the tender was awarded to Ford & Vlahos, a firm of San Francisco attorneys, with John J. Ford at their head, and they appointed Peter Hocking and Kenneth Oliver as their contacts. Between the award of the tender on 13 May 1981 and September 1985 not one of the aircraft was sold, but the Department of Administration granted Ford & Vlahos eleven extensions.

In September 1985 the French Government bought A97-0208 for $3 million, of which just $1 million went to the Australian Government, and she received the civilian registration N445V. She was used to assist the armed struggle in Chad, a former French colony threatened by Libyan-backed insurgents. Next, two more aircraft, A97-0121 and A97-0217, were sold to Aviaco Ltd for $4.5

million, the Australian Government giving approval, but without consulting the US State Department, even though all eleven aircraft were theoretically under the latter's control. The proviso was that the two machines (which took civilian registrations HK-3016X and HK-3017X respectively) be used strictly for non-military, humanitarian duties. Both machines therefore flew out to the States in October 1983, but the US refused to sanction the deal and duly informed the Australian Department of Foreign Affairs. The two aircraft were left stranded, one at the Lockheed facility at Dotham, Alabama, the other in Oakland, California. A third machine, A97-0215, was also purchased by Ford & Vlahos, receiving the civilian registration N4469. She was leased to the US Nuclear Defense Agency for atomic testing on avionics tests, but was returned to Ford & Vlahos and stored in Alabama. In June 1985 she was flown to England, and, after some maintenance work, was used for relief work in the Sudan for the British Government.

Supplier Flight Sergeant Ray Loxley from 1ATS DET Williamtown Air movements, marshals a 36 Squadron RAAF, Hercules, on East Timor, 30 September 1999, during the troubles following the referendum there. (Australian Defence Headquarters, Canberra)

In January 1986, after two years, John J. Ford's exclusive right of sale was terminated and the disposal contract passed to another company, Defence Equipment, whose directors were Peter Hocking and Kenneth Oliver. Next the World Freedom from Hunger campaign, headed by pop singer Bob Geldof, approached the Australian Government for permission to use the unwanted stripped and parked Hercules. Hawke's Government was now in power and the Australian Development Bureau contracted another company, International Air Aid (directors Peter Hocking, Kenneth Oliver and Peter Commins), to handle the $1.7 million refurbishment programme for them. The first aircraft, A97-0207, was moved to RAAF Richmond in January 1986 for the refurbishment to commence, and International Air Aid received $1.5 million for the job. With the civilian registration N22FV, this aircraft flew to Sogerma at Bordeaux, France, for heavy structural checks to be carried out, and was subsequently handed over to the International Red Cross. They, in turn, contracted a company to manage the operational side, appointing Integral Air Aid, Cyprus, whose directors were Peter Hocking, Kenneth Oliver and Peter Commins. The contract between

Integral Air Aid and IRC was later cancelled after the aircraft had flown for only four months, and the whole exercise cost the Australian taxpayer $1.5 million.[31]

Between August 1966 and January 1967 a second batch of twelve C-130E aircraft was purchased, and they joined 37 Squadron in the 86th Wing (Airlift Group), also based at Richmond: A97-159 (c/n 4159), A97-160 (c/n 4160), A97-167 (c/n 4167), A97-168 (c/n 4168), A97-171 (c/n 4171), A92-172 (c/n 4172), A97-177 (c/n 4177), A97-178 (c/n 4178), A97-180 (c/n 4180), A97-181 (c/n 4181), A97-189 (c/n 4189) and A97-190 (c/n 4190).

All two dozen Australian Herks were employed during that country's involvement in the Vietnam War transporting troops, military equipment and supplies and evacuating wounded. Some of these were subsequently used in Antarctic survey work. In September 1977 one of the Australian C-130Es, flown by Flight Lieutenant John Smith RAAF, matched the C-130A's achievement of 100,000 hours of accident-free flying time, covering 31 million statute miles (49,889,664km), the equivalent of fifty-eight round trips to the moon, or 1,200 earth orbits. In achieving

Royal Australian Air Force C-130E A97-167 (c/n 4167) catches the sun as she climbs from Hickam AFB, Hawaii, in June 1968. (Nick Williams AAHS)

---

[31] See the *Hangared* article, 'C130 'A' Hercules', by Mark Farrar, in *Flightpath* magazine, 1988.

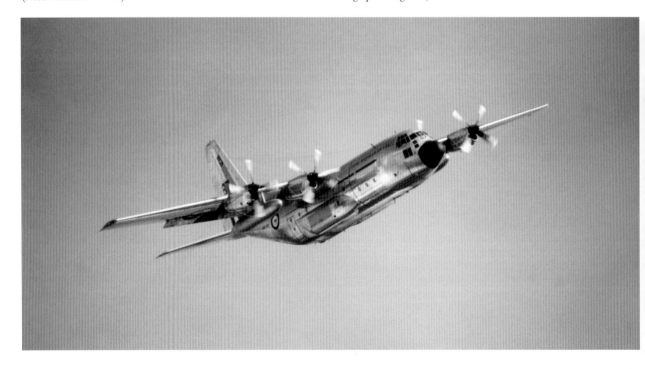

this impressive total No.37's Herks had made the first landing by the light of kerosene flares at night at a devastated Darwin Airport after Cyclone Tracey had wrecked it; had made mercy flights to Fiji, Noumea and Christmas Islands; had re-supplied Australian forces acting as United Nations peace-keepers in Egypt and Pakistan; had flown cargoes as diverse as priceless archaeological exhibits and livestock to China and back; and had ferried wounded troops from Butterworth, Malaysia, to Richmond, NSW, during the Vietnam War.

Between July and October 1978 the C-130As were replaced with twelve new C-130Hs: A97-001 (c/n 4780), A97-002 (c/n 4782), A97-003 (c/n 4783), A97-004 (c/n 4784), A97-005 (c/n 4785), A97-006 (c/n 4786), serial A97-007 (c/n 4787), A97-008 (c/n 4788), A97-009 (c/n 4789), A97-010 (c/n 4790), A97-011 (c/n 4791); and A97-102 (c/n 4793). Some of these have been used for Antarctic supply work.

In 1999 it was the turn of 37 Squadron to have their aircraft replaced by twelve C-130J-30s, between August 1999 and March 2000: the former Lockheed N130JQ (c/n 5440), which became A97-440 and later carried the civilian registration N4080M for a time; A97-441 (c/n 5441), the former Lockheed N130JR (c/n 5442), which became A97-442; the former Lockheed N73232 (c/n 5447), which became A97-447; the former Lockheed N73230 (c/n 5448), which became A97-448; the former

Lockheed N72322 (c/n 5449), which became A97-44; the former Lockheed N4187W (c/n 5450), which became A97-459; A97-464 (c/n 5464), A97-465 (c/n 5465), serial A97-466 (c/n 5466), A97-467 (c/n 5467), and A97-468 (c/n 5468).

187   Royal Canadian Air Force (RCAF) and Canadian Armed Forces (CAF)

The first Hercules to serve with the Royal Canadian Air Force (later the amalgamated Canadian Armed Forces) were four C-130Bs purchased from Lockheed stock, which arrived between October and November 1960. This quartet were the RCAF serials 10301 (c/n 3572), which was sold back to Lockheed, becoming their N4652; 10302 (c/n 3575), also sold back to Lockheed and becoming their N4653; 10303 (c/n 3587), sold back to Lockheed to become their N4654; and 10304 (c/n 3590), which was lost in an accident in Saskatchewan in April 1966. During their RCAF period they all served

A Royal Canadian Air Force C-130E Hercules, serial 130313 (c/n 4066), carrying Military Airlift Command markings, pulls into the sky from Hickam Field Air Force Base, Hawaii, on 31 January 1968. (Nick Williams AAHS)

with No. 435 Squadron. The three survivors were returned to Lockheed in July 1967, who sold them on to Colombia.

Two dozen C-130Es were purchased between December 1964 and August 1968: RCAF serial 10305 (c/n 4020), later 130305; 10306 (c/n 4026), later 130306 (these first two were later modified to carry pallet-mounted training consoles for use as navigation trainers and re-designated C-130(NT)s, then as search and rescue aircraft and finally as early warning aircraft); 10307 (c/n 4041), later 130307, modified to C-130(NT) and later as SAR; 10308 (c/n 4042), later 130308, modified to C-130(NT) and later as an early warning aircraft; 10309 (c/n 4050), later 130309, and lost in a accident at Trenton on 27 April 1967; 10310 (c/n 4051), later 130310, modified to a C-130(NT) then as an SAR; 10311 (c/n 4060), later 130311; 10312 (c/n 4061), later 130312, lost in an accident near Chapais, Quebec, on 15 October 1980; 10313 (c/n 4066), later 130313; 10314 (c/n 4067), later 130314, later modified to early warning role; 10315 (c/n 4070), later 130315, also modified to early warning aircraft; 10316 (c/n 4075), later 130316, also modified to early warning aircraft; 10319 (c/n 4095), later 130319, modified

The Royal Canadian Air Force took delivery of the first four of forty-two Hercules in October/November 1960. One of these, C-130B, 10302 (c/n 3575), is seen over the Rockies toting the Air Transport Command motif and the national flag. She, along with two surviving sisters, was later returned to Marietta, refurbished and sold to Cambodia, in whose service two more were lost in accidents in 1969 and 1982. (Lockheed-Georgia, Marietta via Audrey Pearcy)

to early warning role; 10320 (c/n 4096), later 130320; 10317 (c/n 4122), later 130317, modified to early warning aircraft; 10318 (c/n 4124), later 130318, crashed at Wainwright Army airfield, Arkansas, due to severe icing on 29 January 1989; 10321 (c/n 4191), later 130321, crashed at Wainwright field on 22 July 1993; 10322 (c/n 4192), later 130322, crashed at Alert, Ellesmere Island, North-West Territories, on 30 November 1991; 10323 (c/n 4193), later 130323, modified as early warning aircraft; 10324 (c/n 4194), later 130324, modified as early warning aircraft; 10325 (c/n 4285), later 130325; 10326 (c/n 4286), later 130326, modified as early warning aircraft; 10327 (c/n 4288), later 130326; and 10328 (c/n 4289), later 130328.

Fourteen C-130Hs were diverted to the RCAF from USAF Tactical Air Force allocations between October 1974 and February 1991: RCAF serial 130329 (c/n 4553), which crashed at Namao on 16 November 1982; 130330 (c/n 4555), lost in mid-air collision over Namao with 130331 on 29 March 1985; 130331 (c/n 4559), lost in mid-air collision with 103330 on 29 March 1985;[32] 130332 (c/n 4568), modified to early warning aircraft; 130333 (c/n 4574), modified to early warning aircraft; the former Lockheed N4246M and CAF G-52-18 (c/n 4580), which became 130336; the former Lockheed N4247M and CAF G52-17 (c/n 4584), which became 130337 and later modified as an early warning aircraft; 130334 (c/n 4994), modified to early warning aircraft; 130335 (c/n 4995), modified to early warning role; an unregistered former Lockheed stock aircraft which became 130338 (c/n 5175), 130339 (c/n 5177), modified as early warning aircraft, then modified again for aircrew training aircraft; a former unregistered Lockheed stock aircraft which became 130340 (c/n 5189), modified to aerial tanker role, then later

C-130H of the Royal Danish Air Force, serial B-679 (c/n 4587), carrying red rescue markings on its wingtips, fuselage band and under-nose. (Martin W. Bowman)

re-modified as early warning aircraft; another former unregistered Lockheed stock aircraft which became 130341 (c/n 5200), also modified to an aerial tanker and then re-modified as early warning aircraft; and finally 130342 (c/n 5207), again modified to an aerial tanker and then to an early warning aircraft.

Two late-build L-100-30s, CAF, 130343 (c/n 5307) and RCAF 130344 (c/n 5320), were purchased by the Canadian Armed Forces in March 1996 and modified to C-130H-30s by CAE, Trenton, and given the designation CC-130.

188 Royal Danish Air Force (*Kongelige Danske Flyvevaabnet*)

Becoming the thirtieth nation to operate the Hercules, three C-130Hs carrying USAF serials were acquired under the Mutual Air Aid Programme between April and July 1975, and equipped the *Kongelige Danske Flyvevaabnet*'s Tactical Air Command unit, flying with *721 Eskadrille, Flyvertaktisk Kommando* from their base at Vaerose. These three Herks were the ex 73-1678 (c/n 4572), which became B-678; ex 73-1679 (c/n 4587), which became B-679; and the ex 73-1680 (c/n 4599), which became B-680. All three have been modernised and carry ECM/ESM pods mounted on their wing-tips.

---

[32] The following description of this crash is given in *Propos de Vol* No. 2, 1985, and *Alberta Report*, 8 April 1985. The squadron was tasked to carry out a fly-past in commemoration of the sixty-first anniversary of the RCAF in conjunction with other base aircraft. At the conclusion of the fly-past the three CC-130 crews planned to recover on RWY 29 utilising a low-level 'battle' break manoeuvre. They positioned themselves in echelon right with wing-span spacing. The briefed procedure was to pull up 10° and turn left with 60° of bank maintaining 2g, climbing to 1,000ft (305m) above ground level (AGL) to position themselves downwind. Nos 2 and 3 would follow, each with three-second spacing. After approximately 50° of turn at 900ft (274m) AGL, no.2 collided with the underside of lead aircraft, forward of the port side main gear, punching a five foot square hole in the aircraft floor structure. The no.2 aircraft had its forward fuselage section separated from the aircraft and free-fell into a field. The nos. 3 and 4 propellers separated and landed some distance from the main wreckage. The tail section of the lead aircraft also separated prior to ground impact. Control of either aircraft after the collision was impossible. The four occupants of the lead aircraft and the six occupants of no.2 all sustained fatal injuries. Both aircraft exploded in mid-air and crashed inverted over an area the size of four city blocks. A 300ft × 50ft (91m × 50m) storage building (from which 150 military personnel had left just a quarter of an hour earlier) and several vehicles were destroyed in a very intense fire.

189 Royal Hellenic Air Force (*Elliniki Aéroporia*)

U nder Mutual Aid Programmes the United States allocated four former USAF C-130Hs to the *Elliniki Aéroporia* in 1992, and they joined the Air Materiel Command's *356 Mira, 112 Pterix*. This quartet was 741 (c/n 4622), 742 (c/n 4632), 743 (c/n 4665) and 744 (c/n 4672). They were later modernised, mounting ECM antenna.

No new aircraft arrived to reinforce this initial quartet until September 1975, due to Greece's withdrawal from NATO over the Cyprus question. But from that date through to May 1977 the United States Government allocated eight C-130Hs, diverted from USAF allocations: 745 (c/n 4716), 746 (c/n 4720), 747 (c/n 4723), 748 (c/n 4724), which crashed on Mount Billiuras on 5 February 1991; 749 (c/n 4727), 750 (c/n 4729), which crashed into a mountain near Tanagra on 20 December 1997; 751 (c/n 4732), and 752 (c/n 4734). Some have been re-equipped with MAFF packages for fire-fighting, others for ELS duties.

In 1992 five former USAF C-130Bs were allocated to build up the force: ex 58-0723 (c/n 3518), which became 723; ex 60-0296 (c/n 3597), which became 296; ex 60-0300 (c/n 3604), which became 0300; ex 60-0303 (c/n 3613), which became 303; and ex 61-0948 (c/n 3624), which became 948. These veterans were still in service in 1998.

The Royal Malaysian Air Force (the Tentera Udara Diraja Malaysia) took delivery of six C-130Hs between 1976 and 1980, and this is the first of them, FM2401 (c/n 4656) which was delivered on 26 March 1976. She remained in service for twenty-one years until April 1997, when she was placed in storage. (Lockheed-Georgia, Marietta via Audrey Pearcy)

190 Royal Jordanian Air Force (*Al Quwwat Almalakiya*)

A quartet of former USAF C-130Bs was obtained by the *Al Quwwat Almalakiya* in 1973 and equipped their No. 3 Squadron, which operated from King Abdullah Airport, Amman. These aircraft were the ex 60-0301 (c/n 3610), which became 141, and later was re-numbered 341; ex 60-0302 (c/n 3611), which became 142, and was sold to Singapore in 1976; ex 60-0304 (c/n 3612), which became 140, and later was re-numbered 340; and ex 60-0308 (c/n 3620), which became 143, and was also sold to Singapore in 1976.

These veterans were supplemented by a pair of brand-new C-130Hs – 144 (c/n 4779), which later was re-numbered 744, and then 344; and 345 (c/n 4813) – which were received in June 1978 and April 1979 respectively. In May and July 1982 a second pair of the same type arrived at Amman: 346 (c/n 4920) and 347 (c/n 4929).

Finally, a solitary HC-130H (c/n 4073), the former

USAF serial 64-14857, was acquired in February 1992, receiving the serial 348.

191 Royal Malaysian Air Force (*Tentera Udara Diraja Malaysia*)

S ix new C-130Hs were obtained by the Malaysian Government between March and October, 1976, accepted and sprinkled with holy water at a ceremony by Prime Minister Datuk Hussein Onn. These aircraft equipped the No. 14 (Transport) Squadron based at Subang airfield near Kuala Lumpur: FM2401 (c/n 4656), which was later re-registered as M30-01; FM2402 (c/n 4661), later re-registered as M30-02; FM2403 (c/n 4674), later M30-03, which crash-landed at Sibu, Sarawak, on 25 August 1990; FM2404 (c/n 4685), later M30-04; FM2405 (c/n 4690), later M30-05; and FM2406 (c/n 4697), later M30-06.

A trio of new C-130H-MPs arrived between April and December 1980: FM2451 (c/n 4847), later re-registered as M30-07; the former Lockheed demonstrator N4123M (c/n 4849), which became FM2452, and later M30-08; and FM2453 (c/n 4866), later M30-09. All three were modified to aerial tankers. Finally, six C-130H-30s were obtained between December 1991 and April 1993: M30-10 (c/n 5268), M30-12 (c/n 5277), M30-11 (c/n 5309), M30-14 (c/n 5311), M30-15 (c/n 5316), and M30-16 (c/n 5319).

192 Royal Moroccan Air Force (*Al Quwwat Ali Jawwiya Almalakiya Marakishiya*)

C ommencing in 1976, the *Force Aérienne Royale Marocaine* took delivery of no fewer than seventeen C-130H aircraft in three deliveries, all of which were given civilian registrations. Their primary duties were military logistic support, but they were also invaluable for up-country industrial development haulage and support flights. They also featured in a purely mercantile role with regular produce export runs to Paris with fresh fruit, vegetables, frozen fish and other local products for which there was high demand in France. On the return runs imports of machinery and products were taken back home. One machine, CNA-OM (c/n 4875), was fitted with MAFFS equipment to spray locusts as part of a pest control programme.

The first six aircraft – CNA-OA (c/n 4535), CNA-OB (c/n 4537), CNA-OC (c/n 4551), CNA-OD (c/n 4575), CNA-OE (c/n 4581) and CNA-OF (c/n 4583), with another four: CNA-OG (c/n 4713), CNA-OH (c/n 4717), CNA-OI (c/n 4733) and CNA-OJ (c/n 4738) – were delivered from May 1974. The second delivery comprised a further five – CNA-OK (c/n 4739), CNA-OL (c/n 4742), CNA-OM (c/n 4875), CNA-ON (c/n 4876) and CNA-OO (c/n 4877) – commencing in August 1981, and the last pair – CNA-OP (c/n 4888, N4162M) and CNA-OQ (c/n 4892) – arrived in mid-1982. These last two were equipped with the sideways-looking airborne radar (SLAR) fitted to the port main undercarriage fairing. In addition two KC-130Hs were taken on their strength in November and December 1981 respectively: CAN-OR (c/n 4907, N4216M) and CAN-OS (c/n 4909, N4221M).

A more warlike mission also came the way of the Hercules here, as elsewhere, with operations against the Pollisario guerrilla forces which were actively backed by peaceful Morocco's more extreme Arab neighbours and entering the country via the Western Sahara. Based at Kenitra, the C-130Hs used in this counter-insurgency role had chaff and flare dispenser pods fitted. Two of the Hercules became casualties of this conflict, CAN-OB being shot down and destroyed on 4 December 1976 and CAN-OH destroyed at Guelta Zemmour on 12 October 1981.

193 Royal Netherlands Air Force (*Koninklijke Luchtmacht*)

I t was not until 1994 that the Dutch *Koninklijke Luchtmacht* rather belatedly joined the 'Herk Club' with the purchase of two former Lockheed C-130H-30s for No.334 Squadron, from their base at Eindhoven. This pair were the ex N4080M (c/n 5273), which became serial G273 and was allocated the name *Ben Swagerman*, and ex N4080M (c/n 5275), which became G275 and was named *Joop Mulder*.

194 Royal New Zealand Air Force

T he RNZAF purchased their very first three C-130Hs in March/April 1965, to replace their elderly Hastings transport aircraft in No. 40 Squadron. The original order was actually for three C-130Es and five more of the anti-submarine warfare versions, but the latter were dropped on economic grounds and P-38 Orions ordered instead. What were actually delivered were not C-130Es but the superior C-130Hs, the first being NZ7001 (c/n 4052), which arrived in April 1965. She was operated by No. 40 Squadron based at Whenuapai airfield

near Auckland, and was quickly joined by NZ7002 (c/n 4053) and NZ7003 (c/n 4054). In July 1965, with New Zealand's involvement in the Vietnam War, this trio was kept busy, first airlifting and then supporting Army artillery, support vehicles and personnel to Bien Hoa airfield. These three aircraft also flew missions to China and the Soviet Union (the first to either country by a RNZAF aircraft), and flew in relief operations in Bangladesh, Cambodia and Pakistan. In the period 1972/3, all three aircraft returned to the Lockheed plant to have wing centre-section modifications made which almost doubled their operational life.

This work was continued on a regular basis, and to support the workload, another pair of C-130Hs were acquired in December 1968: NZ7004 (c/n 4312) and NZ7005 (c/n 4313). They entered service in January 1969. Their duties included the evacuation of New Zealand nationals and officials to the safety of Singapore in the humiliating days of 1975. During 1981 all five aircraft again returned to Lockheed for refurbishing of the outer wing panels at a cost of NZ$4.8 million, the last aircraft returning to Whenuapai in October of that year. Since then their work has included regular supply runs down to the McMurdo Sound Airbase in Antarctica.

Royal New Zealand Air Force C-130H RNZAF 7001 (c/n 4052) of No.40 Squadron, on patrol in October 1986. (RNZAF Official)

195 Royal Norwegian Air Force (*Konelige Norske Lufforsvaret*)

In June/July 1969 the *Konelige Norske Lufforsvaret* took delivery of a batch of six C-130Hs for operations with their *335 Skvadron*, based at Gardemoen airfield. They received both military and civilian serials, as well as receiving names from Norse mythology: 68-10952 (c/n 4334), also BW-A, *Odin*; 68-10953 (c/n 4335), BW-B, *Tor*; 68-10954 (c/n 4336), BW-C, *Balder*; 68-10955 (c/n 4337), BW-D, *Froy*; 68-10956 (c/n 4338), BW-E, *Ty*; and 68-10957 (c/n 4339), BW-F, *Brage*.

Very active with NATO and domestic military duties, the Norwegian Hercules have also played a wide humanitarian role down the years. One famous episode on 31 May 1970 saw them flying a whole surgical unit to Lima, Peru, while the same year saw them flying helicopters from Panama,

Vietnam and elsewhere to operate with the US Navy carrier *Guam* anchored off Chimbote, to fly relief missions into the interior.

Overhead aerial view of Royal Norwegian Air Force Hercules C-130H BW-C (c/n 4336) named Balder in flight with special markings over Norway. (Lockheed-Georgia, Marietta via Audrey Pearcy)

196 Royal Saudi Air Force
(Al Quwwat Ali Jawwiya Assa'udiya)

T he following Hercules were purchased by the Saudi Government in several batches down the years. Initially in 1965 they purchased two C-130Es, 451, the former N9258R (c/n 4076), and 452 (c/n 4078). The following year they obtained another pair: 453 (c/n 4128) and 454 (c/n 4136). In 1967 another was purchased, 455 (c/n 4215), and the following year four more: 1606 (c/n 4304), 1607 (c/n 4306), 1608 (c/n 4307) and 1609 (c/n 4311).

In 1970 a pair of C-130Hs was purchased – 1610 (c/n 4396) and 1611 (c/n 4397) – with another pair in 1973: 456 (c/n 4503) and 457 (c/n 4511). These were followed by another six of the same type purchased in 1974: 458

(c/n 4532), 459 (c/n 4539), 460 (c/n 4566), 461 (c/n 4567), 1612 (c/n 4552) and 1614 (c/n 4560).

A single VC-130H, 102 (c/n 4605), was bought in 1977 for use as a VIP aircraft, with square windows, but she was re-registered 111 in 1977.

In 1975 a large order for eight C-130Hs was placed: 463 (c/n 4607), 464 (c/n 4608), 465 (c/n 4609), 1601 (c/n 4612), 1602 (c/n 4614), 1603 (c/n 4618), 1604 (c/n 4633) and 1605 (c/n 4634). A further order for ten more Hercules of this type followed in 1977: 112 (c/n 4737), 466 (c/n 4740), 467 (c/n 4741), 468 (c/n 4751), 469 (c/n 4754), 470 (c/n 4756), 1615 (c/n 4745), 1616 (c/n 4746), 1618 (c/n 4755) and 1619

(c/n 4758). In 1991/92 a fresh order for C-130Hs was delivered, and these were the former N4099R (c/n 5234), which became 472, 473 (c/n 5235), 474 (c/n 5252), 475 (c/n 5253), 1623 (c/n 5254), 1624 (c/n 5267), 1625 (c/n 5269) and 1625 (c/n 5270).

Two VC-130Hs were delivered in 1980 after being converted into VIP aircraft for the Saudi Royal Flight: the former N4099M (c/n 4843), which became HZ-HM5, 1980, re-registered HZ-114 in 1980; and the former N4101M (c/n 4845), which became HZ-HM6, 1980, re-registered HZ-115 in 1980.

Three KC-130Hs were also obtained: 1617 (c/n 4750) in 1977, followed by 1620 (c/n 4872) and 1621 (c/n 4873) in 1980.

Two of the stretched C-130H-30s were purchased in 1992: 471 (c/n 5211) and 1622 (c/n 5212).

Many other Saudi Government Hercules are operated by Saudia. Seven specially converted C-100-30s were operated by Saudia as airborne emergency hospital (medical services) aircraft, C-130H(AEH)s: the former N4253M (c/n 4950), which became HZ-MS05 and later HZ-128; the former N4254M (c/n 4952), which became HZ-MS06; HZ-117 (c/n 4954); the former N4255M (c/n 4956), which became HZ-MS09; the former N4261M (c/n 4957), which became HZ-MS10, and later HZ-129; the former N4266M (c/n 4960), which became HZ-MS14; and the former N4243M (c/n 4986), which became HZ-MS8. There are also four specially converted C-130Hs: the former N4098M (c/n 4837), which became HZ-MS019; the former N4185M (c/n 4915), which became HZ-116; the former N4240M (c/n 4918), which became HZ-MS021 and later MS2; and the former N4190M (c/n 4922), which

Striking view of the Royal Saudi Air Force Herk, (c/n 4078) coded 452, in-flight off the coastline 1976. (Royal Saudi Air Force)

An interior view of one of the seven Saudi Arabian HS (Hospital Ships) specially fitted out L-100-30s. In the front is the operating theatre, which could support two simultaneous operations, while in the centre section beyond can be seen a row of removable seats for medical personnel and medical equipment and supply storage. (via Sven-Ake Karlson)

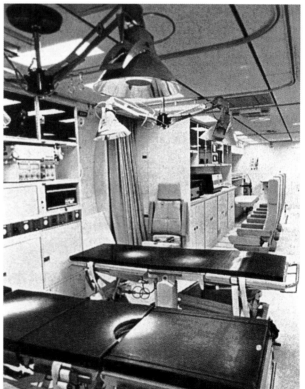

became HZ-MS7. Also there were two VC-130Hs: the former N4098M (c/n 4837), which became HZ-MS019, and the former N4099M (c/n 4843), which became HZ-HM5 and then HZ-114. (See Saudia section for more details.)

197 Royal Swedish Air Force (*Svenska Flygvapnet*)

T he *Svenska Flygvapnet* has always been at the forefront of aeronautical developments and, for the nation's size and neutrality, always one of the best-equipped air forces in Europe. It was no surprise therefore that the Swedes were among the first to see the Herk's great potential, nor that Sweden became the very first air force in Europe to operate the type, even before the RAF had taken on their complement.

The first aircraft, the former USAF C-130E ex 64-0546 (c/n 4039), which had been sold back to Lockheed prior to delivery, was leased by the *Svenska Flygvapnet* as early as February 1965, and was purchased outright that same September, taking the serial 84001. She was assigned to *7 Flygflottilj Transportglygdivisionen*, which operated from Satenas airfield, and they flew her exhaustively in an intensive test programme. Later, in 1968, she was herself leased to the Red Cross for relief flights into Biafra and carried the temporary civilian registration SE-XBT. In August 1987 she was upgraded to C-130H standard.

Performing at Karlsborg on 19 August 1984 is one of the Swedish Air Force Herk C-130Es (382C-8E), serial number 846 (c/n 4885), marked out in test colours. She was later fitted out for electronic countermeasures work. (Sven-Ake Karlson)

Lined up at Karlsborg are several of the Swedish Air Force C-130Es (382C-8E), with ECM underwing pods. They are painted in dark cameo and have black serial numbers; the closest to the camera with crew disembarking is serial 847 (c/n 4887), delivered in May 1985. (Sven-Ake Karlson)

Work being carried out on this Swedish Air Force Herk, serial 847 c/n 4887), at Cambridge Airfield in 1967. (Marshall of Cambridge Aerospace Ltd via Martin W. Bowman)

This first Herk was joined by a second C-130E, 84002 (c/n 4332), which was purchased in May 1969 and similarly brought up to C-130H standard with the installation of the 15LFE engines in February 1982. The Swedish Herks were widely used in the humanitarian role, working with the International Red Cross in Bangladesh and Africa, and with the United Nations peace-keeping forces in the Middle East, in addition to their role as the prime logistical transport for the Air Force.

Sweden purchased six new C-130Hs between October 1975 and 1982, and designated them the Tp 84: 84003 (c/n 4628), 84004 (c/n 4881), which was later ECM-equipped; 84005 (c/n 4884), 84006 (c/n 4885), 84007 (c/n 4887); and 84008 (c/n 4890). The last trio were purchased at a cost of $34 million and were delivered in the first half of 1981.

In 1981 aircraft 841 was in Biafra, which was, according to Lars Olausson, 'a rather hairy operation with

Swedish Air Force C-130H Hercules, serial 841 (c/n 4039) which was modified from a C-130E in 1987. She carries the new (1999) colour scheme of light grey with black markings and carries the national flag on the tail, along with the proud boast, 'First C-130 in Europe', underlined in the national colours of blue and yellow. (Sven-Ake Karlson)

Close-up of the tail markings of Swedish Air Force C-130H Hercules, serial 841 (c/n 4039), in the new light grey colour scheme. (Sven-Ake Karlson)

Fly-past by Swedish Air Force C-130H Hercules, serial 841 (c/n 4039), in the new light grey colour scheme and with her special tail markings proclaiming her to be 'First C-130 in Europe'. (Sven-Ake Karlson)

many aeroplanes in the night searching for the same dimly lit strip'.[33] During Operation 'Bushel' in Ethiopia, 842 and 843 both sustained a great deal of damage from landing on strips bestrewn with loose stones. By 20 August 1987 the following aircraft had these listed flying hours on them:

84001	9,831 hours
84002	8,324 hours
84003	5,447 hours
84004	2,664 hours
84005	2,469 hours
84006	2,718 hours
84007	2,645 hours
84008	2,827 hours

A yearly average of 375 hours.

198 Royal Thai Air Force

Three brand-new C-130Hs were acquired by the Royal Thai Air Force under the US Military Assistance Programme (MAP) and Foreign Military Sales (FMS) scheme via the USAF Aeronautical Systems Division in August 1980: 60101 (c/n 4861), 60102 (c/n 4862) and 60103 (c/n 4863). The Thais thus became the forty-sixth nation to operate the Herky Bird, which replaced the old piston-engined C-123s, and they were flown by No. 601 Squadron, 6 Wing, from Don Muang Airbase near Bangkok.

A single C-130H-30 was added in April 1983, 60104 (c/n 4959), and in December 1988 two more C-130Hs were purchased, becoming serials 60105 (c/n 5146) and 60106 (c/n 5148). These were followed in November 1990 by a second C-130H-30 purchased from Lockheed, 60107 (c/n 5208), and yet another C-130H, 60108 (c/n 5209). Another pair of C-130Hs followed in November and December 1992: 60109 (c/n 5272) and 60110 (c/n 5274). Finally, another pair of the stretched C-130H-30s was obtained in April 1992, becoming 60111 (c/n 5280), which was refurbished as a governmental VIP aircraft, and 60112 (c/n 5281).

[33] Lars Olausson to Arthur Pearcy, dated 26 August 1987, courtesy of Audrey Pearcy.

199 Singapore Air Force (*Republic of Singapore Air Force*)

When the island of Singapore broke away from the Malaysia confederation they set up their own military air arm, the *Republic of Singapore Air Force*, and in 1977 they obtained their first Hercules transport, a former USAF C-130B 58-0725 (c/n 3519). She became 720 and served with No. 122 Squadron, and was converted into a KC-130B aerial tanker in 1988. She was joined in No. 122 Squadron by a second of the same type, the ex USAF 58-0756 (c/n 3557), which became 721 and was later similarly converted to a KC-130B.

Two further C-130Bs were acquired from the Royal Jordanian Air Force, also in 1977: ex 60-0302 (c/n 3611), the Jordanian serial 142, which became RSAF serial 724; and ex 60-0308 (c/n 3620), Jordanian serial 143, which became RSAF serial 725. Again both these were later modified to KC-130Bs. Based at Pay Lebar airfield with No. 122 Squadron, these four aircraft soldiered on until, between January and May 1980, the squadron was reinforced with four new C-130Hs: 730 (c/n 4842), 731 (c/n 4844), 732 (c/n 4846) and 733 (c/n 4848).

A modern tanker was acquired in October 1982, the former Lockheed KC-130H registration N4237M (c/n 4940), which became serial 734. The final addition to date was the acquisition of a fifth C-130H in October 1986, the former Lockheed N73233 (c/n 5070), which received the serial 735.

200 South African Air Force

South Africa, the most prosperous nation in Africa as well as one of the largest, was quick to equip her well-maintained armed forces with the best equipment, and the South African Air Force ordered seven brand-new C-130Bs between November 1962 and 1963: 401 (c/n 3724), 402 (c/n 3749), 403 (c/n 3750), 404 (c/n 3764), 405 (c/n 3765), 406 (c/n 3767) and 407 (c/n 3769). These were operated by No. 28 Squadron of the Air Transport Command, which has its base at Waterkloof, Transvaal.

More would have joined them but for an arms embargo imposed by the United Nations, so the nineteen much-traded civilian L-100-30s of the ubiquitous Safmarine/Safair company (see appropriate section) were earmarked as strategic reserve aircraft to fill the gap. Meanwhile, by high-quality care and maintenance, these seven SAAF Herks continued to operate right up to the present day, despite getting rather long in the tooth! Between 1975 and 1976 they supported clandestine operations in Angola, despite the fact that during the rainy season the landing 'fields' turned to 'sheets of water or large expanses of deep, glutinous mud'. They were also used in the humanitarian role, helping to evacuate the flood of innocent refugees from the fighting area, and at one point 1,604 people were taken from Angola to AFB Waterkloof, near Pretoria. They also operated round-the-clock search-and-rescue missions. In November 1965, for example, two of them conducted a search for the crew of an SAAF Buccaneer that had crashed into the sea near Ascension Island on its way south from the UK. They repeated this mission in October 1969 for the crew of another Buccaneer down in the drink north of Durban, as well as conducting the the hunt for the yacht *Girasol* lost in the Indian Ocean south of Madagascar in 1975 and the coaster *Induna* lost in the same area four years later.[34] No. 28 Squadron also ran a regular shuttle service between Pretoria and Cape Town with up to ninety passengers on webbing seats crammed between pallets of baggage.

When the embargo was finally lifted, two old C-130Bs were obtained from surplus USAF stock in 1997/8: the former USAF serial 58-0731 (c/n 3526), which became SAAF serial 408, and former 58-0734 (c/n 3530) which became SAAF serial 409. Both were re-equipped for the ECM role in 1998. In addition to this elderly pair, three equally vintage former US Navy C-130Fs were purchased around the same time: ex 149787 (c/n 3636), ex 149793 (c/n 3660) and ex 149805 (c/n 3695). All were due to be refurbished but were not and are used for spare parts.

Although, as Colonel Steyn Venter, the South African Air Attaché in London, stated, 'We would love to have the J', he added that, 'with our financial constraints we have to have the upgrade. It will allow us to fly these aircraft for the next twenty years.'[35] Certainly the cost of modernisation by Marshall Aerospace at Cambridge, at £9 million, is only a quarter of that of a new J, but gives the thirty-year-old Bs some 65% of the new aircraft's performance – quite a good deal for the SAAF.

---

[34] See 'The Lockheed C-130B Hercules – Aircraft for all seasons', anonymous article in *SAAF News* magazine, 1980.

[35] See Peter Almond, 'RAF's new Hercules arrives 2 years late', article in *Daily Telegraph*, 25 November 1999.

201 South Korean Air Force (*ROKAF*)

Four Lockheed test C-130H-30s were purchased, two in July 1987 and two in November/December of the same year: the former Lockheed low-altitude parachute eject system (LAPES) test stretched Herk N4080M (c/n 5006), which became ROK serial 5006; former N73232 (c/n 5019), which became 5019; former Lockheed N4249Y (c/n 5030), which became 5030; and former Lockheed N4141T (c/n 5036), which became 5036.

Six new C-130Hs were purchased from Lockheed between October 1989 and February 1990: 5178 (c/n 5178), 5179 (c/n 5179), 5180 (c/n 5180), 5181 (c/n 5181), 5182 (c/n 5182), and 5183 (c/n 5183). All these Herks were operated by the ROK's Air Transport Wing, based at Kimpo airfield near Seoul.

Two further C-130Hs were purchased from Lockheed and joined the first six in March 1990: 5185 (c/n 5185) and 5186 (c/n 5186).

202 Spanish Air Force (*Ejército del Aire Espanol*)

A quartet of brand-new C-130Hs was acquired between December 1973 and April 1974: EAE serial T10-1 (c/n 4520), later changed to 301-01, and later 311-01, which crashed on Gran Canaria in the Canary Islands on 28 May 1980; T10-2 (c/n 4526), changed to 301-02, and later 31-02; T10-3 (c/n 4531), changed to 301-03, and later 311-03, and then 31-03; and T10-4 (c/n 4534), changed to 301-04, then 311-04, and then 31-04. They were initially operated by *Escuadron 301, Mando Aviacion Tactica*, with their base at Zaragoza, Valensuela, but later by *Escuadron 31, Ala de Transporte 31* (hence the serial changes), but from the same airfield.

A solitary new C-130H was purchased in January 1976: TK10-5 (c/n 4642), later 301-05, then 312-10, and finally 31-50. A pair of new-build KC-130Hs followed in February and March 1976: TK10-6 (c/n 4648), later 301-06, then 312-02, and 31-51; TK10-7 (c/n 4652), later 301-07, and then 31-52. Three more new C-130Hs arrived between November 1979 and January 1980 at a price exceeding $18 million: T10-8 (c/n 4835), later 311-05, and then 31-05; T10-9 (c/n 4836), later 311-6, and then 31-06; and T10-10 (c/n 4841), later 312-04, and then 31-07. They operated out of Zaragoza with No. 301 Squadron on logistic, tactical and humanitarian missions. The Air Force on NATO exercises utilised their Herks on paratroop drops, as well as container delivery system (CDS) cargo drops. In

1975 they worked with the International Red Cross in Central Africa hauling food and medicines to drought victims, and the following year assisted the Saharan evacuation by airlifting more than 2,200 people and 4,400,000lb (2,000,000kg) of cargo during 341 sorties. They also worked as pollution control sprayers when the tanker *Uerquiola* sank in the Puerto de la Coruña, airlifting in 613,780lb (278,409kg) of detergent.

Two further KC-130Hs were purchased in November and December 1980: 1620 (c/n 4871), which later crashed at Riyadh, Saudi Arabia, on 24 February 1982; and 1621 (c/n 4874). Both were operated by *Escuadron 32*.

Finally, the former Lockheed C-130H-30 serial N7323D (c/n 5003) was acquired in January 1987, and became serial TL10-01. Later, with *Escuadron 311*, this changed to 311-01, and then 31-01.

203 Sri Lankan Air Force

In January and February 2000 Sri Lanka joined the long line of Herk users when she purchased two former RAF C-130Ks: ex XV203 (c/n 4227), which became serial CR-800, and ex XV213 (c/n 4240), which became serial CR881. Both were due to be modified to C.1P standard.

204 Sudanese Air Force (*Silakh al Jawwiya*)

The forty-third nation to operate the Hercules was Sudan. A batch of six C-130Hs were purchased at $51 million plus for the *Sudaniya* between January and May 1978: 1100 (c/n 4766), 1101 (c/n 4767), 1102 (c/n 4769), which was the 1,500th Hercules delivery; 1103 (c/n 4771), 1104 (c/n 4774) and 1105 (c/n 4775). The plan was for the Sudanese Government to operate them on both economic development and military logistics missions working out of Khartoum Airport.

Lockheed developed a new self-contained and protected high-frequency (H/F) radio antenna which utilised two square feet (0.185m²) of metal and a fibreglass vehicle roof to create a more durable and reliable mobile communications system for the Sudanese operations, which replaced the more vulnerable whip-type antenna. The antenna incorporated all three C-130 communications systems and a very high frequency (VHF) radio system into a four-wheel-drive CJ-7 jeep, and this Mobile Communications Unit (MCU) could be installed in a wide variety of vehicles and even palletised. The MCU contained radio systems for high, ultra high and very high frequency AM and FM bands.

One C-130H of the Sudanese Air Force, 1100 (c/n 4766), has been operated exclusively by the civilian arm, Sudan Airways (see appropriate section for details).

205 Sultanate of Oman

The Sultanate purchased three C-130Hs: former Lockheed demonstrator N4138M (c/n 4878) in February 1981, which became 501; and two brand-new aircraft, 502 (c/n 4916) in February 1982 and 503 (c/n 4948) in January 1983. They all served with No.4 Squadron.

206 Taiwanese Air Force (*Republic of China Air Force*)

Between July and October 1986 the Republic of China on the island of Taiwan received no fewer than twelve new C-130Hs, which became the Republic serials 1301 (c/n 5058), 1302 (c/n 5059), 1303 (c/n 5060), 1304 (c/n 5061), 1305 (c/n 5062), 1306 (c/n 5063), 1307 (c/n 5064), 1308 (c/n 5065), 1309 (c/n 5066), 1310 (c/n 5067), 1311 (c/n 5068) and (c/n 5069). They joined No.10 Squadron and worked out of Pingtung Airbase. Serial 1310 crashed at SungShan airfield, near Taipei, on 10 October 1997.

Another C-130H was purchased from Lockheed in December 1991 and became 1351 (c/n 5215). She was extensively modified for electronic countermeasures operations and also operated out of Pingtung.

In November 1994 another pair of C-130Hs was purchased from Lockheed and became 1313 (c/n 5271) and 1314 (c/n 5276) respectively. In November/December 1994 two additional new C-130Hs were acquired, 1315 (c/n 5308) and 1316 (c/n 5317), and in August a third, 1317 (c/n 5318), joined them.

Finally, another trio of C-130Hs was obtained between August and December 1997: 1318 (c/n 5354), 1319 (c/n 5355) and 1320 (c/n 5358). All are still operational.

207 Tunisian Air Force

The Tunisian *Escadrille de Transport et Communication*, based at Bizerta airfield, operated two brand-new C-130Hs which the Government purchased from Lockheed's stock fleet in March 1985: the former N4249Y (c/n 5020), which although operated by the Air Force was given the civilian type registration TS-MTA, but later became serial Z21011; and the former

N41030 (c/n 5021), which received civilian registration TS-MTB, but later became serial Z21012.

To supplement this pair, seven former USAF C-130Bs were acquired between December 1995 and February 1998: ex 58-0728 (c/n 3523), which became Z21116; ex 58-0751 (c/n 3550), which became Z21115; ex 59-1528 (c/n 3571), which became Z21117; ex 59-1533 (c/n 3586), which became Z21114; ex 60-0299 (c/n 3603), which became Z21118, but sometimes carries the civilian registration TS-MTH; ex 61-0949 (c/n 3625), which became Z21113; and ex 62-3495 (c/n 3721), which became Z21119.

Finally, a single former USAF C-130E was added to the Herk fleet in October 1999: ex 63-7803 (c/n 3869), which became Z21120.

208 Turkish Air Force (*Turk Hava Kuvvetleri*)

F ive new C-130Es were supplied to the *Turk Hava Kuvvetleri* under the Mutual Assistance Programme and joined *222 Filo*, working out of Kayseri Airbase, in December 1964. These were USAF serials ex 63-13186 (c/n 4011), which became ETI-18; ex 63-13187 (c/n 4012), which became ETI-187; ex 63-13188 (c/n 4015),

Turk Hava Kuvvetleri *Hercules, serial ETI-187 (c/n 4012), coming in to land at Ankara*. (Martin W. Bowman)

which became ETI-188; ex 63-13189 (c/n 4016), which became ETI-189; and ETI-494 (c/n 4100), which joined *131 Filo*, but which crashed near Izmir airfield on 19 October 1968.

A further batch of new C-130Es were added under MAP: ETI-947 (c/n 4427) in September 1971; ETI-468 (c/n 4514) in November 1973; and ETI-991 (c/n 4524) in February 1974, which served with *222 Filo*. Most of these aircraft took part in the Turkish paratroop drop which occupied northern Cyprus in 1974 when the island was partitioned, and this led to a United Nations embargo on the supply of further MAP Hercules to this NATO country.

Between December 1991 and August 1992, however, a further seven former USAF C-130Bs were received by the *Turk Hava Kuvvetleri*: ex 57-0527 (c/n 3503), which became 70527; ex 58-0736 (c/n 3532), which became

80736; ex 59-1527 (c/n 3568), which became 591527 but which was returned to the AMARC in 1992 and later sold to the Romanian Air Force (see appropriate section); ex 61-0969 (c/n 3643), which became 10960; ex 61-0963 (c/n 3648), which became 10963; ex 61-2634 (c/n 3670), which became 12634; and ex 62-3496 (c/n 3722), which became 23496. They all fly with *222 Filo* out of Erkilet/Kayseri.

209 Uruguayan Air Force (*Fuerza Aérea Uruguaya*)

In August 1982 a former USAF C-130B, the ex 60-0295 (c/n 3596), was obtained, and received the serial FAU592. After normal service, they used her for supply missions to Antarctica from December 1993. She later took the civilian registration CX-BOX. A second former USAF C-130B, the ex 61-0971(c/n 3668), was obtained in May 1992 and given the serial FAU591, later becoming the civilian-registered CX-BOW. Both these aircraft were operated by *1 Regimento Tactico* from their base at Carrasco, near Montevideo.

In April 1994 the Uruguay Government acquired a third former USAF C-130B, the ex 58-0744 (c/n 3541), from the AMARC park in Arizona, and she became serial FAU593. There is no record that she was ever flown in service by the *Fuerza Aérea Uruguaya* and she was finally struck from charge in July 1997.

210 Venezuelan Air Force (*Fuerza Aérea Venezolana*)

The *Fuerza Aérea Venezolana* placed orders with Lockheed for six new C-130Hs in 1969, and the first quartet was delivered in March 1971 for service with *1 Escuadron, 6 Grupo de Transporte*, working from La Carlota Airbase, near Caracas. The four aircraft were FAZ 3556 (c/n 4406), which subsequently crashed at Caracas on 4 November 1980; FAV4951 (c/n 4407), FAV7772 (c/n 4408), which was also lost in a crash, at Lajes in the Azores, on 27 August 1976; and FAV9508 (c/n 4409). The remaining pair, FAV4224 (c/n 4556) and FAV5320 (c/n 4577), arrived in February and April 1975 respectively.

To replace the two lost Herks others of the same type were ordered, and these became FAV3134 (c/n 4801) in December 1978 and FAV2716 (c/n 5137) in July 1988.

211 Vietnamese Air Force

Although the C-130 had featured largely in the Vietnam conflict from the earliest days of American aid to the beleaguered southern forces, it was not until the final two years of that tragic war that the Republic of Vietnam Air Force (RVAF) received allocations of C-130A Hercules from the USA. Eventually two squadrons, the 435th and 437th, both formed in January 1972 of sixteen aircraft each, were set up, and initially their main duty was the transporting of personnel and equipment up from their base at Tan Son Nhut to the main fighting zones.

The following thirty-two elderly former USAF C-130As were transferred in November 1972 under Project 'Enhance Plus' to replace the C-123K and mainly to work with these two squadrons: the former USAF serial 54-1631 (c/n 3018), later returned to the USAF; 54-1634 (c/n 3021), returned to the USAF; 54-1640 (c/n 3027), returned to the USAF; 55-001 (c/n 3028), later taken over by North Vietnam in a non-operational condition; 55-002 (c/n 3029), burnt out in ground accident at Bien Hoa, 6 April 1972; 55-0005 (c/n 3032), taken over by North Vietnam in a non-operational condition; 55-0006 (c/n 3033), written off April 1975; 55-0008 (c/n 3035), returned to USAF; 55-0012 (c/n 3039), returned to USAF; 55-0013 (c/n 3040), taken over by North Vietnam in a non-operational condition; 55-0016 (c/n 3043), destroyed by enemy action at Song Be, 25 December 1974; 55-0017 (c/n 3044), written off April 1975; 55-0027 (c/n 3054), returned to USAF; 55-0034 (c/n 3061), returned to USAF; 55-0045 (c/n 3072), written off April 1975; 56-0476 (c/n 3084), taken over by North Vietnam in a non-operational condition; 56-0479 (c/n 3087), written off April 1975; 56-0481 (c/n 3089), returned to USAF; 56-0482 (c/n 3090), taken over by North Vietnam in a non-operational condition; 56-0484 (c/n 3091), returned to USAF; 56-0489 (c/n 3097), written off April 1975; 56-0495 (c/n 3103), returned to USAF; 56-0500 (c/n 3108), returned to USAF; 56-0505 (c/n 3113); 56-0518 (c/n 3126), returned to USAF; 56-0524 (c/n 3132), returned to USAF; 56-0532 (c/n 3140), taken over by North Vietnam in a non-operational condition; 56-0542 (c/n 3150), written off April 1975; 56-0543 (c/n 3151), returned to USAF; 57-0460 (c/n 3167), crashed at Phu Bai, near Hue, 2 March 1968; 57-0465 (c/n 3172), written off April 1975; and 57-0472 (c/n 3179), returned to USAF.

Three further C-130As were transferred in August 1973 to replace losses: 56-0519 (c/n 3127), taken over by North Vietnam in a non-operational condition; 56-0521 (c/n 3129), destroyed by enemy action at Song Be,

18 December 1974; and 56-0545 (c/n 3153), returned to USAF.

These Hercules formed the main backbone of the RVAF transport fleet and were efficiently crewed and operated, and had the lowest accident rate of that force, although, due to their age, it was always a struggle to keep them serviced and maintained, and the average serviceability was fourteen aircraft fully operational at any one time. When the North Vietnam regular army increased the use of their Soviet-supplied AAA and SA-7 ground-to-air missiles, the lumbering Herks became more and more vulnerable during supply drops to isolated garrisons, and were forced higher and higher, losing valuable accuracy. The RVAF worked out their own solution to this, after combat tests in which blocks of ice were substituted for equipment. The new method utilised a drop height of between 9,000 and 10,000ft (2,743 to 3,048m) with a delayed-opening parachute which deployed when falling to 2,000ft (610m) altitude. This reduced wind influence and ensured most of the drop arrived in the target zone and not among surrounding North Vietnamese forces. These supply drops were radar-controlled, which overcame the frequent heavy cloud cover as well as the enemy missiles and guns. Nonetheless, the C-130As were still vulnerable to SAMs at the drop height, and flares were carried which were dropped as heat decoys on the occasions when sufficient warning was available.

When the Americans pulled out and left them to it, the lack of heavy bombers was felt, and some C-130As were used as makeshift bombers in the summer of 1974. Under Operation 'Banish Beach', some C-130As were radar-directed at high altitudes over enemy troop concentrations, and parachute-retarded pallets of 55 US gallon (208 litre) oil drums filled with napalm, waste oil or petrol were dropped. These fire bombs ignited on impact and were quite effective against Communist troops caught out in the open or in their trenches. The resulting firestorm could incinerate enemy forces in an area some 1,300ft (396m) long by 700ft (213m) wide. One Hercules was converted to carry an even more lethal bomb load, the 15,000lb (6,804kg) GP *Daisy Cutter*, formerly used by the B-36s. These massive weapons, of which only fifteen were available, were simply rolled out of the tail gate. The effect was demoralising to the enemy, the 500ft (150m) diameter circular blast area 'levelling trees like toothpicks, and leaving nothing but bare ground'. The Communists claimed the B-35s had returned, a story taken up by the compliant Western media, but it was just one lone Hercules delivering the goods. Other loads dropped at this period included 250lb (113kg) bombs which were carried in batches of six-teen to twenty-four at a time and similarly rolled out of the rear door on multiple passes over the enemy positions.

Casualities were few, and mainly in the final days, when all surviving Herks were employed rescuing refugees from the Communist advance, taking 350 of these civilians at a time (normal capacity was 150 maximum). Many C-130s were reclaimed by the USAF after escaping the fall of Saigon, as indicated above, and returned to flying subsidiary duties.

When Tan Son Nhut itself fell to the enemy advance on 20 April 1975, there remained only ten operational C-130As. Seven of these managed to escape to Thailand, while an eighth flew to Singapore when her crew defected. Of those that are known to have fallen into Communist hands, many were in poor or damaged condition, and only two or three of them were briefly employed by them, until lack of maintenance finally grounded them for good.

212 Yemeni Air Force
(*Yemen Arab Republic Air Force*)

Saudi Arabia presented two of its C-130Hs to the *Yemen Arab Republic Air Force* in August 1979: YARAF 1150 (c/n 4825), which later received the civilian registration 7O-ADE, and YARAF 1160 (c/n 4827), which later received the civilian registration 7O-ADD. Both were later operated by Yemeni Airways.

213 Zaire Air Force
(*Force Aérienne Zairoise*)

Between March and July 1971, the *Force Aérienne Zairoise* received three new C-130Hs for service with *191° Escadrille, 19 Wing, d'Appui Logistique*, based at N'Djili Airport near Kinshasa: 9T-TCA (c/n 4411), 9T-TCB (c/n 4416), which was impounded at Malpensa Airport, Milan, in October 1994; and 9T-TCD (c/n 4422), which crashed at Kisangani on 18 August 1974. Some of these were used by President Sese Seko Mobuto on official flights.

Commercial flights with the stretched Hercules were also operated by the Bemba Group for in-country and European air cargo haulage operations, with cargoes as diverse as 20-ton loads of coffee and produce to Belgium and France, returning with farm implements, 35,000lb (15,876kg) D6 bulldozers, water pumps, electric motors and generators, water tanks, ditch diggers, land-rovers, dump trucks, marine engines, medical equipment, frozen meat and dried fish.

Four further C-130Hs were purchased: the first in September 1975, 9T-TCE (c/n 4569), which crashed at Kindu on 14 September 1980; 9T-TCG (c/n 4588) in May 1975, which was also seized at Malpensa in February 1982 and, after receiving the French civilian registration F-ZJEP, joined the *Armée de l'Air* as F-RAPM serial 4588, and later 61-PN; 9T-TCG (c/n 4489) in April 1975, which was re-registered as 9T-TCC and then transferred to *Armée de l'Air* as 4589, and later 61-PN; and 9T-TCG (c/n 4736), which arrived in May 1977 but which crashed near Kinshasa on 19 April 1990, leaving 9T-TCA as the sole survivor.

214 Zambian Air Force

The Government of the Republic of Zambia (GRZ) leased two L-100s: the former Lockheed fleet N9260R (c/n 4101), receiving civilian registration 9J-RCV, and GRZ N9261R (c/n 4109). Both were leased to Zambian Air Cargoes in August 1966. The latter received the civilian registration 9J-RCY and was lost in a ground accident at N'dola Airport on 11 April 1968.

A third L-100, the GRZ-owned 9J-REZ (c/n 4209), was similarly leased to Zambian Air Cargoes in April 1967 and later sold to National Aircraft Leasing (see appropriate section).

The Worldwide Operators of Hercules – Civilian

215 Aboitiz Air Transport

This Manila airport-based company in the Philippines obtained four ex-Australian C-130A Hercules that had never been flown by their RAAF owners: 57-0499 (c/n 3206), the former N22669, which was registered as A97-206 in 1988 and after five years' service was grounded for spares in 1993; 57-0503 (c/n 3210), the former N2267W which was registered as A97-210 in 1988; 57-0504 (c/n 3211), the former N2267W which was registered as A97-211 in 1988; and 57-0506 (c/n 3213), the former N2268G which was registered as A07-213. All were finally sold off to Total Aerospace in Miami in 1998 for spare parts.

216 Advanced Leasing Corporation

A single L-100-30, N82178 (c/n 5048), was delivered to the company. She was subsequently registered to the Transadvaree Corporation, Dallas, Texas. She still flies under the Ardmore Leasing banner.

217 *Aerea Aerovias Ecuatoriansas*

A solitary L-100, N9267R (c/n 4146), built in 1966 and purchased by the Bank of America, was leased to this company in April 1968, but was destroyed in a ground accident at Macuma, Ecuador, on 16 May.

218 Aero Fire-fighting Services

This Anaheim, Orange County, California, company utilised a quartet of C-130As for wildfire control. Veteran pilot for the company, Bill Waldman, originally flew old B-17s for the task from 1969 onward, welcomed the arrival of the C-130s thus: 'With the new-to-us turbine C-130s and P-3 Orions, we can now close the throttles completely. The plane will go downhill like a manhole cover because the engines run at a constant speed and only the propeller blades change pitch.'[36]

One, C-130A N45R (c/n 3104), owned by Roy D. Reagan, was leased in December 1990. Another, N132FF (c/n 3119), was registered in January 1997 but later leased to International Air Response (the former T&G Aviation) in November 1998. A third, N131FF (c/n 3138), was registered in July 1990 and leased to Hemet Valley in June 1991, who sold her to Michael Zincka Leasing, who in turn sub-leased her to the French *Securité Civile* in August 1993 and then, in November 1998, to International Air Response. A fourth, N135FF (c/n 3148), was registered on July 1990 and leased to Hemet Valley, who again sold to Michael Zincka Leasing who sub-leased her to *Securité Civile* in August 1983, and then to International Air Response.

In addition, a single RC-130A (c/n 3227) was bought from Pacific Gateway Investments Inc., also of Orange County, in April 1997 and again leased to International Air Response in November 1998.

219 Aero International

A single L-100-30 Hercules, N8183J (c/n 4796), registered to Rapid Air Transport, Washington DC, in February 1982 was operated by this company in 1982, before being leased to Tepper Aviation.

220 *Aeropostal de Mexico*

Two former USAF C-130As, 56-0487 (c/n 3095) and 56-0537 (c/n 3145), which were leased from Pacific Harbor Capital during 1992, carrying the registrations XA-RYZ and XA-RSG respectively. They were replaced by two former USAF RC-130s, 57-0517 (c/n 3224) and 57-0518 (c/n 3225), leased this time from T&G Aviation in 1993/94, carrying the registrations XA-RSH and XA-RYZ. All these aircraft, painted an overall white colour scheme, worked out of Mexico City for this Mexican Government-sponsored organisation until about 1996.

---

[36] See Don Dowie, 'Fire-fighting', op. cit.

221 AFI International

Two L-100-30 stretched Hercules, N4248M (c/n 4992) and N4269M (c/n 5000), delivered in May 1985 were obtained by this company, the former from the West German company POP, which was to be used for oil exploration in Benin, Nigeria. Both arrived in Libya, with Libyan aircrews aboard, having successfully evaded the US ban on sales to that country. They were used to support Libyan forces infiltrating and fighting in Chad.

222 African AirCargo

This Miami, Florida-registered company operated a single C-130A Hercules, N4469P (c/n 3215) which it purchased from the ITT Commercial Finance Corporation in January 1989,[37] but this machine was later impounded by the US Customs Office at Naples, Florida, and kept at Fort Lauderdale until it was sold to F. S. Conner of Miami, and she was registered to the Zotti Group Aviation company of that city until finally sold for scrap in December 1997.

---

[37] In the January 1988 issue of *Trade-A-Plane* (Crossville, Tennessee), p.127, this aircraft was advertised for sale at a knock-down price of $1.6 million ('Normal retail price $US 3 million'). She was credited in the advertisement with 'Approved Part 91 for Corporate use fully Certified for Enclosed Cargo and Packages. Colour all over White Blue Stripe with Polished Leading Edges.'

223 Africargo

Based in the Congo, two Safair Hercules, (c/n 4600) and (c/n 4606), were utilised by this company.

224 AFTI (Advanced Fighter Technology Integration)

Two pairs of Hercules were operated by this Mojave, California, organisation – (c/n 3122), (c/n 3168) and (c/n 3203), (c/n 3204) – which became AVTEK Flight Test incorporated, working for the US Navy at Point Magu.

225 *Air Algérie*

Two L-100s, N22ST (c/n 4250) and N9232R (c/n 4299), were leased from Saturn in 1981 pending delivery of two (later three) stretched Herks.

Quick-Change Artist! An Air Algérie L-100-30 undergoes a rapid conversion from a cargo aircraft to a passenger airliner. In the photograph below a pallet containing three rows of seats is rolled from a truck into the 55-foot long cargo compartment of the Super Hercules transport. In the left photograph, Hey Presto! the airplane which was a cargo hauler earlier that day has become a widebody airliner. One pallet, containing a galley and lavatory, is inserted in the centre of the aircraft. Air Algérie operated three of the Lockheed L-100-30 aircraft at this date, 26 October 1981. (Lockheed-Georgia Newsbureau via Audrey Pearcy)

Three L-100-30s – 7T-VGH (c/n 4880) with doors fitted to after fuselage, 7T-VHK (c/n 4883) and 7T-VHL (c/n 4886) – were purchased from Lockheed in 1981. These were specially modified versions designed for quick conversion from cargo hauler to passenger aircraft and back again. Lockheed designed a convertible feature by using seven pallets which contained seating for ninety-one-passengers, plus a complete galley and lavatory, which were loaded in via the commercial locking system and locked to the floor in less than an hour.

Of these aircraft, 7T-VHK crashed on landing at Tamanrasset in August 1989, and was a total loss.

226 Air America

The company operated N7951S (c/n 4301) for Southern Air Transport. This organisation also operated Air Force Hercules, including USAF 56-0510 (c/n 3118) before she crashed in Laos on 10 April 1970, on behalf of the CIA in clandestine operations from Laos during the Vietnam War, and has still not given up all its secrets.

227 *Air Atlantique*

Working from Orly Airport, Paris, for SNEAS in March 1995, this company leased a single L-100-30 ZS-RSI (c/n 4600) from Safair for a short period.

228 Air Botswana Cargo (ABC)

This company was formed in 1979 for *ad hoc* charter work worldwide; however, most of their operations were in fact relief missions, and these took them to, among other places, Cambodia, Chad, Cyprus, Ethiopia, Mozambique, Sudan, Tanzania and Uganda. During one particular operation one ABC aircraft was required to move 10,000 tons of supplies in just over three months. Servicing was carried out between schedules and curfew hours to maximise the aircraft's usage, and the task was completed on time.[38]

A single L-100-20, ZS-GSK (c/n 4385), was leased from Safair in November 1984 as their registration A2-AEG for two years. An L-100-30, fitted with fuselage windows for the passenger-carrying module, ZS-JIY (c/n 4691), was also leased from Safair in October 1979 and re-registered A2-ABZ. It was returned in August 1983. A second L-100-30, ZS-JVM (c/n 4701), was similarly leased from Safair in October 1979 and registered A2-ACA, returned to them in February 1987. At various times these aircraft carried the colours of the Lutheran World Federation and the Red Cross of the ICRC of Geneva for work to Asmara along with a pair of Trans-America Hercules, and they also worked in conjunction with Royal Air Force, Belgian Air Force and Swedish Air Force Herks.

229 Air China

Two L-100-30s, B-3002 (c/n 5025) and B-3007 (c/n 5027), were leased from China Eastern Airlines in 1993.

230 Air Contractors

In October 1998, this company leased two L-100-30s, ZS-JIV (c/n 4673) and ZS-JVL (c/n 4676), from Safair, returning them in May 1999.

231 Air Finance

This outfit bought a single L-100-20, N9259R (c/n 4176), from Delta Airlines in September 1983. She was leased to Alaska International Airlines the following month but sold to CTA in September 1977.

232 Air Freight, Ivory Coast

A former Safair L-100-30, TU-TNV (c/n 4698), was briefly registered in September 1991 with this company, but re-registered with Safair the following January.

233 Air Gabon

The Gabon Air Force used this L-100-20 under the civilian registration of TR-KKB (c/n 4710) until she was badly damaged in an accident in May 1983. In December 1986 they bought an L-100-30, the former LAC N4274M (c/n 5024), and registered her TR-LBV.

---

38 See B. W. A. Hartridge (ABC Chief Flight Engineer), 'Botswana airline's part in famine relief', article for *Airborne Lifesavers* in *World Airnews* magazine, June 1987 edition.

234 Air Kenya

Yet another Safair leasing, Air Kenya's L-100-30 ZS-JIV (c/n 4673) tenure was of brief duration in 1992/3 before Transafrik took her over.

235 Airlift International Inc. (AII)

Between May and September 1969 L-100-20 (c/n 3946) was leased from PSL. Both N9248R (c/n 4221) and N9254R (c/n 4222), L-100s, were also reported to have been utilised. Two L-100s were purchased: N759AL (c/n 4225) and N760AL (c/n 4229).

236 Airplane Sales International

In June and October 1996, this Santa Monica, California-based company bought up eleven, inoperational, former US Navy Hercules which had been dismantled, scrapped or relegated as spare parts at the Aerospace Maintenance and Regeneration Center (AMARC) in Arizona. There were two ex-US Navy TC-130Gs – 151888 (c/n 3849) and 156170 (c/n 4239) – which were registered to the organisation as N93849 and N15674 in June 1996, and nine ex-Navy EC-130Qs: 156171 (c/n 4249), re-registered as N34249; 156172 (c/n 4269) as N42699; 156173 (c/n 4277) as N34277; 156174 (c/n 4278) as N14278; 156175 (c/n 4279) as N14279; 156177 (c/n 4281) as N54281; 159469 (c/n 4595) as N54595; 160608 (c/n 4781) as N14781; and 162313 (c/n 4988) as N9239G.

237 Alaska Airlines (ASA)

One L-100, N1130E (c/n 3946), a former Lockheed demonstrator, was leased in March 1965. Another, N920NA (c/n 4101), was leased from NAL in April 1969, and a third, N9263R (c/n 4134), was purchased from Lockheed in April 1966.

An L-100, N9267R (c/n 4146) *City of Anchorage*, was leased from the Bank of America in June 1966. Another, N9277R (c/n 4208) *City of Juneau*, was purchased in April 1967, while a third, N9248R (c/n 4221), was leased from Lockheed in 1968 and modified to an L-100-20 before being sold to Saturn in October 1970.

Nice study of this Alaska International Air L-100 N105AK (c/n 4176) seen on 14 June 1976. (Nick Williams AAHS)

Arctic Airlift. Lockheed Hercules airfreights flown by Alaska International Air carried out what was up to that time the biggest peacetime airlift in history in 1974–5 supporting the booming oil exploration and oil pipeline construction effort in Alaska. Six AIA L-100 Herks flew a seven-day-a-week, 24-hour-a-day airlift of fuel, supplies and equipment to ice and gravel strips along the pipeline and to the North Slope oil exploration area. They hauled an average million pounds a day at the height of the pipeline build-up. Top photo left: an AIA 'Flying Alaska dump truck' N-105AK (c/n 4176) crossing the high Brooks Range on the way to Prudhoe. Right centre: photo from the Hercules windscreen shows the landing strip in the valley at Dietrich, surrounded by jagged mountain peaks. Note the oil pipeline 'haul road' in the valley. Top right: a skid load of vital oil drilling equipment is offloaded from a Hercules at Deadhorse strip, adjacent to Prudhoe Bay. Left centre: an aircraft makes a take-off from Galbraith. Lower right: Herk preparing to take off again from Galbraith after delivering at ATCO modular housing unit, being driven off by truck in background.
(Lockheed-Georgia, Marietta via Audrey Pearcy)

238 Alaska International Air (AIA)

This company provided heavy airlift capacity for the Trans-Alaska Oil Pipeline, hauling more than 1,000,000lb (453,600kg) of air cargo a day during the height of its construction. They pioneered airlifting such equipment into the North Slope.

An L-100-20, N109AK (c/n 4134), was leased in December 1969. A second L-100-20, N105AK (c/n 4176), was leased from Air Finance in October 1973. One L-100, N9227R (c/n 4208), was purchased from National Aircraft Leasing in November 1972 and sold to Saturn the following March, while another, N921NA (c/n 4209), was leased from National Aircraft Leasing in July 1972, but following an accident in February 1973 was sold by insurance company and finally totally destroyed in an explosion at Galbraigh Lake on 30 August, 1984. Another L-100, N102AK (c/n 4234), was leased from National Aircraft Leasing in July 1972, and finally written off in a crash in Alaska in October 1974.

An L-100-20, N103AK (c/n 4222), was leased and then purchased from Saturn in January 1973, while another, N22ST (c/n 4250), was leased from National Aircraft Leasing in October 1975. A third, N104AK (c/n 4300), was leased then purchased in November 1975 from Lockheed and subsequently converted to an L-100-30.

An L-100-30, N101AK (c/n 4248), was similarly leased from National Aircraft Leasing and then outright purchased in December 1977 and subsequently transferred to Markair in 1984. A second, N9232R (c/n 4299), was leased from Saturn in November 1975. Two more L-100-30s, N10ST (c/n 4383) and N11ST (c/n 4384), were leased from Saturn in 1972–6, while another pair, N107AK (c/n 4472) and N106AK (c/n 4477), were leased from Safair in November 1974.

Two L-100-30s, N108AK (c/n 4763) and N501AK (c/n 4798), were purchased in November 1977. The former was, in 1982, leased to Cargomaster before going to Markair in February 1984, while the latter was sold to United Trade International.

239 Alaska World Trade Corporation

A former Pegasus Aviation L-100-30, N2189M (c/n 4582), was registered to this company for a few months early in 1990 before being taken over by Flight Cargo Leasing of Dover, Delaware, in April of that year.

240 Angolan Air Charter (TAAG)

This Luanda-based company also operated as Angolan Airlines and has used Hercules for many years now. Among their diverse roles one was converted with 1,800 US gallon (6,814 litre) internal fuel tanks to haul jet fuel to Menongue, Huambo and Luena.

In January 1999, TAAG obtained a single ex-USAF/US Navy DC-130A, the former 56-0491/158229 (c/n 3099), from CZX at Wilmington, Delaware, with the civilian registration N9724V. She suffered a couple of crashes while operating for the Angolan Government with Unitrans, the second of which, at the 4 de Fevereiro Airport, Luanda, on 10 June 1991, was terminal. Control was lost following an engine failure, and the aircraft, carrying military supplies for the Angolan Ministry of Defence, crashed and caught fire, killing all four crew members and three passengers on board.

In September 1978, Angola Cargo obtained an L-100-20 from CTA, D2-FAF (c/n 4176). She became part of TAAG-Angola Airlines the following April but was scrapped after crash-landing at São Tomé Airport on 15 May. Another L-100-20, D2-FAG (c/n 4222), was similarly purchased from CTA in November 1977, and used by TAAG-Angolan Airlines from the following April, and then Angolan Air Charter. She was twice hit by UNITA action, once while taking off from Luanda in 1982, and again on 5 January 1990, when a missile hit her while she was taking off from Menongue. She crash-landed but was written off.

An L-100-30, N901SJ (c/n 4299), owned by Commercial Air Leasing, was briefly flown for TAAG in 1994 before being leased to Foyle Air, UK. A second L-100-30, ZS-RSC (c/n 4475), operated by Safair but leased out to various companies, also flew in Angola for a brief period in 1987. In October 1992 another Safair L-100-30, ZS-RSI (c/n 4600), was leased for a few months by Angolan Air Charter. A third L-100-30, ZS-JIV (c/n 4673), was leased from Safair for a short spell in 1993, and a fourth, ZS-JVL (c/n 4676), similarly leased from that company in 1996/7. A fifth, ZS-JIX (c/n 4684), was also leased from Safair in 1992 and damaged at Ondjiwa in June of that year. Three more L-100-30s – D2-THS (c/n 4691), with fuselage windows, D2-TAD (c/n 4695) and D2-TAB (c/n 4698) – were also leased for short periods in 1993/4.

Three further L-100-30s were sub-leased from Mitsui Corporation for a short period during the same time: PK-PLU (c/n 4824), PK-PLV (c/n 4826) and PK-PLW (c/n 4828). Finally, another trio of this type – PK-PLR (c/n 4889), which was sub-leased from Heavylift in 1990/91; TR-LBV (c/n 5024), leased from Air Gabon in 1988; and PJ-TAC (c/n 5225), leased to TAAG in 1991 as Angola Air Charter – was still operational, despite battle damage, up to the end of 1999.

Angolan Airlines purchased two new-build L-100-20s from Lockheed in November 1979 at a price in excess of $25 million. These became D2-EAS (c/n 4830) and DS-THA (c/n 4832). The former was destroyed by UNITA anti-aircraft-fire action at Menongue on 16 May 1981, the latter made a belly-landing at Dondo on 8 June 1986.

241 AviSto

A Swiss company, Sogerma, purchased the single ex-Ugandan L-100-30 Hercules, 5X-UCF (c/n 4610), which had been impounded and held at Cairo Airport in April 1998 for use with Medecair in central Africa, and she was assigned their reserved registration of PH-AID.

242 Bank of America

A solitary L-100, N9267R (c/n 4146), built in 1966 was purchased by the Bank of America. She was leased as the *City of Anchorage* in June 1966, and again leased, this time to *Aerea Aerovias Ecuatoriansas*, in April 1968.

243 Bradley Air Services

I n June 1998, this organisation registered this ex NWT L-100-30, C-GHPW (c/n 4799), and that same October leased it to Schreiner.

244 Butler Air Cargo

C al Butler, a pioneer of the early techniques to use aircraft for forest fire-fighting, founded this company which is based at Redmond, east of Seattle, Oregon, close to Microsoft headquarters. About 70% of the company was at one time owned by TBM Inc. This company purchased a single flyable former USAF Hercules C-130A, 56-0531 (c/n 3139), in March 1991, and registered her N531BA. She is currently a stripped-out hulk without electronics or running gear.

245 Canadian Airlines International

F ormed in March 1987 but tracing its routes back through five predecessor airlines: Canadian Pacific Air Lines (CP Air), Eastern Provincial Airways (EPA), Nordair, Pacific Western Airlines (PWA) and Wardair Canada Ltd. This Vancouver-based company has operated leased L-100-30s from time to time.

246 Cargolux

A n L-100-20, CF-PWR (c/n 4355), was bought from PWA in December 1980 and received the registration LX-GCV; it was then leased to United African Airlines the following month. Also, an L-100-30, N9232R (c/n 4299), was leased from Saturn in July 1981 for a number of months.

247 Cargomasters (Australia)

C argomasters leased a pair of L-100-30s, N106AK (c/n 4477) and N108AK (c/n 4763), from Alaska International Air in the summer of 1982, returning them the following year.

248 Certified Aircraft Parts

T his outfit purchased a single former US Coast Guard/USAF, HC-130E (c/n 4158), from WIA in September 1988 for breaking up, selling the cockpit section to Reflections and, finally, the remainder to Asia-Pacific Trading & Simulation PTE in November 1995.

249 Chani Enterprises

B ased in Zambia, this company worked a single former USAF Hercules C-130A, 9J-RTM (c/n 3095), from the British company May Ventures in March 1997.

250 China Air Cargo (CAC)

T wo L-100-30s, B-3002 (c/n 5025) and B-3007 (c/n 5027), were purchased from Lockheed in 1987 by this Shanxi-based company, mainly for fish cargo charter Tianjin–Japan. Both these aircraft were subsequently transferred to China Eastern Airlines in 1991.

Dropping in at Los Angeles International is this L-100-20, N9268R (c/n 4147), of Delta Air Lines. (Nick Williams AAHS)

251 China Eastern Airlines (CEA)

Two L-100-30s, B-3002 (c/n 5025) and B-3007 (c/n 5027), were transferred from China Air Cargo in 1991 and leased to Air China in 1993 and China Air Cargo before being sold to Safair in 1999.

252 *Comercial Proveedorn del Oriente SA (COPROSA)*

This organisation worked a single, damaged, former *Fuerza Aérea Perunana* L-100-20 Hercules, FAP394 (c/n 4358), in October 1994 and registered her OB-1376.

253 Commercial Air Leasing Inc.

In June 1985 this organisation obtained a former Saturn L-100-20, N22ST (c/n 4250), and leased her to IAS/Diamang from 1986. This aircraft was destroyed by mines at Wau, Sudan, while working for the International Red Cross on 2 September 1991. Also, an L-100-30, N520SJ (c/n 4299), was similarly obtained from Saturn at the same date, for subsequent leasing, re-registered N901SJ in April 1988, and was sold to Transafrik in August 1988, who sold her on to the First Security Bank the following month. A second former Saturn L-100-30, N519SJ (c/n 4562), was likewise obtained in May 1988 and re-registered N904SJ. She ended up at the Hamilton Aviation Air Park at Tucson, Arizona, where she was bought by Derco in August 1997.

254 Continental Air Services (CAS)

N9260R (c/n 4101) was the very first L-100 to be delivered to any civilian customer, leased from Lockheed on 30 September 1963. She was sold to GRZ in August 1966. A second, N9261R (c/n 4109), was leased in November 1965 and was also later sold to GRZ at the same time.

255 CZX Productions Inc. (DE)

A single machine, a former USAF/US Navy DC130A, 56-0491/158229 (c/n 3099), was obtained by this Wilmington, Delaware, company in August 1988 from Bob's Air Park at Tucson, Arizona, who sold her on to TAAG, Angola, in January 1991.

Cargo gulper! Delta Air Lines air freighter L-100 N9268R (c/n 4147) is loaded with palletised cargo. (Lockheed-Georgia, Marietta via Audrey Pearcy)

256 Delta Air Lines

Based at Atlanta, Georgia, this well-known company operated a fleet of Hercules for many years on scheduled daily all-freight operations, and increased its freight volume by 92% over six years of C-130 operation. Three L-100s were purchased: N9268R (c/n 4147) in August 1966, and N9258R (c/n 4170) and N9529R (c/n 4176) both in October 1966. All were modified to L-100-20s in 1972.

An L-100, N7999S (c/n 4234), was leased to Delta by National Aircraft Leasing in January 1970.

257 EAS (Europe Air Service) Air Cargo

Based at Perpignan, this company operated a leased L-100-30 for a short period.

258 Echo Bay Mines

A well-travelled L-100-20, CF-DSX (c/n 4303), was obtained from the James Bay Energy Corporation in July 1980, and received the name *Smokey Heel*. She worked with Worldways Canada and her name changed to *Bob Burton* before she was registered to the Florida corporation American Aircraft at Hialeah in July 1988.[39]

---

[39] This aircraft was advertised for sale in the February 1988 issue of *Trade-A-Plane* under the registration N39ST by Transamerica Airlines Inc. of Oakland, 'Fully Equipped for International Operation Including Dual Litton I.N.S.' The advertisement carried the proviso, 'The aircraft is subject to prior sale, commitment or withdrawal from market without prior notice', and no price was mentioned.

259 ENDIAMA

ENDIAMA is the Angolan State Diamond Mining Organisation with mines at Luzamba, Catoca and the Cuanago Valley, the latter under continual threat from UNITA rebels. Based in Angola, they purchased a single Hercules, D2-EHD (c/n 4839), which had already been twice damaged by UNITA action in that country. The aircraft was flown by a Transafrik crew and later re-registered T-650, and was again damaged by UNITA action at Luena in February 1992 and repaired in Portugal. Returning to Luanda, she continued her dangerous work until UNITA finally got her at the fourth attempt, shooting her down at Huambo on 2 January 1999.

260 Ethiopian Airlines (RRC Air Services)

Two Hercules L-100-30 aircraft were leased from RRC Air Services, after being in storage since 1984/85: ET-AJK (c/n 5022) and ET-AJL (c/n 5029) in July 1988. ET-AJL was lost in a crash south of Djibouti on 17 September 1991. A third, ET-AKG (c/n 5306), was purchased in November 1996.

261 Evergreen International Aviation Inc.

Evergreen Holdings, which included Evergreen International Aviation and Evergreen Helicopters, were originally established at McMinnville, Oregon. Following the Senator Frank Church hearings, in 1975 the CIA was pressured to sell off its lucrative business front companies, and this included Marana Field, which was taken over by Evergreen. The manager of the CIA's proprietary airlines, George Dole, worked for Evergreen, as did former CIA pilots Gary Eitel and Dean Moss, the latter of whom died in mysterious circumstances.[40]

The company grew rapidly with government contracts, and currently has seven subsidiary companies, one of which specialises in air cargo. In February/May 1999 they bought two former USAF WC-130E Hercules, 61-2365 (c/n 3688) and 64-0552 (c/n 4047), from Wright-Patterson

---

[40] See John Titus, 'Evergreen Pilot murdered on Weapons Flight', article in *Portland Free Press*, March/April 1994; and 'Air Force Investigates Evergreen', article in *Portland Free Press*, May/June 1996 issue.

airfield, Ohio, after both had been retired from service. Both aircraft were ex-stock from Western Intentional Aviation salvage yard at Tucson, Arizona.

Due to heavy debts and financial problems, in December 1997 the company announced that an 'unnamed' financial institution would help buy back $125 million of bonds, but the sell-off of some aircraft assets seemed inevitable. Both Hercules were offered up for re-sale in January 2000, and are located at the Pinal Air Park, Marana, Arizona, pending their disposal. Their attributes are listed as upgraded wing modifications completed in 1986 and 1988, low flight times (19,485 and 20,357 hours respectively) and the fact that both aircraft were well maintained by the US Air Force (any rumoured covert CIA backing and usage is *not* mentioned!).

262 *Fédération Européenne des Sociétés* (EFIS)

A French company, with headquarters at Chateauroux, they employed a single Hercules L-100-30, F-GNM (c/n 4695), which they leased from Safair, between February 1996 and May 1997.

263 First National Bank of Chicago

A single L-100-20, N92656R (c/n 4300), was purchased by the bank on behalf of Interior Airways, who leased at various periods from 1968 until she was sold to AIA in October 1975. AIA had her modified to an L-100-30.

264 Flight Cargo Leasing Inc.

Based at Dover, Delaware, this organisation registered a former Alaska World Trade L-100-20, N2189M (c/n 4582), in April 1990 and leased her to Tepper Aviation and Rapid Air Transport for eastern European operations.

265 Flight Systems Inc. (AVTEL Flight Tests Inc.)

Three ex-USAF DC-130As – 56-0514 (c/n 3122), 57-0496 (c/n 3203) and 57-0497 (c/n 3204) – were operated by Flight Systems for the US Navy between April 1986 and October 1990, and by AVTEL Flight Tests Inc. at Mojave, California, and Donaldson

Center, Greenville, South Carolina. The first aircraft was finally scrapped for parts at the end of 1993, while the other two went to Point Magu.

266 Flying W Airways (FWA)

The company flew this L-100-20, a former Lockheed demonstrator, as N50FW (c/n 3946) under lease to PSL in 1969 before she was leased to Airlift International. They also leased two other L-100-20s, N30FW (c/n 4302) and N50FW (c/n 4303), from the Giraud Trust in April 1964, before they went to the subsidiary RDA that same December. Finally, two further L-100-20s, N60FW (c/n 4358) and N70FW (c/n 4364), were purchased from Lockheed in July 1970, but later went back to Lockheed as N785S and N7986S respectively and were re-sold to the *Fuerza Aérea del Peru* instead.

267 Ford & Vlahos

This company is headed by John J. Ford, assistant secretary of T&G Aviation and head of a firm of attorneys in San Francisco who act for Pacific Harbor Capital. On their behalf Southern Cross, owned by Multitrade, duly acquired seven unused RAAF C-130As – 57-0500/N2267B (c/n 3207), 57-0501/N2267N (c/n 3208), 57-0503/N2267U (c/n 3210), 57-0504/N2267W (c/n 3211), 57-0505/N2268A (c/n 3212), 57-0508/N2268V (c/n 3215) and 57-0509/N2268W (c/n 3216) – out of storage from Laverton RAAF base (N2267W from the School of Technical Training, Wagga) and re-registered them N22FV (November 1985), N4445V (September 1986), N12FV (March 1986), N5394L (July 1984), N13FV (October 1983) and N15FV (September 1986) respectively.

The first was used for the Band Aid relief flights in Ethiopia and operated by International Air Aid for the International Red Cross until April 1986. Three others (the second, fifth and sixth) were originally to be sold to the Government of Colombia, but this was blocked by the US Government, and instead they were registered to Ford & Vlahos as in August 1983. The second was finally sold to *Securité Civile* for the Chad Government in October 1979, and the fifth was embargoed at Oakland, California, until returned to the RAAF in November 1986. The third and fourth were also returned to the RAAF in 1986, then leased to Hayes Industries, Alabama, the following month. The sixth was eventually sub-leased to the US Nuclear Defense Agency, then stored at Chico, California, and later

operated by International Air in the Sudan in 1985 before being registered to ITT Commercial Finance Corporation in August 1986.

268 Fowler Aeronautical Services

This company, based at Van Nuys airfield, California, obtained four former unused RAAF C-130As – N205FA (c/n 3205), N207GM (c/n 3207), N213DW (c/n 3212) and N216CR (c/n 3216) – which had been originally registered to Ford & Vlahos (see appropriate section) but returned to the RAAF. They were registered by Fowler in 1989 for re-sale. The first was returned to the RAAF in 1990 and was demolished for parts and training 1990/1; the second and fourth were eventually registered to IEP, IEPO at Chatsworth, California, in September 1992; the third was sold to Peter Suarez at Van Nuys in July 1994.

269 Foyle Air UK

Based at Luton Airport, this company utilised three Hercules aircraft over a four-year period. An L-100-30, registration N901SJ (c/n 4299), was leased from Commercial Air Leasing in January 1994 for use as an oil spill spraying aircraft, as was a second of the same type, N908SJ (c/n 4300), the following year, and a third, N923SJ (c/n 4301), in 1997.

270 Frameair (TAC Holdings)

A single L-100-30, PJ-TAC (c/n 5225), was purchased by this Netherlands Antilles company in August 1991 and subsequently leased to TAAG as Angola Air Charter in April 1993. A second, (c/n 5307), was ordered in February 1992, but cancelled in January 1996. She was subsequently sold to the Canadian Armed Forces in March 1996. Four further L-100-30s – S9-NAD (c/n 4475), ZS-JVL (c/n 4676), D2-TAD (c/n 4695) and D2-TAB (c/n 4698) – were leased from Safair to TAC Holdings (Frameair) at various times for work for the Angolan Government.

271 Globe Air Inc.

This holding company had four of the ubiquitous and much-touted former Safair L-100-30s registered to it for a while, most of which were operated by Saturn before going into storage and being re-sold. They were N517SJ (c/n 4558), which was registered in April 1987 but crashed on initial training flight at Travis Air Force Base on the eighth of that month; N904SJ (c/n 4562), which was assigned from Saturn in July 1995, but which was in storage at Tucson until sold by Hamilton Aviation to Derco in August 1978; N250SJ (c/n 4565), registered in April 1987 and later re-registered as N515SJ, operated by Saturn and stored at Tucson, being returned to Globe Air and finally also sold to Derco in August 1997; and N516SJ (c/n 4590), registered in April 1987 and re-registered as N516SJ in July, being operated by Saturn. This last was also stored at Tucson 1993–5, returned to Globe in March 1996, and sold to Lynden Air Cargo in July 1997.

272 Hawkins & Powers

This Wyoming-based concern had two C-130As, the former USAF 56-0496 (c/n 3104) and USAF 56-0507 (c/n 3115), registered as N8053R and N8055R in May 1989. They leased one of the Hercules to British Aerospace Corporation and the other to Multitrade International, a company linked to a previous C-130 sale. Both eventually went to Roy D. Reagan in August 1998.

Three more C-130As – the former USAF 56-0534 (c/n 3142), 56-0535 (c/n 3143) and 56-0538 (c/n 3146), which later served with the US Forest Service – were obtained from Hemet in 1988/89 and registered N131HP, N132HP and N130HP respectively.

Finally, they acquired another quartet of C-130As – the ex USAF 57-0459 (c/n 3166), obtained in February 1990 and registered N135HP; 57-0482 (c/n 3189) in March 1989, and registered N133HP; 57-0511 (c/n 3218) in October 1990, and registered as N134HP; and 57-0513 (c/n 3220), which was obtained for spare parts in August 1998 and registered N8230H.

273 Hayes Industries

Based in Birmingham, Alabama, this company leased a former RAAF C-130A, 57-0508/A97-215 (c/n 3215), from Ford & Vlahos in November 1983, and sub-leased her out to the US Nuclear Defense Agency in 1984. She was stored at Chico, California, for a while, before being utilised by Sudan International Aid the following year, and was finally taken over by the ITT Commercial Finance Corporation in August 1986. The company became Pernco Aerospace Incorporated in 1989.

274 Heavylift

This Stansted-based company has leased six L-100-30s from various owners down the years: N15ST (c/n 4391), ZS-JIX (c/n 4684), PK-PLU (c/n 4824), PK-PLV (c/n 4826), PK-PLW (c/n 4828) and PK-PLR (c/n 4889).

275 Heavylift International

This Sparks, Nevada-based corporation purchased two former USAF C-130As, N487UN (c/n 3095) and M537UN (c/n 3145), from Pacific Harbor in March 1995 and re-sold the former to May Ventures, GB, and the latter to Bush Field Aircraft Corporation, who sold her on to Aero Corporation in January 1999.

276 Hemet Valley Flying Services Incorporated

This Californian fire-fighting company, based at Hemet, originally operated eighteen ex-Navy Grumman S-2 Tracker and thirteen ex-Army Cessna O-2 push-pull spotter aircraft for the job. They upgraded and added punch when they purchased or leased several much-travelled ex-USAF, ex-Forestry Service C-130As as water bombers. Jim Venable, President of the company, said that their C-130s retained their original cabin pressurisation and air-conditioning, unlike other operators of the type who removed such equipment in order to carry more retardant,[41] but there *may* have been other reasons for this. Hemet re-registered them, among them N137FF (c/n 3092), which remained at Tucson until sold to Mace Aviation in August 1998; N134FF (c/n 3104), N132FF (c/n 3119), which was leased to FAASA before going to Aero Firefighting Service Company in 1997; N131FF (c/n 3138), in 1998, before she went to Michael Zicka Leasing in September 1989 and was again leased back, this time from Aero Firefighting in June 1991 and sub-leased to *Securité Civile* in France in 1993. They acquired six further C-130As – N132FF (c/n 3142), N133FF (c/n 3143), N134FF (c/n 3146), N135FF (c/n 3148), N136FF (c/n 3149) and N138FF (c/n 3227) – most of which were also sub-leased and finally sold to Aero.

---

[41] See Don Dowie, 'Fire-fighting', op. cit.

277 Herc Airlift Corporation

A single former RAAF C-130A, 57-0508/A97-215 (c/n 3215), registered N4469P, was leased by this organisation from the ITT Commercial Finance Corporation for a while in 1987, when she was named *Lennie Marie*.

278 HSL Company

B ased in Dallas, Texas, this company obtained a single L-100-30 direct from Lockheed which was registered N8213G (c/n 5055).

279 Hunting Air Cargo

T his company leased three former Safair L-100-30s: N920SJ (c/n 4561) in March 1994; ZS-RSI (c/n 4600) in March 1996; and ZS-JIY (c/n 4691) in February 1997.

280 Inter-Agency Ecological Program (IEP) – IEPO

B ased at Chatsworth, California, in 1992 this organisation registered two former RAAF C-130A Hercules, 57-0500/A97-207 (c/n 3207) and 57-0509/A97-216, (c/n 3216) as N207GM and N216CR respectively.

281 IAAFA (Inter-American Air Force Academy)

B ased at Homestead Air Force Base, three former USAF Hercules were employed as ground training aircraft: a C-130A, 56-0517 (c/n 3125) and a C-130B, (c/n 3537), both of which were destroyed in a hurricane on 24 August 1992, and a C-130B-II, 59-1531 (c/n 3579).

282 Intercargo Services (ICS)

T his French-based company operated a single L-100-30 on behalf of Zimex in 1990, F-GFZE (c/n 4698), which was re-registered to Zimex as HB-ILG before being re-registered to her original owners, Safair, the same year.

283 Interior Airways

B ased at Fairbanks, Alaska, this company operated one L-100-20, N9265R (c/n 4300) for the First National Bank of Chicago from 1968 before first leasing and then selling it to Alaska International Air in 1975.

Five L-100s were leased from National Aircraft Leasing: N921NA (c/n 4209) from 1969 to 1972; N760AL (c/n 4229) in 1967, which crashed at Prudhoe Bay, Alaska, on 24 December 1968; N7999S (c/n 4234) in April 1969; N9262R (c/n 4248) in November 1969; and N9266R (c/n 4250) in December 1968. They hauled scientific equipment and other supplies to scientists on the ice island in the Arctic, some 300 miles (483km) north of Point Barrow, Alaska, having to land on an ice strip only 3,400ft (1,036m) long and 6ft (1.8m) thick. They also moved oil drilling equipment into the North Slope.

All these aircraft were subsequently transferred to Alaska International Air.

284 International Aerodyne (IA)

O ne L-100, N9262R (c/n 4248), was purchased in 1968 and passed to National Aircraft Leasing.

285 International Aviation Services (IAS)

H eadquartered at Shannon, Eire, and with a subsidiary at Guernsey, Channel Islands, this company leased several L-100-30s, including N3847Z (c/n 4839), in December 1984. They later merged with Transmeridian Air Cargo at Luton Airport in the UK and became British Cargo Airlines.

286 International Aviation Services – IAS Cargo Airlines (UK)

O ne L-100-30 was briefly operated for *Air Algérie* by this UK-registered company in 1989, 7T-VHK (c/n 4883), but was written off in a crash at Tamanrasset on 1 August of that year. They later became part of Dan Air London.

287 International Aviation Services – IAS (Guernsey)

Several leased from SAT/TAMAG including N521SJ (c/n 4250) in 1986 and TAM69 (c/n 4759) in 1989, while ND-ACWF (c/n 4839) was purchased from Wirtschafsflug of Frankfurt in December 1984 and re-registered D2-EHD, and was operated for Diamang before being damaged by a UNITA missile in 1986 and subsequently sold to ENDIAMA.

288 International Telephone & Telegraph (ITT) Commercial Finance Corporation

In August 1986, this corporation registered the former RAAF C-130A, 57-0508/A97-215 (c/n 3215), from Ford & Vlahos and leased her to the Herc Airlift Corporation and others before finally selling her to African Air Transport of Miami in June 1988.

289 Investment Capital Xchange

Based at Helena, Montana, this organisation registered a solitary former Lockheed L-100-30 Hercules, N898QR (c/n 5032), in December 1997.

290 Jamahiriya Air Transport

This Tripoli-based company operated two L-100-30 stretched Hercules: N4248M (c/n 4992), which became 5A-DOM, and N4269M (c/n 5000) Delivered in May 1985, the former, from the West German company POP, was to be used for oil exploration in Benin, Nigeria. In fact they flew to Libya, with Libyan aircrews aboard, successfully evading the US ban on sales to that country. 5A-DOM was subsequently hijacked by its defecting aircrew and flown to Egypt in March 1987, but the aircraft was later returned to Libya, despite its illegal origins.

291 James Bay Energy Corporation

This hydro-electrical supply company was based in northern Quebec, and bought a single L-100-20, RP-C98 (c/n 4303), from the Government of the Philippines in September 1973 and leased her to Quebecair for operations. There were two Quebecair aircrew working twelve round-the-clock shifts per day flying from Schefferville with foodstuffs, fuel and other essential supplies for the construction workers, including thousands of gallons of beer, to the outlying camps on the complex of reservoirs, dykes, dams and powerhouses, before she was finally sold to Echo Bay Mines in July 1980.

292 Larkins, Gary R.

This Auburn, California, company registered a former Time Aviation C-130A, N9539G (c/n 3224), in July 1982, and another ex Time Aviation aircraft, a DC-130A, N3149B (c/n 3230), was similarly registered with the company before both went to Humberto Montano in Arizona.

293 LESEA – Lester E. Sumrail Evangelistic

A single C-130A, the former USAF 55-0025 (c/n 3052), was registered N226LS from the *Fuerza Aérea Perunana* in 1990 and christened *Mercy Ship Zoe* for use in relief work. She later carried the name *Feed the Hungry* before being held on the ground at Stansted and then subsequently at South Bend, Indiana, where she was offered for sale.

294 *Lineas Aéreas del Estade* (LADE)

A single Lockheed L-100-30 demonstration aircraft, N4248M (c/n 4891), was purchased by *Fuerza Aérea Argentina* in December 1982. Re-registered LV-APW in February 1982, she was operated by the LADE company.

295 Lockheed-Georgia Company (GELAC)

Although the Lockheed company has registered many completed Hercules on their books, as the Lockheed Aircraft Corporation (LAC) prior to their sale, they only actually retained five Hercules for their own use, mainly as demonstrators. These included an L-100, N1130E (c/n 3946), which was leased out and later converted to an L-100-20.

An L-100-20, N4174M (c/n 4412), originally sold to Kuwait in April 1971, was re-purchased in May 1982 and became the famous high-technology test bed (HTTB) aircraft (see appropriate section for further details).

An L-100-30, N4110M (c/n 4839), was built in March 1980 and retained as a demonstrator until sold to Wirtschaftsflug in October 1981, but she returned to Lockheed in November 1983 and was sold to Guernsey, Channel Islands, in December 1984.

A second L-100-30 demonstrator, N4170M (c/n 4891), was an all-white aircraft with a red stripe for LADE, but was sold to the Argentine Air Force in December 1982.

A KC-130H, N4237M (c/n 4940), was retained as a tanker demonstrator until sold to the Singapore Air Force in July 1987.

296 Lynden Cargo

This Alaskan-based company obtained five former Safair/Saturn L-100-30 Hercules including NJ903SJ (c/n 4590), purchased in July 1997 and re-registered as N403LC in 1997; S9-NAJ (c/n 4606), re-registered N401LC in 1999; D2-TAB (c/n 4698), purchased in February 1997 and re-registered N402LC; and N909SJ (c/n 4763), purchased in May 1999 and re-registered N404LC. The fifth L-100-30 was another former Safair aircraft, ZS-OLG (c/n 5025), which was leased in July 1999.

297 L-100 Leasing

Yet more of the much-circulated former Safair aircraft briefly found their way to this organisation. Two L-100-30s: ZS-RSJ (c/n 4606), operated in Angola by SFAir in 1987 and returned to Safair the following year, and ZS-JJA (c/n 4698), returned to Safair in 1987.

298 Maple Leaf Leasing

Two L-100-20s were registered to this company: the former Zambian Air Cargoes 9J-RBW (c/n 4129), which was purchased in 1969 and leased to Pacific Western, being rebuilt as a L-100-20 after crash damage and finally sold to Pacific Western in 1977, and former Lockheed and National Aircraft Leasing N7960S (c/n 4355), which was leased and then sold to Pacific Western in 1977.

299 Markair

Markair utilised several L-100-30s, including the former Alaska International Air machines N101AK (c/n 4248), leased and then sold to Transamerica International Airlines in 1984; N104AK (c/n 4300), also leased to Transamerica and sold to Saturn in 1987; N107AK (c/n 4472), sold to Saturn in 1992;

N106AK (c/n 4477), in 1984, which it leased to Zantop International and then sold to Saturn; and N108AK (c/n 4763), which was sold to Saturn in 1991.

300 May Ventures UK

This British company purchased a single, much-travelled C-130A, N487UN (c/n 3095), in 1995 and registered her 9J-AFV with the name *Tanganyika*. She was operated by Shabair in Zambia and then went into storage at Johannesburg until being sold to Chani Enterprises in 1998.

301 Megatrade

A single former Lockheed L-100-30 was registered N8218J (c/n 5056), in 1993 by this company, but five years later she was registered under the same number to Ruftberg of Dallas, Texas.

302 Merpati Nusantara Airlines

This Indonesian airline based at Djakarta Airport operated two Hercules L-100-30s, PK-PLS (c/n 4917) and PK-PLT (c/n 4923), which were purchased by the Indonesian Government in 1982 and leased to Pelita before going to Merpati in 1990 and 1986 as their PK-MLS and PK-MLT respectively. Both were placed in storage in the early 1990s and subsequently sold to *Tantara Nasional Indonesia-Angkatan Udara* (TNI-AU).

303 Micronesia Aviation Corporation

In 1993 a former RAAF C-130A, 57-0506/A07-213 (c/n 3213), was leased by this company from the Philippines Air Force, who had her in storage at Manila airfield for many years. Registered RP-C3213, she carried the name *Equator Traders* but was eventually obtained by Total Aerospace for spare parts.

304 Military Aircraft Restoration Corporation

In August, 1986 a former USAF C-130A, 57-0518 (c/n 3225), was registered by this Anaheim, California, corporation and finally sold to *Aeropostal de Mexico* in 1993. Likewise, a second former USAF C-130A, 56-0500 (c/n 3108), was registered to this corporation as N223MA in February 1992 but utilised by the United Nations in central Africa 1994/5, before being offered up for sale as spare parts.

305 Mitsui Corporation

T hree L-100-30s – PK-PLU (c/n 4824), PK-PLV (c/n 4826) and PK-PLW (c/n 4828) – were purchased by this company in July 1979 and leased to Pelita.

306 Montano, Huberto

T his Arizona-based company acquired via Gary R. Larkins two former Time Aviation Hercules: a C-130A, N9539G (c/n 3224), in July 1982, and another ex-Time Aviation aircraft, a DC-130A, N3149B (c/n 3230). Both ended up as scrap at the Western International Aviation yard at Tucson.

307 Multitrade Aircraft Leasing

B ased in Las Vegas, Nevada, this company acquired a single former USAAF C-130A, 56-0500 (c/n 3108), from the Air Force in July 1990 and registered her N223MA, naming her *The Phoenix*. She was used in central African operations and registered to Military Aircraft Restoration in 1992. They leased another from Hawkins & Powers. The company's subsidiary, Southern Cross, flew in a number of RAAF C-130s.

308 National Aircraft Leasing

A long with Pepsico Air Lease, this company owned Hercules aircraft for lease to various operations. An L-100, N920NA (c/n 4101), was purchased from GRZ in March 1969 and leased to ASA, then Saturn, before being modified to an L-100-30 in November 1972. A second L-100, N9227R (c/n 4208), was purchased from ASA in 1967 and sold in turn to AIA in November 1972. Her sister, N921NA (c/n 4209), was purchased from GRZ in 1969 and leased to various companies before being damaged in February 1972. The insurance company sold the aircraft on to AIA.

Two L-100s, N7999S (c/n 4234) and N9266R (c/n 4250), were purchased in 1969 and 1968 respectively and were both leased to Interior. A third, N9262R (c/n 4248), was obtained from International Aerodyne in 1968 and leased to Interior Airways

(see appropriate section).

A single L-100-20, (c/n 4355), registered N7960S by Lockheed, was purchased by this company and Maple Leaf Leasing in November 1969 and leased to Pacific Western Airlines, which later purchased the aircraft in January 1977.

309 NASA (National Aeronautics and Space Administration)

A standard C-130B, 58-0712 (c/n 3507), which had been modified as the C-130BLC (boundary layer control) test bed, and re-converted as an NC-130B, had been employed by NASA at the Johnson Space Center in Texas from July 1968. In September 1969 this aircraft was purchased and received a new registration, N707NA, being re-registered as N929NA in October 1973. Extensively modified, she was named *Earth Survey*, which reflected her role, and served until 1982, when she resumed the N707NA registration. Fitted with type-15 engines in October 1996 she was flown from NASA Dryden before going into non-flyable storage in October 1999.

A standard US Navy EC-130Q, 161494 (c/n 4896), originally delivered in September 1981 and serving with VQ-3 and VQ-4, was used by NASA at Wallops Island in December 1991 as a remote sensing research aircraft for a period before being grounded and broken up for spare parts. A second EC-130Q, 161495 (c/n 4901), and a third, 161496 (c/n 4904), both with similar histories, were registered to NASA in October and November 1992, the former taking the registration N427NA.

310 NOAA (National Oceanic and Atmospheric Administration)

F ormerly the Research Flight Facility (RFF), the aeronautical arm of the Environmental Research Laboratories, the US Commerce Department's National Oceanic and Atmospheric Administration (NOAA) operated two WC-130B Hercules in the 1970s conducting atmospheric research which included participation in such international ventures as the International Field Year for the Great Lakes (IFYGL) in 1971 and the Global Atmospheric Research Program's Atlantic Tropical Experiment (GATE) in 1974.

In August 1970 the NOAA took over a WC-130B, 58-0731 (c/n 3526), and this received the registration N6541C under the Department of Commerce in March

1972. This machine was operated out of Miami with the name *NOAA's Ark* and was re-registered N8037 before converting back to a standard C-130B again in 1981 and resuming USAF duties.

A US Navy EC-130Q, 8209 (c/n 4932), was allocated to NOAA in May 1992 and later was assigned to the National Center for Atmospheric Research at Denver, Colorado, in January 1997. She was struck off for salvage in 1997.

An L-100-30, N4281M (c/n 5032), which had been stored at Lockheed between 1985 and 1988 and registered to Worldwide Trading at Delroy Beach, Florida, in January 1989, was re-registered N898QR in April 1989 and flew in an overall white paint scheme with NOAA decals until October 1993, when she was struck off.

These aircraft carried additional equipment in order to measure weather elements and position, and a wide variety of cloud physics instrumentation for sampling the interiors of clouds, including an infra-red (IR) temperature radiometer, ice-nuclei counter, aerosol detector, liquid water content sensors and a hydrometer foil sampler. In 1974 the WC-130B was modified to carry the airborne weather reconnaissance system (AWRS), a minicomputer-centred airborne meteorological data system developed by Kaman Aerospace Corporation. She could also carry the Omega dropsonde, which sensed temperature, humidity, pressure and position (or winds); the position-sensing capability used an Omega-updated inertial navigation system. She also had side nose radar and vertical cameras providing time-lapse photographic coverage. Thus fitted out, she took part in the National Aeronautics and Space Administration's *Skylab* earth-sensor experiments, and was extensively used in the development of new remote-sensing techniques for use aboard satellites. She was also heavily involved in weather modification experiments, carrying four seeding racks on each side of her fuselage containing a total of 416 silver-iodide flares. A push-button firing mechanism located at the visiting scientist station built onto the flight deck, and connected to an electrical sequencer, was used to ignite and launch the flares during cloud penetration flight.

A typical year's period of service for *41-Charlie*, as the Herk was christened, was the logging of 478 hours and 45 minutes' flight time in 1972, which included Project 'Storm Fury' (63 hours); Hurricane research (63 hours 50 minutes); Naval Research Laboratory projects (142 hours 30 minutes); laser profilometer research (20 hours 20 minutes); fisheries research (19 hours 15 minutes); National Center for Atmospheric Research projects (2 hours 15 min-

utes); NASA projects (27 hours 5 minutes); and hail project support (71 hours 55 minutes), along with essential calibration and proficiency (66 hours 35 minutes).

311 NSAF (National Science Foundation)

L C-130Rs operated by the US Navy for the NSAF included 7704 (c/n 4725) and 7705 (c/n 4731). Former EC-130Qs of the US Navy allocated to the NSAF were 161496 (c/n 4904), 8209 (c/n 4932) and 162312 (c/n 4984). The last was fitted with an extended sampling boom to the starboard forward fuselage in November, 1998 and used for atmospheric research, based at Boulder, Colorado, and taking the civilian registration N130AR from October 1993.

A single LC-130H, 93-1096 (c/n 5410), built in December 1995, became the *City of Christchurch, NZ* and is still flying with the Foundation.

312 Northwest Territorial Airways

T his Yellowknife, Canada, company operated six Hercules aircraft. A single L-100, C-FPWK (c/n 4170), was leased from Pacific West Airlines in April 1981, and while being used as a fuel tanker it was burnt out on 11 April. Of several L-100-30s which served, C-FNWF (c/n 4562) and C-FNWY (c/n 4600) were leased from Safair during the years 1979–82, while ZS-JIV (c/n 4673) was leased from Safair in 1996/7. Finally, yet another L-100-30, C-GHPW (c/n 4799), was leased in 1983 and purchased outright in 1987 from Pacific West Airlines and utilised by the Red Cross in Angola in the following years, carrying the name *Captain Harry Sorenson*, before being sold to Bradley Air Services.

313 Pacific Gateway Investments

A single former fire-fighting C-130A, N138FF (c/n 3227), from Hemet Valley Flying Service, was registered to this Orange County, California, company in January 1990, who leased her back to Hemet Valley for several years until she finally became an Aero Fire-fighting machine in 1997.

314 Pacific Harbor Capital Inc.

B ased at Portland, Oregon, this company is a subsidiary of PacifiCorp which, according to some claims, has CIA links.[42] The company registered a former T&G Aviation C-130A, N120TG (c/n 3095), in 1993 and leased her to *Aeropostal de Mexico* at Mexico City in 1993/4, and then sold her to Heavylift International in 1995. A second C-130A, N130RR (c/n 3145), was obtained from Roy D. Reagan in 1990 as a fire bomber, but she then became a normal transport plane with T&G Aviation and was also leased to *Aeropostal de Mexico*, returning to Pacific Harbor in 1993 as N537UN and, after a spell at the Marana (Pinal Air Park), was also sold to Heavylift International in 1995.

315 Pacific Western Airlines (PWA)

Pacific Western Airlines, a Vancouver, British Columbia-based company, obtained a single L-100, N92623R (c/n 4134), leased from Lockheed

and then to ASA in 1963 before being sold to the latter in 1966. A second, CF-PWO (c/n 4197), the former Lockheed-registered N9269R, became number 382 in May 1967 and was leased to TMA in 1967.

The range of cargo hauled by their C-130s includes breeding cattle from Canada to Japan, with textiles coming back in return, and oil rigs all over the world, from the Canadian Arctic to the Middle East, Africa and South America. At one period in 1971, a PWA Herk was temporarily based at Resolute Bay in the Canadian Arctic for over a month, lacking a hangar or indeed any kind of shelter in temperatures that plummeted as low as −70°C, but was able to operate.

A third L-100, N109AK (c/n 4129), was leased from Maple Leaf Leasing in March 1969 as number 383, and, after being damaged in an accident at Eureka, North West Territories, in August 1968, was re-built as an L-100-20 and leased to Alaska International Air.

---

[42] See *Seattle Post Intelligencer*, 25 October 1975 issue. In the 1975 Senate hearings Senator Frank Church stated that the holding company for all the then CIA airlines was 'The Pacific Corporation'. See John Titus, 'Who's Who in the C-130 Scandal (an Update)', article in *Portland Free Press*, March/April 1997 issue.

This civilian Hercules L-100 (Model 382) AP-AUT belonged to Pakistan International Airways and was one of two of the type operated by that company. She is seen here in pristine condition on her delivery. (Lockheed-Georgia, Marietta via Audrey Pearcy)

An LC-100-20, CF-PWC (c/n 4361), was purchased in December 1969 and became number 384. She was finally lost in an accident in Zaire on 21 November 1976. Another L-100-20, CF-PWR (c/n 4355), was leased from Maple Leaf Leasing in November 1969 and became number 385. She was sold out to PWA in January 1977, who sold her on to Cargolux in December 1980. A third, CF-PWK (c/n 4170), was purchased from Delta Airlines and became number 386. She was leased to NWT in April 1981 and lost in their service. A solitary LC-100-30, C-GHAW (c/n 4799), was purchased in December 1978, becoming number 387. She was leased and then finally sold to NWT in 1983.

PWA operated mainly between November and May, servicing both the DEW Line radar chain and later the Panarctic Oils oil-drilling sites in the arctic regions of Alaska and Canada, flying to within a few hundred miles of the North Pole. The cargo was mainly drill rigs, bulk fuel, equipment, personnel and supplies, and in one case an entire oil-rig community: houses, rigs, fuel and food. They landed anywhere that had an ice depth of 54in (1.37m) which was capable of supporting the L-100, conditions which limited their period of operation. In order to operate in such sub-zero conditions PWA's engineers invented a pre-heating system for the propellers to engine start, utilising bleed from the APU. Outside this period PWA shifted their supply missions to Cornwallis, Ellesmere and Melville islands where they landed on gravel air strips and sandbars.

Pacific Western Hercules also operated 'air charter' work for oil rigs to Ethiopia, and diamond mine support in Angola, according to Harry Zelinski (although these missions might not have been what they seemed), along with airlifting two F-104 StarFighter aircraft at a time from Europe to Canada for overhauls.

316 Pakistan International Airlines (PIA)

Two L-100s, AP-AUT (c/n 4144) and AP-AUU (c/n 4145), were purchased directly by the Government of Pakistan in October 1966 for the national airline PIA, and became their 64144 and 64145 respectively.

317 Pegasus Aviation Incorporated

A former *Force Aérienne Gabonaise* L-100-30, TR-KAA (c/n 4582), was purchased by the company in 1989 and re-registered N2189M; she was re-registered to the Alaska World Trade Corporation in March 1990. A second L-100-30, this time one of the former Safair fleet, 9Q-CBJ (c/n 4796), was taken out of storage at Brussels Airport in 1989 and registered N123GA. She passed into the hands of Rapid Air Transport the same year.

318 Pelita Air Services

This Indonesian Government-sponsored company, headquartered at Djakarta, operated six L-100-30s, three of which were officially accepted at Marietta on 18 December 1981 by the Ambassador Mr Danoedirdjo Ashari. Others were leased from Mitsui Corporation in July 1979: PK-PLU (c/n 4824) *Bina* (and later *Toili*); PK-PLW (c/n 4828) *Sentiaki* (and later *Nimbo Krang*); PK-PLR (c/n 4889) *Sitiung*; PK-PLS (c/n 4917) *Rimbo Bujang*, with doors; PK-PLT (c/n 4923) *Pasir Pangarian*; and PK-PLV (c/n 4826) *Hanonan*.

Their initial role was as part of the Indonesian transmigration air lift programme under Operations 'Relita' I, II and III, when 500,000 families (2,500,000 people) were transported by air, 128 people per trip, from over-populated areas of the country to less settled regions. In a six-month period in January to June 1981 alone, 100,000 passengers and 14,000,000lb (6,350,400kg) of cargo were shifted. After a decade of service many were sub-leased to a wide variety of companies (see appropriate sections), PK-PLV being lost in a crash at Kai Tak airport, Hong Kong, on 24 September 1994. Others went to *Tantara Nasional Indonesia–Angkatan Udara* in April 1994 (see appropriate section).

319 Pemex (*Petroleole Mexicanos*)

A single L-100-30, XC-EXP (c/n 4851), was purchased from Lockheed Aircraft Corporation in April 1980. They used her until the early 1990s, when she went to the *Fuerza Aérea Mexicana* as their number 10611.

320 Philippines Aerotransport (PADC)

The Government of the Philippines took delivery of its first Hercules in April 1973, with two more in July and August. These were used to airlift agricultural produce like corn, rice, tomatoes and bananas across the many islands of the republic. They also transported millions of fingerlings, seedlings and plants to support the nation's green revolution. Other hauls carried thousands of school books to the southern islands from Manila to spread education, and, of course, oil construction, road and bridge-building supplies have also been hauled by the Herky Bird all over the 7,000-island archipelago.

A former Lockheed L-100 demonstration aircraft converted to a L-100-20, N50FW (c/n 3946), was obtained by the Philippines Government in 1973 as their RP-97, but was sold to PADC five years later. After being placed in storage the Philippines Air Force took her over again in 1995. An ex-Saturn L-100-20, N30FW (c/n 4302), was purchased by the Philippines Government in August 1973 and became this company's RP-C99 in 1978. She was re-sold to UAA in 1982. A third L-100-20, N40FW (c/n 4303), was obtained by the Philippines Government in 1973 and leased as RP-C98 before being sold to the James Bay Energy Corporation. Two more L-100-20s were direct sales from Lockheed to the Philippines Government, in 1973 and 1975: the first, N7967S (c/n 4512), was sold to the company in 1983 and flown for eight years before being broken up for spares, while the second, RP-C101 (c/n 4593), was leased and then stored at Manila before being used by the Philippines Air Force in the 1990s.

321 PSCI (Power Systems Conversions/ Improvements, Inc.)

A single C-130A, the former refurbished Snow Aviation's N130SA (c/n 3035), was registered to this Fayetteville, Arizona, organisation in 1997.

322 PSL Air Lease Corporation

The PSL Air Lease Corporation operated a single L-100-20, the former Lockheed demonstrator N50FW (c/n 3946), in 1969, which was operated by the Flying W organisation.

323 Questline

Registered in Florida with one Hercules, the former USAF C-130A 56-0491 (c/n 3099), this organisation flew her in Angola on behalf of the Government, but she crashed and burnt out at Luanda on 10 June 1991.

324 Rapid Air Transport

This Washington DC-based company operated two former Pegasus L-100-30 Hercules, N2189M (c/n 4582) and N8183J (c/n 4796), from 1989 and has leased them out to a variety of users since that time.

325 Roy D. Reagan

A former USAF man based in Oregon, Roy Reagan established a network of contacts and became a successful broker of former US military aircraft on the open market. He and Fred Fuch, a former director of the Forest Service programme, are said to have held talks with the Department of Defense and General Services Administration officials in Washington DC and convinced them that any C-130s transferred would remain strictly under Forest Service control for forest and range-land fire-fighting duties. In 1987 Reagan and Hemet Valley Flying Services came up with the idea of doing a deal whereby surplus aircraft from the Davis-Monthan park would be exchanged for outdated fire-fighting aircraft and the latter given to air museums around the country. A trio of Air Force generals involved in the discussions later testified that they didn't understand that the titles of the C-130s would leave Government control, or else they would not have approved of these exchanges.

Former CIA pilot Gary Eitel's contention is that the Hercules would be used to fight fires during the fire season, but used for clandestine operations during the off-season. Both the CIA and the Forestry Service deny such collusion, however, but a University of Georgia history professor, William Leary, has revealed that from the 1950s the two agencies colluded in such covert activity in south-east Asia and that they together set up Intermountain Aviation, which worked from the Pinal Air Park in Marana until it was taken over by Evergreen in 1975.[43]

Republican Congressman Curt Weldon, of Pennsylvania, investigated the crash of one of these aircraft in Angola in which Robert Weldon, his nephew, was killed, and claimed it was on a CIA mission at the time and that Reagan had sold the aircraft to Dietrich Reinhardt (who had owned St Lucia Airlines) and Peter Turkelson in 1986, both of whom,

---

[43] See William Leary, *Perilous Missions*, University of Alabama Press, 1984.

so the Congressman claimed, had CIA connections.[44]

True or not, Mr Reagan certainly handled some much-travelled and hand-changed C-130A Hercules: former USAF 56-0487 (c/n 3095), ex MASDC, Tucson, and registered N6585H in January 1991, which went to T&G Aviation in January 1991; 56-0491 (c/n 3099), in October 1986, which went to World Wide Aeronautical Industries in 1986; 56-0496 (c/n 3104) and 56-507 (c/n 3115), both from Hawkins & Powers Aviation in May 1989, the first of which went to Aero Fire-fighting Service in December 1990, the second back to Hawkins & Power; and 56-0537 (c/n 3145) as N537TM in August 1989, which went to Pacific Harbor Capital Inc. in December 1990.

---

[44] See John Titus, 'Who's Who in the C-130 Scandal (an Update)', article in *Portland Free Press*, March/April 1997. Both Reagan and Fuch were convicted of conspiracy in April 1998 concerning twenty-two C-130s, and sentenced to terms of imprisonment by Judge William Browning. See David E. Hendrix, 'Whistleblower case takes aim at reputation of Forest Service', article in *The Press-Enterprise* (Riverside, California), 5 April 1998, and Tim Steller, 'Aircraft in scam may have flown for CIA', article in *The Arizona Daily Star*, 1 April 1998, and subsequent story in 2 April 1998 issue.

Safair, the South Africa-based company, operated a fleet of fifteen Hercules airfreighters. The one shown here, ZS-GSK, named Boland (c/n 4385) in their service, is an early model L-100-20 ZS-GSK, which was later superseded by the L-100-30 type.
(Arthur Pearcy via Audrey Pearcy)

326 Ruftberg

This Dallas, Texas company obtained a single L-100-30, N8218J (c/n 5056), from Mega Trade in 1998.

327 Safair Freighters

Formed in 1969 and based at Jan Smuts Airport, Johannesburg, Republic of South Africa, this company, a subsidiary of Safmarine and Rennies Holdings Ltd, has been the major Hercules user, with no fewer than twenty-one aircraft utilised on lease, charter and haulage to a huge variety of companies. Their Hercules fleet has traditionally also been available as a military reserve unit should the need arise.

A solitary L-100-20, (c/n 4385), was leased from Safmarine (see below).

A fleet of seventeen L-100-30s was widely utilised with the following aircraft in service with the company at various dates from December 1972. Many were leased out to other companies before being finally sold out. These stretched civilian Herks were registrations ZS-RSB (c/n 4472), ZS-RSC (c/n 4475), ZS-RSD (c/n 4477), ZS-RSE (c/n 4558), ZS-RSF (c/n 4562), ZS-RSG (c/n 4565), ZS-RSH c/n 4590), ZS-RSI (c/n 4600), ZS-RSJ (c/n 4606), ZS-JIV (c/n 4673), ZS-JVL (c/n 4676), ZS-JIW (c/n 4679), ZS-JIX (c/n 4684), ZS-JIY (c/n 4691), ZS-JIZ (c/n 4695), ZS-JJA (c/n 4698) and ZS-JVM (c/n 4701). One of these, ZS-RSI (c/n 4600), was leased to DHL at Luton in 1995 and worked to Boulogne.

Another L-100-30 was purchased in November 1978 and leased to SCIVE in Zaire as their 9Q-CBJ (c/n 4796).

Finally, two further L-100-30s were purchased from China Eastern Airlines in May 1999, ZS-OLG (c/n 5025) and ZS-JAG (c/n 5027), the former being leased to Lynden Air Cargo.

328 Safair Freighters (USA)

New Jersey-based subsidiary which operated three Hercules L-100-30s purchased in late 1974/early 1975: ZS-RSE (c/n 4558), which became N46965 and went to Globe Air in April 1987, crashing at Travis Air Force Base on the eighth of that month; ZS-RSG (c/n 4565), which became N250SF, was subsequently leased and re-leased, and was registered to Globe Air and sold and re-sold; and ZS-RSH (c/n 4590), which became N251SF and was subsequently leased and operated by Saturn while registered to Globe Air before being sold and re-sold.

329 Safmarine

single L-100-20, (c/n 4385), was delivered to this company in August 1970 and registered ZS-GSK *Boland*. She was immediately leased to Safair and was purchased by that company in February 1980.

330 St Lucia Airways

Owned by Dietrich Reinhardt, in May 1984 this company purchased a single L-100-20 aircraft, J6-SLO (c/n 4129), which was named *Juicy Lucy* and was allegedly used on covert CIA missions to smuggle

Saturn Airways L-100-30, N12ST (c/n 4388) being loaded with a jet engine at night. (Lockheed-Georgia, Marietta via Audrey Pearcy)

missiles into Iran by Oliver North during the embargo and also to supply ammunition and supplies to UNITA in Angola, before being sold to Tepper Aviation.[45]

331 SATRON Inc. (SATCO)

This El Segundo, California-based organisation operated two L-100-20s, the former *Fuerza Aéra Perunana* FAP 395 (c/n 4364), leased by this company as their OB-R-1004, and FAP 396 (c/n 4450) as OB-R-956, in 1976, but both were lost in accidents, the former crashing at Tarapoto on 19 February 1978, the latter crash-landing at San Juan on 24 April 1981.

---

[45] See John Titus, 'Who's Who in the C-130 Scandal (an Update)', article in *Portland Free Press*, March/April 1997.

332 | Saturn Airways (Trans-International)

Before becoming part of Trans-International (TIA) this company operated a large fleet of nineteen Hercules of varying types. Many of its early operations were LOGAIR daily freight-hauling runs to various air force bases in the CONTUS (Continental USA) area. One Hercules of this company hauled out the earth station to Beijing, China, for use during the ground-breaking first visit of President Richard Nixon. Another was chartered by the Disney Corporation to fly camera crew and equipment to worldwide locations for Disneyworld movie sets.

One L-100-20, N24ST (c/n 4101), was leased from NAL in June 1972 and was later modified to a L-100-30.

An L-100, (c/n 4134), registered N16ST, was purchased from ASA in July 1971 and modified to an L-100-30 in April 1972.

An L-100-20, N19ST (c/n 4147), was purchased from Delta in September 1973, and was subsequently modified to an L-100-30 in March 1974. This aircraft, which had undergone two "stretch" modifications since being first delivered to Delta in 1966 – to -20 and then, with Saturn, to -30 – achieved fame with TIA as being the first of that type to achieve 30,000 hours flying time. This milestone was reached during a LOGAIR/QUICKTRANS military charter supply route flight from Tinker AFB, Oklahoma, to Hill AFB, Denver, Colorado, with Captain Bill Thomas at the helm.

As the Oakland, California-based Transamerica company they airfreighted oil rig parts into the Guatemalan jungle for Texaco. In 1981, they undertook a similar operation when two Transamerica L-100-30s were leased to the Chevron Overseas Petroleum Company, airlifting a 1,500,000,000lb (680,388,555kg) oil-rig from Port Sudan to primitive air strips at Adar, El Muglad and Malaka in the Sudan, along with 200,000 US gallons (757,082 litres) of diesel and aviation fuel and rig support equipment, in under thirty days flying around the clock. Five rotating aircrew were used, with each flight crew resting for fourteen hours after each duty day at Khartoum.

A second L-100, N18ST (c/n 4208), was purchased from Alaska International Air in January 1973 and was modified to an L-100-30 in February 1973.

An L-100-20, N9248R (c/n 4221), was purchased from ASA in October 1970, but almost at once crashed at McGuire Air Force Base. Her sister, N13ST (c/n 4222), purchased at the same time, was later leased and then sold to Alaska International Air. A third, N14ST (c/n 4225) *Bozo*, was later converted to an L-100-30.

An L-100-30, N37ST (c/n 4248), was leased from Transamerica in July 1987 and then purchased outright in October. An L-100-20, N22ST (c/n 4250), was leased several times from National Aircraft Leasing and then finally purchased in September 1991, then leased out to various parties until she was mined and destroyed in the Sudan in September 1991 while working for the International Red Cross.

Four more L-100-20s were acquired by Saturn. One, N38ST (c/n 4300), was first leased from Markair, then purchased in October 1987. A second, N7951S (c/n 4301), was leased from Air America in November 1968 and sold outright in July 1970. She was returned, modified to an L-100-30 in September 1971 and sold outright to Saturn in January 1974, registered N23ST. A third, N7952S (c/n 4302), was purchased from the Girard Trust subsidiary RDA in February 1973. The fourth, (c/n 4333), was leased from Lockheed in May 1970 and subsequently purchased outright in October 1972 as N17ST *Wimpy* and was subsequently modified to an L-100-30.

Two L-100-20s, (c/n 4383) and (c/n 4384), were purchased in June 1970 and were registered as N10ST *Rudolph* and N11ST *W. C. Fields* respectively. Both were subsequently modified to L-100-30s in February 1971 and leased to Alaska International Air. They were followed by two L-100-30s (c/n 4388) and (c/n 4391), in December 1970 and June 1971 which received the civilian registrations N12ST *Schnozz* and N15ST *Barney G.* The latter was leased to Southern Air Transport and crashed at Kelly Air Force Base on 4 October 1986. A further pair of L-100-30s, N20ST (c/n 4561) and N21ST (c/n 4586), were purchased in November 1974 and April 1974 respectively. They subsequently went to TIA in December 1976.

Saturn achieved early fame by carrying the largest ever shipment for the service-contracted LOGAIR system, a mean 50,058lb (22,706kg). It regularly shipped podded and crated Rolls-Royce RB.211-22B engines for the Lockheed L-1011 TriStar jet transport from Short Brothers & Harland's plant in Belfast, Northern Ireland, over to Marietta.

333 | Saudia

Fourteen Hercules aircraft have been operated by this company for the Saudi Government. Seven specially converted L-100-30s were purchased from Lockheed Aircraft Corporation in 1983: the former N4242N, which became HZ-MS05 (c/n 4950), modified as a hospital aircraft prior to delivery; the former N425M, which became HZ-MS06 (c/n 4952), modified as a dental hospital aircraft prior to delivery; HZ-MS11 (c/n 4954), delivered as the personal VIP aircraft of Sheikh Ibrahim; the former N4255M, which became HZ-MS09 (c/n 4956); N4261M, which became HZ-MS10 (c/n 4957); N4266M, which became HZ-MS14 (c/n 4960); and the former N4243M, which became HZ-MS08 (c/n 4986), all of which had also been converted to hospital aircraft prior to delivery.

Another L-100-30, N15ST (c/n 4391), was leased from Saturn in March 1978.

Four C-130Hs: the former N4098M (c/n 4837), which was modified to a surgical hospital prior to delivery and became HZ-MS019; the former N4185M (c/n 4915), purchased in September 1982 and converted to a VC-130-H in 1995, and operated by the company as part of the Saudi Royal Flight; the former N4240M (c/n 4918) and N4190M (c/n 4922), purchased in March and May 1982 respectively and converted to hospital aircraft prior to delivery, which became HZ-MS021 and HZ-MS07.

Two VC-130Hs: the former N4098M (c/n 4837),

purchased from Lockheed in January 1980, which was modified as a surgical hospital aircraft prior to delivery, and which became HZ-MS019; and the former N4099M (c/n 4843), purchased from Lockheed Aircraft Corporation in July 1980, operated by the company as a VIP aircraft of the Saudi Royal Flight as HZ-HM05, re-registered HZ-114 in February 1981. Of these special aircraft, HZ-MS05 and HZ-MS10 were later stripped of their medical equipment and re-converted to orthodox L-100-30s.

334 Schreiner Airways

Based at Schiphol, Netherlands, Schreiner of Leiden has operated six different leased Hercules L-100-30s: PH-SHE (c/n 4895), leased from Gabon 1989/90; N909SJ (c/n 4763), leased from Saturn

A fine study of Southern Air Transport's livery on Air America's N7951S (c/n 4301). (Arthur Pearcy via Audrey Pearcy)

1992/3; ZS-JVL (c/n 4676), leased from Safair in 1997; ZS-JIV (c/n 4673), leased from Safair in 1998; ZS-JIY (c/n 4691), leased from Safair in 1998; and C-GHPW (c/n 4799), leased from Bradley Air Services in 1998.

335 *SCIBE-Society Commerciale, Zaire*

A single L-100-30, 9Q-CBJ (c/n 4796), was leased by this organisation from Safair in November 1978. Their itinerary included three flights to Bunia, Zaire, which transported 132,000lb (59,874kg) of equipment to construct a slaughterhouse. A flight to Gbadolite took 20 tons (18,144kg) of cargo, including cars, spare parts and household appliances, returning with 16 tons (14,515kg) of fresh produce.

336 SFAir

A French regional air carrier, based at Bordeaux, which flew cargo missions throughout Europe and Africa and first began flying in April 1981. After the French civil aviation authority, *Direction Générale de l'Aviation Civile* (DGAC), issued a provisional certificate for the Hercules, an L-100-20, N4174M (c/n 4412), was leased from Lockheed between July 1983 and February 1984.

An L-100-30, ZS-RSI (c/n 4600), was leased from Safair in April 1981 and was registered F-WDAQ; a second, F-GFAS (c/n 4606), from L-100 Leasing was operated for Africargo in the Congo in 1987; while a third, ZS-JJA (c/n 4698), was also leased from Safair from May 1984. These aircraft were transferred to Jet Fret in 1988 before returning to their owners.

337 Shabair

T his Zambian company operated a single C-130A Hercules, the May Ventures 9J-AFV (c/n 3095), during 1995/6.

338 Snow Aviation International Inc.

B ased in Ohio, the company bought a single C-130A, N130SA (c/n 3035), from Aero Corp at Lake City, Florida, in 1995 which had allegedly been destined for modernisation for the Peruvian Navy, but which was never paid for. Under Snow Aviation's auspices this modernisation was carried out in 1995 and she was registered to PSCI Inc. in 1997.

339 South African Airways (SAA)

T wo further former Safair L-100-30s were leased to South African Airways from 1974: ZS-RSB (c/n 4472) and ZS-RSC (c/n 4475).

340 Southern Air Transport (SAT)

T his Miami, Florida-based outfit became a high user, with twenty-three Hercules passing through its hands down the decades. Their haulage record included electronics equipment, textile equipment, construction helicopters and jet engines; they even used one Herky Bird to transport meat from Argentina to Chile and airlifted oil-drilling equipment to Ecuador.

One L-100-30, N916SJ (c/n 4134), was leased from Saturn to commemorate the company's fiftieth anniversary, carrying the name *Southern Air Transport 50 Years 1947–1997*, in March 1983 before being sold to Transafrik. Another, N9232R (c/n 4299), was converted to an L-100-30 in January 1974 after an early accident in February 1972.

An L-100-20, N7984S (c/n 4362), was purchased by Saturn in December 1969 and became N522SJ in November 1985.

An L-100-30, N106AK (c/n 4477), was purchased by Saturn in February 1992 and re-registered N906SJ for leasing.

Purchased by Safair and registered as ZS-RSE (c/n 4558), this L-100-30 was later registered to Safair Freighters in the United States.

There were also several former Saturn/Safair-operated aircraft – including N920SJK (c/n 4561), N519SJ (c/n 4562), N250SF (c/n 4565), N921SJ (c/n 4586), N251SF (c/n 4590) and N108AK (c/n 4763) – utilised (see appropriate sections).

341 Southern Cross Airways

O wned by Multitrade, this aircraft operator brought in a number of former RAAF Hercules for use by private firms. One of these aircraft, it was claimed, was involved in the Mena, Arkansas, CIA operation. Another – (c/n 3215), allegedly tail-coded N69-P – was stated to have operated on Roy Reagan's certificate on contract for the US Nuclear Defense Agency and was allegedly busted by the DEA in Miami, Florida, on a cocaine-smuggling mission. This aircraft was sold to a US customs agent and flown to T&G Aviation to be refitted, and then went on to work in Africa.

The California company certainly briefly operated a former RAAF C-130A, 57-0508/A97-215 (c/n 3215), in 1986 for Herc Airlift, who leased her from ITT Commercial Finance Corporation. She was later sold to African Air Transport, a Miami-registered company, in June 1988, who subsequently sold her to African Cargo, Miami, in January 1989. She was impounded at Naples, Florida, by US Customs and stored at Fort Lauderdale before being sold to F. S. Conner, Miami, in March 1995 and registered to Zotti Group Aviation, Miami, in May of that year.

342 Suarez, Peter

nother former RAAF C-130A, 57-0505/A97-212 (c/n 3212), was purchased by this Van Nuys, California, outfit from Fowler Aeronautical Service in July 1994 and re-registered N130PS, ending up for sale by Kreuger Aviation Inc., California, from October 1996.

343 Sudan Airways

ne C-130H of the Sudanese Air Force, 1100 (c/n 4766), was operated by the civilian arm, Sudan Airways, between 1983 and 1991 and registered initially ST-AHR and then ST-AIF.

344 TAB (*Transporte Aéreo Boliviano*)

former RC-130A re-converted to a standard C-130A, 57-0521 (c/n 3228), was purchased by the *Fuerza Aérea Boliviana* in October 1988 and became their TAM69. Painted white overall, she was operated by the company as CP-2184 until going into storage at La Paz in 1997.

Two C-130Hs, TAM90 (c/n 4744) and TAM91 (c/n 4759), were purchased by the *Fuerza Aérea Boliviana* in July and October 1977 respectively and operated by TAB on their behalf. The former was lost in a night crash into the sea off Tacumen, Panama, on 28 September 1979; the other was leased to IAS/Transafrik for United Nations operations in Sudan and Angola, and was twice damaged in this risky work. She was finally returned to Bolivia in January 2000.

The Bolivian Government purchased a single L-100-30 from Lockheed in October 1979, the former N4083M (c/n 4833), for the *Fuerza Aérea Boliviana* which became their TAM92 and was leased and operated for them by TAB as CP-1564. In 1988 this aircraft was sub-leased to

Transafrik and destroyed on 16 March 1991 by enemy action close to Malanje, Angola.

345 T&G Aviation (International Air Response)

ith the late Jack Chisum as Vice-President, in 1968 this established organisation was based in Chandler, Arizona, and obtained six former USAF C-130A Hercules for modification into fire-fighting water bombers: 54-1631 (c/n 3018) in October 1989 and registered N117TG; 56-0478 (c/n 3086) in October 1989 and re-registered N116TG; 56-0487 (c/n 3095), via Roy D. Reagan, in January 1991 and re-registered N120TG; 56-0537 (c/n 3145), via Pacific Harbor Capital, in December 1990; 57-0512 (c/n 3219) in October 1989 and re-registered N118TG; and 57-0517 (c/n 3224), via Valley National Bank of Arizona, in October 1990, already registered as N9539G before the company became International Air Response (IAR) in 1998.

Woody Grantham purchased two of these C-130s from Roy Reagan for $688,000 and had US State Department approval for the work; the other three C-130s were exchanged for two helicopters and two obsolete aircraft, following a request from US Republican John Jay Rhodes in 1991.[46] Some T&G Forest Service Hercules were contracted for the Bechtel Corporation via MARTECH to haul oilfield equipment to the Gulf in the aftermath of the war, but were accused by Evergreen and Southern Air of also illegally running in whisky to Kuwait, and the aircraft were ordered to return to Marana, Arizona, according to some sources.[47] Jack Chisum himself was subsequently knocked down and killed by a car in Arizona.

International Air Response, with Woody Grantham as its President, currently works out of Chandler Memorial Airport, located south of Chandler and 20 miles (32km) from Phoenix. The field is leased from the Gila River Indian Community, a World War II-built field with a 9,000ft

---

[46] See Jay Reynolds, 'Major Deceptions on Contrails Unmasked (Part 3)', Veritas News Service, 26 April 1999.

[47] See NewsHawk ® Inc., via David Hoffman, Haight Ashbury Free Press, 'C-130s Said Diverted From US Forest Service Duty by CIA', 31 October 1999.

(2,743m) asphalt runway.[48] At least three of the original six C-130s are still operational – N116TG, N117TG and N118TG – and are based at Chandler during the winter months, moving out to locally sited airfields according to the wildfire threat pattern and in conjunction with the US Forest Service.

346 TBM Inc.

This company, founded in 1957 by Henry Moore, Doug Gandy, Harvey Miller, Bob Nunch, Milt Watts, Bob Phillips, Wayland Fink, Jim French and Elmer Johnson, originally based at Redmond, Oregon, and then at Tulare, California, was named after the US Navy's Avenger torpedo bomber, in particular the variant built by General Motors during the war (the TBM), which was the first aircraft when purchased at a military surplus sale. They have been in the air tanker business since 1959 and have provided continuous state and federal air tanker services since that time as aerial fire-fighters. They cover the areas of Fresno and Ramona in California, Fort Smith and Fort Huachuca in Arkansas, Silver City in New Mexico, Minden in Nevada, West Yellowstone in Montana and Pocatello in Idaho.

The company obtained four old former USAF C-130A Hercules: 54-1639 (c/n 3026) in 1990, unregistered as used for spare parts; 56-0473 (c/n 3081) in 1989, re-registered N473TM; 57-0466 (c/n 3173) in 1989, re-registered N466TM; and 57-0479 (c/n 3186) via US Forestry Service in 1991, re-registered N479TM. Two Hercules are still flying.

347 Tepper Aviation

A Florida-based company with one L-100-20, used for operations in Angola. The former St Lucia Airways J6-SLO, (c/n 4129), which was purchased in 1988 and re-registered N9205T *Grey Ghost*, crashed at Jamba on 27 November 1989. Two L-100-30s were also leased for operations in Eastern Europe and the US Government: N2189 (c/n 4582), from Flight Cargo Leasing in 1990, which went to Rapid Air in 1995; and N8183J (c/n 4796) in 1989 from Rapid Air.

---

48 See Jay Reynolds, 'Major Deceptions on Contrails Unmasked (Part 3)', Veritas News Service, 26 April 1999.

348 Time Aviation

A Sun Valley, California-based company with two ex-USAF aircraft: a C-130A, the former 57-0517 (c/n 3224) in 1981 and registered N9539G; and a DC-130A, 57-0523 (c/n 3230), registered N9539Q, with both of these going to Gary R. Larkins the following year.

349 Transafrik

Working out of São Tomé and Príncipe, this African company has used twenty-five Hercules, both purchased and leased, over the years. A single C-130H, TAM69 (c/n 4759), was leased from *Fuerza Aérea Boliviana* in 1987 for UN operations in Sudan and Angola, and was damaged by UNITA action, and also later by an accident at Mongu Airport, before being returned to the FAB in January 2000.

Seven L-100-20s have been used, including S9-CAW (c/n 4300), operated by Transafrik for TWL Ltd, Mauritius, from 1998; S9-CAV (c/n 4301), bought from Saturn in 1998; S9-NAI (c/n 4303), bought from American Aircraft Corporation, Florida, in 1988, but finally brought down by UNITA action at Luanda Airport on 9 April 1989 and written off; and S9-NAL (c/n 4385), bought from Safair in 1989 and used by the United Nations in Africa. Two more, N522SJ (c/n 4362) and N910SJ (c/n 4383), were bought from Saturn in 1999, while N901SJ (c/n 4299) was also bought in 1999 from Commercial Air Leasing, but immediately re-sold to First Security Bank.

No fewer than fifteen L-100-30s have been employed, of which six – N916SJ (c/n 4134), L-100-30, S9-CAX (c/n 4248), S9-BOQ (c/n 4388), N905SJ (c/n 4472), S9-BOP (c/n 4477) and S9-CAO (c/n 4561) – were bought from Saturn in 1998/99. Two of these have been lost to date: S9-CAO (c/n 4561) was destroyed by UNITA action on 26 December 1998 and S9-BOP was written off in an accident at Luzamba, Angola, on 27 December 1999.

Three others – S9-CAI (c/n 4562), bought from Derco in 1998; S9-CAJ (c/n 4565), bought from Globe Air in 1999; and N921SJ (c/n 4586), bought from Hamilton Aviation, Tucson, in 1999 – were purchased.

Seven more L-100-30s have been leased down the years: CP-1564 (c/n 4833), leased from *Fuerza Aérea Boliviana* in 1988 but shot down by UNITA forces in Malanje, 16 March 1991; D2-EHD (c/n 4839), owned by ENDIAMA but flown by Transafrik, damaged by UNITA action several times, finally being shot down by a SAM missile while in cruise at FL170, 20 miles (32km) from

Huambo on 2 January 1999, with the loss of all three crew members and six passengers; S9-CAY (c/n 4208), operated by Transafrik for TWL, Mauritius, from 1998; S9-NAD (c/n 4475), leased from Safair for United Nations work in Cambodia in 1992 and returned in 1993; S9-NAJ (c/n 4606), leased from Safair in 1989, damaged in a mid-air collision on 30 January 1990, continued work for United Nations worldwide and returned to Safair 1992; ZS-JIV (c/n 4673), leased from Safair 1993; and S9-NAT (c/n 4695), leased from Safair 1991–93.

350 Trans-Latin Air (TLA)

Based in Panama, used one former USAF C-130A, 57-0517 (c/n 3224), from Valley National Bank of Arizona and the Marana Air Park and re-registered HP1162TLN in 1990, but she went to T&G in 1992.

351 Trans-Mediterranean Airways (TMA)

A solitary L-100, the ex Lockheed N9269R (c/n 4197), was leased in 1967 but crashed at Cayaya, Peru, on 16 July 1969.

352 Uganda Airlines

This Kampala-based company registered a single L-100-30, N108AK (c/n 4610), purchased from Page Airways in August 1975 and becoming their 5X-UCF. She worked for Uganda Air Cargo, carried the name *The Silver Lady* and had a host of misadventures, including fire damage and being impounded twice, before finally being sold to AviSto of Switzerland for Medecair.

353 United African Airlines

This Libyan company used several Hercules aircraft. An ex-Philippines Government L-100-20, PI-99 (c/n 4302), was purchased in 1982 and re-registered 5A-DJR. A former Cargolux L-100-20, LX-GCV (c/n 4355), was leased in 1981 and re-registered 5A-DHJ, later as 5A-DHI0. A Lockheed L-100-30, N501AK (c/n 4798), which had been originally purchased from Alaska International Air by United Trade International in 1979 but impounded at Tripoli in October of that year, was leased in January 1980. Also the two L-100-30s, 5A-DOM (c/n 4992) and TY-BBU (c/n 5000), which beat the blockade were claimed to be registered with the company before they were transferred to Jamahiriya Air.

354 United Trade International (UTI)

A former Alaska International Air L-100-30, N501AL (c/n 4798), was purchased in 1979 but impounded at Tripoli that October and later went to United Arab Airlines (see appropriate section).

355 Unitrans

Dietrich Reinhardt briefly utilised a TAAG C-130A, N9724V (c/n 3099).

356 *Wirtschaftsflug*

This Frankfurt-based German company purchased a former L-100-30 demonstrator from Lockheed in October 1981, registered her D-ACWF (c/n 4839), and used her on charter flights throughout Europe, the Middle East and Africa. She returned to Lockheed in November 1983.

357 Worldways

The Echo Bay Mines' L-100-20, CF-DSX (c/n 4303), was utilised by this Canadian company in 1983, when she was named *Bob Beaton*.

358 World Wide Aeronautical Industries

This Ashland, Oregon-based company was among the many who handled this former USAF/USN C-130A, 56-0491/158229 (c/n 3099), obtaining her from Roy D. Reagan in December 1986 and transferring her to Bob's Air Park at Tucson the following year.

359 Worldwide Trading

Based at Delroy Beach, Florida, with a single ex Lockheed L-100-30, N4281M (c/n 5032), which was re-registered N898QR in April 1989 and went to Investment Capital Xchange in 1997.

360 Yemenia

Yemen Airways, based at Sanaa, have operated two C-130H Hercules which were given to them by Saudi Arabia in 1979: 7O-ADE (c/n 4825) and 7O-ADD (c/n 4827).

Zambian Air Cargoes operated five L-100-20s, one of which, N9261R (c/n 4109) is seen in flight. On 11 April 1968, she was involved in a ground collision with her sister aircraft (c/n 4137) at N'dola airport and both were complete write-offs. (Lockheed-Georgia, Marietta via Audrey Pearcy)

361 Zaire Air Services

T his company leased two Hercules from the all-embracing Safair in 1988: an L-100-30, (c/n 4606), in 1982, which was damaged in a ground collision; and an L-100-20, ZS-GSK (c/n 4385), re-registered 9Q-CHZ in 1988.

362 Zaire Cargo

A lso leased by this company from Safair in 1985 were three L-100-30s: ZS-RSC (c/n 4475) in 1985, re-registered 9Q-CZS; ZS-RSJ (c/n 4606) in 1982, re-registered 9Q-CZA; and ZS-JIY (c/n 4691) in 1983/4, also re-registered as 9Q-CZS.

363 Zambian Air Cargoes

P urchased in April 1996 was an L-100-20, (c/n 4129) *Alexander*, which was sold to Maple Leaf Leasing in 1969. Two L-100s purchased in April 1966, N9261R (c/n 4109) and 9J-RBX (c/n 4137) *Ajax*, were lost in a ground collision at N'dola on 11 April 1968.

This company also used three more L-100s 9J-RCV (c/n 4101), 9J-RCY (c/n 4109) and 9J-REZ (c/n 4209) – which it leased from the Government of Zambia (GRZ) in August 1966 and April 1967 (see appropriate section).

364 Zantop International

This organisation leased a solitary former Alaska International Air L-100-30, N106AK (c/n 4477), from Markair from April 1986 to March 1991.

365 Zimex Aviation

Two more much-traded former Safair L-100-30s saw brief service with this company: HB-ILG (c/n 4698) in 1988 and HB-ILF (c/n 4701) in Angola in 1987, the latter shot down by UNITA while taking off from Cuito Airport on 14 October 1987.

366 Zincka, Michael, Leasing

Michael Zincka Leasing had two fire-fighting C-130As on their books in 1989, the former Hemet Valley Aviation N131NF (c/n 3138) and N136FF

(c/n 3148), and they were later registered to Aero Fire-fighting Service who leased them back to Hemet, who sub-leased them to the French Government agency *Securité Civile* for two years.

367 Zotti Group Aviation

After being purchased by F. S. Conner of Miami from the US Customs pound at Fort Lauderdale, Florida, a much-travelled C-130A, N4469P (c/n 3215), was registered to this organisation in May 1995, and broken up there over the next two years.

Appendix One

Chase the Herk – Strange Happenings!

The murky world of covert actions, with allegations of misuse of C-130s obtained from the Arizona bone-yards for all manner of CIA operations, including arms smuggling and drug importation, continue to abound, but whether or not every one of Gary R. Eitel's many claims are true, the complications are so labyrinthine that tracking down the many ramifications seem almost beyond human powers.

To give just one example from many, in 1990 the US Forest Service is alleged to have transferred two aircraft to TBM Inc. TBM transferred them to Roy Reagan, who sold them to T&G Aviation. Woody Grantham of T&G in turn is alleged to have sold them to Pacific Harbor Capital, who then sold them back to T&G. In 1993, the same two aircraft were transferred by T&G back to Pacific Harbor Capital, as a repossession according to the two companies, as a sale according to a Federal Aviation Administration document, according to John Titus as part of a 'sheep-dip' cleansing operation.

Although during investigations US Attorney Claire Lefkowitz stated that no evidence of CIA involvement with the Forestry Service and ex-service C-130s was found[49] the rumours persist. The exchange of twenty-eight C-130 and P-3 aircraft for ageing World War II fire-fighting aircraft belonging to such companies as Hemet Valley Flying Services, Hawkins & Powers Aviation, Greybull, Wyoming, TBM Inc./Butler Aircraft, Aero Union Corporation, Chico, California, T&G Aviation, Heavylift International and Pacificorp, Portland, Oregon, remains shrouded in some confusion, although current operations have been declared legitimate enough.[50] The General Services Administration stated in September 1995 that these exchanges were illegal and instructed the Forest Service to recover all the aircraft.

Whatever happened with the Contras in Nicaragua and the drug deals, along with all the other allegations of misuse, one thing is clear: the full story has not yet been told. The highly mysterious deaths of many of the people who may have known some aspects of the story are a warning that not everything is as it seems about this peculiar aspect of the C-130's otherwise unblemished and splendid history.[51]

---

[49] See Tim Steller, 'Aircraft in scam may have flown for CIA', article in *The Arizona Daily Star*, 1 April 1998.

[50] See Jay Reynolds, 'Major Deception on Contrails Unmasked (Part 3)', Veritas News Service, 26 April 1999.

[51] See Gary Null, *The Strange Death of Colonel Sabow* (www.garynull.com/Documents/sabow/htm), where, among others, computer specialist Tom Wade, Marine Colonel Jerry Agenbroad and Marine Colonel James E. Sabow all died sudden and violent deaths in the same manner as Jack Chisum of T&G. See also Alexander Cockburn & Jeffrey St Clair, *Whiteout: the CIA, Drugs and the Press*, Verso Books, 1999; Peter Dale Scott & Jonathan Marshall, *Cocaine Politics: Drugs, Armies and the CIA in Central America*, University of California Press, 1998; Gary Webb, *Dark Alliance: The CIA, the Contras and the Crack Cocaine Explosion*, Seven Stones Press, 1998.

Appendix Two

Summary

Model	First Delivered	Delivery Ceased
C-130A	1956	1959
C-130B	1959	1963
C-130E	1962	1974
C-130H	1964	1998
C-130H2	1978	1992
C-130H3	1992	1997
C-130J	1996	–
L-100	1964	1968
L-100-20	1968	1981
L-100-30	1970	1998
C-130H-30	1980	1997

Close up and personal. Seen from the photographing aircraft, this RAF Hercules, 217, makes a picture of controlled power. (RAF Public Relations via Martin W. Bowman)

Appendix Three

Model List

Model	Applied to	From c/n	Initial Customer
82	XC-130	1001	US Air Force
182-1A	C-130A, C-130D	3001	US Air Force
182-2A	RC-130A	3217	US Air Force
282-11B	C-130B	3724	South African Air Force
282-1B	C-130B, HC-130B	3501	US Air Force
282-2B	HC-130B	3594	US Coast Guard
282-3B	KC-130F	3554	US Marine Corps
282B-3B	C-130, KC-130F	3554	US Marine Corps
282-4B	C-130E	3651	US Air Force
282-7B	C-130B	3546	Indonesian Air Force
282C-6B	LC-130F	3562	US Navy
382-12B	HC-130H, HC130P	4036	US Air Force
382-13B	C-130E	4011	Turkish Air Force
382-14B	C-130H	4052	Royal New Zealand Air Force
382-15B	C-130E	4020	Royal Canadian Air Force
382-16B	C-130E	4091	Brazilian Air Force
382-17B	L-100	3946	Lockheed Aircraft Corporation
382-19B	C-130K	4169	Royal Air Force
382-20B	HC-130N	4363	US Air Force
382-4B	C-130E	3609	US Air Force

Model	Applied to	From c/n	Initial Customer
382-4B	EC-130E	4158	US Coast Guard
382-5E	C-130H	4900	US Air National Guard
382-8B	C-130E	3779	US Air Force
382B-10C	L-100	4221	Aircraft International Incorporated
382B-14C	L-100	4234	Lockheed Aircraft Corporation
382B-1C	L-100	4101	Continental Air Services
382B-2C	L-100	4129	Zambian Air Cargoes
382B-3C	L-100	4134	Lockheed Aircraft Corporation
382B-4C	L-100	4144	Pakistan International Airlines
382B-5C	L-100	4146	International Aerodyne
382B-6C	L-100	4147	Delta Airlines
382B-7C	L-100	4208	Alaska Airlines
382B-8C	L-100	4197	Lockheed Aircraft Corporation
382B-9C	L-100	4209	Zambian Government
382C-01F	MC-130H	5236	US Air Force
382C-02F	C-130H	5213	Japanese Air Force
382C-03F	C-130H	5137	Venezuelan Air Force
382C-04F	C-130H	5141	Chad Government
382C-05F	MC-130H	5265	US Air Force
382C-06F	C-130H	5179	Republic of Korea
382C-07F	C-130H	5215	Taiwan
382C-10D	C-130E	4294	Imperial Iranian Air Force
382C-11D	C-130E	4304	Royal Saudi Air Force
382C-11E	C-130H	4875	Royal Moroccan Air Force

Model	Applied to	From c/n	Initial Customer
382C-11F	KC-130T	5219	US Marine Corps
382C-12D	C-130E	4308	Argentinian Air Force
382C-12E	KC-130H	4907	Royal Moroccan Air Force
382C-13D	C-130H	4312	Royal New Zealand Air Force
382C-13E	C-130H	4878	Sultanate of Oman
382C-13F	C-130H-30	5224	Algerian Air Force
382C-14D	C-130H	4334	Royal Norwegian Air Force
382C-14E	C-130H	4879	Abu Dhabi
382C-14F	C-130H	5238	US Air Force Reserve
382C-15D	C-130E	4314	US Air Force
382C-15D	C-130E	4404	US Air Force
382C-15E	C-130H	4890	Indonesian Air Force
382C-15F	C-130H	5209	Royal Thai Air Force
382C-17D	C-130E	4365	Imperial Iranian Air Force
382C-17D	C-130E, C-130H	4386	Greek Air Force
382C-17F	C-130H-30	5208	Royal Thai Air Force
382C-18D	C-130H	4366	Libyan Republic Air Force
382C-18E	C-130H	4939	US Air Force Reserve
382C-18F	KC-130T-30	5260	US Marine Corps
382C-19D	C-130H	4396	Royal Saudi Air Force
382C-19E	C-130H	4916	Sultanate of Oman
382C-19F	AC-130U	5256	US Air Force
382C-1D	C-130	4115	Imperial Iranian Air Force
382C-1E	C-130H	4861	Royal Thai Air Force

Model	Applied to	From c/n	Initial Customer
382C-20D	C-130H	4406	Venezuelan Air Force
382C-21D	C-130H	4411	Government of Zaire
382C-21F	C-130T	5255	US Naval Reserve
382C-22D	C-130H	4441	Italian Air Force
382C-22E	HC-130H-7	4931	US Coast Guard
382C-22F	C-130H	5278	US Air National Guard
382C-23D	C-130H	4436	Argentinian Air Force
382C-24D	C-130H	4430	Israeli Defence Forces
382C-24E	C-130H	4936	Egyptian Air Force
382C-24F	HC-130H(N)	5294	US Air National Guard
382C-25D	C-130H	4456	Imperial Iranian Air Force
382C-25E	C-130H	4911	Algerian Air Force
382C-26E	C-130H	4915	Saudi Arabian Government
382C-26F	C-130H	5175	Canadian Armed Forces
382C-27C	L-100-20	4450	Portuguese Air Force
382C-27D	HC-130H	4507	US Coast Guard
382C-27D	HC-130H	4528	US Coast Guard
382C-27E	C-130H	4976	Japanese Air Force
382C-27F	C-130H-30	5211	Saudi Arabian Government
382C-28D	LC-130R	4508	US Navy
382C-28E	C-130H	4920	Royal Jordanian Air Force
382C-28P	C-130H	4458	Safair
382C-29D	KC-130H	4503	Lockheed Aircraft Corporation
382C-29E	KC-130H	4940	Singapore Air Force

Model	Applied to	From c/n	Initial Customer
382C-29F	C-130H	5234	Saudi Arabian Government
382C-2D	C-130E	4159	Royal Australian Air Force
382C-2E	C-130H	4842	Singapore Air Force
382C-30D	C-130H	4515	Lockheed Aircraft Corporation
382C-30F	C-130H	5253	Saudi Arabian Government
382C-31D	C-130E	4519	US Air Force
382C-31F	C-130T	5298	US Naval Reserve
382C-31F	C-130T	5304	US Naval Reserve
382C-32D	EC-130Q	4595	US Navy
382C-32E	C-130H	4918	Saudi Arabian Government
382C-32F	KC-130T	5302	US Marine Corps
382C-33D	C-130H	4542	US Air Force
382C-33E	C-130H	4948	Sultanate of Oman
382C-33F	C-130H	5310	US Air National Guard
382C-33F	C-130H	5321	US Air Force
382C-34C	L-100-30	4610	Government of Uganda
382C-34D	C-130H	4530	Israeli Defence Forces
382C-34E	KC-130T	4974	US Marine Corps
382C-35D	C-130H	4535	Royal Moroccan Air Force
382C-35E	C-130H	4968	US Air National Guard
382C-35F	C-130H	5312	US Air Force Reserve
382C-36D	C-130H	4588	Government of Zaire
382C-36F	C-130T	5341	US Naval Reserve
382C-37C	L-100-20	4706	Peruvian Air Force

Model	Applied to	From c/n	Initial Customer
382C-37D	C-130H	4591	Imperial Iranian Air Force
382C-37E	HC-130H-7	4947	US Coast Guard
382C-37F	C-130H	5272	Royal Thai Air Force
382C-38D	C-130H	4572	Royal Danish Air Force
382C-39D	C-130H	4552	Royal Saudi Air Force
382C-39F	KC-130T	5339	US Marine Corps
382C-3D	C-130	4128	Royal Saudi Air Force
382C-40D	C-130H	4580	Abu Dhabi Air Force
382C-40F	AC-130U	5279	US Air Force
382C-41D	C-130H	4579	US Air Force
382C-42D	C-130H	4556	Venezuelan Air Force
382C-42E	C-130H	4964	Colombian Air Force
382C-42F	C-130H	5360	US Air National Guard
382C-43D	KC-130R	4615	US Marine Corps
382C-43F	C-130H	5380	US Air Force Reserve
382C-44E	C-130H	5015	Japanese Air Force
382C-45D	C-130H	4570	Brazilian Air Force
382C-46D	C-130H	4605	Royal Saudi Air Force
382C-46E	C-130H	5008	US Air National Guard
382C-47D	KC-130H	4625	Brazilian Air Force
382C-47E	LC-130H	5007	US Air National Guard
382C-47F	LC-130H	5402	US Air National Guard
382C-48D	C-130H	4576	Argentinian Air Force
382C-48E	KC-130T	5009	US Marine Corps

Model	Applied to	From c/n	Initial Customer
382C-49D	C-130H	4619	Nigerian Air Force
382C-49E	MC-130H	5004	US Air Force
382C-4D	EC-130Q	4239	US Navy
382C-4E	VC-130H	4843	Royal Saudi Air Force
382C-50E	HC-130H-7	4993	US Coast Guard
382C-50E	C-130H	5058	Taiwan
382C-51D	C-130H	4553	Canadian Armed Forces
382C-51F	KC-130T	5385	US Marine Corps
382C-52D	C-130H	4653	Israeli Defence Forces
382C-52F	C-130T	5383	US Naval Reserve
382C-53D	KC-130H	4660	Israeli Defence Forces
382C-53F	C-130H	5389	US Air Force Reserve
382C-54D	C-130H	4622	Greek Air Force
382C-54E	C-130H	4983	Abu Dhabi Air Force
382C-54F	C-130H	5271	Taiwan
382C-55D	KC-130H	4642	Spanish Air Force
382C-55E	C-130H-30	4986	Saudi Arabian Government
382C-55F	C-130T	5404	US Naval Reserve
382C-56D	C-130H	4628	Royal Swedish Air Force
382C-56F	KC-130T	5411	US Marine Corps
382C-57D	C-130H	4656	Malaysian Government
382C-57E	HC-130H-7	5028	US Coast Guard
382C-57F	C-130H	5417	US Air National Guard
382C-58D	KC-130R	4702	US Marine Corps

Model	Applied to	From c/n	Initial Customer
382C-58E	KC-130T	5040	US Marine Corps
382C-59D	C-130H	4716	Greek Air Force
382C-59E	MC-130H	5041	US Air Force
382C-59F	C-130T	5429	US Naval Reserve
382C-5D	C-130E	4202	Brazilian Air Force
382C-60D	C-130H	4737	Royal Saudi Air Force
382C-60E	C-130H	5038	US Air Force Reserve
382C-60F	C-130H	5435	Japanese Air Force
382C-61D	KC-130H	4750	Royal Saudi Air Force
382C-61E	HC-130H-7	5031	US Coast Guard
382C-61F	C-130H	5318	Taiwan
382C-62F	C-130H	5358	Taiwan
382C-63D	C-130H	4704	Philippines Air Force
382C-63E	C-130H	4994	Canadian Armed Forces
382C-64D	C-130H	4707	Egyptian Air Force
382C-65D	LC-130R	4725	National Science Foundation
382C-65E	C-130H	5020	Tunisian Air Force
382C-66D	C-130H	4736	Government of Zaire
382C-66E	C-130H	5070	Singapore Air Force
382C-67D	C-130H	4713	Royal Moroccan Air Force
382C-68D	KC-130R	4768	US Marine Corps
382C-68E	C-130H	5088	Japanese Air Force
382C-6D	C-130E	4276	Imperial Iranian Air Force
382C-69D	C-130H	4747	Cameroon Air Force

Model	Applied to	From c/n	Initial Customer
382C-70D	HC-130H	4757	US Coast Guard
382C-70E	KC-130T	5085	US Marine Corps
382C-71D	C-130H	4780	Royal Australian Air Force
382C-71E	C-130H	5071	US Air National Guard
382C-72D	C-130H	4744	Bolivian Air Force
382C-73D	C-130H	4749	Portuguese Air Force
382C-73E	MC-130H	5026	US Air Force
382C-74D	C-130H	4743	Ecuadorian Air Force
382C-74E	C-130H	5093	US Air National Guard
382C-75D	EC-130Q	4781	US Navy
382C-75E	C-130H	5108	Japanese Air Force
382C-76D	C-130H	4768	Sudanese Government
382C-76E	HC-130H-7	5023	US Coast Guard
382C-77D	C-130H	4761	Philippines Air Force
382C-77E	MC-130H	5091	US Air Force
382C-78D	C-130H	4772	Portuguese Air Force
382C-79D	C-130H	4765	Government of Gabon
382C-79E	HC-130H-7	5106	US Coast Guard
382C-7D	C-130E	4285	Canadian Armed Forces
382C-80D	C-130H	4815	US Air National Guard
382C-80E	C-130H	4990	Brazilian Air Force
382C-81D	C-130H	4792	Ecuadorian Air Force
382C-81E	C-130H	5122	US Air Force Reserve
382C-82D	KC-130H	4814	Argentinian Air Force

Model	Applied to	From c/n	Initial Customer
382C-82E	C-130H	5138	Japanese Air Force
382C-83D	C-130H	4779	Royal Jordanian Air Force
382C-83E	KC-130T	5143	US Marine Corps
382C-84D	C-130H	4801	Venezuelan Air Force
382C-84E	HC-130H-7	5121	US Coast Guard
382C-85D	EC-130Q	4867	US Navy
382C-85E	C-130H	4998	Brazilian Air Force
382C-86D	C-130H	4825	Northern Yemeni Government
382C-86E	AC-130U	5139	US Air Force
382C-87D	C-130H	4812	Ecuadorian Air Force
382C-87E	MC-130H	5130	US Air Force
382C-88D	C-130H	4852	US Air National Guard
382C-88E	C-130H	5151	US Air Force Reserve
382C-89D	C-130H	4813	Royal Jordanian Air Force
382C-89E	MC-130H	5173	US Air Force
382C-8D	C-130E	4287	Brazilian Air Force
382C-8E	C-130H	4881	Royal Swedish Air Force
382C-90D	C-130H	4829	Government of Niger
382C-90E	C-130H	5170	Japanese Air Force
382C-92D	C-130H	4835	Spanish Air Force
382C-92E	C-130H	5114	French Air Force
382C-93E	C-130H-30	5146	Royal Thai Air Force
382C-94D	C-130H	4838	Indonesian Air Force
382C-95D	C-130H	4841	Spanish Air Force

The elegance of N130JA (c/n 5408), the first RAF C-130J-30. (Lockheed Martin Aeronautical Systems Company via Martin W. Bowman)

Model	Applied to	From c/n	Initial Customer
382C-95E	KC-130T	5174	US Marine Corps
382C-96D	KC-130H	4872	Royal Saudi Air Force
382C-96E	C-130H	5188	US Air National Guard
382C-97D	C-130H-MP	4847	Malaysian Government
382C-97E	AC-130U	5228	US Air Force
382C-98D	KC-130H	4871	Spanish Air Force
382C-98E	HC-130(N)	5202	US Air National Guard
382C-9D	LC-130R	4305	US Navy
382C-9E	C-130-MP	4898	Indonesian Air Force
382E-11C	L-100-20	4299	Lockheed Aircraft Corporation
382E-13C	L-100-20	4300	First National Bank of Chicago
382E-15C	L-100-20	4302	Flying W Airways
382E-16C	L-100-20	4412	Government of Kuwait
382E-18C	L-100-20	4350	Lockheed Aircraft Corporation
382E-20C	L-100-20	4362	Lockheed Aircraft Corporation
382E-19C	L-100-20	4355	Lockheed Aircraft Corporation
382E-21C	L-100-20	4333	Lockheed Aircraft Corporation
382E-22C	L-100-20	4383	Saturn Airways
382E-25C	L-100-20	4385	Safair
382E-26C	L-100-20	4358	Lockheed Aircraft Corporation
382E-29C	L-100-20	4512	Lockheed Aircraft Corporation
382E-33C	L-100-20	4593	Philippines Government
382E-44C	L-100-20	4830	Government of Angola
382E-47C	L-100-20	4850	Government of Peru

Model	Applied to	From c/n	Initial Customer
382G-23C	L-100-30	4388	Lockheed Aircraft Corporation
382G-28C	L-100-30	4472	Safair
382G-30C	L-100-30	4582	Government of Gabon
382G-31C	L-100-30	4558	Safair
382G-32C	L-100-30	4561	Saturn Airways
382G-35C	L-100-30	4673	Safair
382G-38C	L-100-30	4763	Alaska International Air
382G-39C	L-100-30	4796	SCIBE Zaire
382G-40C	L-100-30	4798	Alaska International Air
382G-41C	L-100-30	4800	Indonesian Air Force
382G-42C	L-100-30	4799	Pacific Western Airlines
382G-43C	L-100-30	4824	Pelita Air Services
382G-45C	L-100-30	4833	Bolivian Air Force
382G-46C	L-100-30	4839	Lockheed Aircraft Corporation
382G-48C	L-100-20	4851	Petroleole Mexicanos
382G-50C	L-100-30	4834	Government of Dubai
382G-51C	L-100-30	4880	Air Algérie
382G-52C	L-100-30	4889	Pelita Air Services
382G-53C	L-100-30	4891	Argentinian Air Force
382G-54C	L-100-30	4893	Ecuadorian Air Force
382G-57C	L-100-30	4917	Pelita Air Services
382G-58C	L-100-30	4895	Government of Gabon
382G-59C	L-100-30	4949	Government of Kuwait
382G-60C	L-100-30	4950	Saudi Arabian Government

A busy scene at the hangar of Marshall of Cambridge Aerospace as work is carried out on three of the RAF's Hercules fleet. With leading edge removed, the wing form can clearly be seen, along with the tail form on the rear aircraft. (Marshall of Cambridge Aerospace via Martin W. Bowman)

Model	Applied to	From c/n	Initial Customer
382G-61C	L-100-30	4956	Saudi Arabian Government
382G-62C	L-100-30	4992	Alliance Funding International
382G-63C	L-100-30	4954	Saudi Arabian Government
382G-64C	L-100-30	5000	Alliance Funding International
382G-65C	L-100-30	5024	Government of Gabon
382G-67C	L-100-30	5022	Ethiopian Airlines
382G-68C	L-100-30	5048	Advanced Leasing Corporation
382G-69C	L-100-30	5025	China Air Cargo
382G-70C	L-100-30	5225	Frameair
382G-71C	L-100-30	5307	Frameair
382G-71C	L-100-30	5320	Canadian Armed Forces
382G-72C	L-100-30	5306	Ethiopian Airlines
382T-09F	C-130H-30	5184	Government of Chad
382T-10F	C-130H-30	5187	Egyptian Government
382T-16E	C-130H-30	4894	Algerian Air Force
382T-20E	C-130H-30	4933	Cameroon Air Force
382T-20F	C-130H-30	5226	French Air Force
382T-21E	C-130H-30	4925	Indonesian Air Force
382T-25F	C-130H-30	5264	Portuguese Air Force
382T-28F	C-130H-30	5268	Government of Malaysia
382T-30E	C-130H-30	4919	Algerian Air Force
382T-34F	C-130H-30	5277	Government of Malaysia
382T-38E	C-130H-30	4959	Royal Thai Air Force
382T-38F	C-130H-30	5280	Royal Thai Air Force

Model	Applied to	From c/n	Initial Customer
382T-39E	C-130H-30	4961	Government of Dubai
382T-3E	C-130H	4864	Indonesian Air Force
382T-40E	C-130H-30	4962	Nigerian Air Force
382T-41E	C-130H-30	5001	Nigerian Air Force
382T-44F	C-130H-30	5309	Government of Malaysia
382T-45E	C-130H-30	4987	Algerian Air Force
382T-50F	C-130H-30	5273	Royal Netherlands Air Force
382T-51E	C-130H-30	5006	Republic of Korea
382T-52E	C-130H-30	5003	Spanish Air Force
382T-56E	C-130H-30	4997	Algerian Air Force
382T-62E	C-130H-30	5030	Republic of Korea
382T-91E	C-130H-30	5140	French Air Force
382T-94E	C-130H-30	5150	French Air Force
382U	C-130J-30	5523	Lockheed Aircraft Corporation
382U-04J	WC-130J	5451	US Air Force Reserve
382U-06J	C-130J-30	5478	Royal Air Force
382U-07J	WC-130J	5473	US Air Force Reserve
382U-08J	C-130J-30	5469	US Air National Guard
382U-09J	EC-130J	5477	US Air National Guard
382U-11J	KC-130J	5488	US Marine Corps
382U-12J	WC-130J	5486	US Air Force Reserve
382U-13J	C-130J-30	5495	Italian Air Force
382U-16J	C-130J-30	5491	US Air National Guard

Model	Applied to	From c/n	Initial Customer
382U-17J	EC-130J	5490	US Air National Guard
382U-31J	C-130J-30	5520	Italian Air Force
382U-32J	EC-130J	5527	US Air National Guard
382U-33J	KC-130J	5515	US Marine Corps
382U-48F	C-130J-30	5413	US Air Force Reserve
382V-01J	C-130J-30	5443	Royal Air Force
382V-03J	C-130-J	5440	Royal Australian Air Force
382V-05J	C130J-30	5446	Royal Air Force
382V-30J	C-130J-30	5517	US Air National Guard
382V-31J	C-130J-30	5510	Italian Air Force
382V-34J	C-130J-30	5521	Italian Air Force
382V-49F	C-130J-30	5408	Royal Air Force
392C-93D	C-130H	4837	Saudi Arabia

Appendix Four

Museum Hercules

Quite a number of retired C-130s found their way into various air museums in the USA and elsewhere, although not all of them are on public display, it should be noted. (Some others were preserved as gate guards or static displays, but with the cutting back of the US defence budgets these are gradually being dismantled.)

1: USAF serial 53-3129 (c/n 3001) *First Lady*, USAF Armament Museum, Eglin, Florida.
2: USAF serial 54-1626 (c/n 3013) *Vulcan Express*, USAF Museum, Wright-Patterson AFB, Ohio.
3: USAF 54-1630 (c/n 3017) *Azrael*, USAF Museum, Wright-Patterson AFB, Ohio.
4: USAF serial 55-0014 (c/n 3041) *Jaws of Death*, Robins AFB Museum.
5: USAF serial 55-0023 (c/n 3050) *City of Ardmore*, Linear Air Park, Dyess AFB.
6: USAF serial 55-0037 (c/n 3064) *Sayonara*, Octave Aerospace Museum, Rantoul Aviation Complex, Chanute, Illinois.
7: USAF serial 56-0509 (c/n 3117) *Raids Kill Um Dead*, Hurlburt Field Memorial Air Park.

8: USAF serial 57-0453 (c/n 3160) *Nite Train to Memphis*, National Vigilance Park, Fort George G. Meade, Maryland. Dedicated to the C-130 aircrew lost over Armenia in 1958.
9: USAF serial 57-0457 (c/n 3164), Pima Air Museum, Tucson, Arizona.
10: USAF serial 57-0478 (c/n 3185), Museum of Aviation.
11: USAF serial 57-0485 (c/n 3192) *Snowshoe*, Minnesota Air National Guard Historical Museum.
12: USAF serial 57-0490 (c/n 3197), Empire State Air Museum, Schenectady County Airport, New York.
13: RAAF serial A97-214, RAAF Museum, Point Cook.
14: USAF serial 57-0514 (c/n 3221) *Miasis Dragon*, Selfridge Military Air Museum.
15: USAF serial 57-0526 (c/n 3502), Hill AFB Museum, Salt Lake City, Utah.
16: USAF serial 62-1786 (c/n 3732), USAF Museum, Wright-Patterson AFB, Ohio.
17: US Navy serial 159348 (c/n 4601), TACAMO facility Static Park at Tinker AFB, Oklahoma.

Royal Air Force Hercules XV211 (c/n 4237), with prominent refuelling probe, sets up a racket as her engines roar prior to take-off. (Martin W. Bowman)

Appendix Five

C-130 Hercules Major Sub-Contractors

C-130A–H

Allison Division, General Motors, Indianapolis	Engines
Alcoa, Pittsburg, Pennsylvania	Aluminium Forgings etc.
Avco, Nashville, Tennessee	Empennage
Collins Radio, Cedar Rapids, Iowa	General Avionics
Garrett Corporation, Los Angeles and Phoenix	Environmental Controls
General Electric, Binghampton, New York	Electrical Generators
Goodyear Company, Akron, Ohio	Brakes
Goodyear Aerospace, Rockmart, Georgia	Fuel Cells
Hamilton Standard, Windsor Locks, Connecticut	Propellers
Honeywell Corporation, Minneapolis	Fuel Quantity Gauges
Kaiser Aluminium, Oakland, California	Aluminium Forgings etc.
Martin-Marietta, Torrance, California	Aluminium Castings etc.
Menasco, Burbank, California	Landing Gear
Rohr, Chula Vista, California	Nacelles
Ronson Hydraulics, Charlotte, North Carolina	Flight Controls
Scottish Aviation, Prestwick	Fuselage Side Panels
Sperry-Vickers, Jackson, Michigan	Hydraulic Pumps
Stainless Steel Products, Burbank, California	Ducting
Texas Instruments, Dallas, Texas	Radar System (APQ 122)

C-130J

Aero-Maoz	Lighting Systems
Aerostructures Corporation	Wings, Wing Components and Empennages
Aerotech World Trade Ltd	Databus Test Analysis & Simulation Systems
AiResearch	APUs
Airtechnology Group	Fans, Fan Heaters, Motors, Generators, Switches & Sensors
Alliant Defense	Missile-warning System
Ametek Aerospace Gulton-Statham Products	Aviation Sensors & Instrumentation
Ametek Rotron Technical Motor Division	Brushless Motors, Fans & Blowers
ATC Power Systems Inc.	AC/DC and DC/DC Power Supplies
Aviation Spares International Ltd	Military Aircraft Spares
Avionic Display Corporation	High-resolution, Active Matrix, Flat-panel, Liquid Crystal Displays (LCD)
BCF Designs Ltd	Databus and EMC Test Solutions
B. F. Goodrich Lighting Systems	Lighting Systems
Downey Aerospace, Staverton, Gloucestershire	Composite Propellers
DRS Headland Ltd	Airborne Video Systems for Flight Test and Mission Data
Filtronic Components Ltd	Microwave Subsystems
Filtronic Components Ltd	Airborne Surveillance and Targeting
Flight Dynamics (Collins-Kaiser)	Holographic Head Up Display (HUD)
GFM GmbH	Ultrasonic Cutting and High-Speed Routing Machines

Hella Aerospace GmbH	Aircraft Lighting Systems
Honeywell	Dual embedded INS/GPS and Digital Mapping Systems
Judd Wire	Insulation Systems for Electrical Wire and Cable
Lockheed Martin	Infra-red Countermeasures System
Lucas Aerospace	Full-Authority, Digital Engine-Control System
Mercury Computer Systems	High Performance Real-Time Multicomputers
Metronor ASA	High-Precision Portable Co-ordinate Measuring Machines
MPC Products Corporation	Electromechanical Components and Systems
Northrop Grumman	Colour Weather and Navigation Radar
PTC	Integrated Software Solutions for Aircraft Development
Radom Aviation Systems Ltd	Aircraft Upgrades and Modifications
Rolls-Royce	Turbo-prop Engines
ROTRAN Simulator Logistics Ltd	Flight Simulator Relocation
Saft	Aircraft Batteries
SBS Technologies Inc.	MIL-STD-1553, ARINC 429 & Telemetry Products
Senior Aerospace	Metallic and Non-metallic Products and Systems
SKY Computers Inc.	High-Performance Real-Time Multicomputers
Timken Aerospace & Super Precision	Speciality Bearings
Torotel Products Inc.	Magnetic Components
Tracor	Countermeasures Systems
Westinghouse	Weather/Navigation Radars

Pacific Western L-100-20 N926R (c/n 4197) is towed on arrival at company HQ. (Lockheed-Georgia, Marietta via Audrey Pearcy)

Bibliography

Archer, Bob & Dorr, Robert F. & Hewson, Robert, 'Lockheed C-130 Hercules' in *World Air Power Journal*, Vol. 18, pp 50–109, Aerospace Publishing Ltd, 1992.

Archer, Bob, & Keep, Mike, *Lockheed C-130 Hercules*, Aviation News/Sky Books Press, 1979.

Badrocke, Mike & Gunson, Bill, *Lockheed Aircraft Cutaways: The History of Lockheed Martin*, Osprey, 1998.

Ballard, Jack S. *Development and Employment of Fixed-Wing Gunships 1962–1972*, Office of the Air Force History, 1982.

Bowers, Ray L. *Tactical Airlift: The United States Air Force in Southeast Asia*, Office of Air Force History, 1983.

Bowman, Martin W. *Lockheed C-130 Hercules*, Crowood Publishing, 1999.

Brown, Albert, *C-130 & the Blue Angels*, privately published via A4 Sky Jt, 1981.

Bunrin-Do, *Famous Airplanes of the World, No. 79 Lockheed C-130 Hercules*, Tokyo, 1976.

Caidin, Martin, *The Long Arm of America*, E. P. Dutton and Co., 1963.

Caidin, Martin, *The Mighty Hercules*, E.P. Dutton and Co., 1964.

Campbell, R. L. *Tasks of Hercules*, Lockheed-Georgia, 1975.

Chinnery, Philip D, *Any Time, Any Place: Fifty Years of the USAF Air Commando and Special Operations Forces 1944–1994*, United States Naval Institute, Annapolis, 1994.

Cockburn, Alexander & St Clair, Jeffrey, *Whiteout: the CIA, Drugs and the Press*, Verso Books, 1999.

Dabney, Joseph Earl, *Herk, Hero of the Skies*, Cobblehouse Books, 1986.

Davis, Larry, *Gunships: A Pictorial History of Spooky*, Squadron/Signal Publications, 1981.

Drendel, Lou, *C-130 Hercules in Action*, Aircraft No. 47, Squadron/Signal Publications, 1981.

Francillon, Rene J., 'C-130 Hercules Variant Briefing Parts 1, 2 & 3', *World Air Power Journal*, Vols 6–8, Aerospace Publishing Ltd, 1991–2.

Gaines, Mike & Goulding, James, *Hercules*, Jane's Aircraft Spectacular, 1985.

Hinebaugh, *Flying Upside Down*, United States Naval Institution, Annapolis, 1999.

Jolly, Randy, *Air Commandos*, Aero Graphics, 1994.

Kyle, James H., *The Guts to Try*, Primer Publications, 1994.

Laming, Tim, *Hercules: The C-130 in Service*, Motorbooks International, 1992.

Leader, Ray, *Colours and Markings of the C-130 Hercules*, Colours and Markings, Vol. 7, 1987.

Leary, *Perilous Missions*, University of Alabama Press, 1984.

Lee, Robert Mason, *Death and Deliverance*, Macfarlane Walter & Ross, 1992.

McGowan, Sam, *The C-130 Hercules: Tactical Airlift Missions, 1956–1975*, Tab Books Inc., 1988.

Mackintosh, Ian, *C-130 Pictorial*, Airline Publications, 1979.

Mason, Francis K., *Lockheed Hercules*, Patrick Stephens Ltd, 1984.

Maxell, H. G., 'History of the Hercules . . . with pilot's report', *Air Classics* magazine, June 1974.

Middleton, Peter, 'Antarctic Shuttle', *Flight International* magazine, January 1985.

Mikesh, Robert C., *Flying Dragons: The South Vietnamese Air Force*, Osprey, 1988.

Morris, M. E., *C-130: The Hercules –Airpower* No. 1009, Presido Press, 1989.

Morse, Stan (ed), *Gulf Air War Debrief*, Aerospace Publishing, 1991.

Muniandy, A., *Erks on Herks*, Hercules Publishing House, 1995.

Nye, Frederick F., *Blind Bat: C-130 Forward Air Controller: Ho Chi Minh Trail*, Eakin Publications, 2000.

Olausson, Lars, *Lockheed Hercules Production List, 1954–2001*, privately published, 2000.

Orr, Kelly, *From a Dark Sky: The Story of US Air Force Special Operations*, Presidio Press, 1996.

Peacock, Lindsay, *The Mighty Hercules: The First Four Decades*, RAF Benevolent Fund, 1994.

Pearcy, Arthur, *A History of US Coast Guard Aviation*, Airlife, 1989.

Pereira, Wilf, *RAF Lyneham: Hercules Super Station in Action*, privately published, 1990.

Pierce, K. J., 'The Lockheed Hercules', series of articles in *South-East Air Review WLAG* – November 1966–March 1967 editions.

Reed, Arthur, *C-130 Hercules*, Modern Combat Aircraft 17, Motorbooks, 1984.

Reed, Chris, *Lockheed C-130 Hercules and its Variants*, Schiffer Publishing Ltd, 1999.

Robbins, Christopher, *Air America: The Story of the CIA's Secret Airlines*, Putnam, 1979.

Selby, Earl and Miriam, *Hercules: Work-Horse of the Air*, Readers Digest, 1983.

Scott, Peter Dale & Marshall, Jonathan, *Cocaine Politics: Drugs, Armies and the CIA in Central America*, University of California Press, 1998.

Turner, Paul St John, *Lockheed Hercules*, Profile No. 223, Profile Publications, Windsor, 1971.

Vaughan, David Kirk, *Runway Visions: An American C-130 Pilot's Memoirs of Combat Airlift Operations in Southeast Asia 1967–1978*, Verlinden Productions Inc., 1986.

Webb, Gary, *Dark Alliance: The CIA, the Contras and the Crack Cocaine Explosion*, Seven Stones Press, 1998.

White, Molly O'Loughlin, *The Foodbirds: Flying for Famine Relief*, Bookmarque Publishing, 1994.

Wilson, Stewart, *Dakota, Hercules and Caribou in Australian Service*, Australian Airpower Collection, 1991.

The EC-130E squadron based at Harrisburg IAP, Pennsylvania, is 193 SOS. This photo taken on 20 December 1999 shows the special antennae on the vertical tail surfaces and elsewhere on these aircraft. Not bad for a 'Logistics' squadron. (Kevin R. Smith)

Index